Robert Hutchinson is a fellow of the Society of Antiquaries of London and the author of *The Last Days of Henry VIII*, *Elizabeth's Spymaster*, *Thomas Cromwell*, *House of Treason*, *Young Henry* and *The Spanish Armada*. He was Defence Correspondent for the Press Association before moving to Jane's Information Group to launch *Jane's Defence Weekly*. He has a doctorate from the University of Sussex and was appointed OBE in the 2008 Honours List.

# ROBERT HUTCHINSON

THE AUDACIOUS CRIMES OF

## Colonel BLOOD

THE SPY WHO STOLE THE
CROWN JEWELS & BECAME
THE KING'S SECRET AGENT

W&N
WEIDENFELD & NICOLSON

A W&N PAPERBACK

First published in Great Britain in 2015
by Weidenfeld & Nicolson
This paperback edition published in 2016
by Weidenfeld & Nicolson,
an imprint of the Orion Publishing Group Ltd,
Carmelite House, 50 Victoria Embankment,
London EC4Y 0DZ

An Hachette UK company

1 3 5 7 9 10 8 6 4 2

Copyright © Robert Hutchinson 2015

The right of Robert Hutchinson to be identified as the
author of this work has been asserted by him in accordance
with the Copyright, Designs and Patents Act 1988.

A CIP catalogue record for this book
is available from the British Library.

ISBN 978-1-780-22610-1

Printed and bound by CPI Group (UK) Ltd, Croydon, CRO 4YY

The Orion Publishing Group's policy is to use papers
that are natural, renewable and recyclable products and
made from wood grown in sustainable forests. The logging
and manufacturing processes are expected to conform to
the environmental regulations of the country of origin.

www.orionbooks.co.uk

*To Gavin and Caroline, Rob and Matthew;*
*Jo and John, Bertie and Charlie*

# Contents

# List of Illustrations

1 Unknown man, formerly known as Thomas Blood, attributed to Gilbert Soest. Oil on canvas, 1670s. (© National Portrait Gallery, London)

2 Thomas Blood by George White. Mezzotint, early 18th century. (© National Portrait Gallery, London)

3 James Butler, First Duke of Ormond, by William Wissing. Oil on canvas, *c.* 1680–5. (© National Portrait Gallery, London)

4 Sir Joseph Williamson after unknown artist. Oil on canvas, 1660s. (© National Portrait Gallery, London)

5 Henry Bennet, First Earl of Alington, after Sir Peter Lely. Oil on canvas, *c.* 1665–70. (© National Portrait Gallery, London)

6 Charles II after Sir Peter Lely. Oil on canvas, *c.* 1675. (© National Portrait Gallery, London)

7 George Villiers, Second Duke of Buckingham, by Sir Peter Lely. Oil on canvas, *c.* 1675. (© National Portrait Gallery, London)

8 Barbara Palmer, Duchess of Cleveland, after Sir Peter Lely. Oil on canvas, *c.* 1666. (© National Portrait Gallery, London)

9 Charles II by John Michael Wright. Oil on canvas, *c.* 1661–2. (Royal Collection Trust/© Her Majesty Queen Elizabeth II 2014)

10 The Martin Tower in the north-east corner of the Tower of London. (© Historic Royal Palaces)

11 Colonel Blood stealing the regalia from the Tower. Colour lithograph, English school, 19th century. (Private collection/© Look and Learn/Bridgeman Images)

12 Colonel Blood's daggers. English or Scottish, 1620. (© Royal Armouries)

# *Acknowledgements*

This book could not have been written without the tireless and enthusiastic support of my dear wife, who has shared with me the complexities of seventeenth-century Irish politics and the conspiracies against the crown and government of Charles II.

I am very grateful to Heather Rowland, Head of Library Collections, and Adrian James, Assistant Librarian, at the Society of Antiquaries of London; Kay Walters and her team at the Athenæum Club library; the staff at the University of Sussex library at Falmer, East Sussex and the National Archives at Kew and in the Rare Books, Manuscripts and Humanities reading rooms at the British Library. My thanks are also due to the staff at the Bodleian Library; to my researchers Hilda McGauley of 'Records of Ireland' for her assistance at the National Library of Ireland and especially to Denise A. Harman for her hard work at the Lancashire Record Office. Lastly, I am particularly grateful to Robert C. Woosnam-Savage, Curator of European Edged Weapons at the Royal Armouries, and to my good friend Philip J. Lankester, Curator Emeritus, for their very kind help with Colonel Blood's ballock daggers.

At Weidenfeld & Nicolson, Alan Samson has, as always, been encouraging and helpful, as has Lucinda McNeile, and I would like to record my gratitude to my meticulous editor Anne O'Brien and to David Atkinson for compiling the index and to my agent Andrew Lownie. Any errors or omissions are entirely my responsibility.

Robert Hutchinson
West Sussex, 2015

# Prologue

*So high was Blood's fame for sagacity and intrepidity ... [he was believed] capable of undertaking anything his passion or interest dictated [no matter] how desperate or difficult.*

Biographia Britannia, 1747–66.[1]

Colonel Thomas Blood is one of those mysterious and charismatic characters in British history whose breathtaking exploits underline the wisdom of the old maxim that truth can be stranger than fiction.

An attempted coup d'état in Ireland and his involvement in countless plots to assassinate Charles II and to overthrow the lawful government of England, Scotland and Ireland in the late seventeenth century won him widespread notoriety in the three kingdoms. Little wonder, then, that Charles II's ministers publicly branded him the 'Father of all Treasons'.[2] With a substantial price on his head, dead or alive, Blood became a hunted man throughout the length and breadth of the British Isles.

But this extraordinary fugitive from justice was far from cowed by any hue and cry pursuing him in the dark, filthy alleyways and back lanes of London or Dublin. Paradoxically, the tighter the net was drawn around him, the more audacious this 'notorious traitor and incendiary'[3] became.

Blood's attempt to steal the Crown Jewels from within the protective high walls of the Tower of London in May 1671 propels him to the top of a very select group of bold outlaws who have preyed upon the riches of the English royal court down the years.

In the mid-fourteenth century, 'Adam the Leper' cheekily

snatched property belonging to Edward III's buxom and matronly queen, Philippa of Hainault.[4] A few decades before, in 1303, Richard of Pudlicott raided Edward I's treasury in the Chapel of the Pyx inside Westminster Abbey, assisted by its sub-prior and sacristan. Today we would recognise the crime as a medieval 'inside job'.[5] Richard was hanged and reportedly his skin was flayed off his corpse. Tradition maintains (wrongly) that this was nailed upon a wooden door of that sacred edifice, near the Chapter House, as a terrible warning to lesser mortals who covet the wealth of their sovereign lieges.[6]

Almost four centuries on, Blood was no mere thief, no matter how brazen his crime. He was an incorrigible adventurer who, not for the first time, eventually turned his coat to live a perilous existence as a government spy, or double agent, for Charles II's secret service in their battle to counter both internal and external threats to the uncertain Stuart crown.

His skill at avoiding retribution was so adroit that when he finally went to meet his Maker, there was a prevalent belief that he had managed to cheat even the Grim Reaper himself. The alehouses of Westminster and Whitehall buzzed with stories that the old soldier had not died but was only up to his usual tricks. Was his demise just another of Blood's clever stratagems to fool his many powerful enemies at the royal court? Was death his ultimate cunning disguise?

Such was the full tide of rumour running across London that the government was forced to exhume Blood's body from his grave in Tothill Fields chapel to demonstrate publicly the mouldering truth. The colonel's swollen and rotting cadaver was only identified at a grim inquest in Westminster by a witness recalling the inordinately large size of one of his thumbs.

His was a complex character, full of contradiction and inconsistency. He possessed strong nonconformist religious beliefs, pledging himself daily to be 'in serious consideration . . . of Christ and what he has done' and not to be 'slothful in the works of ye lord'. He claimed to shun wine, strong drink and any kind of 'excess in recreations or pomp or in apparel . . . quibbling or joking . . . all obscene and scurrilous talk'.[7]

Sometimes he erred from this straight-and-narrow godly path. Blood was also an arrogant, eccentric fantasist with a very persuasive manner, reinforced by buckets of Irish charm and armed with a neat turn of phrase that proved useful in a tight spot. That lyrical word 'blarney' might have been created especially for him. And, in truth, his escapades, conducted under a multitude of aliases and assisted by a wardrobe packed full of disguises, left no swash unbuckled, no outrage untested, no crime too great to attempt. Many a daring man of action would resemble more a meek, pious Vatican altar boy by comparison.

Thomas Blood came from a family whose origins, appropriately, lay in a thirst for adventure. The Irish branch traces its origins to Edmund Blood, a minor member of the Tudor gentry, from the tiny hamlet of Makeney, near Duffield in Derbyshire,[8] who sailed off to Ireland in 1595 as an ambitious twenty-seven-year-old cavalry captain seeking fame and fortune – or, more bluntly, the simple plunder of war or the joyful sequestration of an enemy's land and property.

He joined Queen Elizabeth I's army to fight in what became a bitter nine-year war against the Irish magnate Hugh O'Neill and his allies, who sought, like so many others before and after, to finally end the alien English rule of the Emerald Isle.[9] During a stormy sea passage over to Dublin, Blood's first wife, Margaret, inconveniently gave birth to a son, which at the gracious request of a fellow passenger and comrade-in-arms, the Earl of Inchiquin,[10] was appropriately christened 'Neptune'.

Edmund quickly discovered that the discomforts of soldiering were not to his taste. He resigned his commission and acquired 200 acres (81 hectares) of land near Corofin in Co. Clare, along with nearby Kilnaboy Castle[11] and later Bohersallagh House,[12] possibly through the influence of Inchiquin, his old travelling companion and later commanding officer, who already owned property in the area.

Extra income was opportunely earned by stopping ships sailing north along the Clare coast to Galway or south to Limerick and politely inviting their captains to hand over sizeable quantities of cash in return for the promise of a safe passage onwards. The presence of armed men in cutters, probably based at Lahinch in Liscannor Bay, was a persuasive reason to accept gracefully such imperative suggestions. Some may regard this traditional pastime as a protection racket, others as pure piracy – but no one dared suggest there was any conflict with the sober Presbyterian religious beliefs that the Blood family had practised after arrival in Ireland.

In April 1613, Edmund was elected as one of two members of parliament for the nearby borough of Ennis in the Irish House of Commons, as part of the Dublin government's cynical redrawing of constituencies to guarantee a permanent Protestant majority. Edmund was then described as *generosus* or gentleman.[13] After two years' service as an MP, he hauled himself further up the greasy pole of social status by receiving a grant of heraldic arms,[14] the choice of bucks' heads as charges probably inspired by his love of hunting.

He had two more sons, Edmund (died 1615) and Thomas, by Margaret.[15] On his wife's death, he married Mary Holdcroft, or Holcroft, of Lancashire[16] although family tradition suggests he had a third wife before he died *c.*1645.[17] By Mary, he had a fourth son, William, born at Kilnaboy in 1600.

Neptune, the eldest, was ordained a minister in March 1623 and became the dean of Kilfenora in 1663, as well as vicar general of the diocese thirteen years later. He was a feisty Protestant churchman, serving with King Charles I at Oxford during the first English Civil War,[18] and continued the lucrative family tradition of exacting money from hapless ships sailing along the coast of Co. Clare. After parliamentary forces stormed Drogheda and Wexford in September and October 1649 and put their citizens to the sword, Neptune's boats were burnt by Cromwell's troops, but he was given three grants of confiscated land as compensation for his loss of the coastal business.[19] He rescued the silver communion plate from both Christchurch and St Fin Barr's cathedral in the city of Cork to prevent its theft or destruction by the Ironside soldiers and, after the restoration of the monarchy, paid the two churches more than

£18 in 1665 so he could continue to use the sacred vessels in his own cathedral at Kilfenora.²⁰

Thomas, the third son, born at Kilnaboy in 1598, became an ironmaster in Sarney, Dunboyne, Co. Meath, eleven miles (17.9 km) north-west of Dublin. Some sources describe him as a black-smith, but this belittles his status, as he enjoyed a profitable business exporting iron ingots to England. Unfortunately, nothing is known about his wife. In 1621 he purchased an estate in Co. Meath from William Cooke and seventeen years later bought 500 acres (202 hectares) in Co. Wicklow.²¹

As befits a man of such mystery, the early life of Thomas Blood junior remains obscure and contradictory. He was born at Sarney in early 1618,²² probably the elder son of the marriage, as there are tenuous reports of a William Blood, born around 1620, who died some two decades later at Dunboyne. He apparently had at least one sister. Blood's parents were described as 'serious, honest and of no inferior credit and possessions in the country where they lived' according to Colonel Blood's first biographer in 1680.²³ He emphasised that they took care 'that their offspring should not degenerate from the virtues and repute of his ancestors [*sic*] by forming and shaping his condition according to the rules of a strict and sober education . . . to preserve him from those extravagancies that usually attend metalled and active spirits'. The youngster may have been sent to Lancashire for his education, in the care of his stepgrandmother's family.

In March 1640, Charles I granted property in the barony of Dunboyne to the Bloods, including houses, quarries, orchards and gardens of the hamlet of Suppocke, amounting to sixty acres of arable land and ten acres of pasture (totalling twenty-eight hectares), together with five cottages, at an annual rent of 5s 6d (27.5p).²⁴ (A cousin, Edmund, is recorded as owning a mill, seven tenements and seventy acres of land in Dunboyne at the same time, property he bought in July 1621.)²⁵ Thomas Blood junior received further generous grants, in June 1643, of the 'towns and lands of Sarney, Braystown and Foylestown in the barony of Dunboyne and five hundred acres of unprofitable mountain in Glenmalure, alias

The Glinns, in Co. Wicklow,' the latter award sounding distinctly parsimonious.[26] Our future adventurer lived not at Sarney but at Ashtown, in today's western suburbs of Dublin.[27]

This new mark of royal favour was probably a reward for Blood's support for the crown during the rebellion of Irish Catholics that broke out in Ulster in October 1641 over the loss of the best agricultural land to Protestant settlers and increasing fears over the future of the Catholic faith in Ireland.[28] The Irish aristocracy and clergy formed a 'Catholic Confederation' the following summer, based at Kilkenny, which became the *de facto* government of two-thirds of Ireland. There were other grave consequences across the Irish Sea. The means of restoring English rule in Ireland became one of the catalysts of the Civil War between King and Parliament, as the MPs sought control of the army sent to defeat the rebels and also the power of veto over royal appointees as its commanders.

Like all such Irish conflicts, it was a bloody affair with neighbour pitted against neighbour, and the opportunities for plunder and vengeance were eagerly seized by both sides. Blood's dour Protestant uncle Neptune later claimed mordantly that in Co. Clare he had goods worth £180 looted from him, as well as being deprived of church benefices worth £140 a year and his cattle stolen by 'Hugh Hogan and Teige O'Brien of Caherminnane'. His home at Kilnaboy had been demolished and he had lost £120 in debts owed him by Catholics. More vividly, the clergyman reported the murder of two Presbyterian settlers, George Owens of Kilfenora and Michael Hunt of Moghna who, he claimed, had been killed by Teige and Simon Fitzpatrick of Ballyshanny.[29]

Thomas Blood had been appointed a justice of the peace at the remarkably early age of twenty-one in 1640 and probably had fought against the rebels in the spring of 1642 when James Butler, First Duke of Ormond, led a series of Royalist army attacks to clear the districts around Dublin of Confederation forces.

Although the Irish war was still continuing unabated, Blood heeded the clarion call to arms issued by his beleaguered monarch when Charles I defiantly raised his royal standard at Nottingham on 22 August 1642.

A 'Captain Bludd' served in Sir Lewis Dyve's regiment of Royalist infantry as quartermaster after May 1643. Although this unit was much reduced after the hard fighting of the Cornish campaign of August 1644, it formed the garrison of the twelfth-century Sherborne Castle, Dorset, in October that year. Many of his brother officers are known to have come from Dorset and Somerset, which suggests that hasty local recruiting had filled gaps caused by heavy casualties. More would fall when the walls were breached and the fortress surrendered to parliamentary forces under Sir Thomas Fairfax after an eleven-day siege the following August.[30]

It may be that if Blood was at the siege of Sherborne, he either escaped or, if taken prisoner, was freed on parole to return to Ireland after his father's death at Sarney in 1645.[31] There is some circumstantial evidence that he rejoined the Royalist army when fighting was renewed in 1648 in what became the Second Civil War. His contemporary biographer and apologist 'R.H.' – possibly Richard Halliwell, one of his cronies and fellow conspirators in the years to come – maintained that Blood 'gave his prince all the assistance his personal valour was capable to afford him; wherein he performed several good pieces of good service'.[32]

One of these exploits may have been his role in an audacious (some may say recklessly foolhardy) attempt to kidnap Colonel Thomas Rainborowe,[33] commander of the parliamentary forces besieging Pontefract Castle in Yorkshire.

A Royalist army had been defeated by Oliver Cromwell at the three-day battle at Preston, Lancashire on 17–19 August 1648 and one of their generals, Sir Marmaduke Langdale, was captured. He was taken to Nottingham and black rumours swept through Pontefract's 500-strong garrison that Langdale would be executed within sight of the castle walls unless they immediately capitulated.

Captain William Paulden, one of their more daredevil officers,[34] decided to snatch Rainborowe and exchange his life for that of Langdale. He and twenty-two hand-picked volunteers crept out of the castle at midnight on 28 October and rode the twelve miles (19 km) to Doncaster where the parliamentary commander was billeted in an inn, preparing for godly worship on the Sabbath morrow. Blood may have been one of them.

Four assailants safely reached Rainborowe's lodgings and announced they held an urgent message for him from Cromwell. The ruse worked: they were admitted and promptly seized the parliamentary commander and his lieutenant, bundling both down into the street and their waiting horses. The colonel suddenly realised he was confronted by only four men and shouted 'Arms! Arms!' to rouse his sleeping troops in the town. Amid the confusion, one of his would-be kidnappers grappled with Rainborowe, dropping his uncocked pistol on the ground. The lieutenant picked it up – but before he could open fire, was cut down ruthlessly. Rainborowe was stabbed in the neck and when he tried to stagger to his feet, was run through his body with a sword, killing him on the spot.[35]

The Royalists rode out of Doncaster, across the bridge over the River Don, and headed back north to Pontefract, sweeping up fifty prisoners on the way.[36]

Blood's biographer, 'R.H.', maintained that most people believed that he was 'the contriver and [an] associate' in 'this bold and desperate adventure'. However, he acknowledged that Blood 'frequently disowned the fact himself' and it would therefore 'be a crime to impute the honours of other men to a valour that has no need of these shifts'.[37]

As we shall see, Blood never shrank from claiming the benefits of notoriety for his adventures, so it is strange that he should deny any part in such a daring escapade. And yet, this adventure bears some of the hallmarks of his later outrages: a grievance nurtured; a bold attempt to exact vengeance and a hostage taken.[38] Years later, in 1671, Prince Rupert, the dashing and impetuous Royalist cavalry general, generously described Blood as a 'very stout, bold fellow in the royal service'.[39] Amid all those officers in the Royalist armies, why would he remember Blood, unless he had been involved in a remarkable feat of arms? There is one additional piece of circumstantial evidence that may link Blood with this botched and bloody attempted kidnapping. It is known that Rainborowe's regiment took an important role in the siege of Sherborne Castle in

1645[40] and the attack on the parliamentary commander may well have satisfied a grudge, a personal desire for revenge for an incident during the fighting.

Afterwards Blood, always the realist with a cynical eye on the bigger picture, may have believed that the Royalists were finally and irrevocably defeated. Charles I had been beheaded outside the Banqueting House in Whitehall with one blow of an axe by a masked executioner on the bitterly cold afternoon of Tuesday, 30 January 1649. Any chance that the Stuarts would be restored to the crown of England and Scotland seemed nigh impossible. By 1650, Blood was in Lancashire and, self-betterment overcoming the niceties of hopeless loyalty, had switched sides, becoming a cavalry cornet, then promoted lieutenant in the parliamentary army.[41] He may have served briefly under Cromwell in Ireland after the Roundhead general landed with 8,000 infantry and 4,000 cavalry of the New Model Army at Dublin in August 1649 at the start of a campaign which was to crush the Irish rebellion after four years' hard fighting.[42]

Blood had ended seven years of war still a junior officer in the military command structure. As the years passed, his well-developed ego allowed him to rise up through the ranks to self-appointment as a colonel. But now he had something else on his mind – his requirement for a wife.

The parish registers of Newchurch, Lancashire record the wedding there of *Thomas Bloud gen*[erosus] *et Maria Holcrofte* on 21 June 1650.[43]

Blood had done well for himself.

His seventeen-year-old bride was the elder daughter of Lieutenant Colonel John Holcroft and his wife Margaret, of Holcroft Hall, a late-fifteenth-/early-sixteenth century farmhouse with stone mullion windows which still stands today.[44] He apparently had met her through Holcroft's eldest son Thomas, a fellow parliamentary soldier[45] or possibly through connections with his stepgrandmother's family.

The Holcrofts came to this part of Lancashire in the mid-fourteenth century.[46] Thomas Holcroft was a 'gentleman servitor' at the coronation of Anne Boleyn at Westminster in 1533. Three years later his brother John Holcroft contributed fifty-three soldiers to the Earl of Derby's contingent fighting against the rebels of the Pilgrimage of Grace who sought an end to the suppression of the monasteries. The Holcrofts did well out of the Reformation: Thomas was granted local friaries at Warrington, Preston and Lancaster, and portions of the lands of Whalley Abbey, Cartmel Priory and Vale Royal Abbey in Cheshire.[47] At the end of Henry VIII's reign, two members of the family served as commissioners evaluating the valuable chantries at Stretford and Manchester in February 1546.[48]

From 1640, Blood's father-in-law was MP for Liverpool in the Short Parliament and then mayor of the city in 1644. Two years later he was elected MP for Wigan but was excluded from Parliament in Pride's Purge on 6 December 1648, arguably the only successful military coup d'état in English history.[49]

John Holcroft was an important local parliamentary hero, having been involved in one of the first skirmishes in the prelude to the Civil War. On 15 July 1642, Holcroft, still a plain 'Mr', together with his fellow local militia commissioners, tried to deny Manchester to the forces of the crown. The Royalist high sheriff of Lancaster, Lord Molyneux, and Lord Strange had just sat down to a convivial meal after a busy day recruiting troops in the city, when they heard that Holcroft was only streets away at the head of a large force 'with soldiers armed with pikes and muskets, with their matches lighted and cocked, also a drum beating'. Molyneux ordered them 'in his majesty's name to lay down their arms, keep the peace and cease the tumult but Mr Holcroft ... charged him with disobedience to [the] law'. In the confusion that followed, Strange was shot at three times before he and the high sheriff fled the town. One of their pursuers, Richard Percival, a 'linen webster' of Kirkmanshulme, was killed by a pistol bullet, supposedly the first man to die in the English Civil War.[50] In March 1643, Holcroft commanded a small force of 600 musketeers defending Lancaster. After they were driven into the castle, the frustrated Royalists set the town ablaze.[51]

Mary Holcroft was married from Holcroft Hall and, nine months later, the couple's first-born son, Thomas, was baptised at Newchurch on 30 March 1651.[52] Over the years, the couple were to have six more children: four sons – William, Holcroft (born *c.*1657), Edmund and Charles – and two daughters, Mary and Elizabeth.[53]

Blood returned to Ireland and his wife joined him there later in 1651. He apparently received a grant of more land in lieu of army back pay and so impressed Henry Cromwell (Oliver's fourth son), lord deputy and later lord lieutenant of Ireland, that he was appointed a parliamentary commissioner.[54] His biographer says Cromwell looked upon Blood 'as a person fit for employment and promotion ... the main use he made of his authority was to assert and uphold, as much as lay within his power, the Protestant and English interest in that kingdom'.[55]

So we leave Thomas Blood, happily chasing and chastising Irish Catholic rebels – or do we? There is one report that, around this time in his career, he served as a footman, under the alias 'Allen', to one of the regicides[56] – one of the fifty-nine who condemned the king at his trial in Westminster Hall and afterwards signed the death warrant. On one hand, this seems unlikely, as Blood would have been a man of some means in Ireland and would hardly have been employed as a mere retainer, even to a person of influence in the Commonwealth government. On the other, 'Allen' was one of his favourite aliases in the years to come and possibly Blood cunningly believed that such employment might prove advantageous, close to the new egalitarian seat of power.

Oliver Cromwell, Lord Protector of the realm since December 1653, died in Whitehall on 3 September 1658 from the effects of malaria and a kidney infection. He was fifty-nine. His son Richard succeeded him, but stable governance descended into confusion as various factions fought for political supremacy. Many guessed correctly that the days of England as a republic were numbered.

On 8 May 1660, Parliament proclaimed that the exiled Charles II had been the lawful monarch since the execution of his father in 1649. He was crowned in Westminster Abbey on 23 April 1661.

These momentous events across the Irish Sea reached out and radically changed the lives of Thomas Blood and his growing family in ways they could hardly have dreamt of in their worst nightmares. Ruin was about to befall the Bloods of Sarney, Co. Meath.

# I

## Capture the Castle

*Things of this nature, in my humble judgment, must not be dallied with, but be crushed in the very egg and a rebellion is easier prevented than suppressed.*

Roger Boyle, Earl of Orrery and president
of Munster, to Charles II, 23 May 1663[1]

Wholesale state confiscation of Catholic and Royalist lands in Ireland followed Oliver Cromwell's brutal suppression of the Irish Confederation rebellion. Superficially, this seemed to be the action of an impecunious administration in London confiscating traitors' property simply to meet the vociferous demands of New Model Army veterans in Ireland for their eighteen months' arrears in pay.[2] English governments had taken this harsh step before and were prepared to repeat it in the future.

However, the objective was far more malevolent than a mere juggling of hard-pressed state budgets.

The Rump Parliament's Act of Settlement of Ireland in August 1652 authorised the summary execution of the leaders of the defeated uprising. It also established a legal framework to seize sufficient land to reward those 'adventurers' (or rather speculators) who had funded English efforts to put down the insurrection to the tune of £10 million from 1642, as well as recompensing, in kind, the 12,000 English troops still serving in Ireland.[3]

Many Royalist and almost all the Catholic landowners, particularly those living in Ulster, Leinster and Munster, lost all or part of their estates. Even those who played no part in the rebellion were penalised. Those living in Ireland between 1 October 1649 and 1 March 1650 who had not 'manifested their constant good affection to the interest of the Commonwealth of England' lost one third of their lands. Before these punitive measures were implemented, 60 per cent of Ireland's land was in Catholic hands. Afterwards, their holdings had plummeted to about 8 per cent – and much of this acreage produced poor agricultural yields.

Worse still, Cromwell planned a coldly calculated programme of ethnic cleansing, perhaps defined more accurately as social engineering. Around 50,000 Irish men, women and children were deported to Jamaica, Barbados and the smaller Caribbean islands of St Kitts, Nevis and Montserrat to work as indentured labourers on sugar and tobacco plantations.[4] Landowners were told in July 1653 that they must move to Connacht (the smallest and poorest of the four Irish provinces) and its counties of Mayo, Galway, Sligo, Leitrim and Roscommon, all west of the River Shannon. The only alternative offered to this banishment was to be summarily hanged; reputedly, Cromwell himself demanded that the Irish must go 'to Hell or Connacht'.

These newly designated Irish homelands were intended to be tribal reservations, in all but name, their populations hemmed in by water – either by the river or the North Atlantic. To reinforce the point, a one-mile (1.61 km) wide security zone was established along the eastern perimeter of Co. Clare and reserved for armed military settlers 'to confine the transplanted and to cut them off from relief by sea'.

Furthermore, a £20 bounty was offered for the arrest of Catholic priests. Assisting or sheltering them became a capital offence. In the forlorn hope that the faith would wither and die in their absence, priests were incarcerated in an internment camp on Inishbofin, a bare rocky island,[5] measuring 3.5 by 2.5 miles (5.7 by 4 km), seven miles (4.35 km) off the coast of Co. Galway.

With the massacres of Wexford and Drogheda of 1649 still vivid in their memories, it is no surprise that Catholic landowners upped sticks and left hearth and home to obey Cromwell's penal edict. Popular myth talks darkly of wholesale depopulation, but in reality many remained on their former property as tenant farmers, serving absentee English landlords.

To ensure the profitable and most efficient distribution of the sequestered lands, a radical and intensive mapping survey of Ireland was undertaken by William Petty, one-time physician-general to the Commonwealth army in Ireland. Assisted by 1,000 men, the 'Down Survey' took three years to complete from 1655 and its results allow us to see precisely how the riches of Ireland were divided up, as its scale was generally forty perches to an inch, one perch equalling twenty-one feet (6.4 metres).[6]

Thomas Blood, as a former parliamentary soldier, was one of those who benefited from this redistribution of other people's assets. In addition to his old property in Sarney and in Co. Wicklow, the survey shows him with land holdings in the parish of Athboy in Driseog, Co. Meath, formerly owned by the Protestant Royalist Edward Scurlocke. These totalled 237 acres, which he shared with Trinity College, Dublin, and another old parliamentary comrade-in-arms, Nathaniel Vincent. Elsewhere in the county, at Moyagher, in the barony of Lune, Blood held a one-third share in 843 acres, formerly owned by Catholics named as James White, John Begs and another only identified as —Plunkett from Rathbone. At Kilpatrick, in the barony of Margallion, Blood now held 66 acres in his own right and shared 562 acres (of which 270 were categorised 'unprofitable') at Brittas in the parish of Nobber in the same barony with James Watson, both parcels of land once owned by a Catholic called Patrick Cruice.[7]

Together with the 500 acres of unprofitable mountainside at Glenmalure and his 220 acres in Sarney, Blood thus had ownership of or part share in a total of 2,428 acres.

Suddenly, by the shifting fortunes of war and the rich bounty of state intervention, he had become a very well-heeled gentleman indeed.

All this was to change dramatically after the restoration of the monarchy in 1660. Two years later, the Irish Parliament passed an Act of Settlement[8] which ordered that the Cromwellian settlers and the demobilised Commonwealth soldiers surrender some or all of their allotted lands to 'old English' Royalists and the so-called 'innocent Catholics' who had played no part in the Irish Confederation rebellion but had lost their property.[9] All the plaintiffs had to do would be to lodge a formal claim and prove their original title to their lost acres. The new settlers would be compensated with awards of an equal amount of land elsewhere in Ireland, according to the legislators.

Each case was to be decided by a seven-man Court of Claims – made up of seven imported English gentlemen to allay Protestant misgivings about the process.[10] Within six months, between 5,000 and 6,000 Irishmen applied for restitution of their property, and of the 600 cases heard during this short period, more than 85 per cent were successful and their lands restored. On top of this flood of claims, it was discovered there was not nearly enough vacant land to hand over to the newly dispossessed. The plan was unworkable and the seeds of discord and resentment took root in the fertile soil of Irish bitterness.

As a direct result, Thomas Blood forfeited his possession of 1,426 acres granted under the 1652 Act of Settlement – or almost 85 per cent of the property handed over to him by a generous Roundhead Parliament. Of the lands left to him, the 270 acres at Brittas were acknowledged to be barren and unprofitable, as were those previously granted by Charles I in the Wicklow Mountains. He was left with just 220 acres at Sarney that could yield any kind of profit on which to live.

At one stroke, his wealth and hopes of future prosperity had been destroyed. He had been dispossessed by statute. One report says he was forced to move from his hometown of Sarney to Dublin and lodge with his Scottish brother-in-law William Leckie (or Lackey), a fellow of Trinity College, Dublin, former Presbyterian preacher in Co. Meath and now a local schoolmaster.[11] His landlord was a voluble and vocal advocate of using armed force to restore the lands of dispossessed Protestants.

Blood's continuing poverty is perhaps revealed by the later petition of a Dublin butcher called Dolman. On 30 June 1663, the slaughterman sought the legal assistance of James Butler, First

Duke of Ormond (lord lieutenant of Ireland since 1661), to re-cover an 'outlandish bull and cow' of which he had been unlawfully deprived by Blood, described in the petition as a 'lieutenant in the late army'. His petition was approved and presumably the butcher had his animals returned. As to whether they came back dead or alive, history is silent.[12]

His financial and legal troubles were not confined to Ireland. In Lancashire, his father-in-law, Lieutenant Colonel John Holcroft, had died and was buried at Newchurch on 22 April 1656, virtuously bequeathing £80 a year to the curate of the village.[13]

Holcroft's death came at an inopportune time, as far as the con-venient settlement of his estate was concerned, for his executors found themselves confronted by an administrative nightmare. A legal action had begun four years earlier over the ownership of Holcroft's manor of Pursfurlong and property called 'Great and Little Wooldens' in the hamlet of Cadeshead in Lancashire. This litigation stemmed from the estates, debts and last will of another local magnate, Edward Calveley, who died in November 1636.[14] Depositions had been taken from witnesses in 1652 which sug-gested that Holcroft had sustained Calveley when he was in straitened circumstances and the estate was bought by Holcroft, who raised the money by selling his rights to the tolls levied on the roads in Manchester. Evidence was given that 'several great sums of money and gold' had been brought by horse and that the parliamentary officer had moved into the property 'and was ac-counted the owner by the country'.[15] Events then became more menacing. At the Lancashire midsummer Quarter Sessions held at Ormskirk in 1657, the colonel's widow Margaret swore on oath that on

> the twelfth day of February in the night time, Thomas Holcroft of Holcroft esquire; Hamlet Holcroft the younger of Culcheth, gent[leman], Joseph Key, Robert Drinkwater, husbandmen and Richard Dean Milner, all of Holcroft, forcibly and riotously w[i]th swords ... and other weapons did enter into ... [the] house of this infor[mant] ...

The document is badly torn[16] and, frustratingly, the *lacuna* rules out any chance of explaining why Margaret's eldest son and another member of her late husband's family, together with three henchmen, should break into her home at dead of night, armed to the teeth. In the light of events that we shall explore later, it seems likely this was somehow connected with the division of Holcroft's estates.

A flurry of court actions now assailed Blood's embattled in-laws over their extensive property holdings throughout north-west England. In 1660, Robert King brought a civil case against 'Mary Holcroft, relict of John Holcroft' and John Benbow, over an earlier conveyance made by Christopher Trentham of his estate in Cheshire to Holcroft.[17] To complicate matters still further, during the Easter and Trinity legal terms of 1661, depositions were taken in a fresh action brought by John Calveley against the son, Thomas Holcroft, his mother and others over the ownership of the manors of Holcroft, Cadeshead, Barton-upon-Irwell and Pursfurlong and lands in Culcheth, Risley, Atherton and Wigshaw, all in Lancashire.[18] As we will see, the intransigence of the issue was to deepen as the years passed and, as usual in such cases, only the lawyers profited.

Therefore, as far as Thomas Blood was concerned, on top of the problems of a growing family in Ireland and an unexpected dramatic downturn in his fortunes, immediate fulfilment of his wife's expected inheritance rights seemed less than certain. His future looked decidedly bleak, if not hopeless.

There were others in Ireland in the same sorry plight and feelings amongst the English and Scots Protestant population began to run high. Anger and resentment became widespread and there were furious demands for action to redress perceived injustices.

A further factor in the growing agitation amongst the nonconformists was the Act of Uniformity of 1662[19] which made use of the new *Book of Common Prayer* compulsory during church services and decreed that officiating ministers had to be ordained by bishops. Any clergyman who refused to take an oath swearing allegiance to the terms of the Act faced ejection from his living. This legislation imposed the established Anglican Church and its rites and form of prayers on the population and further alienated Presbyterians and other dissenting ministers and their congregations.

Fear of violence and unrest multiplied like an unseen contagion throughout Ireland. In October 1662, the Dublin government was forced to order that unauthorised stockpiles of gunpowder should be surrendered by 10 December under amnesty. A second proclamation in November banned anyone other than MPs and enlisted soldiers from openly carrying weapons.

Another disturbing straw in the wind was the continuing losses, apparently from pilfering, of weapons from the army's arsenals in Ireland. An inventory drawn up in June 1663 showed major losses of arms since the last stock-taking nine months before: 112 modern firelock muskets were missing; 848 older matchlock muskets, 837 bandolier belts with powder cartridges; 80 cavalry carbines; 93 pikes; 80 pistols and 3,499 swords. While in the normal course of events some may have been discarded because of age and others sent for repair, there were inevitable suspicions that some of these weapons had found their way into the hands of nonconformist dissidents – more than enough to equip a well-armed regiment of rebels.

More perturbing, perhaps, was the absence of twenty-three 'great guns of all sorts'. Again, this may have been because these cannon were no longer regarded as fit for use; of the remaining artillery, only forty guns were 'sufficiently mounted' for service in combat.[20]

In early 1663, an intercepted letter written by Irish nonconformists was palpably designed to be both inflammatory and seditious. It purported to be penned by a Catholic and aimed to trigger antipopish hysteria with its talk of 'crushing the fanatic [Protestant] officers [in the army] by peeling their rind and imprisoning some of the leading men' as part of a plot to make the army in Ireland wholly Catholic.[21]

Protestant settlers believed it was high time to sweep aside the niceties of political protocol and make a stand in the defence of their interests. On 13 February 1663, Sir Audley Mervyn, speaker of the Irish House of Commons, delivered an eloquent and powerful address to Ormond in the presence chamber of Dublin Castle.

It must have been uncomfortable listening for Ormond as Mervyn rambled on, employing colourful, sometimes almost apocryphal prose, in a thirty-page speech designed to demonstrate the great anger felt by his MPs and their constituents. He began with dire warnings that popery still posed a grave danger to the Anglican religion in Ireland:

> Believe it sir, whatever delusive tenets have been broached of late, the contrary has been written in blood, not in his majesty's kingdom, but wheresoever the Papal power has been exalted.
>
> Persons preferring the reformed religion are but tenants for their lives and fortunes till a time of slaughter is appointed.

Mervyn then moved on to the unrest and disquiet over the restitution of lands under the 1662 Act of Settlement: 'We have been asked to speak for the people, who had we not spoken for them would certainly have spoken for themselves ... The alarm that Hannibal is at the gates is hot throughout the Protestant plantations'. They were being treated unjustly: 'The law says "All hail Protestants of Ireland" but if the execution is dissonant we are crucified under a glorious inscription of mockery.'[22]

Just over two weeks later, the Irish Commons reinforced their message to Ormond's government by approving a motion pledging that they would apply 'the utmost remedies to prevent and stop the great and manifold prejudices and inconveniences which daily did and were like to happen to the Protestants of Ireland by the proceedings of the Commissioners'.[23] The vote did nothing to dampen the dangerous powder trail of discontent and protest.

The lives and well-being of the commissioners were now being threatened and in London Charles II was quick to lend them his royal support in what was becoming an impossible task:

> We have heard there have been several threats and disrespects used to you by some turbulent and unquiet persons to discourage or at least [harass] you in the execution of the trust committed to you.

We shall loyally support you against all such affronts and are pleased with your impartiality.[24]

No wonder the acrid, sharp smell of insurrection began to creep through the streets of Dublin. That month, the lord lieutenant warned Charles II that the army in Ireland was so ill-prepared that it was impossible to predict how far a rising might succeed:

This general discontent will not, I hope, cause any disturbance but if it should, the army is in a very ill state to repress [it], for there is nothing in the Treasury to draw or keep it together . . .

If we cannot keep the army together it will always be in the power of a few desperate men to start a commotion with regard to which no one can say where it would end.[25]

Ormond waited until 9 March before he made his official response to the Irish MPs' resolution. He did not mince his words, reproaching them for having caused so much 'general uneasiness' that many English-born Protestants 'had been frightened into selling their lots and adventures at vile and under rates or compounding with the old proprietors on very ill terms'.[26]

In making his admonishment, Ormond was aware that a conspiracy to stage a coup d'état in Dublin was under way. On 4 March, he had received a letter from Philip Alden, a shady lawyer, a dealer in forfeited estates and a known agent of the former parliamentary general and regicide Edmund Ludlow, who after the restoration had escaped to Switzerland to save his head.[27] Alden had been recruited by an army officer, Colonel Edward Vernon, as a double agent at the beginning of 1662 to monitor the activities of nonconformist 'fanatics' in Ireland. Now he was proving his mettle.

His encrypted note to the lord lieutenant – sent direct as his 'handler' Vernon was away in London – provided sketchy details of a political conspiracy against his administration involving some Irish MPs.[28] Ormond replied immediately, demanding to know 'who are at the head of the design for taking [Dublin] castle'.[29]

According to the spy, the plot had been under way since the

beginning of 1662 with a 'close committee, being most of the members of [the Irish] Parliament' sitting daily in Dublin with the objective of overthrowing Ormond's government and engaging 'England, Scotland and Ireland in a new civil war'.[30] Confirmation came the same day from a soldier named Jenkin Hopkins, who had been reportedly sounded out about joining the insurrection by a Lieutenant Turet. Further credence to the reports was provided by later news of the discovery of a parallel plot in Durham, but there the principal conspirator, Paul Hobson, had escaped.[31]

The attempt on Dublin Castle was originally planned for 9 or 10 March, but the conspirators brought forward the date to Thursday, 5 March – just twenty-four hours after Alden revealed it to Ormond – because Sir John Stevens, constable of the castle, was due to mount the guard that day. He was blissfully unaware there were traitors within his garrison. A sergeant and fifty privates had joined the plot and, having obtained arms and powder 'out of the store by the folly of the storekeeper's boy, resolved to make their attempt on the outer gate'.[32] Ormond organised a hasty plan to thwart the coup attempt with loyal troops, but the plotters got wind of it and fled the city.

Two days later Ormond wrote to Chancellor Hyde describing how the plot to 'surprise this castle' had been discovered. He admitted ruefully that he could not 'boast much of being master of the temper necessary for the government of as ill a sort of people as inhabit any part of the earth. I am destitute of the power which should make them good [and] to keep them from doing hurt'.[33] The same day, he wrote to Henry Bennet (the previous year appointed one of Charles II's secretaries of state), announcing he was deeply engaged 'in the examination of a conspiracy for taking this Castle and me in it'.

He had discovered 'no one better in it than [Captain] William Hewlett who has been accused of bragging that it was he that had murdered the last king'.[34] Ormond added: 'These fellows evidently take courage from the [Irish] House of Commons and if they change not and become more temperate, I shall presently make use of the power I have to separate them either by prorogation or for good and all. They will [create] less harm apart than together.'[35]

At least the chastened Irish Commons pulled back from confrontation. On 11 March they responded to Ormond's biting words with a short, somewhat cringing response:

> Our address was certainly misinterpreted if it was taken to mean anything disloyal to the king.
>
> Our only wish was to lay before you and the Commissioners of Settlement certain considerations in order that you might take resolutions upon them.
>
> The House believes that you have done much to establish the Protestant religion and English interest. We never intended by the orders we made to trench upon your grace's prerogative and hope that those who made the late plot against the castle will receive condign and speedy punishment.

They concluded with the promise of steadfast assistance 'against all opponents of the king's authority'.[36]

A week later, Ormond sent for Alden 'for fear of discovery of our correspondence'. A face-to-face meeting was required to elicit more information to help find 'the bottom of the plot . . . in some way that it may not spoil the use of future intelligence'.[37]

Two days later in London that inveterate gossip Samuel Pepys heard of the conspiracy in a coffee house near St Paul's churchyard:

> I heard how there had been a surprisal of Dublin by some discontented Protestants . . . and it seems the Commissioners have carried themselves so high for the Papists that the others will not endure it.
>
> Hewlett and some others are taken and clapped up and they say the king has sent over to dissolve Parliament there who went very high against the Commissioners.
>
> May God send all well![38]

The Irish government was meanwhile frustrated by its lack of evidence against the handful of minor players swept up after the aborted coup – mostly former parliamentary officers now working as 'discontented tradesmen' in Dublin. Ormond was exasperated at the failure to discover and then prosecute the ringleaders: 'The design to surprise the castle sticks at Hewlett', he complained to Secretary Bennet. 'We can trace no further – not even to get enough evidence to incriminate him legally.'[39] He admitted to the king that 'we find a difficulty in inculpating people in connection with the recent plot against the Council and Parliament . . . Since yesterday I have heard that some go about persuading the English that the Irish had a plot to destroy them'.[40]

His irritation was exacerbated by widespread rumours that Edmund Ludlow had been involved in the plot and, if so, had cannily escaped his net. John King, First Baron Kingston, reported that the regicide was said to have been in Ireland

> until the last week and I think he came here when the last design [plot] in England failed him . . .
>    He went from Limerick with a vessel pretended for the discovery of a Brazil[41] and under that shelter [cover] has been fitting with arms, ammunition, provisions [for] the two or three months past.[42]

Ormond continued to fear a fresh insurrection and was right to be cautious. By mid-April he knew the conspiracy to seize Dublin Castle had been resurrected by a wider and more capable group of conspirators. The news had come from a spy dispatched to Waterford, Kilkenny and Tipperary to act as an agent provocateur, pretending to recruit dissidents to the banner of rebellion. The agent, identified only by his initials 'P.A.' (noted on his report by a recklessly careless Ormond), indicated that two army officers, Major Alexander Staples and a Colonel Wallace, had joined the plot.[43] This time, the lord lieutenant decided to sit tight, allow the plot to come to fruition, and catch the conspirators red-handed.

Informing the king of this new danger, the lord lieutenant said the conspiracy involved 'the same kind of people' as were responsible for the former. He believed it was a real threat because of the 'unusual meetings and preparations ... about the same time in several parts of the kingdom'.[44] Secretary Bennet, in response, inquired if Ormond had any new information about the plot and whether he could discover 'any connections with England and Scotland ... [where] there is certainly much combustible matter if a fire should ever break forth, from which God keep us'.[45]

Doubtless inflamed by his brother-in-law's incendiary polemics, Blood was deeply involved in the first plot – but the precise role he played remains frustratingly opaque. During 1662, Blood was said to be active recruiting supporters amongst former parliamentary soldiers in Dublin[46] and at Christmas that year he and William Leckie had journeyed north to Ulster to sow sedition amongst the Scottish Presbyterian settlers. Here he received some promises of support, with the Scots agreeing to 'rise in arms and second the design of taking the castle'.[47]

The part he played in the revived conspiracy is rather more transparent. Although the informer Alden contemptuously plays down his role, dismissing 'Lieutenant Blood' as merely an 'agent [whom] they sent upon errands and not the chief of the rebels as generally reported to be',[48] it is clear he was much more than just a humble messenger boy.

'Thomas Blood of Sarney' heads the list of wanted men named in the government proclamation promulgated after the second plot unravelled, and Blood was supposedly the author of the rebels' declaration, printed for general distribution after the successful capture of both Ormond and Dublin Castle.[49] He looms large in the accounts of the conspiracy given under interrogation, as he was to lead the assault on Dublin Castle and claimed, according to one informer, to have planned the coup d'état 'for three-quarters of a year'.[50] Mere mention of Blood's name was enough to send a cold shiver of apprehension down the spines of both the Irish and English governments in the months and years to come.

Vernon commented to Bennet that while the lord lieutenant had 'nipped the last little design in the bud, there is now one in blooming which (if it take) he will be surer to gather it when it is full ripe, which will be in a short time'. At the heart of the conspiracy was one Stephen Charnock, a former chaplain to Henry Cromwell, Parliament's lord deputy in Ireland for two years from 1657. Charnock, said Vernon,

> was private, not stirring out of his lodging but on his coming and departure it's good to have an eye on him but by a very curious [careful] hand, lest he, finding himself suspected may cause a jealousy [hamper] upon our intelligence.

Government spies had established that this new conspiracy was part of a much more ambitious plan to overthrow the monarchy – with concurrent uprisings by radical nonconformists in England and Scotland. Charnock had

> told the villains [plotters] that they were so hampered in England they could not stir 'till the ice was broken here or in Scotland' (which is said to be very forward) and he assured them of £20,000 ready in [the] bank.
>
> He proposed Henry Cromwell as ... their general which was generally rejected.
>
> The Scotch designers [plotters] seem to lean towards [establishing a new] Commonwealth and did not positively refuse Ludlow for their ... captain.

In England, Vernon warned, there were 'rich discontents' who had to be closely watched, 'being there is so much money stirring and my Staffordshire intelligencer [spy] assured me they had notice from London that God had raised them up considerable friends beyond their expectation but at that time, the Lord's harvest was not ripe'.

> I could say more, but it is unwise to do so without [using] a cypher. There are some postmasters on the road who are subtle fellows and have actually served as intelligencers and officers to the rebels.[51]

The Irish government imposed new security measures to counter the insurrection. On 4 May, two orders in council were signed. The first, designed to secure at least the temporary loyalty of royal troops, regulated military pay and organised the payment of arrears. The second directed 'the return to his majesty's stores in Dublin and in various other cities and towns, of arms formerly taken from thence' – an administrative attempt to neutralise at least some of the weapons and munitions that had been stolen over the previous few months.[52]

Ormond was confident he had the measure of the plotters. 'The design ... ripens very fast and is very far spread, yet my greatest care is not to let the conspirators find they are discovered lest they desist' he told the king on 16 May.

> I want evidence and matter sufficient to make examples of some of them ... Nothing would contribute [more] to the future settlement and peace of this kingdom.
>
> I do not doubt but that knowing what I do of their actions and intentions, I shall be able to resist and apprehend them in the very act of their attempting the castle ...

The lord lieutenant assured Charles: 'I would not have acted upon my own responsibility in this matter but that I cannot, in all probability, [because of slow communications] have your directions. God preserve your majesty's person and government from this wicked generation.'[53]

Three days later, he instructed the governors of Carrickfergus, Derry and Galway to search diligently for conspirators and take action to secure the loyalty and security of their garrisons.[54]

Matters were now coming to a head.

That same day, Colonel Alexander Jephson, MP for Trim in Co. Meath, had approached Sir Theophilius Jones at his home in Lucan, eight miles (13 km) south of Dublin, with an incredible offer. Jones, a former governor of Dublin under the Protectorate and, since 1661, scoutmaster[55] of Ireland, had a case set down for hearing by the reviled Court of Claims.

Jephson's horse had cast a shoe and while the two awaited its re-shoeing at a nearby blacksmith's forge, Jones had invited his visitor into his home. In the buttery, a tankard of ale, a bottle of cider and a plate of meat were ordered up and, as they awaited these refreshments, Jephson laid his hand 'on a large sword which he had by his side'.

> He said he had not worn that sword for thirteen years before and had made his will and left his wife and thirteen children behind him and was going to Dublin where ... he and many more men were resolved to adventure their lives and they ... doubted not to secure the English interest.
>
> They were assured of the castle[s] of Dublin and Limerick, Waterford and Clonmell.

Jones, doubtless open-mouthed at this revelation, could only stammer out that this 'seemed a very high undertaking' and required 'many weighty considerations for effecting it, particularly a good army and money to maintain it'. Jephson assured him there was no problem there.

> We want not an army, for there are 15,000 Scots excommunicated in the north by the Bishop of Down and the rest of the bishops, which were ready within two days and they doubted not that our army would join with them.
>
> And they had a bank of money in Dublin sufficient to pay off all the arrears of money both in Oliver's [Cromwell] time and since the king came in.

Naturally, Jones asked him where all this cash had come from.

> He did not know from whence the bank of money should come, if not from Holland and that he [saw] three or four firkins [casks containing cash] carried into Mr Boyd's house and he himself could carry out of the bank £500 tomorrow.

Jephson threw all caution aside and revealed more details of the plot to an incredulous Jones.

There were 1,000 horse [cavalry] in Dublin ... which Sir Henry Ingoldesby was to appear with as soon as the castle was taken and a flag put up.

They intended to offer no violence to any [who] ... opposed them. That the lord lieutenant was to be seized ... but to be civilly treated. That several other persons were to be secured and Jephson was to seize the Earl of Clancarty⁵⁶ and Col. Fitzpatrick. Every party had particular orders to surprise all of the guards in the city.

Six ministers in Dublin who went about in periwigs but laid them by when they were in prayer ... were to be in the street to see that no plunder or disorder should be committed.

This was to be a godly rebellion then. Thousands of copies of a declaration had been printed ready for distribution after Dublin Castle and the city had been taken. These would set out the manifesto for the uprising: securing the 'English interest' in the three kingdoms (which had been ruined by 'the countenance given to popery'); restoration of all the estates in Ireland possessed by the English on 7 May 1659 and re-establishment of the church along the nonconformist principles of the Solemn League and Covenant. There was no suggestion of a return to a republic.

Jephson, carried away by his own enthusiasm, even rashly disclosed the rebels' passwords: 'For the king and English interest'.

What of that offer to Sir Theophilius Jones? Jephson promised him that after capturing Dublin, he would become the commander of the rebels' '20,000-strong army'. There was no risk, he added:

[He] should run no hazard in it but might sit still and not appear until the whole work was done.

There were two amongst the conspirators who did not trust Jones, the colonel told him, believing him to be 'too great a creature of the

Duke's [Ormond] . . . but these [views did] not prevail', all the rest being for the good knight.[57]

After Jephson rode back to Dublin, cock-a-hoop that the rebels had a commander-in-chief in waiting, Jones began to worry that there were elements of self-delusion in those wild claims of support. He wrote down a detailed account of this seditious conversation and, in fulfilment of the beliefs of the doubting Thomases amongst the conspirators, early the following morning revealed everything to Ormond.

That night, 20 May, three nonconformist ministers met in Dublin to seek God's blessing on the enterprise.

Blood was staying at the Bottle Inn near the city's St Patrick's Gate. Together with his brother-in-law, William Leckie, he and two other plotters, Lieutenant Richard Thompson (deputy provost-marshall for Leinster) and James Tanner (a Dubliner who was formerly a clerk to Henry Cromwell's secretary) met at the White Hart, further along Patrick Street, to finalise the arrangements for the coup. After their meal ended, they were joined by Jephson, two men from his Trim constituency called Ford and Lawrence, and a Captain Browne.

The remaining conspirator who attended this cosy gathering was the informer Philip Alden.

Over the preceding days there had been much acrimonious debate about whether to kill Ormond or merely to take him hostage. Some maintained that the lord lieutenant had been 'a great patron to the English and the Protestant religion' and therefore should be spared. The more ruthless among them countered that Ormond was unwaveringly loyal to the king and 'his interest in the kingdom and the army' was so strong that, if spared assassination, '[at] one time or another he would prevail against them'. Their arguments prevailed and the plotters finally agreed to kill him after the castle had been stormed.[58]

Lawrence urged them to strike now, even though they only had ten cavalrymen at their disposal instead of the 120 planned – or the 1,000 horse that Jephson had earlier boasted of.[59] Later, Alden reported:

It was resolved by the confederates not to stay [delay] longer (having greater numbers with their arms, garrisons and towns as they gave out and believed) to second them in that country, in Scotland and England, but the next morning to surprise the castle of Dublin and afterwards to march northwards to join the Scots.

The plan was simple. Six men, including a Dublin shoemaker called Jenkins, would enter the castle about six o'clock the following morning by its Great Gate, disguised as petitioners, exercising their ancient right to seek redress from the lord lieutenant for legal wrongs done them. They would walk to the back gate leading from Ship Street (or Sheep Street as it was known then) and await the arrival of a delivery of bread. The baker would drop his basket of loaves and, in the confusion, the sentinels at the gate would be overpowered.

Blood and about one hundred former parliamentary officers and soldiers would then sweep into the castle, capture it and seize Ormond. He apparently had no intention of killing the viceroy. Lord Dungannon's troop of soldiers would be lured away by men commanded by one Crawford. William Warren, brother of Colonel Abel Warren, would recruit some of the cavalry at Trim, lately under Sir Thomas Armstrong's command.[60] Once the castle and its arsenal of weapons had been secured – indicated by a flag being hoisted on its highest tower – rebel cavalry would patrol the city streets, dispersing any bands of loyal soldiers they encountered. The nonconformist ministers would use their godly influence to prevent any looting in Dublin. Then the insurgents, reinforced by others rallying to the Protestant flag, would head north to Ulster to join up with a hastily recruited army of Scots settlers, and so sweep on to a glorious victory over the Irish government and the papists.

But more prudent counsels soon prevailed among the conspirators.

Even the most optimistic recognised as the evening wore on that they had too few troops with which to hold the city, let alone guard its gates. Their doubts were intensified by a row with the two landladies who were putting up some of Blood's assault party for the night. Worried about their possible incrimination in such dark matters discussed on their premises, these doughty proprietors 'kept up such a clamouring and threatened to discover them' to the government unless the would-be rebels quit their house immediately. Fearing the next day's attack had been compromised, caution overcame confidence and it was decided around nine o'clock that Wednesday night that it would be prudent to delay the coup d'état until the following week when another 500 cavalry were expected to arrive in Dublin as reinforcements.[61]

Alden alerted Colonel Vernon to the change in plans by eleven o'clock.[62] After the information was confirmed, the lord lieutenant was awakened at four the following morning in his opulent quarters in Dublin Castle.

Ormond decided to take no more chances. He pounced on the plotters immediately.

## 2

## Escape and Evasion

*There is one Blood that was very notorious in this late wicked plot and is fled . . . who has a small house and £100 a year of land in . . . Dunboyne . . . now forfeited to his majesty. I have begged this of the king; the duke and duchess of York and the earl of Bath will speak for me.*

Sir Gilbert Talbot to Joseph Williamson,
13 June 1663[1]

Twenty-four would-be rebels were detained during the early morning raids ordered by the lord lieutenant. As troops continued to kick down the doors of tenements and taverns in Dublin in their frantic hunt for conspirators, those already held were marched, manacled and under heavy guard, into Dublin Castle for interrogation – ironically, the very fortress they had planned to seize. Among these grim-faced men under close arrest was Philip Alden, the government's slippery prize informer. Was his detention the action of an over-enthusiastic officer, who arrested everyone in sight? Or was it a clever ploy by his spymaster Ned Vernon to preserve the agent's cover amongst the conspirators?

Six of the plotters now locked up in the castle's south-west Bermingham Tower[2] were former army officers: the voluble and indiscreet Irish MP Alexander Jephson and his brother colonels Edward Warren and Thomas Scott, who had both served under Henry Cromwell; captains John Chambers, Theophilus Sandford and Lieutenant Richard Thompson. Six prisoners had been cavalry troopers in the parliamentary army: Thomas Ball of Dublin; Robert Davies, John Biddell, John Smullen, John Griffin and William

Bradford. Two were nonconformist ministers – Blood's brother-in-law William Leckie and Edward Baines, once a pastor at St Patrick's Cathedral, Dublin, and another chaplain to Henry Cromwell.[3] The remainder were smaller fry, including John Foulke, the son of a former governor of Drogheda, the innkeeper Andrew Sturges and James Tanner, who very soon was to sing his heart out in a desperate attempt to save his own neck.

Amongst the evidence seized that morning were copies of the rebels' public declaration of their objectives – one copy set out in Blood's bold, straggly handwriting. It described forcefully the plight of those Protestants dispossessed of their lands:

Having long expected the securing . . . of our lives, liberties and estates as a reasonable recompense [for] that industry and diligence exercised by the Protestants of this kingdom in restoring his majesty to the exercise of his royal authority, instead, we find ourselves, our wives and children, without mercy, delivered as a prey unto these barbarous and bloody murderers, whose inhumane cruelty is [registered] in the blood of 150,000 poor Protestants[4] [since] the beginning of the war in this kingdom.

The king, claimed this manifesto, had 'suffered himself to be seduced by evil councillors' and the result was that 'the bloody Papists' were 'the first that tasted of his royal clemency in settling them in their justly forfeited estates'. Moreover, Ormond had [admitted] 'keeping a correspondence with several of the said murderers during their hostility, as appears by his certificates on their behalf to the Court of Claims.

We may undoubtedly conclude . . . that evil is determined upon us and before it [can] be executed . . . to stand upon our just and necessary defence and to use all our endeavours for our self-preservation . . .

And to the end [that] no well-minded Protestants in the three kingdoms may be afraid to stand by us in this our just quarrel, we declare we will stand for that liberty of conscience proper to everyone as a Christian for establishing the Protestant religion in purity, according to the Solemn League and Covenant[5] [and we call] for the restoring of each person to his lands as they held them in the year 1659 and discharging of the army's [pay] arrears.

The declaration ended with the defiant: 'In all which, we doubt not the Lord of Hosts, the mighty God of Jacob, will strengthen our weak hands.'[6] Copies of the rebels' statement, which had been 'fixed in several parts' of the Irish capital, were torn down and on one sheet someone had scribbled a brief narrative of the plot and the names of the principal conspirators – some arrested, others who had made their escape. Among the latter was Blood, described as 'Captain Blood' – apparently now having reverted to his more senior rank in the Royalist army.[7]

The lord lieutenant reported to Bennet on 23 May on his efforts to destroy the insurrection:

I made full preparations and was so ready that if the attack on Dublin Castle had been made, as was intended, on the 21st of this month, the conspirators would, I think, have been taken in their own snare.

But thinking they were discovered, these conspirators who, up to nine o'clock on Wednesday night, were ready to carry out their design, feared to do so on the following morning.

It then became necessary to seize the conspirators and we arrested some and shall arrest more.[8]

In the days and nights that followed, Ormond conducted many interrogations of the detainees in person, assisted by his 'trusty secretary' Sir Paul Davies, sometimes calling in his advisers to suggest specific questions.[9] As a result of what he heard, he was quietly confident that his prisoners would be 'inclined, I think, to save themselves at the expense of accusing others' and despite 'the nicety of our laws' – the requirement for convincing proof presented before a judge and jury – 'we shall be able to make examples of some of these conspirators'.[10]

This skilful and none-too-gentle questioning revealed the scale of the plot and Vernon warned Sir Joseph Williamson in London that 'many persons of note are implicated in it'.[11] The veteran Scottish soldier Sir Arthur Forbes at Newton, Co. Meath, reported widespread talk of an imminent rebellion: 'There is just ground to suspect some sudden design against the State. The people generally hereabouts, seem to apprehend present trouble.'[12]

As part of the fallout from the abortive coup, the vultures were beginning to gather around the estates and possessions of those accused of involvement – now potentially forfeit to the crown and thus obtainable by those happy fortunates who enjoyed royal favour.

First out of the traps was Francis Aungier, Third Baron Aungier, the English MP for Arundel, Sussex, and governor of Westmeath and Longford.[13] In a helpful postscript to his letter to Bennet on 23 May, he acknowledged having seen a list of imprisoned suspects, which included the name of Major Alexander Staples. 'He has a good estate [worth] £500 a year in Tyrone, which will be worth getting. Act quickly, or you will be too late', Aungier warned the secretary of state in Whitehall.[14]

Winston Churchill,[15] one of the despised commissioners in the Court of Claims, had recognised the same golden opportunity. The next day, he too wrote to Bennet, seemingly affecting no great desire to 'gain by these forfeits'. Then, shamelessly, he moved on to reasons why he should be so rewarded.

> But owing to the duty which I here discharge I was more exposed, even than my brothers [fellow commissioners] to danger in the event of this design being successful, I think I may not unreasonably put in for a small proportion among the rest.
>
> Among the twenty or more who are about to be proclaimed traitors . . . there is one Major Abel Warren that has a newly acquired estate of about £400 or £500 a year – most of it such as cannot be taken from him without any previous reprisal.
>
> If the king will grant it, I think I shall be able to reserve it out of the jaws of the Act of Settlement . . .
>
> I need not tell you how 'dry' our employment is here; clogged

with clamour without any certainty of profit. I am only anxious to serve the king.[16]

Any hopes of immediate profit from the downfall of the conspirators, however, were dashed by the lord lieutenant's suggestion that Charles II should delay 'engagements for the estates of those found guilty' which should be used for 'the king's service and [for] the rewarding of those who discovered the plot'.[17]

This did not deter Sir Gilbert Talbot's naked avarice. A few weeks later, he asked Williamson blatantly:

> I ask your honour's pardon for this trouble [but] his majesty promised me on my parting [that] if I could find out any small grant, I should have it.
>
> There is one Blood, that was very notorious in this last wicked plot and is fled, who has a small house and £100 a year of land in the barony of Dunboyne ... of his ancient ancestry but now forfeited to his majesty.
>
> I begged this of the king; the duke and duchess of York and the Earl of Bath will speak for me.

He concluded confidently: 'I doubt not your honour's favour'.[18]

Ormond moved quickly to prorogue the Irish Parliament until 20 July to prevent MPs fomenting any opposition to his measures to secure the kingdom. Furthermore, he published a proclamation to demonstrate that he still retained a firm grip on law and order in Ireland. This described how 'certain wicked persons of fanatic and disloyal principles disaffected to his majesty's just and gracious government' had conspired to raise 'disturbances in Ireland and

> especially to attack his majesty's castle of Dublin and seize the person of us, the lord lieutenant, in order to their carrying on their mischievous contrivances or renewing bloody confusions throughout this kingdom from which evils this realm and all his majesty's subjects ... [which] have been but newly released [by the restoration of the monarchy] ...

We look upon these odious conspiracies as the mischievous contrivances of some fanatic and disloyal persons of desperate fortunes as well as of desperate and destructive principles who endeavour to amend their own condition by the ruin of others ...

We think it well to make it known for the quieting of all honest men that we direct ... the presidents of provinces, mayors of corporations and sheriffs and justices of the peace to arrest and imprison all such persons as they shall within their several areas find to have a hand in this conspiracy.[19]

Ormond had taken an enormous risk in deploying troops, with their uncertain loyalties, to crush the would-be rebellion. Vernon acknowledged frankly that those soldiers ordered to round up the conspirators were 'not without corruption', but only trusted officers 'who had always served his majesty were acquainted with [the plot] and no other'.[20]

Continuing fears of military subversion lay behind the publication of another proclamation the next day, ordering officers to 'repair to their said quarters and there to attend their ... duties, notwithstanding any licence formerly granted for [their] absence ... Wherefrom they may not fail as they will answer [to] the contrary at their peril'.[21] Vernon was typically more forthright, believing that the 'naked truth' was that there were only 'four troops [of cavalry] in Ireland [that] I dare [give] my word for'. Six troops of horse had rounded up the suspects, 'yet upon my conscience, had the enemy attacked them, they [would have] beaten our [soldiers]'.

I confess I saw little safety in this kingdom before the design was broke[n] but my Lord Arran's regiment and a few old cavaliers and the prudence of a government must protect us for a time, by making the English and Irish balance each other.

Vernon then turned to the fate of his spy Alden:

My friend will be able to do us good service and I will endeavour to protect him. He is now in prison but if I can manage it he shall leap out of prison into England, where nothing can stir but that he will be able to detect it.[22]

It soon became apparent that many leading conspirators had evaded arrest, slipping quietly out of Dublin before they could be detained. Roger Boyle, Earl of Orrery and president of Munster, harboured some rather snide criticisms of Ormond's tactics, and claimed some kudos for himself in foiling the plot. In a pointed letter to the king on 23 May, he announced that he had learned of the conspiracy on 8 May and had

> spent the night in writing dispatches which I sent to the lord lieu-tenant, giving him full account of the plot and stating where its conspirators met in Dublin; who are the heads, whom they employ into Scotland and whom to the north of Ireland, [and] also that they intended speedily to surprise your castle and city of Dublin, his grace's person and the State there.
>
> I advised that the chief fanatics in the country should at once be secured to prevent their designs from being executed, for I could not but believe some dare not attempt that wickedness unless many were engaged in it.
>
> I considered also . . . how ill the army was paid . . . the soldiers yet unclothed . . . [and most] parts of the kingdom unsettled . . . If a fire should be kindled . . . no one knows how far it might burn.
>
> But his grace was rather inclined to give the conspirators more rope to hang themselves, being confident that we could quell the rebellion when it took place.
>
> I cheerfully submitted to his view and kept on sending him what news I received.

Orrery had then diligently arrested 'the most fractious Presby-terians, Independents, Anabaptists[23] and Quakers in the southern Ireland – for some bragged, at their arrest in Dublin, that though prevented, they would soon meet us [to fight] in the field. I therefore acted promptly.' In another sly dig at Ormond, he added:

Things of this nature, in my humble judgment, must not be dallied with, but be crushed in the very egg and a rebellion is easier prevented than suppressed ...

There is one Capt. Browne, governor of Liverpool under the usurper, who lies in Dublin, [and who holds] a correspondence between the fanatics of England and Ireland. I have sent his grace notice of where he lies, for if his papers be took, they may discover much.[24]

On 23 May, Ormond and his Council of Ireland issued yet another proclamation, this time offering rewards of £100 (£12,500 in today's money) for the arrest of thirteen conspirators wanted by the government.

The name of Thomas Blood headed the list.

In its ponderous, verbose fashion, the proclamation noted that by 'the blessing of God' the government had 'discovered and disappointed a traitorous conspiracy'. Although many plotters were apprehended, others had 'found means to escape, namely Lieutenant Thomas Blood late of Sarney near Dunboyne, Co. Meath; Colonel Daniel Abbot; Major Abel Warren; Andrew McCormack, lately a pretended minister of Magherally in Co. Down; Robert Chambers, another minister; Col Gilbert Carr, commonly called Gibby Carr; John Chamberlin, late of Dublin, brewer; John Fooke esquire, late of Ardee, Co. Louth; Lieutenant John Ruxton, late of the same place; Major Henry Jones, late of Stillorgan, Co. Dublin; Lieutenant De la Rock; Major Alexander Staples, late of Derry; Lieutenant Colonel William Moore, who was recently disbanded from the army, after being garrisoned at Galway and Athlone.

We therefore, by this proclamation, in his majesty's name, strictly charge and command all and every the said forenamed persons that within eight and forty hours after publishing this proclamation ... he and they do render his and their persons to us, or to any one of his majesty's Privy Council or to one of the Justices of the Peace.

Wherein, [if] they or any of them fail, we do hereby declare and publish them and every one of them so failing, to be rebels and traitors against his majesty, his crown and dignity and to be accordingly prosecuted by all his majesty's good subjects.[25]

Failing any such surrender, this handsome reward would be paid to anyone who handed over one of the conspirators to a sheriff before 24 June. Those who harboured them or failed to deliver them to justice would be declared 'rebels and traitors against the Crown'. All the majesty and force of the law had been thrown at Blood and his co-conspirators.

Ormond busied himself dispatching instructions the length and breadth of Ireland to destroy the conspiracy, root and branch. He warned Colonel Gorges in Derry that, the plot to capture Dublin having failed, 'attempts upon other places will probably be laid aside. Yet, lest desperation should drive on some ... the utmost vigilance is recommended. It is certain that the conspirators had some intelligence in Derry, by means of one Staples, some of whose former company are ... in that garrison still.'[26]

Orrery dutifully ordered his governors and garrison commanders to hunt down the fugitives in this 'horrid plot' with 'all possible diligence' and to reward generously any who captured them for 'their pains and service'.

I have already found some of the emissaries of those traitors, who endeavoured to impose upon the soldiery by telling them the foulest lies imaginable, thereby to debauch [corrupt] them to their rebellious party.

The soldiers were so loyal and honest as to discover to me this seducer, whom forthwith I apprehended and have sent up a prisoner to his grace, to receive his due punishment ...

The soldiers that so loyally and honestly discovered this villain I have rewarded with money and him that first revealed it I have made a corporal that they may see there is more advantage in being a good subject than in being a knave.[27]

Such was the climate of fear now in Ireland that no man, fugitive or pursuer, could be entirely sure of the loyalty or the motives of anyone. Rumours and accusations spread like dry leaves blowing in the wind.

Robert Green in Dublin told Colonel James Walsh that 'disguised men have been passing about these parts' and there had been suspicious night meetings,[28] and at Loughbrickland in Co. Down John Thompson reported an example of bold Irish opportunism. 'Much mischief is being done here by unruly persons spoiling [robbing] people's houses in the night under [the] pretence of taking prisoners for being [in] the plot.'[29] Poor Major Thomas Barrington wrote pitifully to the Irish Secretary Sir George Lane on 22 May after hearing that his name 'has been mentioned' during the investigation of the conspiracy. He now 'expects every hour to be arrested, to his disparagement' but if he was given safe conduct and the protection of some guards, he would come instantly to Dublin Castle and clear his name.[30]

Still fearing the flight of some of the plotters, on 30 May Ormond signed a warrant for the removal of Dubliners who lived in rooms overlooking the city's quays and replacing them with soldiers 'for the better security of the city'.[31]

Nine days after the plot was broken, Ormond reported to Charles II that the conspiracy could well be rekindled 'unless we show that we are prepared to foil such attempts and [demonstrate] that they mean absolute ruin to the contrivers'.

They will never be put down, however, till the army is so paid that we can march out with a great part of it to any spot where disturbance may break out.

I find that the conspirator[s] relied much on the existence of divisions in your majesty's court and councils and unless these [are] diminished, the recent attempt will be repeated.

I enclose an intercepted letter from a person on whom I cannot yet light [name]. I think the information which he contains was furnished by Gibby Carr, who, I am sure, was lately here and a prime conspirator and is said to have been a remonstrator in Scotland.[32]

The lord lieutenant acknowledged that, despite further arrests having been made, 'it would be impossible to get full evidence against any of the conspirators but at the price of pardoning some to give testimony against the rest. I shall select for pardon those who most deserve it and who can tell the most.'[33]

The same day, Vernon announced triumphantly that the arrested plotters were now telling the truth 'and say that the design was . . . wholly Presbyterian and was [alive] long before [the dissent over] the commissioners' [decisions on land claims]:

> Blood, one of the chiefs, and Col. Gibby Carr are certainly . . . fled to Scotland.
>
> [Henry] Cromwell may, I think be concerned, for many of the rebels named him for general and his own chaplain, Charnock, came privily hither and [?]proposed him [and] told them they had £20,000 ready in England and that on any good success, the [Royal Navy] fleet would revolt.
>
> But in a short time, I shall be able to give you the truth, for my friend [Alden] . . . has increased his reputation [with the conspirators] by his obstinacy upon his examinations.[34]

Meanwhile, one of those arrested on 21 May had pragmatically decided to make a clean breast of all he knew, much to his interrogators' delight. James Tanner was brought before Ormond and dictated a long and detailed deposition. He did not hesitate to name names – and that of Thomas Blood featured prominently among them. Early that April, he claimed, Blood had proudly brandished a letter addressed to him from Stephen Charnock announcing that Henry Cromwell would lead the coup.

Shortly after, Charnock had arrived from England and lodged at the home of a Mr Phillips, a glover, of Castle Street, Dublin, where Tanner met him, together with Blood and Major Alexander Staples.

> Blood told [the] witness that he had spoken of the matter to Col. Robert Shapcott who had advised him to speak of the design only

to one person at a time in order to secure secrecy. Blood had also [said] that Col. Alexander Barrington was in the said design.

The interrogators showed Tanner one of the plotters' declarations and he identified the handwriting as Blood's, 'as he knew his writing well'.

Blood had told him 'that the taking of the castle had been put off until 21 May when Col. Abel Warren would arrive in Dublin'. A curiously imprudent, if not boastful, Blood also disclosed that Captain John Chambers would raise forces in Co. Louth to support the rebellion 'which would be brought hither by one Fooke, whose Christian name he [Tanner] knew not'.

Chamberlin told him that McCormack, a Scottish minister, had been lately at Dublin and came in disguise to see in what readiness they were for the design and that he went into the north [of Ireland] and that they expected to hear from him the Tuesday next before 21 May . . .

[Major] Staples, when departing from Dublin, told witness that he was going to deal with the Scots [settlers in Ulster] for their conjunction [assistance] in the design of taking the castle and that he would try to secure Derry.

Since then, [the] witness had heard from Staples that men were coming in to him apace and that he was to send a man to Newry to carry news from one to the other and that when they heard that the castle was taken, they in the north would take the field.

[Tanner] did not know Col. Gilbert or 'Gibby' Carr, but Blood had told [him] that the lord lieutenant had sent horse to arrest Carr at Blood's house and that Carr . . . was now in the north collecting men to aid the design.[35]

Ormond recognised a familiar name in Tanner's five pages of breathless testimony – an individual who had caused him much trouble before. He told Bennet that the main instigators of the plot were members of the Irish House of Commons, some of whom he had now imprisoned. 'One of these is called Shapcott, a lawyer, and a very leading man in the House, of a bold and seditious spirit and it is likely that the Commons may, if they meet, call . . . for his trial with which we may not be ready to proceed. I do not know what appeals or declarations this may lead to and this is the reason against summonsing Parliament.'[36] Accordingly, the meeting of the Irish Parliament was postponed to 25 August and later to 1 October.

This was a wise move on Ormond's part, as disorder and confusion seemed likely to continue in Ireland, although he had nearly fifty prisoners under lock and key. Sir Nicholas Armorer told Joseph Williamson: 'The jails are full of these rogues and we have enough to hang them and most of the party. Now is the time to smite them.'[37] Sir Thomas Clarges observed: 'This kingdom is in great disorder. Both the ancient and new English Protestants are very bigoted in their opinions and zealous against the Irish . . . The settlement of this kingdom will be one of the knottiest pieces in the king's government.'[38] Ned Vernon admitted the English settlers were discontented 'and the Irish do not carry themselves prudently, being too much puffed up'.[39]

The lord lieutenant was delighted to receive royal endorsement for his tactics and actions, being told by Bennet that Charles II had his letter detailing the discovery of the plot 'to be twice read to him' and had 'notified his approval, as well as the extension of mercy to certain participators willing to give evidence as of the speedy execution of the chief criminals'. In general, the king had approved of Ormond's 'vigour and steadiness in abiding the plot'.[40] He wrote back to Whitehall, expressing gratification for the king's reaction and promising that 'no time will be lost in trying those who are [held] and indicting those who are fled, but the lawyers tell me great care must be taken in putting together evidence as any flaw may lead to a failure and the prisoners are too well friended not to have any point taken which is to their advantage'.[41]

He also urged the arrest of Stephen Charnock, who had fled to London via Chester, using the alias of 'Clark' – information given him by James Tanner, now a much-relieved recipient of the royal prerogative of mercy. This 'pretended minister . . . is deeply implicated in the late plot' and after going to England

and whilst the plot was in contriving, he wrote hither a letter signifying that if the business was ripe here a person (not named in
the letter but interpreted by one Thomas Blood . . . to be Henry
Cromwell) would soon be here 'to seal the writings' but [this was]
interpreted by Blood to be 'head the party' [or *coup*].

Charnock lodges with Robert Littlebury, stationer, at the sign of
the Unicorn in Little Britain [in London][42] and Littlebury can say
where he is if he is not there.

It is absolutely necessary that he be sought out and
apprehended . . .[43]

Ever co-operative, Tanner disclosed that letters to Charnock
should be addressed to Littlebury but have the letter 'C' inserted
below the address, so the minister would know they had been sent
by the Dublin conspirators. 'Unless you go warily', he warned
Sir George Lane, 'you will hardly meet with Charnock.' He also
penned a letter to Charnock himself.[44]

Additional proof of Tanner's value as a turncoat came a few days
later, when he wrote to another plotter, Major Staples, urging
him to turn himself in and 'make an ingenuous confession of his
whole knowledge of the plot. The evidence is clear', he warned
him, adding ominously: 'and the law will condemn us all. The duke
[Ormond] inclines to mercy.'[45]

Arrests continued throughout Ireland and, with seventy suspects
now crowding the prison in Dublin Castle, there was a need to
find additional accommodation to house the detainees. Eventually,
a nineteen-year lease was procured on Proudfoot's Castle, a four-
storey square tower on the city quay wall alongside the River Liffey
at the southern end of Fishshamble Street, and work began on its
conversion into a new jail.[46]

Ormond remained worried about the chances of convicting the
conspirators, taking advice from Patrick Darcy, 'a learned counsel'[47] lodging at the Boar's Head, Dublin, on a number of occasions
in May and June on various points of law.[48] The lord lieutenant
reported that Sir James Barry, First Baron Santry,[49] chief justice of
the Irish court of King's Bench, 'who is an honest man and good

lawyer, thinks that the prisoners should be tried by a special commission ... I have ordered him to consult with the other justices and king's counsel and agree on the easiest and quickest way of proceeding'.[50] Later Ormond acknowledged that, in deciding to 'proceed promptly to prosecute the conspirators', he had 'overruled the scruples of some of the judges'.[51]

Vernon had few doubts about the legal methodology necessary to win successful convictions. In a letter to Williamson, he radiated confidence not only that the prosecutors possessed sufficient proof against the ringleaders, but also that an existing criminal law could be deployed effectively:

[There is] an excellent statute of tenth [year] of Henry VIIth.[52] 'Tis but ten lines but they are pithy and make [clear] that all persons who shall design against the lord lieutenant [or] deputy or stir up the Irishry against the Englishry or Englishry against the Irishry are, to use their own words, guilty of treason.

It is plain that we are in danger between two rebellious people and I, between two stools, am going to the ground.

Whilst serving my prince here, my own family wants me. You taste the delights of England whilst I eat shamrocks.[53]

In a further attempt to suppress Presbyterian unrest, on 16 June, Ormond and his Irish Council signed a proclamation instructing the presidents of the Irish provinces to arrest all 'such ministers or pretended ministers that you find cause to suspect (to have had any hand in the late conspiracy or to be likely, by their preaching,) to seduce the people from their due obedience and subjection to his majesty's authority, ecclesiastical or civil'.[54] He also signed orders for the seizure of unauthorised firearms, ordering searches in the city and county of Dublin. Confiscated weapons should be placed 'in a secure place' and anyone who did not surrender their firearms 'shall be deemed disaffected to the king and will be proceeded against accordingly'.[55]

Lieutenant Colonel Robert Shapcott had also been arrested in Ireland and Charles II himself wrote to Ormond instructing that the prisoner be sent to London for interrogation 'before me or such as our Privy Council appoint' to find 'more effective proof against him'. The king ordered: 'You shall send him over here in custody and see that he speaks to none save when his custodians are present.'[56]

One in, one out. Due to Vernon's behind-the-scenes machinations, Philip Alden managed to escape from the Dublin Castle prison a few days afterwards by clambering out through a barred window. To the outside world, this disconcerting jailbreak appeared to be the result of careless or lax security; indeed, Ormond blamed the 'negligence' of the constable of the castle. Ned Vernon kept up the pretence, writing to Secretary Williamson, rather tongue-in-cheek, on 19 June:

> You will hear how that most notorious villain Alden broke prison. Great efforts are being made to find him and the constable of the castle, a very knave, [has been] turned out about him.[57]
>
> The rogues (dissident Presbyterians) are very pleased at his escape as it is believed that he knew much of all their designs in England and Ireland . . .
>
> So subtle was the knave that 'tis not imagined how he broke loose, for the window bar that he broke was upon the top of all the castle in the highest turret.
>
> If he comes to Whitehall I know you will secure him.[58]

The first batch of prisoners were arraigned at the bar of the King's Bench court in Inns Quay, Dublin[59] on 25 June, among them Leckie, Edward Warren, Alexander Jephson and Richard Thompson. All pleaded 'not guilty' to charges of treason.

But the government's judicial retribution on the rebels had an ill-starred beginning. After the prisoners were called into the dock, there was, according to Sir George Lane, 'an unlucky accident which frightened the whole court in so much that the judges were disturbed and even ready to rise'.

Private John Fellows, one of the soldiers standing guard, was 'discomposed' by the large, noisy crowd thronging the courtroom, and accidentally fired his musket, the bullet killing another soldier nearby. Immediately, everyone assumed that an audacious rescue of the prisoners was under way – a belief shared by the men in the dock,

> especially Mr Leckie who smiled very pleasantly when he saw the disorder but when he saw there was no redemption, he quickly changed his leering countenance.[60]

When order was finally restored, the trial was resumed. Leckie, in a loud, rambling outburst from the dock, claimed the devil had possessed him and went 'stark mad, blaspheming God and affecting to be Christ', reported Vernon. Because of his sudden insanity, his case was deferred.

Other conspirators would face trial in the new law term. Those found guilty 'will die penitent Christians, desiring that their brethren, the Presbyterians, may be carefully watched, for there is a thorough engagement amongst them both in England and Ireland and Scotland and this [they confessed] without desire of their lives but by way of repentance, being worked to it by Dr Parry and others [of Ormond's] chaplains, from whom they received the Sacrament this day', according to Vernon.[61]

On 22 June, the lawyer Darcy had written to Ormond, enclosing twenty-nine names of the members of the grand juries of the county and city of Dublin who had been sworn in to try the conspirators. He was less than sanguine about the outcome of their judicial deliberations: 'I know so few of them that I cannot tell what to say unto them but I fear that . . . not many of them are fit for the business now to be agitated'.[62] Darcy also passed on some disquieting gossip:

> This morning . . . Sir John Ponsonby said openly in the presence of his old gang that in this trial of the prisoners they [the government] would find themselves deceived . . .
>
> Ponsonby and others pretending to [know the] law [maintain that] the conspiracies and declarations without [being] done is no treason.[63]

The lawyer urged the lord lieutenant to follow three simple courses of action to avoid disaster in prosecuting the would-be insurgents. Firstly, he should choose 'old Protestants' as jurymen; secondly, he should act with speed; and finally, the words of the indictments should be selected carefully or 'the king and your grace may be the sufferers when it may be too late to call the fact treason'. He concluded: 'The God of heaven preserve the king and his interests.'[64]

Leckie, Warren, Thompson and Jephson appeared again in court on 1 July and the indictment was read out to Leckie. Vernon, who must have attended the hearing, reported that the jury were all 'able discreet persons of good estates' with Sir John Percival acting as foreman. Sir William Domville, attorney general, and Sir John Temple, solicitor general for Ireland, in two eloquent speeches

showed the practices in all ages both by the Mosaical law,[65] the Saxon, Norman and our more modern laws, how conspirators against princes were most severely punished.

About six witnesses were then called, Col. Scott, Capt. Sanford and persons engaged with them to prove the [scope] of the design, both in Ireland, England and Scotland . . .

How they intended to march through Scotland with this English army whom they thought their own; that 20,000 Scots in the north of Ireland would keep the Irish employed whilst the English invaded England with what party they could raise in Scotland . . .

That it was a covenant design and driven on by the pretended clergy of that gang, many of which met in periwigs the day before the design to ask a blessing on it.

Domvile also called eight witnesses against Leckie 'who all proved the charge against him'.

Then there was another sensation in court. 'A most handsome woman . . . with very great soberness and more prudence than usual in that sex' swore that she was with Leckie's wife (who had just given birth at her home near Dunboyne), when the troopers arrived to arrest her husband.

Mrs Leckie expressed great fear that the attack on Dublin castle had been discovered but afterwards she was much cheered with a belief that though her husband was taken and condemned, yet his pardon would be obtained by two persons [who] were bold and so much concerned for him that they would not be denied.

These mystery men of power and influence were named in court as Sir Audley Mervin, speaker of the Irish House of Commons (and Ormond's *bête noire*) and John Clotworthy, First Viscount Massereene, *custos rotulorum* of Co. Londonderry and a prominent and vocal champion of Irish Presbyterians. In the event, while official suspicion over their loyalties remained, no action was taken against them.

Leckie, in his defence, would 'not admit the truth of the whole of the charge but put himself upon the law and was not free to say or answer more'. The previous night he had suffered another apparent bout of madness, but at the bar 'his Presbyterian spirit was very calm and he said little'.

The jury promptly found him guilty.[66]

Despite his earlier grave doubts about the outcome of the trial, the 'learned counsel' Patrick Darcy was delighted by its progress. He told Ormond on 3 July that never in his life had he 'met with better management by lawyers of a matter [of procedure] than that shown by Sir William Domville against Lackes [Leckie]. Nor was ever evidence better managed by all the King's Counsel.'[67]

A week later, Warren, Jephson and Thompson were brought back to court for sentence. Baron Santry, the increasingly infirm chief justice, employed striking biblical references and language to leave them in no doubt as to the heinousness of their crimes and promised death and damnation for all rebels. Sternly, he condemned them to suffer the terrible fate of all traitors: death by hanging, drawing and quartering.[68]

Such executions turned the scaffold into a veritable butcher's block of gore and suffering. The victim was initially hanged by the neck but cut down from the gallows while still alive. He then was castrated and his vital organs ripped out and burnt before his eyes. Finally the corpse was beheaded and hacked into quarters, and the body parts displayed in public spaces as a dreadful deterrent to those who rashly contemplated conspiracy against their king.

Robert Leigh, Williamson's agent in Dublin, told him: 'Leckie, having turned mad within two days (or feigned himself so) was brought to the bar but escaped sentence – the law being not able to take hold of a madman and so was carried across in a cart back to his prison. Some people pity their cases here, but not I.'[69]

Sir George Lane noted that Leckie was 'stark mad and is therefore reprieved, though if he should recover his wits, [there would be a delay] until the next [law] term because till then death cannot be pronounced upon him'. He had arranged that reports of the trial proceedings should 'be collected carefully for the press, so that the world may see the horridness of this wicked plot'. Copies would be printed and sent for distribution in England.[70]

Leckie had meanwhile reportedly tried to cheat the executioner 'by knocking out his own brains in prison' but had survived this apparent suicide attempt.[71]

One of those condemned, Thompson, deputy provost-marshal for Leinster,[72] wrote 'a declaration' from his Dublin Castle cell on 5 July about his 'unhappy role in the late plot', naming Blood as the man who drew him into the failed conspiracy:

First, that Thomas Blood late of Sarney ... was the first person that I ever heard make mention of the plot.

He assured me that their aim was to surprise the castle and city of Dublin for the accomplishment of which ... he had many friends both in the city and in the regiment and particularly two sergeants in the regiment whose names he would never tell me though I oft pressed him and also that he expected seven hundred men out of the north from among the Scots before the appointed day of surprise to assist them in the act ...

Second, he mentioned no less than 30,000 Scots (if occasion offered itself) who were ready to prosecute the design or to draw into the field the particular persons he would never name whom he corresponded with [except] only one, Mr Hart, a Scotch minister, as I take it, of the north . . .

Third, when I urged (that in case the designs failed) to know what sanctuary we might have to secure ourselves in, he assured me that Drogheda was made fit to receive [us] by which means I could never tell but I apprehended his way still was to [win over] some inferior officers and the common soldier and upon these hopes I conceive he [would] remove his family into Drogheda.

Thompson had overheard conversations between Blood and others about the city of Derry and the 'general disquiet of the army' which they hoped to exploit. Blood had also talked about an old conspiracy to rescue the leading Scottish covenanter Archibald Campbell, First Marquis of Argyll, who had been accused of treason and imprisoned in the Tower of London in 1660. A plan to liberate him, also involving Gibby Carr, was abandoned after he told them he was an 'infirm man and ancient, therefore they should desist until a more seasonable time – or that they should await God's pleasure'.[73]

In his covering letter to the confession, Thompson asked Ormond to be 'pleased graciously to accept these last words of a dying man which not the fear of death but a sense of duty forces the writer to present to your grace'. He stressed:

I call God to witness that I was no contriver but drawn by Mr Blood into these plots for which great sin I beg pardon from God, the king and your grace and all good people.

And give me leave to make this last protestation that if your grace shall please to employ me as a witness to [help] find the contrivers and depths of this design I shall use the utmost of my endeavours.

This I beg of your grace, not as a design . . . for fear of death but to make some satisfaction for my past crimes.[74]

Despite his contrition and anxiety to make amends, it was inevitable that Thompson would still die for treason, but because of his confession, his sentence was commuted to simple hanging.[75]

What of the fugitive conspirators who, despite every effort, still eluded capture?

The 'minister' Andrew McCormack had managed to escape to Scotland before the round-up of Presbyterian clergy. Colonel 'Gibby' Carr had been reported in Scotland and then, rather embarrassingly, was said to have been living in Rotterdam in Holland, according to an official certificate signed by the city's borough masters and governors, provided by Jacob Vortius.[76] A few weeks later, Bennet told Ormond that Carr's wife, who was then living in London, had 'produced testimony from magistrates in Rotterdam that he had been constantly seen there these six months'. He added, a trifle cynically: 'Perhaps 'tis a bought testimonial only.' Ormond commented later that if these statements were 'authentic, let me say they are here [regarded as being] much in the wrong'. There were some in Dublin who would 'swear they saw him in the north about the 23rd of May, two days after the plot was to have been executed'. He concluded more in hope than expectation: 'He should come here where he will be heard if he has a fair defence.' One can detect frustration and asperity in this response, but the lord lieutenant's black mood may have been affected by his painful gout and 'an extraordinary indisposition of the spleen'.[77]

Bennet had more bad news in the same letter: despite the most meticulous of inquiries, no trace of Charnock had been found in London.[78]

And what of Thomas Blood? Although the spymaster Vernon believed him beyond reach in Scotland, he apparently remained stoically in Dublin for three days while the arrests and searches continued around him. Probably believing the city was becoming too hot to hold him, Blood headed north, using the alias Thomas Pilsen, to seek shelter with his Presbyterian cronies. James Milligan was later arrested and questioned over his concealment of the fugitive[79] and was described as 'Blood's only guide and protector in Co. Antrim'. He had hidden him at his mother's home in Antrim while she was away and had been dispatched by Blood with a message for his wife who had moved to Drogheda and was living 'in a house beyond the bridge next [to a tavern] of the King's Arms'.[80]

There were fears that Blood was planning to assassinate Ormond and the lord lieutenant was warned 'to have about his person a sufficient guard'.[81]

He had a number of narrow escapes while on the run from the government manhunt. His later notes of the times when God had provided him with deliverance mention an incident at Loughbrickland, a small village south of Banbridge in Co. Down, near the main Dublin–Belfast road, and another 'in the wood', unfortunately with no more information as to what happened or the precise location. He also eluded arrest after being betrayed 'by false brethren'.[82]

Blood hid in the hills and mountains in the north of Ireland, sometimes in the unlikely guise of a Catholic priest. At one stage he even sheltered with a group of 'papists'. Using other aliases and disguises, he headed for the wastes of Co. Wicklow, where he was sheltered in the home of a minister called Cox. There, he corresponded with a fellow fugitive, the Dublin brewer, John Chamberlin, probably early that August. Blood tried hard to keep faith with his dreams of rebellion, believing that 'most of our friends are safe, as I understand by the [list of] prisoners' names ... [and] that many were taken up that were not concerned [in the plot]'. Therefore, he had 'hopes yet to advance that broken interest' by trying to recruit supporters for a fresh insurrection amongst former parliamentary cavalry troopers in the area.

> I have no confidence in the Scots ... they stick so to the king's interests, though I have laboured with some of them of a small sort to come along with me.
> I can prevail little yet I doubt not to pick up some.[83]

An additional slip of paper attached to this letter contained instructions for the bearer, listing friends who could provide assistance and information.[84]

Daringly, and not without a touch of arrogance, Blood then returned to Dublin to visit his wife and children, who had gone back to the city. Even though their lodgings must have been watched, he spent a 'night and part of a day' with them, before departing brazenly 'at the gates at noonday and through the streets'.[85]

Meanwhile, those who had played key roles in foiling the conspiracy were contemplating their rewards for their services to the crown. On 14 July, Ormond wrote to Charles II recommending Vernon, 'who was mainly instrumental in discovering the late plot. He has on all occasions served the king well.'[86] Vernon left Dublin en route to London the next day – almost certainly with the spy Philip Alden in tow, who doubtless had spent the three weeks in a Dublin safe house. If the lord lieutenant had been disingenuously unaware of the true nature of the informer's escape, he now knew the full extent of Vernon's plans, as he wrote to the lord chancellor in London:

Col. Vernon will bring a friend of his and of the writer to see the chancellor. He is the man by whose honesty and industry, notice was given of the late [traitorous] design . . . He cannot appear here and be any longer useful in that way. But 'tis hoped that he may be useful in England.[87]

The day of Vernon's departure also marked the executions of Warren, Jephson and Thompson at Gallows Green, situated where today's Lower Baggot and Fitzwilliam streets intersect in Dublin. Sir George Lane, the Irish Secretary, was very sparing in detail in his businesslike account of their deaths sent to Bennet:

The speeches of Warren, Thompson and Jephson will show you that they are executed.

The first died like a Christian. The other two had made the world believe, before they came to the place of execution, that they would do their duty by confessing their guilt and exhorting the people to loyalty, obedience and the renunciation of popery.

But this was clearly only a feint in expectation of pardon, for their speeches, which they had penned beforehand, declared their seditious thoughts.[88]

Perhaps it was a politician's reluctance to be the bearer of bad news, or just plain bureaucratic reticence, but Sir George's report lacks much of the drama and pace of what really occurred that summer morning on the scaffold.

Happily, Robert Leigh, Williamson's shrewd agent in Dublin, was also an eyewitness to events and his vivid narrative provides us with a glimpse of the horror and pandemonium that followed the arrival of the prisoners at the place of execution, after being bumped and battered as they were dragged along the cobbled streets from Dublin Castle, tied on to three sledges or sheep hurdles.

The renegade MP Alexander Jephson was the first to die. Standing on the scaffold, bizarrely still wearing his hat, he made a 'large speech', counselling the crowd around him to avoid sin at all costs. He acknowledged his own crime of concealing treason but said that his death was caused by 'none but the vile Papists'.[89] The condemned man then meekly handed his hat to the hangman who

> immediately turned the ladder and with it Jephson, who held fast by the same to save his life as long as he might, but that would not do.

With Jephson still hanging from the gibbet, there was sudden commotion, described by Leigh as a 'hot alarm'.

> Everyone betook themselves to several defences, most part that had arms, besides the guard to their [weapons], and those who had none to their heels, who, tumbling over one another as they ran (and some on horseback amongst them) did some mischief, [such] as breaking legs and arms and some children killed.

Panic and fear spread through the Dublin streets – 'all began to shut up their shops and a great many to betake themselves to the castle' for safety. A company of infantry was sent to reinforce the sheriff's halberdiers who were guarding the prisoners.

Thompson and Warren who stood by the gallows foot, only pin-
ioned by the arms, began to pluck up good heart, but the sheriff
holding Thompson by the one hand and his sword in the other,
did let neither stir.

Eventually, order was restored and Warren was pushed towards
the gibbet ladder. He made 'a tedious troublesome discourse' to
play for time, 'and looking several ways about him, as we supposed,
for help'. Warren spoke of his 'just and righteous cause which now
lies in the dust [but which] someday would terrify the greatest
monarch'.[90]

Tired of this diatribe, the sheriff interrupted him and Warren
asked angrily 'why a dying man should not have the liberty to speak
his conscience?' Unnerved by the earlier alarm and fearing an im-
pending rescue attempt, the sheriff had become jumpy and hustled
Warren up the ladder 'so that in some discontent and much against
his stomach, he was turned over, though he held as fast as he could
by the ladder and then by the rope that Jephson hung by'.

It was then Thompson's turn to be executed. Leigh reported:
'He made a modest speech, acknowledging his crime, saying he was
drawn in by one Blood, who made his escape and, having declared
himself for the Church of England and prayed for the king, he cast
himself off resolutely. There I left all three, wishing all the rest of
their fellow plotters were with them.'

What triggered the panic? Some claimed afterwards that a pair
of coach horses had escaped and run amok in the crowd. Others
believed firmly 'it was done maliciously with [the] intention to
rescue the prisoners'.[91] Was Blood's reputation, as a man of action
who would risk all to liberate his friends even at the eleventh
hour, the catalyst for the Dublin crowd's terror? Or was there a
real attempt to snatch the prisoners off the scaffold, which came
to naught?

Warren's widow Elizabeth later appealed for financial assistance,
placing the blame for her husband's fate squarely on Blood's shoul-
ders. At a 'time of great sickness [he] was wrought upon by the
pestilential insinuation of one Blood to join with him in his plot

against the castle of Dublin'. She pleaded for what was left of his forfeited estate to be remitted to her and her seven children.[92]

Leckie remained in Dublin's Newgate prison, no doubt still ranting and raving, for many months. At about six o'clock on the evening of 14 November he escaped.

It was an enterprising rescue. Leckie apparently exchanged clothes with his wife in order to fool the guards as he broke prison. He was assisted by two men, also disguised as women, who had filed through the bolts holding fast his cell door. Sir George Lane, unusually voluble, described the aftermath:

> [They] conveyed him to Little Thomas Court and lodged him over the gate of the court in the hollow of the wall.
>
> On Sunday, a gentleman living near that place, [sent] his servant into the city [and on his] return, discovered Leckie in woman's attire endeavouring to [get off] the wall and he, seeing the servant, desired him to procure a ladder to help him down.

The servant told his master in Little Thomas Court about what had happened and, looking out of the window, saw Leckie on the wall. They ran out and overtook him as he was walking towards a clothier's shop.

> On being asked who he was, Leckie confessed his name and escape ... and was brought to Little Thomas Court and kept there until he was returned to Newgate.

On 18 November, the Scottish minister was back at the bar of the Court of King's Bench. The judge, Sir William Ashton, told him:

> What a remarkable work of God it was that he, who before had feigned madness on purpose to elude the sentence of the law, had, by his own act [of] escaping out of prison discovered himself and demanded what he had to say why judgment should not pass against him, according to law.

He said he only escaped because of the miseries and hardships of prison and thanked God he was in a better condition to answer for himself than when he was last in that place.

As he offered nothing material, sentence was pronounced upon him.[93]

Leckie was brought out for execution on 12 December. Rumours swept through the 2,000-strong crowd that his brother-in-law, Blood, was on his way to rescue him and the news led to a repeat of the panic that had thrown the earlier executions into chaos. This time, even the executioner briefly fled, leaving Leckie standing forlornly on the scaffold, with the halter round his neck.

But there was no sudden liberation.

When order was eventually re-established, he was quickly kicked off the gallows ladder.[94]

When the Irish Parliament at last met again in October 1665, eight MPs were named as conspirators: Alexander Staples (Strabane); Abel Warren (Kilkenny town); Thomas Scott (Co. Wexford); two members for Ardee, John Roxton and John Chambers; Thomas Boyd (Bangor); Robert Shapcott (Wicklow); and the executed Alexander Jephson (Trim). Those still living were expelled and disqualified from any public office, civil or military.[95]

Staples, who claimed to have warned about the plot, was eventually pardoned, despite the king's initial refusal, saying that troublesome Ireland had 'more need of examples of justice than mercy'.[96] Shapcott also received a pardon in 1666.

Blood and the others remained hunted men, forever on the run.

# 3

## *A Taste for Conspiracy*

*The fanatics of Ireland were represented by Lieutenant Colonel William Moore . . . and one Mr Blood and Mr Alden, two notorious villains of this country.*

The Earl of Orrery to Secretary Arlington
8 November 1665.[1]

Charles II's remarkably efficient intelligence operations were created by just one man: Sir Joseph Williamson, the second surviving son of an impecunious Cumberland vicar, a fellow of Queen's College, Oxford and the former keeper of the king's library in the Palace of Whitehall in Westminster. This colossal power, focused in the hands of one man, mirrored the extensive overseas and domestic spy networks established a century before by Sir Francis Walsingham, Williamson's doughty Elizabethan predecessor, to defend the last Tudor monarch from Catholic intrigue and her Protestant realm from Spanish invasion.[2]

We all learned at school (those that still teach traditional English history) that the reign of that 'Merry Monarch' Charles II swept away the bleak, joyless edicts of Oliver Cromwell's republican regime and returned a broad smile to the face of drab old England. Elements of popular culture such as bawdy and licentious drama, the 'filthy exercise' of maypole dancing – even the ungodly Christmas mince pie[3] – had fallen victim to dour Puritanical proscription, but these were happily now revived to gladden the hearts of Charles's subjects.

Reality was somewhat different. Life was not always quite so merry. Behind that gorgeous and glittering façade of a new-found, confident monarchy, the Restoration government was confronted in the 1660s with a seemingly endless wave of dangerous uprisings and plots that endangered both king and realm, not only in Ireland, but also in England and Scotland. In truth, these were hazardous times. The risk of assassination, by bullet, bomb or silent crossbow bolt, never seemed far away for Charles, his brother James, Duke of York,[4] or George Monck, First Duke of Albermarle, the major player in restoring Charles II to the throne.

Williamson, created one of the two secretaries of state in 1662, alongside Henry Bennet, frankly acknowledged the perils:

> I find a spirit of malice has everywhere insinuated fears and jeal-
> ousies into the people, which it must be the care of prudent men
> to exercise and cast out, 'ere it possess them too far.[5]

Desperate times require desperate measures. The state mon-opoly of a General Post Office was set up in 1660[6] and this nationwide mail-delivery system became the main weapon of Stuart counter-espionage through the regular interception, read-ing or copying of private citizens' letters at its headquarters in Cloak Lane (near Dowgate Hill, in the City of London), under Thomas Witherings, who enjoyed the splendid title of 'postmaster of England'.[7]

An example of Williamson's covert postal intelligence operations (while pursuing an increasingly cold trail left by Thomas Blood) were his instructions issued in August 1666 to intercept 'all let-ters coming from Ireland, addressed to John Knipe [of] Aldersgate Street (London) or going to Ireland, addressed to Daniel Egerton of Cock [Cook] Street, Dublin'.[8] He hoped this correspondence would indicate the movements, or plans, of those under suspicion for plotting crimes against the state.

Of course, many letters written by conspirators (or, for that matter, government informers) would not be in plain text – the risk of such vital information falling into the wrong hands was just too great. Ciphers were often employed, based on a simple principle of letter or symbol substitution. Without a key for decoding, encrypted letters appeared to be mysterious gibberish to the reader.

In the late seventeenth century, these codes were far less sophisticated than today's complex encryption methodologies. And they had one major failing. Whatever letter, number or symbol is substituted, its original frequency of use is retained in the enciphered message. Thus, by analysing the incidence of the letters on the page, it was possible to establish which consonant or vowel each substituted letter represented. The greatest vulnerability of such codes therefore is the frequency in which vowels occur in words – for example, 'e' accounts for 13 per cent of all letters used in any kind of prose, whereas 'z' is used less than 1 per cent of the time. Once the letters or symbols for vowels and commonly used letters such as 't' have been isolated, the secrecy of the message becomes fatally compromised.

For the nineteen years he ran his spy network, Williamson employed a number of code-breakers such as the Oxford mathematician Dr John Wallis[9] and the German theologian and diplomat Henry Oldenburg, who translated letters in foreign languages.[10] Sir Samuel Morland, another of his cipher experts, perceived his work as being of high importance and value to the crown as 'a skilful prince ought to make a watch tower of his general post office ... and there place such careful sentinels as that, by their care and diligence, he may have a constant view of all that passes'.[11]

Morland was also a prolific and ingenious inventor[12] and in 1664 the king spent three hours, accompanied by Bennet and probably Williamson, in a late-night visit to the mail interceptors' 'secret room' at Cloak Hill. Fascinated, Charles watched demonstrations of various primitive mechanical machines that could open letters without trace, replicate wax seals, forge handwriting, and copy a letter (possibly by pressing dampened tissue paper against the inked handwriting) 'in little more than a minute'.[13] It was an impressive demonstration of the formidable covert surveillance capability of the king's secret service. Years later Morland reminisced:

With these [machines] the king was so satisfied that he immediately put [them] into practice as they were and competent salaries
appointed for the same and this practice continued with good success till the fire of London consumed both the post house and all
the engines and utensils belonging to the premises.

Equally important to the Stuart government's intelligence-
gathering were the informers who, as in Walsingham's time,
comprised an army of mainly social misfits, criminals and turncoats
who were prepared to risk their lives supplying information about
the internal enemies of the state, in return for the grant of a royal
pardon for past delinquencies or simple monetary gain. Sometimes
they were rewarded in kind. In May 1667, William Garret petitioned Williamson for the post of tide-waiter in the customs[14] in
recompense for his regular supply of useful intelligence to a previous secretary of state, Sir Edward Nicholas.[15]

Unsurprisingly, the life expectancy of the members of this
raggle-taggle corps of spies was frequently all too short. Only a
handful managed to enjoy lengthy careers to match those of Joseph
Bincks, who informed on religious radicals and was still operational a decade later, and William Huggett, who had served the
parliamentary general Thomas Kelsey, governor of Dover Castle
in Kent, in the 1650s and was still spying for Williamson twenty
years afterwards.

The penetration and reach of this ever-changing group of spies
and informers was extraordinary throughout the three kingdoms,
particularly so in England. No man could believe himself entirely
immune from arrest for any injudicious words spoken drunkenly
in a rowdy tavern, or for being seen in the company of suspected
persons in the street.

Many of these agents collected their pay and received fresh instructions during furtive visits to Williamson's office on the ground
floor of Whitehall Palace,[16] or more often at a nearby safe house,
rented specifically for these clandestine meetings.[17] We know that
one informer, William Leving (whom we shall meet shortly), made
a number of such visits to 'Mr Lee', apparently a codename for

Williamson, 'when necessity required it', at times varying between seven and nine o'clock in the evening, presumably therefore under cover of darkness.[18]

Intelligence-gathering is always inherently expensive. In 1674, a payment of £4,000 was made to the two secretaries of state to fund their undercover operations – equivalent in today's spending power to more than £15 million.[19] The money was drawn from government income derived from the unpopular hearth or chimney tax, which was levied on the number of fireplaces in dwellings to pay for the royal household's costs.[20] These secret service funds were also employed for a multitude of other purposes, many having nothing to do with espionage, such as the £30 paid to Leonard Manning in December 1679 for his extensive tree-planting in the New Forest (then in Hampshire) and the £375 paid out in part payment for the funeral of 'Mrs Elinor Gwynn' at St Martin-in-the-Fields, Westminster.[21] We know her better as the actress Nell Gwynn, one of Charles II's many mistresses and mother of his two bastard sons. She died on 14 November 1687 at her comfortable home at 79 Pall Mall in St James's after suffering a stroke. This area of government income was evidently treated more like a handy contingency fund to hide embarrassing or inconveniently timed expenditure than a fully fledged departmental budget.

The twilight world of domestic espionage was a crowded one. As well as agents employed by regional magnates or the governments in Ireland and Scotland, noblemen such as George Villiers, Second Duke of Buckingham, also employed their own private 'intelligencers' to spy on rivals at court or gather indiscreet information useful in furthering their political ambitions.

The duke had squandered an estate reputed to be the largest in England through his reckless extravagance and a misguided trust placed in a succession of employees who cheerfully appropriated his money. He was ruthlessly ambitious with a short-fused temper which sometimes escalated into violence, as when he came to blows with the Marquis of Dorchester and ripped off his wig during parliamentary business in December 1667. Both peers were briefly sent to the Tower to cool their heels, if not their tempers.

Buckingham's servants unfortunately followed their master's bad example: in August 1663 they fought a pitched battle among themselves in the courtyard of his London home when many were 'hurt and the porter, it is thought, will not recover'.[22] Nine years later his cook was executed for murdering his counterpart in George Sondes First Earl of Feversham's household.

Back in the murky world of espionage, Williamson's everyday domestic adversaries were an unlikely alliance of religious nonconformists such as Presbyterians, Anabaptists and the occasional Quaker who objected to the legal imposition of liturgical rites laid down by the established Church of England. There were also many former parliamentary soldiers who fervently sought a return to a righteous, godly republic in place of the unrestrained hedonism of Charles II's monarchy.

The most zealous opponents, if not fanatics (to use a word frequently employed in official correspondence) were the Fifth Monarchists. They based their religious and political beliefs on the prophecy in the Bible's Book of Daniel[23] that four ancient monarchies (the Babylonian, Persian, Macedonian and Roman civilisations) would precede the new kingdom of Christ. The year '1666' held especial significance for them because of its resemblance to '666', or the 'Number of the Beast', described in the Book of Revelations[24] – which identified the Antichrist whose kingdom would herald the end of worldly rule by wicked mortals. When Christ appeared, as King of Kings, in His Second Coming, the Fifth Monarchists keenly anticipated becoming the new generation of saints in a thousand-year reign.

There was nothing in their creed to gainsay a pre-emptive strike on England's body politic to prepare for this longed-for Second Coming. As far as they were concerned, Charles II was both a despot and a traitor to King Jesus.[25] Over four days from Sunday, 6 January 1661, fifty well-armed Fifth Monarchists, wearing full armour, roundly defeated musketeers sent to disarm them in the City of London. They later fought 700 troopers from the Life Guards, as well as an infantry regiment, for more than half an hour in running battles in Wood and Threadneedle streets in the heart of the city. Forty were killed in the fighting, including six Fifth Monarchists, one with the spine-chilling nickname of 'Bare-bones', who had barricaded themselves in the Helmet tavern in Thread-needle Street and refused any quarter.[26] Their leader, the wine cooper Thomas Venner, who had been shot three times in this last, desperate stand, was hung, drawn and quartered as a traitor on 19 January 1662 at Charing Cross. Twelve of his brethren were also executed.[27]

Through this crazy world of violent religious fervour strode Thomas Blood, whose assorted allies constantly crossed the non-conformist religious divides. Standing four-square in the way of his political and personal aims and objectives were the establishment figures of Ormond in Ireland and the two secretaries of state and spymasters, Bennet and Williamson.

Like Walsingham before him, Williamson sought to manipulate public opinion by the use of information, or propaganda, to pro-mote the government's standing through the medium of newsletters and the *London Gazette*, its official journal, 'published by authority' and sent by post to subscribers up and down the country.[28] Regular news from up to fifty sources in the British Isles, notably customs officers, governors of garrisons and postmasters, filled its columns and short précis of dispatches from English embassies overseas yielded intriguing snippets of foreign news.

In 1668, Lorenzo Magalotti, an Italian philosopher, author and later a diplomat, met Williamson during a hectic week-long trip to Windsor, Hampton Court and Oxford. He described him as 'a tall man, of very good appearance, clever, diligent, courteous and ... very inquisitive in getting information'.[29] Samuel Pepys first met him in February 1663 at the dinner table of the well-heeled Thomas Povey. He was not impressed: Williamson, he confided to his diary, was 'a pretty knowing man and a scholar but it may be [he] thinks himself to be too much'.[30] Three years later, Pepys had changed his opinion dramatically, declaiming enthusiastically: 'Mr Williamson, who the more I know, the more I honour'.[31]

However, that other great Restoration diarist, John Evelyn, sneered at Williamson's rapid promotion up through the tiers of government and his burgeoning influence at court. In July 1674, Evelyn was at Windsor and wrote that Sir Henry Bennet had let Williamson 'into the secret of affairs, so that there was a kind of necessity to advance him and so by his subtlety, dexterity and insinuation he got now to be principal secretary, absolutely [Bennet's] creature – and ungrateful enough'.[32] Like so many others in Tudor and Stuart public service, Williamson, knighted in 1672, managed cunningly to exploit every available opportunity to create wealth for himself: in 1668, he was said to be worth £40,000 a year in ready cash, or nearly £6 million at today's values.[33] God, Williamson pointed out piously, was the 'real author of every good and perfect gift'.[34]

The senior secretary of state, Henry Bennet, was a son of the landowner Sir John Bennet who owned property in Harlington, Middlesex. He was another Oxford man, going up to Christ Church, and he had fought in the Civil War, suffering an honourable scar across the bridge of his nose during a brutal skirmish at Andover on 18 October 1644, when the king's vanguard drove William Waller's parliamentary troops helter-skelter out of the Hampshire market town. Bennet joined the exiled royal court at St Germain, near Paris, three years later and was knighted in 1657. Fluent in Latin, Spanish and French, on 15 October 1662 he became secretary of state, despite the opposition of his many enemies at court such as Lord Chancellor Clarendon and Buckingham, who became ever more jealous of the influence Bennet, with his Catholic sympathies, wielded so dexterously with the king. For his faithful services, he was created First Earl of Arlington on 14 March 1665.[35]

As far as intelligence-gathering was concerned, Bennet was ultimately responsible for all espionage and surveillance activity, but it was Williamson who ran the agents and other operations on a day-to-day basis.

According to Clarendon, in the early 1660s, Charles II had grown so weary of the incessant rumours of potential uprisings, 'that he had even resolved to give no more countenance to any such information, nor to trouble himself with inquiry into them'.[36] A case, perhaps, of 'wolf' being cried too many times by his spymasters.

But growing evidence of a potential insurrection in the north of England captured even the king's jaded attention.

When the would-be rebels met in Durham in early March 1663, they took a 'sacramental engagement or vow, not only of secrecy but also to destroy without mercy all those who [would] oppose [them]' especially Albemarle and Buckingham. Agents were sent to Dublin, to London (where a council of radicals had been set up) and to the west of England to synchronise the timings of rebellion. They drew up a manifesto, bursting with righteous indignation, containing a veritable litany of the terrible evils they saw about them – blasphemy, adultery, drunkenness, swearing, the all-pervasive papists, the Anglican Church's worship of idols, unemployment and unfair taxes (ironically, including that on chimneys). The green and pleasant realm of England had now become a vivid reincarnation of biblical Sodom and Gomorrah. To eradicate such widespread sinfulness, they were ready to risk their lives 'for the reviving of the good old cause' – as it was better 'to die like men than live worse than slaves'.[37]

Local officials knew full well that 12 October had been set as the date for the rebels to make their move and two days earlier, in a carefully orchestrated operation, the 'principal officers and agitators' were arrested across north-east England while the militia mobilised near Pontefract in Yorkshire, reinforced by 1,000 men from Buckingham's own regiment. Apart from a few minor acts of violence, the rebellion was surgically cut out before it could even spring into life.[38] Most of its leaders were captured, such as Captain John Mason, detained while hiding in Newark-on-Trent, Nottinghamshire, but who later managed to escape from Clifford's Tower in York in July 1664 with three other men involved in the abortive uprising.[39] Others remained dangerously at large, like John Atkinson, a former soldier turned stocking-weaver, who, having stained his face, masqueraded as a labourer in Co. Durham.

Durham-born William Leving was among the conspirators arrested and thrown into York Castle. Together with his father, he was to raise his native city under Captain Roger Jones, alias 'Mene Tekel'.[40] Leving had been a junior officer in Sir Arthur Heselrige's

Parliamentarian regiment and served with him when he was governor of Newcastle. Leving supported the vain and ambitious General John Lambert[41] over his failed attempts to resist the House of Commons' control of the New Model Army in 1659. As a consequence, Leving forfeited both his commission and the back-pay owed him.[42] Such ill-luck, or more pertinently, his frequent bad judgement, was to dog him in his future career as a government spy.

Sir Thomas Gower, governor of York, whose own all-pervasive spy network in north-east England had been a major factor in the suppression of the insurrection, claimed to have two witnesses ready to testify against Leving, with incontestable evidence that would hang him. But Sir Roger Langley, high sheriff of Yorkshire, believed his prisoner would be of more value to Charles II's government alive and well, serving as an informer, than as a rotting corpse hanging from a gibbet as a deterrent to would-be rebels. He suggested to Bennet:

> If a way could be found to get Mr Leving out of the jail so that he
> would not be suspected by his own party, he might be of great use,
> for he assures me he would not question to let you know some of
> the names of some of the [rebel] council now in London.[43]

Langley gave him £10 as pocket money and dispatched him to London in May 1664, where he spent some time in the Tower. From there he wrote enthusiastically to the secretary of state, boasting that, in return for his freedom, he could 'give an account of every plot that may be hatched between London and the [River] Tweed' on the Scottish borders. To cloak his espionage activities, he suggested that his escape should be faked and he could then 'shift as a banished man'.[44] To outwardly confirm his undying loyalty to the cause of rebellion, he still corresponded with his fellow conspirators, pledging he would happily accept any suffering before betraying them.[45]

His 'escape' being successfully contrived sometime in July 1664, Leving was soon about his business. Employing the alias 'Leonard Williams', he quickly infiltrated the radical Presbyterian council in the capital, which was busy planning an attack on the king and court at Whitehall Palace, as well as seizing the Tower of London. Blood was named as one of the leading lights in this audacious conspiracy.

The adventurer had left Ireland, probably in the last three months of 1663, and arranged a clandestine meeting with his mother-in-law Margaret Holcroft in Lancashire, when he was almost captured. After travelling about the north of England with Williamson's agents hard on his heels, Blood fled to Holland at the beginning of 1664, where he was befriended by the Dutch admiral and naval hero Michiel de Rutyer, who was 'pleased to admit [him] into his society and honoured with an entertainment answerable to that respect and affection which he bore the nation of England'.[46]

Sometime around March 1664, Blood returned to London and 'fell in with the Fifth Monarchy men, resolving to venture all in ... their interest' as he found them 'to be a bold and daring sort of people like himself and their principles so suiting with his discontents'. Tellingly, Blood judged them 'very proper for his management' as his maxim was always 'never to put his confidence in any that were not engaged either by principle or interest to his designs'.[47] The fanatical Fifth Monarchists matched that requirement precisely.

On 12 September 1664, Bennet's intelligence service produced a list of thirteen persons 'now in London who go about in disguise and under other names'. Among those listed are John Atkinson (alias Peter Johnson) and Captain Lockyer (alias Rogers) and a Mr Allen. Above this last name is written, in the same hand but in a different ink: 'His name is Blood'. Williamson added a note at the end of the list: 'The chief meeting house is at a widow's in Petty France and my informer [says] they have got money for the imagining of a design which they intend to set in London and to that end are [planning] how they may become masters of the Tower.'[48]

This threat was taken seriously by the state. The same day, orders were issued for the repair of the Tower of London and for stretching chains across its access from the city – 'the key to be kept by the Master of Ordnance'. The public were also prohibited from the Thames wharf alongside the fortress.[49]

In December 1664, there were unconfirmed reports that Blood and his two fellow conspirators in the Dublin Castle plot, the Presbyterian minister Andrew McCormack and Colonel Gibby Carr, had slipped into the north of Ireland, landing in the vicinity of Rostrevor in Co. Down. It was also rumoured that 300 muskets had been shipped in from Scotland for use by rebel forces. Despite strenuous searches, no traces of the fugitives could be found.[50]

A list of the following year, written on one sheet of paper, has the 'names of various persons suspected to be in and about the City of London this 22 May'. 'Blood alias Allen' is included in a list of seven men who met at the Swan near Coleman Street and sometimes at the home of 'Robert Melborne, a silk thrower in Shoreditch'. Of these plotters, Timothy Butler and Christopher Dawson were the 'persons entrusted to buy arms'.[51]

Leving's regular reports began in 1665, having received payments of £20 each for himself and a fellow informer, John Betson, for spying services rendered to Bennet. The spy complained about the miserliness of his pay: 'The money is insufficient. I have run great hazards and spent much money in the cause. A good reward would encourage Mr Betson and tend much to the king's service', he told Bennet.[52] Soon after, he repeated his pleas for more generous remuneration 'having caused the taking of sixteen at once, some more considerable than [John] Atkinson',[53] who had fled to London from Yorkshire after the collapse of the northern rebellion the year before.

Atkinson was detained and questioned in the Tower. He admitted his acquaintance with Blood, Lockyer and other conspirators, as well as having been 'engaged by the [Ana]baptists of desperate fortune'. But he had 'wearied of their selfish designs and looked for an opportunity to [unmask] them'. He disclosed the addresses of some of the plotters – but warned that if any were arrested, the others would flee immediately and would be difficult to hunt down.

Leving also reported on his progress to his erstwhile mentor, Sir Roger Langley in York:

> In March 1663, Atkinson was active in the design and got a [rebel] council together – namely Blood, Lockyer, Captain Wise, [Captain Roger] Jones, Carew[54] and Major Lee. They mean to take houses near the Tower and Whitehall, gather arms, and destroy the king, [the] Dukes of York and Albemarle and lord chancellor [Clarendon]. Atkinson knows where most of these persons lodge and will tell anything else wanted [if] pinched . . . to a confession.[55]

Blood's first biographer, Richard Halliwell, describes the work of this secret committee 'of which Mr Blood was head'. To ensure their security, they were protected by 'a Court of Guard, seldom less than thirty [men] a day' while they met at the Widow Hogden's house in Petty France, Westminster.[56]

> At this committee all orders were given out, all manner of intelligence brought, examined and all things sifted and debated in reference to their grand design.

Then Blood began to suspect that two of his fellow conspirators had become traitors to the cause. Either 'out of remorse or [in] hopes of reward, [they] had begun to make some discovery of this project at court.

> He appointed to meet the two persons at a certain tavern in the city, who were no sooner come according to their summons, but he took them both prisoners and from thence carried them to a certain place of darkness, which they had found out and hired for their convenience.[57]

This 'place of darkness' was probably a room or cellar in a tavern in Coleman Street, a notorious 'hotspot' of dissent and sedition in the seventeenth century, or its side street, Swan Lane.[58] Harking back to his own career in the military, Blood 'very formally' called together a court martial of his own 'and tried the two men for their lives'. They were found guilty and sentenced to be shot dead by an impromptu firing squad within forty-eight hours.

When the time for execution came, they were both brought to the stake and being without any other hopes, were forced to prepare for death.

Then, at the very point of despair, Mr Blood was so kind as to produce them a pardon and so releasing them and giving them their freedom, bid them go to their master and tell them what they had done ... and that they should ask him to be as favourable to his soldiers [plotters] when they fell under his mercy.[59]

It is very plausible that one of these two men was William Leving. His description of undergoing a similar ordeal at the hands of the conspirators, and Blood's biographer's account of his own kangaroo court, chime remarkably.

Leving's narrative begins one cold Sunday evening in February 1665,[60] when he was asked by two friends to attend a secret meeting. They escorted him through 'many turnings into an obscure place' where he was suddenly confronted by a group of men who, threatening him with pistols and swords, angrily accused him of being a spy. Leving, of course, denied this vehemently but was held a close prisoner for two days, always demanding to know the identity of his accuser. He later learned it was Henry North, a fellow government informer, and an 'intelligencer' in the pay of Buckingham. As far as the conspirators were concerned, Leving was guilty of rank treachery and betrayal, but curiously they decided not to kill him. Instead, he was simply released, with his solemn promise not to meet Bennet or any of his agents.[61]

At the end of March 1665, Leving sought to return to his home city of Durham to induce his friends to confess to involvement in the abortive rebellion and accordingly requested Bennet, now Earl of Arlington, to provide him with 'protection under the king's hand and seal'. The result was not nearly as grand as Leving had hoped: he was given a single sheet of paper, on which was written his 'certificate of employment', to be waved under the noses of sheriffs and magistrates if he faced arrest or imprisonment:

This is to certify [to] all whom it shall concern that the bearer hereof William Leving is employed by me and consequently [is] not to be molested or restrained upon any search or inquiry whatsoever.

Henry Bennet[62]

This document proved useful that May when Leving was arrested in Leicestershire but was released after proving his identity and credentials as a servant of the crown.

Despite his anxious protestations, Leving was ordered to remain in London that hot summer, all through the height of the epidemic of bubonic plague that killed 100,000 (or 20 per cent) of the capital's population. To forestall the risk of infection, the royal court fled first to Hampton Court in July, then moved on to Salisbury in Wiltshire and finally ended up in Oxford in September, accompanied by Parliament and the high courts of justice. Back in London, victims were locked in their houses and their doors daubed with the words 'Lord have mercy' as a warning to others not to enter. Between one and three of the occupants died in most infected homes. Grass grew in the streets, and because domestic animals were believed to pass on the 'Great Plague', special 'dog killers' were employed, slaughtering 40,000 dogs and 200,000 cats. Leving lost most of his family to the disease, which in reality was spread by fleas living on the city's prodigious population of black rats.[63] Blood survived the plague, which he confidently saw as a sure and certain sign that God smiled on his involvement in sedition and rebellion aimed at transforming this ungodly nation.[64]

At the end of October 1665, the Presbyterian factions held a clandestine conference at the Liverpool home of Captain Brown, the former Cromwellian governor of the city,[65] to plan new insurrections in England, Scotland and Ireland. Orrery, in Dublin, soon learned details of their deliberations from his 'fanatic intelligencer', who sent him news of 'the transactions of that wild people'. The Irish contingent was represented by Blood and his fellow Dublin Castle plotter, Lieutenant Colonel William Moore. The third member of this delegation was our old friend Philip Alden, still working undercover as an effective government informer.

As a result of this strategy meeting, two rebel agents were dispatched to Scotland 'to revive their party there'. Moore also travelled to Ireland, 'and having shaven his head, now wears a great bushy periwig[66] and is gone into the borders of Munster. From thence, [he] is to go ... to the Scots of Ulster to incite them into new rebellions', Orrery reported to Arlington:

> I have sent some trusty spies after him, who, I hope, may apprehend him. They have had lately numerous meetings in [Dublin] at the house of Capt. Sands and at the house of one Mr Price where they rail bitterly against his majesty's authority and particularly against my lord lieutenant and myself by name.
>
> They promise their party great things after Christmas.[67]

In February 1666, another of Orrery's spies reported that Blood could be found at the home of his old associate, Colonel Gibby Carr, 'in the north of Ireland or at his wife's, near Dublin'. They planned to seize the city of Limerick in the province of Munster. Now came news that the Liverpool meeting of the 'fanatics' had delayed any general uprising until the Royal Navy were busy fighting the Dutch (in the Second Anglo-Dutch War) and the government was distracted by this foreign threat.[68] They claimed to have 10,000 cavalrymen on call but would march to Scotland 'in small numbers'.[69] Orrery informed Ormond that Blood and a man called George Aires were living under assumed names and 'may be caught, if care is used, going out of the house of one Cock or Cooke, a brewer at the Coombe in [south] Dublin'.[70] He suggested watching the brewer's house 'by some who know their faces well. Otherwise they may escape the search.'[71]

He enclosed an extraordinary two-and-a-half-page letter which seems to have been written by Dame Dorcas Lane, wife of the Irish Secretary Sir George Lane, to her husband about an admission made to her by a conspirator regarding 'a damnable plot which has been hatching this year or two against his majesty and all the nobility of the three nations'. All the castles and fortresses in Ireland would be surprised and all those who resisted 'would be put to the sword'. It had been postponed from New Year's Day but 'is very soon to be put into execution'. Her informant had 'laid out a sum of money to the promoting of this devilish design' and they 'had corrupted the most part of all the soldiers that are in any strongholds' – including Dublin Castle, which had cost them 'many a piece of gold'. He made Dame Dorcas swear a sacred oath to keep secret what she had heard.

> When this man told me first of the business, truly I thought he was mad or drunk ... that he should tell a silly woman a business of that great weight and therefore I thought little of it.
>
> But a day or two after ... he came here again ... [and] implored me with fresh protestations to keep his counsel.
>
> I [appeared] to like his design on purpose to sift him as well as I could, but I could not get from him the names of any of the plotters.
>
> For all my oath, my conscience tells me I ought not to keep secret so damnable a design that threatened the death of so many innocent souls and knowing that the Great God of Heaven forced him to discover this business to me, [I ought] not to conceal it.

Dame Dorcas was only too well aware that she held her informant's life in her hands: 'it is not fit that I should, by the discovery of the plot, be the cause of his death'. After all, she had only been told of its existence so that she could 'provide for the safety of me and mine'. She told her husband:

> I beg that my name may not be mentioned but that you will pretend that he heard this from some other source.
>
> I forget to tell you that their pretences are for liberty and religion but I am sure [that] murder and treason never came from God.
>
> They do believe that God has [had] a hand in it since they have not been discovered all this while.[72]

Perhaps finding counter-intelligence operations in Ireland too efficient, Blood returned to England. He had other important business to transact, seemingly to further the nonconformist cause. Under the alias of Morton,[73] Blood landed in the United Provinces of the Netherlands in March 1666, accompanied by the Fifth Monarchist John Lockyer, en route for a meeting with the old parliamentary cavalry commander Edmund Ludlow, who was innocently engaged in writing his memoirs, safely exiled among the sympathetic Swiss in Lausanne under the name 'Edward Phillips' – a pseudonym based on a variation of his mother's maiden name.[74]

The aim was to escort Ludlow to Paris, together with the fugitive regicide Algernon Sidney, to negotiate substantial funding from the French and their Dutch allies for yet another uprising in England. Unfortunately, Blood and Lockyer were arrested as suspected English spies by the Dutch in Zeeland, as they possessed no passports or other means of identity.[75] However, they managed to talk their way out of detention, assisted by another exiled regicide John Phelps, who was making one of his periodic visits to the Netherlands from his home in Switzerland.[76]

Therein lies a mystery. Joseph Williamson's address book, covering the period 1663–7 and containing more than 150 names, includes a frustratingly vague entry concerning correspondence with a 'Mr T.B.' in Zeeland[77] who was writing letters from Holland to a 'Thomas Harris' in London – one of the cover names then used for the secretary of state's office in Whitehall. Was this spy Thomas Blood? Had he become a double agent working for the government? Was he now involved in a covert operation to persuade Ludlow to move from the safety of Switzerland so he could be assassinated, or at least kidnapped and brought to trial in England? Some kind of subterfuge was patently under way, else why did Blood feel the need to use an alias when he was ostensibly amongst friends? There are more questions than answers – not surprising, given the elusive, enigmatic figure of Thomas Blood. The evidence is not wholly conclusive, but it may go some way to explaining why he so miraculously escaped capture so often and his later generous treatment by Charles II and his government after the most outrageous of his adventures.[78]

Yet, at the same time, matters very damaging to Blood were being decided in Dublin. On 2 April 1666, Ormond sent a draft grant of lands to London 'in favour of Captain Toby Barnes who served King Charles I and the present king in Ireland and abroad'.[79] Those lands were Blood's remaining property, which had been forfeited to the crown since he was declared a traitor. Nine days later Charles II wrote back to Dublin, signifying his assent:

> In remembrance of Sir Toby's service . . . we direct you to take steps
> for granting him, under the Great Seal, a lease at such rent and or
> a term as you think fit of the town and lands of Sarney, Braystown
> and Foylestown in the barony of Dunboyne, Co. Meath and five
> hundred acres of unprofitable mountain at Glenmalure, alias The
> Glinns, Co. Wicklow, formerly belonging to Thomas Blood of
> Sarney, lately attainted of high treason.[80]

This was hardly a sensible action to preserve the loyalty of a double agent. Or was it a case of purely bad timing and bureaucratic ineptitude – or, indeed, a method to preserve and enhance Blood's reputation within insurgent circles?

Certainly Blood, or Morton, failed in his mission to escort Ludlow to Paris. The parliamentary general was not impressed by Blood when he and John Phelps talked to him in Lausanne and anyway he was wary of travelling as he had heard of 'several persons sent out of England to destroy the friends wheresoever they may be met with', according to his intercepted letter.[81] Doubtless the assassination of the regicide John Lisle by three Royalist agents in a churchyard at Lausanne almost two years before was also still fresh in his memory. Nor did Ludlow trust the Dutch, pointing to the arrest of the three regicides Miles Corbet, John Barkstead and John Okey in the Netherlands by Sir George Downing, the English ambassador there, in 1661.[82] This, said Ludlow, was 'an act of treachery and bloodguilt' for which the Dutch should repent 'before God's servants could join with them'.

After much 'heart-searching', Ludlow refused to budge from the anonymous safety of Switzerland. Blood was equally unimpressed by the republican hero, believing him 'very unable for such an employment' and much more interested in 'writing a history as he called it'.[83]

Meanwhile Arlington, focusing on the problems of the naval war against the Dutch, was slow off the mark to appreciate the dangers of new unrest in Ireland. He warned Ormond the following August that Blood 'and other notorious conspirators would resort' to Ireland, with the aim of spreading sedition throughout the ranks of the militia. 'Some of my informers have offered to go to Ireland', he added, but, perhaps believing that local knowledge paid the best dividends, declined to send them, unless Ormond specifically asked for assistance.[84]

Williamson had received intelligence from one of his spies, Captain John Grice, a former parliamentary agent, who also reported that Blood and Captain Roger Jones (the infamous 'Mene Tekel') had 'gone to Ireland ... to do mischief'.[85] Grice had generously offered his services to arrest them, suggesting that a good man to detain would be the innkeeper of the Black Boy at Oxmantown, 'who will know [of] any plot in Ireland'.[86]

Although the adventurer had returned to London from Europe in the early summer of 1666,[87] Orrery, attending the lord lieutenant on a progress through the province of Munster that September, was convinced of Blood's permanent presence in Ireland. Accordingly, he had 'put all the province on their guard in case of disturbance. Those who are in arms here are of one mind in their loyalty', he assured Arlington.[88]

One spy told Sir George Lane that 'John Breten in Bride's Alley [Dublin] a tobacco man [and] one Johnson, a shoemaker in St Patrick's Street' would know where the fugitives were.

The man that keeps the Black Boy [tavern] in Oxmantown in [north] Dublin ... [this] was the place where Blood lay. It had his horses or [he] caused them to be brought [to] him that morning that he made his escape from Dublin.

The man's name I have forgotten but you may find him out for his wife is blind.[89]

Like the 'Scarlet Pimpernel' of another era, Blood was seemingly here, there and everywhere. He was accused of starting the Great Fire of London, which began about one o'clock in the morning of 2 September 1666 in the bakery of Thomas Farriner in Pudding Lane and went on to consume most of the medieval city before it burned out three days later.[90] 'Divers strangers, Dutch and French were during the fire apprehended upon suspicion that they contributed mischievously to it who are all imprisoned', reported the *London Gazette* at the time.[91] Much later, Israel Tonge, the unhinged confederate of the rabid anti-papist Titus Oates, suggested that Blood had a 'share' in starting the fire and claimed it was a 'Popish-French Louvestin [Republican] plot, Blood being the agent for the latter'.[92] Another culprit, named in a letter to Charles II, was Captain John Mason. These all proved to be idle allegations. Williamson published a memorandum which concluded that 'after many examinations by . . . his majesty's ministers, nothing has been found to argue [that] the fire in London [was] caused by other than the hand of God, a great wind and a very dry season'.[93]

Amid the chaos and destruction caused by the Great Fire, Arlington reported to Sir George Lane on 6 September that Blood had been reported in Lancashire but had travelled to London and came near to arrest after the fire had broken out.[94]

Five weeks later, Arlington had changed his mind about strengthening the intelligence network in Ireland, dispatching his own agents (Leving and later his fellow spy William Freer, or Fryer) to Dublin. Leving was armed with another letter of protection to show to the lord lieutenant: 'The bearer of this letter is sent into Ireland to endeavour to take Blood and his conspirators. His true name is Ward but he goes by the name of Williams.'[95] The spymaster was being cautious about the identity of his agent, using two separate aliases for Leving.

It is particularly difficult for an agent to operate in the strange environment of a different country. Who you know, after all, is more important than what you know. Leving, however, managed to infiltrate the Presbyterian community in Ulster, delivering 'information concerning Blood and other conspirators who are fled from Ireland' to Ormond on 16 November.[96] He and Freer spent ten weeks in Ireland before returning to England in December. Leving's last message from Ireland regretted that he had not detained Blood or 'Mene Tekel' in Ireland. He had, however, met several of their acquaintances and had passed on the intelligence he had gained from them to Ormond.[97]

Meanwhile, in Scotland, one Presbyterian rebellion had actually come to pass. Although seemingly unpremeditated – it was triggered on 13 November 1666 by soldiers bullying an old man in Dalry, Kirkcudbrightshire, about his unpaid fines for not attending authorised church services – there had been signs that an insurrection was already being planned. Four townsmen rescued the victim, shooting a corporal in the stomach and disarming four other soldiers. As feelings rose, 200 men rode to Dumfries and kidnapped Sir James Turner, the local military commander (still wearing his nightgown and feeling 'indisposed') and shamefully disarmed his two infantry companies, before throwing them into prison.[98] From there, the rebellion escalated rapidly, with the rebel force growing to about 2000-strong. The rebels maintained steadfastly their loyalty to Charles II, yet demanded the end of episcopal rule in the Church in Scotland, a restoration of Presbyterianism and that deprived ministers should be returned their livings.[99]

Three days later, the Scottish Privy Council mobilised its forces under Lieutenant General Thomas Dalziel. It was wary of support for the rebels from a 'fifth column' of collaborators, so in the Scottish capital of Edinburgh security was tightened at the gates, the night watch reinforced and the militia ordered to swear an oath of allegiance to the government in London.[100] On the morning of 28 November, the rebels, depleted by desertion to just over 1,000, fought Dalziel's troops at Rullion Green, seven miles (11.3 km) from Edinburgh. They defended a snow-covered hilltop position, and despite fighting desperately were defeated at sunset after three charges by government troops. About fifty rebels were killed and

120 captured in the night pursuit that followed.[101] One of those killed was the minister Andrew McCormack, Blood's fellow conspirator in the Dublin Castle plot.[102]

Evidence for Blood's involvement in the Pentland uprising is scant. Viscount Conway was told of his role there by Charles II himself soon after its defeat and Orrery also informed Ormond of Blood's participation, based on information received from Arlington.[103] An almost contemporary report from Sir Philip Musgrave, *custos rotulorum* of Westmorland, in April 1667 mentioned 'one Blood, who was among the Scotch rebels last winter and in last year's insurrection in Ireland'. He had been spotted in Westmoreland 'at a rigid Anabaptist's [house] with whom he corresponds'. More recent authorities maintain that he was present when the Presbyterian forces were routed but escaped unharmed.[104] Strange then that Blood's name does not appear on the government list naming the Scottish rebels' leaders.

Warrants for his arrest were issued in London on 19 January 1667[105] and on 2 March – the latter granted to Leving, permitting him to seize Blood, Timothy Butler, Captain Lockyer and others together with 'any instruments of war that may be in the places where they are seized'. The prisoners had to be brought to Arlington for interrogation if arrested in London or Westminster, 'or in the country, before the nearest deputy lieutenant or justice of the peace'.[106] But the bird had apparently flown from the capital. On 21 January, Grice reported Blood in his old stomping ground of Lancashire, living 'about Warrington or Manchester' under the name of 'Allen' or 'Groves'. He planned to remain in the area until the end of February.[107]

Blood had had enough. He decided to withdraw from the dangerous world of espionage. Casting around for a more 'safe and quiet way to get a livelihood' he made the bizarre decision to become a doctor, practising at Romford, Essex, under the assumed name of 'Ayliff'. Without any medical qualifications, one wonders what became of his patients. His wife Mary and his eldest son, Thomas, were sent to live in an apothecary's shop in Shoreditch, north of London, where they changed their name to Weston.[108]

Aside from his own charlatan medical practice, Blood had suddenly become a law-abiding citizen.

But his apothecary's hat and gown were merely another cover to mask his true activities. His greatest adventures were yet before him.

# 4

## *A Friend in Need*

*Two of the soldiers . . . singled [Blood] out and drove him into a court-yard where he made a stand, his sword in one hand and his pistol in the other.*

Remarks on the Life and Death of the fam'd Mr Blood[1]

The government's secret service was slowly but surely closing in on the devout conspirators. One of its spies, Captain William Leving, alias Leonard Williams, requested another warrant from Williamson on 28 February 1667 for the arrest of fifteen ringleaders of a new plot against the government. These included Colonel Henry Danvers, Captain John Lockyer, Timothy Butler, Ralph Alexander and Majors Blood and Lee. Our adventurer had promoted himself again.[2] Every attempt to capture the revolutionaries failed, however.

Espionage was never a very lucrative trade in the late seventeenth century. Though the work was, by definition, highly dangerous, the recompense was frequently less than generous. Moreover, the embryo intelligence service was sometimes slipshod in making the regular payments promised to its agents. Leving therefore always seemed painfully short of money.[3] To bolster his uncertain income, he was compelled to become a part-time highwayman, initially in Leicestershire and then in the green hills and dales around Leeds, Yorkshire, partnered by his fellow informer, the equally impecunious William Freer.

Leving's new career of holding up and robbing coaches and horsemen at pistol point proved less than successful. His victims may have stood but rarely did they deliver. He was soon apprehended by the local constables and on 18 May 1667 found himself in a dirty, rat-infested cell in York Castle.[4] Freer managed to evade capture and went to ground in Leeds.[5] A crumpled piece of paper, bearing a 'warrant for passing on the king's affairs' – his 'get-out-of-jail card' – was discovered in the pocket of Leving's coat and revealed his true identity and occupation to the startled authorities.[6]

Unfortunately it did not work. Arlington had other plans for his hapless spy.

Leving was taken to London and thrown into the city's Newgate prison. From there he wrote a plaintive letter to Arlington on 11 July, explaining how he had unwittingly fallen into a life of crime. It was a familiar story of an innocent abroad, easily influenced by hard-drinking criminals who made glib promises of easy earnings:

> Being without hopes of employment, I went to visit some friends in Leicestershire . . . [but] fell into ill company and offended, but did not hurt any man's person and thus got into prison.

Always anxious to demonstrate his worth to Arlington, Leving added that while locked up in York Castle he had not been idle. The spy had met 'a person of good descent and estate who is willing to lay aside his business and be the king's agent, not from fear or necessity but conscience'. Leving boasted: 'He can discover any treachery and either foreign or domestic conspiracy.'[7]

Two days later, he wrote a panic-stricken note to Williamson, having heard he was to be removed from Newgate to appear as a prosecution witness in the imminent trial in York of Captain Roger Jones ('Mene Tekel'), John Atkinson and Robert Joplin, all of them insurgents from the failed northern rebellion in England of 1663. A public appearance in court was not a prospect to be savoured for an informant whose faceless anonymity was his sole protection against bloody retribution in the dark, friendless world he inhabited.

Predictably, answer came there none to his pleas. On 20 July a warrant was issued to the keeper of Newgate authorising him to arrange for Leving to be returned to York under protective custody for his testimony at the assizes. The same day, Sir John Robinson, lieutenant of the Tower of London, was also instructed to organise 'the safe conveyance' of Captain John Mason to face trial for treason – and almost certain condemnation as a traitor – at the same circuit court.[8] Mason had been a major thorn in the government's side for years, having been a key player in the northern rebellion and numerous conspiracies ever since. Now informer and arch-rebel were to become unlikely and uncomfortable travelling companions on the Great North Road.

Both prisoners were to cover the 210 miles (339 km) to York on horseback, guarded by seven cavalry troopers under the command of Corporal William Darcy, the escort drawn from the Duke of York's Horse Guards regiment.[9] Leving had probably been ordered to report on his fellow prisoner's conversation during the six-day journey and try to draw out incriminating evidence which could later be used against him. He must also have been worried that, with such a high-profile rebel as John Mason, the small military cavalcade would be liable to attack on some lonely road en route to the north of England.

Leving had every reason to be uneasy about his unwanted ride to York.

At about seven o'clock on the evening of Thursday, 25 July 1667, the party was ambushed in a narrow lane between the small villages of Darrington and Wentbridge, south-east of Pontefract, West Yorkshire, just twenty-five miles (40 km) from York.[10]

This rescue mission was led by Thomas Blood.

Almost inevitably, because of the harum-scarum way the adventurer undertook his daring escapades, strong elements of what we would recognise as tragi-comedy permeated every aspect of the enterprise. The prisoner who had to be goaded into making his escape to freedom. The death of a nervous barber from York, Mr Scott, who had only joined the military escort for protection on the last stretch of this perilous road, because it was a notorious haunt of highwaymen. Blood being unhorsed three times because he had forgotten to tighten the girth of his horse's saddle. So the list goes on. Overall, the exploit came to resemble more the madcap adventures of the Keystone Cops than Errol Flynn's recklessly brave displays of derring-do.

The reported size of Blood's rescue party varied: a London newsletter, published five days afterwards, said the troopers were attacked by 'thirteen stout horsemen'[11] but Corporal Darcy, in his official dispatch, estimated the number of assailants as 'half a score' – or ten.[12] Certainly, Blood was accompanied by a couple of old comrades-in-arms, the Fifth Monarchist Captain John Lockyer (who had been involved in an anti-government conspiracy in Nottingham in 1663),[13] Timothy Butler, who acted as quartermaster and armourer in this and other conspiracies, together with 'several others'.

Blood must have received a very timely tip-off that Mason – for whom he held 'a particular affection and friendship' – was being taken north. He was also provided with accurate intelligence about the strength and armament of Corporal Darcy's section and their likely route. Escort and prisoners departed London, most likely on the morning of 20 July, and Blood and three associates followed that night 'without [top] boots, upon small horses and [with] their pistols [hidden] in their trousers to prevent suspicion'. But it was 'a good way' north of Newark, Nottinghamshire, before the pursuers picked up the escort's trail.

Richard Halliwell, Blood's contemporary biographer, takes up the story:

> At one place, they set a sentinel to watch [Mason] coming by. But whether it was out of fear, or that the person was tired with [such] a tedious expectation, the sentinel brought them no tidings, either of the prisoner or his guard.
>
> Mr Blood and his companions began to think their friend so far before them upon the road that it would be in vain to follow him.

This was the fifth day out from London. The next twenty-four hours would see Mason securely behind bars in York, well beyond the reach of his rescuers. Despite despairing of their chances of success, Blood relentlessly urged his party on. That evening, they

stopped at an inn at Darrington[14] in Yorkshire where they decided
to spend the night before returning to London, having failed ab-
jectly in their mission. Then, unexpectedly, they had a stroke of
luck.

They had not sat long in a room next the street, condoling among
themselves [on] the ill success of a tedious journey and the misfortune of their friend, before the convoy came thundering up to the
door of the same inn with their prisoners.

Mason, they later discovered, had unwittingly recommended this
same Darrington inn 'as being best known to him' to give 'his
guardians the refreshment of a dozen of drink' after a long and
dusty day in the saddle.

There Mr Blood had a full view of his friend and the persons he
had to deal with.
   He [ordered] a small supper, [to be eaten] at the fire, so that he
had but very little time for consultations [with his comrades].
   Captain Mason's [escort] did not intend to alight [stop] so that
[Blood] only gave general directions to his associates to follow his
example in whatever they saw him do.

In haste, the hopeful rescuers threw money down on a table as
payment for their food and drink and told 'the woman of the house
that since they had met with such good company they were resolved
to go forward' rather than return to London. 'Captain Mason went
off first upon a sorry beast and with him the commander of the
party and four more' – leaving three troopers to quietly finish their
ale in the inn parlour.
   Blood and his nervous, edgy associates, anxiously awaiting the
soldiers' departure, must have found it unbearable to suffer this
delay before finally going into action. One trooper at last emptied
his pint-pot, mounted his cavalry charger and rode off, followed a
little later by his remaining two comrades.
   Outside in the inn yard, Blood and a companion were horsed

and waiting impatiently for these last two laggards to leave. He had realised that if he could neutralise these troopers as quickly as possible, he would improve vastly the chances of successfully snatching Mason from a weakened escort. But how far ahead were the advance party?

[They] soon overtook them. These four rode a little time together. Mr Blood on the right hand of the two soldiers and his friend on the left.

Upon a sudden, Blood laid hold of the reins of the horse next to him, while his friend, in observation of his directions, did the same on the other hand. Having ... by surprise dismounted the soldiers [they] pulled the bridles and sent the horses to pick their grass where they pleased.

These two being made sure of, Mr Blood pursued his game, intending to reach the single trooper.

But he being got to the rest of his fellows, now reduced to six and a barber of York ... Mr Blood [rode] up, heads the whole party and stops them.

Darcy and his troopers were surprised by his sudden appearance and apparently believed this grubby horseman to be either drunk or mad. Naïvely, any notion of a trap did not enter their heads. Accordingly, with the disdain of soldiers towards a mere civilian standing in the way of their duty, they tried to hustle Blood off the road, striking his horse with their switches, 'exercised with more contempt than fury'. Then, in the nick of time, he was joined by his fellow assailant.

'Rough blows' were exchanged as precursors to a fierce mêlée, as the remainder of Blood's attackers rode up. Both sides traded pistol shots and continually wheeled their horses in their attempts to strike a telling, fatal blow with their swords.

Amid the confusion of yells, curses and flat, reverberating gunshots, Mr Scott, the unfortunate barber of York – despite shouted 'warnings that were oft given him' not to meddle in a business that did not concern him – joined in the clash of arms enthusiastically.

He 'laid about him [with his sword] with more zeal than discretion'[15] but was soon lying lifeless on the ground, the first casualty of the fight. Whether he died by blade or bullet is not known. Given his luck on this fateful day, he was probably killed by a stray shot or a ricochet.

Mason, mounted on his 'thirty shilling steed', had meanwhile blithely ridden on ahead and, glancing back with surprising *sang-froid*, wondered what on earth was going on behind him.

> He conjectured it at first to have been some intrigue against him, as if the troopers had a design to tempt him to escape which might afterwards prove more to his prejudice.
>
> He came back, at which time Mr Blood cried out to him: 'Horse, horse, quickly' – an alarm so amazing at first that he could not believe it to be his friend's voice when he heard it.

Incongruously, Mason had decided to dismount as the fighting raged about him. But at last, Blood's desperate shouts galvanised him into action. Catching the reins of a stray horse that had lost its rider, he jumped into the saddle and galloped off.

As the skirmish continued, Blood managed to fall off his mount three times, 'occasioned by his forgetfulness' in not tightening a new girth to his saddle, which the ostler had loosened at the inn after his arrival. Tired of crashing painfully to the ground and not a little discomfited, perhaps, by his own stupidity in the face of danger, he unwisely decided to fight it out on foot, despite the huge disadvantage he created for himself in combating mounted adversaries who knew very well how to handle their weapons. He had already suffered four flesh wounds from close-quarter pistol shots:

> Two soldiers singled him out and drove him into a courtyard, where he [defiantly] made a stand, his sword in one hand and his pistol in the other.
>
> One of the soldiers, taking that advantage of his open body, shot him near the shoulder-blade of his pistol arm at which time he had four other bullets in his body that he had received before.

The soldier . . . flung his discharged pistol at him, with [such] a good aim and violence that he hit him a stunning blow just under the forehead, upon the upper part of the nose between the eyes, which for the present amazed [stunned] him that he gave himself over for a dead man.

Yet resolving, like a true Cock of the Game,[16] to give one sparring blow before he expired – such is the strange provocation and success of despair – with one vigorous strike of his sword, he brought his adversary with a vengeance from his horse and laid in a far worse condition than himself at his horse's feet.

Blood, brimful 'of anger and revenge', was about to run the fallen trooper through with his blood-stained sword when Mason (who astonishingly still had not fled the scene), shouted to 'hold and spare the life of one that had been the most civil person to him on the road'. Blood reluctantly drew back his sword, lowered it and grudgingly spared him. For him, this was no time for chivalry, or compassion for a helpless enemy, but as far as his friend was concerned, common courtesy always should be rewarded – even in the heat of battle.

Mason then joined Blood in 'mastering' the other trooper and 'the victory, after a sharp fight that lasted about two hours' was complete.

Two soldiers were reported dead (incorrectly as it transpired), as was the ill-starred York barber. Three troopers had been unhorsed and the rest wounded.

Though the encounter happened in a village, where a great number of people were spectators of the combat, yet none would venture the rescue of either party, as not knowing which was in the wrong or which in the right.

[They] were therefore wary of being arbitrators in such a desperate contest where they saw the reward of assistance to be nothing but . . . death.[17]

Let history not condemn them for their timorous inaction.

Discretion is, after all, the better part of valour and they at least lived to tell the tale to their grandchildren.

Leving, like the terrified villagers, had escaped involvement in the brutal skirmish. As the bullets began to fly, he mounted a stray horse and galloped off to hide in a convenient house a short distance away.

After Blood and his accomplices had departed triumphantly with the rescued Mason, he emerged from his bolthole to meekly surrender himself to a wounded and panting Corporal Darcy. The spy that night reported to Arlington that he had gone back to Darrington only to summon assistance for the soldiers when the fighting began, 'but the people, being sore afraid . . . ran into their houses and not one appeared'.

The leaders of the assailants were only too familiar to Leving. He named them as 'Major Blood, Lockyer and Butler'.

A magistrate and prominent member of the local gentry named Stringer had arrived breathlessly to take charge at the scene after galloping from his home a few miles away at Sharlston. He summoned a local surgeon to treat the wounded troopers and Leving gave him and his fellow justices 'directions as to the country known by Captain Mason [and] [they] have sent the hue and cry[18] after them'. Leving suggested to Arlington that anyone who could recognise Mason and Blood in a crowd should be stationed in the northern outskirts of London, as they were probably heading for the capital.[19]

The post from York was delayed 'so as to give Lord Arlington full information' and two days later, Mascall, Williamson's man in the city, provided further details of the attack. He claimed Blood and his men were equipped with helmets, gauntlets and body armour; if so, they must have picked up these breast- and back-plates and 'head pieces' from a cache known to them somewhere along the road from London.

At the first action, they fired upon the soldiers' backs without saying a word or making any show of force . . .

It appeared they [were] resolved to kill Leving, who is come in, along with the gentlemen who were able to travel, three or four of whom are believed to be mortally wounded.

Scott, a citizen of York, being in the soldiers' company, was slain outright.

The rogues had taken such care that they secured all the passes [entrances] to the field by several footmen and their accomplices.[20]

Four days after the attack, Darcy, still recovering from his wounds whilst lodging at the Black Swan, in York's Coney Street, sent his two-page official report to the office of Sir Charles Wheeler, an officer in Prince Rupert's Horse, in Old Palace Yard, Westminster.[21] Any letter describing the failure of a mission is a difficult one to write for a young, aspiring soldier and, in selecting his words, he was properly aware of the importance of the value of military horses:

As I am bound, I thought fit to give you an account of our late sad misfortune upon Thursday last in the evening about six or seven of the clock at Darrington, a small village in Yorkshire.

We were set upon in a narrow lane in the rear by half a score, as near as [I] can judge, well-armed men who, after they had fired some pistols [at] us, said: 'Deliver, or you are all dead men'.

Whereupon I presently faced about and we fought with them [for] half an hour till we were so disabled we could engage them no longer; Procter being shot through the body, Knifton through the arm, Lobley through the thigh, Hewet into the back and I wounded in the hand and head. My horse [was] shot in the leg.

Lobley, Proctor and Jackson's horses were carried away.

I shot one and got another of their horses. One had mounted Singleton's horse, but Lobley dismounted him and recovered it again.

Only now did Darcy acknowledge the loss of his prisoner:

They rescued Mason and we sent the hue and cry after them.

Three of them are known by Leving, the prisoner who is sent to

York Castle, and he has discovered them to Justice Stringer to be Lockyer, Butler and Blood.

A gentleman of York, being behind, was slain.

I was forced to have the assistance of the country, none being left with me but Singleton and Jackson. The other[s] were left behind, but alive. I took all possible care of them. They will want money, as it will be three months before they are able to stir.[22]

The hunt was now on for Mason and Blood and his accomplices for a crime generally regarded among the gentry as 'a most insolent act against the king and the government'.[23] Predictably, the renegade Cromwellian Edmund Ludlow, safe in comfortable exile in Switzerland, saw Mason's rescue as 'agreeable work for the Lord'.[24]

After the fight at Darrington ended, the fugitives had wisely separated and sought safe houses in which to hide, which they reached within a few days.

Blood 'rode all that night and lost his way', his body and clothes 'covered with blood and gore from top to toe'. He managed to find an unidentified friend's house (presumably within thirty miles of Darrington and still in Yorkshire) where his gunshot wounds were treated by a local surgeon, who was undoubtedly well paid for his silence.[25] There he 'lay close' to recuperate.[26] Afterwards, Blood, true to form, disappeared from sight.

In London, John Betson, another government informer – and a crony of Leving – believed he could organise the arrests of 'some of Mason's friends'. He had lined up a potential traitor within the Presbyterian dissident community, but warned that 'he wants money'.

Betson had blotted his copybook with Arlington when he complained, a few weeks earlier, about the ungenerous £10 of secret service cash he had received as a reward for the role he played in Mason's earlier detention. 'I will be satisfied with £40 and your lordship's favour', he had told the spymaster smugly.[27] Now the informer sought an urgent meeting with Arlington. 'I will wait upon your lordship this morning and desire that you will not be in a passion against me', though he added meekly, 'I justly deserve it.

I would rather die than offend again.'[28] He also sought the king's pardon for past crimes and misdemeanours.

The government published another proclamation for the arrest of Blood on 8 August, offering £100 for his capture, that of his accomplices, and of Mason.

> Whereas we have been informed that John Lockyer, Timothy Butler and Thomas Blood (commonly called Captain Blood) with several other persons did lately in a most riotous and rebellious manner, at Darrington, near Wentbridge in the county of York, violently set upon and assault the guard entrusted with the care of conducting one John Mason, a prisoner for treason, from Our Tower of London to Our City of York in order to [stand] his trial there.
>
> [They] having killed [*sic*] and desperately wounded several of the guard and others, did rescue and carry away the said Mason and do lurk in secret places and not submit themselves to justice.

The lord lieutenants of the English counties, justices of the peace, mayors, bailiffs and subjects were 'straightly charged' to be diligent and 'use their best endeavours to search for and apprehend' these fugitives 'in all places whatsoever'. Those who concealed or harboured them would be 'proceeded against with all severity'.[29]

Meanwhile, Leving at least had received a blanket reprieve on 31 July, 'if found guilty only of felony'.[30] He was back in York Castle, still scared about his day in court as a witness. As a last resort, he wrote to Robert Benson, the clerk of York assizes, asking to be 'excused [from] witnessing anything against Jones, Atkinson or Joplin [as] they are men I have nothing to say against, having been very little concerned with them'. Leving used his good service as one of the government's informers to justify his request, emphasising: 'During my compliance [association] with the fanatics, I was always faithful to them and after my eyes were opened, I knew better and his majesty was graciously pleased to pardon and employ me.'[31]

It was the last letter written by a man who was always terrified that one day those whom he had betrayed to Charles II's secret service would find him and wreak their bloody vengeance.

That day of retribution had finally arrived. Scribbled on the front of Leving's one-page letter was a note declaring it was found on the dead body of the writer on 5 August. Leving had been tracked down and poisoned within the supposed security of York Castle. He was quickly and quietly buried in one of the city's cemeteries.

Who was his murderer?[32] Superficially, Thomas Blood appears the prime suspect. He had recognised Leving during the skirmish at Darrington and must have guessed that he was on his way to bear witness against his fellow would-be rebels at York. He must also have grasped that Leving had identified him and his accomplices Lockyer and Butler during Mason's rescue and would pass on this information to the authorities in an attempt to ingratiate himself. Blood therefore had ample reason to be motivated by revenge and, because he was still in Yorkshire (within reach of York Castle), he might have had the opportunity to administer the poison, using one of his many disguises. His experience as a sham apothecary might also have provided the knowledge about which poison to employ, if not the means.

Revenge, as we will see, was always a powerful, insistent driver in Blood's actions, goading him into committing ever more audacious crimes and outrages. Yet somehow, his direct involvement in Leving's death seems unlikely.

To him, the means was always part of the intended message to the wider world in all his exploits. The use of poison never featured in Blood's *modus operandi*, as he preferred to employ spectacular, if not flamboyant, methodology in his escapades, rather than using such a silent and ambiguous technique in lethal retribution.

Blood was also seriously wounded, and just eleven days after the Darrington affray was probably in no fit state to travel far, no matter how compelling the reason. He may, however, have been able to smuggle an easily concealed small bottle of poison into York Castle and to arrange for it to be put into Leving's food or drink, either by a sympathiser to his cause, or someone easily corrupted by a generous bribe.

Another potential suspect is John Atkinson, who had fled to London after the collapse of the projected rebellion in Yorkshire and had been betrayed by Leving in the spring of 1665. As one of those Leving was going to testify against in the forthcoming trial, he also had a strong and immediate personal motive and was held in York Castle at the time of the murder, although, presumably, his movements within the prison were constrained.[33]

Finally there is the august personage of George Villiers, Second Duke of Buckingham. Leving had fallen foul of this powerful nobleman by providing evidence against him after allegations had been made that he had plans to assist those plotting against the crown. Buckingham had recently been freed from the Tower of London after trumped-up charges of treason against him were withdrawn[34] and he may have found it prudent to neatly remove one of the witnesses against him. Others who had crossed him were also to die in mysterious circumstances.

Tellingly perhaps, Buckingham later deemed it necessary to fend off, rather ambiguously as it turned out, accusations of poisoning made against him. He wrote: 'Let any man show that [he was] really poisoned and he will do me the greatest kindness imaginable. Let the matter of fact be proved and I'll undertake to tell for what reason it was done.'[35] So Buckingham had the motive and certainly the means to order Leving's murder.

Meanwhile, William Freer, Leving's friend and fellow informer, had the misfortune to come up before a stern and testy magistrate called White at Wakefield, Yorkshire, accused of highway robbery. Like Leving before him, Freer offered up a document to spring him from jail – this time a pardon from the king for his crimes. Again, it failed to work, as White judged it invalid because it lacked the royal seal.

Freer begged Arlington to write 'two or three lines' within nine days to the magistrate to arrange his freedom, otherwise he was to be sent to York Castle. The prospect terrified him because of the 'danger of being poisoned by the same that did it to Mr Leving'.

He had not been wasting his time before his arrest. Freer 'had caused one man to be taken who was able to give account of several that are contributors to hiding persons who were with Blood and Butler in Yorkshire'. They posed no danger to the state 'as they dared not trust one another'.[36]

His desperate pleas and his industrious collection of intelligence all came to nothing. On 28 September, Freer was in York Castle, still appealing to Arlington to write to Justice White 'who committed me, and another justice, to procure my liberty, the king having promised me my life'. Probably from contacts among the prisoners, he had received stunning news:

Blood is dead and the rest of them are in London. I hope when at liberty to give an account of [Timothy] Butler.

If one who came from London and was lately in the Tower were promised his life, he could inform of all persons concerned.[37]

The news about Blood was completely untrue. Whether this was disinformation, planted by friends of Blood to cover his tracks, can only amount to conjecture. Perhaps it was just wishful thinking on Freer's part. Certainly, the manhunt continued for the fugitives with no diminution in effort or intent on the part of the authorities.

Others were swept up by the search for the fugitives. In late September, Sir Philip Musgrave, *custos rotulorum* of Westmorland, reported on the 'safe keeping' by the garrison in Carlisle Caste, Cumbria, of one Elton, a lieutenant serving Mason in the former parliamentary army. The prisoner was an Anabaptist, 'a stubborn, ill-principled man, with nothing to maintain himself. I therefore wish him a quick remove' from Carlisle.[38]

Despite the name of 'John Mason' appearing in a list of prisoners held in Windsor Castle that September,[39] he remained happily at large. Three years later, we find him keeping a tavern in London and utterly undaunted. He was still conspiring to overthrow the government.[40]

After his wounds healed, Blood once again decided to stay away from conspiracies and returned to his old quack practice at Romford in Essex[41] where he resumed his alias of Doctor Ayliff or Allen. His wife Mary and her family remained in the apothecary's shop in

Shoreditch, just north of the city of London, still using the cover name of Weston.

His son Thomas was apprenticed in 1667 to a Scottish apothecary in Southwark, the former parliamentary army surgeon Samuel Holmes.[42] His servant noted that he was 'very poor in clothes while he lived [there]' but afterwards 'dressed very fine'.[43] However Thomas quit after six months to work in Romford, firstly to sell drugs to its gullible citizens alongside his father, then to try his hand independently as a grocer. He may also have worked as a mercer – dealing in textiles, fabrics, especially silks, velvets and other costly materials. The former tailor-turned-grocer Samuel Weyer was employed by the two Bloods at Romford but was sacked by them.[44]

Then young Thomas fell into a 'debauched life' and his father wrote ruefully about his son's growing 'wickedness'.[45] Finding himself falling heavily into debt, he became a highwayman in Surrey, preying on the affluent passing trade to raise cash, operating under the alias of 'Thomas Hunt'. Clearly he enjoyed some success, as Holmes's sister, Mrs Elizabeth Price, believed him to be worth £500, and as a twenty-one-year-old 'lusty' highwayman he may also have made some progress in the affairs of the heart as she recalled him being a servant 'to a young gentlewoman'.[46]

Crime never pays and it was not long before 'Thomas Hunt' fell into the clutches of the law. He appeared before Chief Justice Keeling and Judge Morton at the Surrey county assizes at Guildford on 4 July 1670, accused of assaulting, with intent to rob, John Constable near Croydon the previous May. He was fined 100 marks, or £67, and thrown into the Marshalsea prison in Southwark.[47]

His father moved to Southwark to be close to his son and lodged with Barnaby Bloxton, tailor, at Winchester House, using the pseudonym 'Dr Alec'. Blood asked his landlord to stand surety for his son, but Bloxton refused. Instead he helpfully introduced him to the brewer William Mumford.[48] Mumford agreed, as did William Gant of Wapping in Essex, and both men put up the requisite money. 'Thomas Hunt' was freed after a month on their bond guaranteeing his good behaviour for seven years.[49] On 17 October, the failed highwayman recovered his sword, belt and pistol from the Lambeth constable Thomas Drayton, signing a receipt, witnessed by his brother Edmund.[50]

Blood senior returned to Romford with other things on his mind.

The origin of the well-known phrase 'revenge is a dish best served cold' is highly debatable.[51] Certainly it describes very aptly Thomas Blood's beliefs or personal creed. Specifically, he had waited patiently for more than seven years to inflict a terrible revenge on one particular enemy.

Now he saw his chance for vengeance.

# 5

## *An Incident in St James's*

*The execrable design to assassinate the duke of Ormond has alarmed
all the country ... It has opened all men's mouths and thoughts to
speak their liking for him as well as their detestation of the attempt.*

Robert Benson to Williamson
24 December 1670.[1]

In the late seventeenth century, built-up London petered out at the
western end of Piccadilly.[2] Clean air and the bucolic fields and lanes
of the flat Middlesex countryside began at Tyburn Lane, which led
north to the city's traditional place of execution for felons, very near
today's Marble Arch.[3] In 1660 a windmill stood at the other end
of Piccadilly, at the start of the highway to Reading in Berkshire
and onwards to Bristol, known as the 'Great West Road'. Along the
north side of this unpaved street stood half a dozen grand mansions,
including the newly completed Clarendon House, the short-lived
residence of Lord Chancellor Clarendon, which cost him between
£40,000 and £50,000 to build.[4]

After Clarendon's fall from power in August 1667, the house was
rented by the Duke of Ormond for a few months in 1670.[5] It was
an impressive London home for the former lord lieutenant of Ireland[6] – a huge three-storeyed E-shaped building, with two wings
and a central cupola behind a courtyard, set back from the street at
the T-junction of Piccadilly with St James's Street. There were two
imposing wrought-iron gates barring its entrance, flanked by por-
ters' lodges, each one embellished with blind columns on the street
façade. The grounds extended to thirty acres (12.14 hectares) of

former agricultural land, including the twenty-four once owned by 'the widow Austin of the "Eagle and Child" [tavern] in the [nearby] Strand'.[7] Ormond had served as lord steward of the royal household since the Restoration and was appointed lord high steward of England in March 1661; the mansion was a convenient base for his ceremonial duties at court.

St James's Street, which began to be built up at the beginning of the century, ran south from Piccadilly, down a gentle slope to Henry VIII's red-brick palace of St James, erected in 1531–6 on the site of a medieval hospital for leprous women.[8] The impressive tall twin-towered gatehouse fronting Pall Mall still bears the old ogre's royal cipher. This wide street, earlier described as a 'quagmire' by the diarist John Evelyn, was paved over in 1661 and was later celebrated across London for the fashionable coffee and chocolate houses scattered among the twenty-four dwellings that lined the road.[9]

It was at the top end of this street, after seven o'clock on the evening of Tuesday, 6 December, 1670 that Blood staged another outrage that rocked the royal court, triggered a feverish House of Lords investigation and became a sensation throughout all of Charles II's realms. Blood, together with four or five desperadoes, including his eldest son Thomas, dragged Ormond from his coach in a violent attempt either to kidnap or assassinate the former Irish viceroy.

His crime bore all the hallmarks of a carefully planned operation. Reliable intelligence must have been obtained from a well-wisher (or someone within Ormond's household who was corruptible) indicating that the lord high steward would attend a state function in the City of London that day. Blood was also provided with the precise time of the duke's return and his route homewards.

Ostensibly, it was an act of pure revenge. Blood and his fellow assailant, Lieutenant Colonel William Moore, who now lived in Gray's Inn Lane, London, had irretrievably lost their Irish estates when they were attainted as traitors in the aftermath of the bungled Dublin Castle plot of seven years before. Both held Ormond personally responsible for their continuing impoverishment, as did the younger Blood, who similarly had lost any hope of his inheritance. Their hatred of the duke burned still bright despite the passing of the years.

If our adventurer – by dint of yet another self-promotion now enjoying the exalted rank of colonel – relished a certain vicarious notoriety before, his exploits now became infamous. After such an audacious crime, committed on the very doorstep of a royal palace, Charles II's government left no stone unturned to find and arrest Blood and his outlaw accomplices.

Yet the blue-blooded aristocrat quite possibly at the heart of the conspiracy was left unquestioned and untouched by the forces of law and order as he strutted vaingloriously within an arm's breadth of the monarch himself.

It was a propitious time for such an attack, as London was distracted and enthralled by the pomp and splendour of a grand state visit. The Second Anglo-Dutch War had ended three years earlier after de Ruyter's flotilla broke the chain booms defending the River Medway in Kent, burned some English warships moored at Chatham and jubilantly towed away the *Unity* and the flagship *Royal Charles* as prizes. After this national disgrace, the treaty signed on 31 July 1667 at Breda Castle restored peaceful relations between the two rival naval powers.[10]

William, Prince of Orange arrived in England on a five-month visit, primarily to collect an embarrassingly large debt of 2,797,859 guilders (about £280,000) owed to the Dutch House of Orange by the Stuarts. Of course, the perpetually cash-strapped Charles II could not repay the loan and William eventually agreed magnanimously to reduce it by £100,000. No wonder he was royally entertained, even though the king's continuing indebtedness, coupled with the lingering shame of the successful Dutch naval attack on the Medway, must have made Charles, for all his gamecock bravura, an uncomfortable and uneasy host.

But the English monarch had other, more sanguine, reasons to lavish his hospitality on the twenty-year-old princely guest in his household. His Portuguese wife, the Catholic Catherine of Braganza, whom he had married in May 1662, had failed in the first duty of any royal consort down the ages: to produce the all-important healthy heir to the throne. She had endured four tedious pregnancies but, sadly, all resulted in miscarriages and stillbirths, the last in June 1669.[11] James, Duke of York, Charles's younger brother and the heir presumptive to the throne, was also a Catholic and this posed almost insurmountable problems, in many eyes, to his peaceful succession. To dampen down or divert parliamentary and popular disquiet, Charles conceived the idea of marrying off Mary, James's eldest surviving daughter, to the staunchly Protestant William, even though she was eleven years his junior and still played with her dolls in the royal nursery.[12]

On Saturday, 3 December, Charles, his queen and the Prince of Orange (who was fresh from an agreeable visit to the academic splendours of the University of Cambridge) appeared incognito 'at the merriments usual at this time of year at The Temple [in London] where they were entertained with dances of all kinds to their very great satisfaction'.[13] The following Tuesday, the prince was feasted in the Guildhall's fifteenth-century great hall by the lord mayor, Sir Richard Ford, and the affluent Corporation of the City of London. After the banquet, William was graciously pleased to review the city's trained bands of citizen soldiers marshalled outside in the courtyard facing Gresham Street.

Ormond, now an infirm sixty-year-old, had been invited to the function and left the Guildhall sometime after five o'clock by coach to return westwards across the City of London to Clarendon House. Unusually, his vehicle did not have straps fitted at its back for his liveried retainers to hang on to; indeed, the duke had somewhat heartlessly fixed a large number of projecting iron spikes on the carriage to prevent them from enjoying the ride. Instead, they had to pant along behind or beside the coach on each side of the street. He normally was attended by six tall footmen carrying torches or *flambeaux* to light the way – some running ahead, shouting this proud warning to bystanders: 'Make way for the Duke of Ormond!'[14]

The weather was stormy, as it had been for the last fortnight.[15] As Ormond's coach wended its slow way through the crowded and filthy streets, Michael Beresford, a parson from Hopton in Suffolk, was strolling in the Piazza in Covent Garden, a large colonnaded open space situated between St Martin's and Drury lanes which had been completed by the classical architect Inigo Jones in 1637.[16] There, he told Arlington later, he recognised a man called Thomas Allen, dressed smartly and wearing a fine brown periwig on his head. Beresford had formerly known him as a footman to Sir Michael Livesey, another Puritan signatory to Charles I's death warrant who had fled for his life to the Netherlands in 1660.[17] This was indeed Thomas Blood, as usual hiding behind one of his favourite aliases.

'Allen' walked past the parson several times before he stopped, turned back and politely inquired his name. Beresford, in turn, asked him to confirm his identity and he replied: 'Allen – and that Sir Michael Livesey was living'. Where was Allen lodging in London? He would not say but added that he 'had been in Ireland and [was] lately come over' and had relations on the Isle of Sheppey in Kent. Allen's reticence and evasiveness troubled Beresford so much that he continued his questioning.

What was Allen doing here? 'Nothing at all.'

Would Allen like to drink a pint of wine with him (probably in the nearby Shakespeare tavern)? Allen unfortunately had to refuse the kind invitation.

'What was Sir Michael Livesey [doing] in town?' Ignoring the question, Allen – 'looking ghastly' – blurted out: 'There are bad designs at foot.'

'What!' exclaimed an astonished Beresford, then added: 'We have had too many already.' Allen responded with the cryptic comment: 'We are all desperate.'

As the pair walked northwards towards Long Acre in the gathering dusk, a messenger boy came up and told Allen enigmatically: 'The horses have gone before' and he immediately strode off without even saying a word of farewell, leaving behind a perplexed and discomforted parson standing alone in the street.[18]

This surreal meeting must have ended sometime after six-thirty. The planned rendezvous for Blood's accomplices was a large hostelry called the Bull Head tavern[19] in Old Spring Gardens at Charing Cross, about fifteen minutes' walk away from Long Acre.[20]

Matthew Pretty, who drew pints of ale from the tavern's barrels, and its young potboy, William Wilson, testified afterwards that five men in cloaks, armed with swords, had earlier arrived there on horseback and had ordered drinks.

> They having drunk about six pints of wine – canary,[21] sherry and white wine – two pints of each and one of them [told] the drawer to draw good wine for they were graziers.[22]
>
> Then the drawer asked if they knew Mr West, a grazier, who is dead and if they knew Mr Poultney, a grazier of Blackwall. They said, yes, they knew them.

The drawer recalled that one of their horses was 'a reddish dark colour with a bald face' and its rider was a 'tall, lean, pale-faced man with short-black hair' who said he would not take £10 for his old bald horse yet. The potboy believed this man to 'be a Portuguese' and remembered him only too well as he had sometime before taken a message to his lodgings and he had not only beaten him but refused to hand over a tip. Pretty said two of the others were young; 'about twenty-six years' old, he estimated with curious precision.

Both witnesses said that 'near the hour of seven o'clock' a man wearing a cloak walked into the tavern – this must have been Blood – just as one of the duke's linkmen ran past, shouting: 'Make way here for the Duke of Ormond!' At the same time everyone saw the duke's coach trundle by outside in the darkened street, followed by his breathless retainers.

The 'graziers' and the new arrival paid for and drank another two pints of white wine. After fifteen minutes, they called for three white clay pipes of tobacco and left hastily, taking the tobacco with them. The horsemen rode off at 'a great pace' west towards the Haymarket or Pall Mall, leaving their change and some of their wine undrunk. This was consumed appreciatively by the potboy[23] and Pretty probably pocketed the coins.

As well as Blood, his son (still employing the pseudonym 'Thomas Hunt') and Lieutenant Colonel Moore, this party also included the Fifth Monarchist Captain Richard Halliwell (or Holloway).

Another member was called Simons, of whom little more is known, although this may be the alias of another Fifth Monarchist, William Smith, who helped to arrange Mason's rescue back in July 1667.[24]

Ormond's coach and footmen continued their stately progress down Pall Mall and at its end, at St James's Palace, wheeled right, up the unlit slope of St James's Street, drawing ever nearer to Clarendon House at the top end of the cobbled road. After a long, tiring and probably tedious day of diplomacy and polite conversation, home was at last in sight for the elderly duke. Any idea of an ambush would not have entered his thoughts.

Blood's party then struck.

Henley, the coachman, high up on the vehicle's box in front, heard shouts from a rider suddenly coming up alongside him, warning that there 'was a dead man' lying in the street ahead and 'bade him stop the coach'.

He pulled tightly on the reins, the coach came to a sudden, jerking halt and the collars and bridles of the horses were seized. Two riders aimed their pistols at the terrified coachman's head.

Behind the coach, an assailant pointed a brace of pistols at the chest of a footman called Exby and swore that he would be shot dead instantly if he moved a muscle in any attempt to help his master.[25] The other retainers were scattered by the horsemen and fled for their lives.

Ormond was no doubt sprawling on the floor of the coach after its unexpected and violent halt. His first reaction was that he was the victim of a simple, sordid robbery by highwaymen.[26]

He was quickly disabused.

After threatening to pistol-whip him, Blood bundled him out of the carriage and down on to the filthy cobbles. Despite Ormond's struggling, he managed to pin a paper to his chest that spelt out the reasons for his capture and execution.[27] Blood then manhandled him up behind 'Hunt', sitting astride his horse. Refusing Ormond's gabbled offer of forty guineas (£42) in ready cash and £1,000 worth of jewellery in return for his immediate release, they tied their victim to the younger Blood with a short length of cord.[28]

Blood then galloped off westwards down Piccadilly, heading for

Tyburn Lane, apparently to check if there was a noose still hanging from the triple gibbet at the north end of the road. His plan was to ignominiously hang Ormond as a common malefactor from the public gallows.

Amid all this noise and confusion in the darkness, the coachman seized his chance of escape, whipped up his horses and raced the short distance up to Clarendon House.

The other attackers began to follow Blood, with 'Thomas Hunt' (his protesting prisoner behind him) coming up last. He had been instructed by his father 'to ride through thick and thin till he got to the place appointed'.[29]

But the duke was made of stern stuff. Not for nothing had he served as a military commander in the Irish Confederation Wars of 1641–7 and later against Parliament's army in Ireland, suffering the full rigours and discomforts of campaigning in a wet Irish winter. The old soldier began to struggle violently against his bonds. 'Hunt' was unable to subdue him as he was hampered by holding his sword and bridle in one hand and a pistol in the other.

The assailants had ridden a 'good way past Berkeley House'[30] before the plan for the ambush began to unravel.

Ormond managed to knock the firearm out of 'Hunt's' hand and then heaved him out of the saddle by jerking his foot beneath one of his captor's legs. Both assailant and prisoner fell off the wheeling, panicky horse and rolled over several times in the filth and mire of Piccadilly. The duke landed heavily on top but still managed to snatch the sword out of Hunt's grasp.

Torches and voices were approaching in the darkness and 'Hunt' cut the duke's bonds, remounted and rode off, his friends firing a ragged volley of pistol shots at Ormond, lying winded in the mud. Whether due to the dark or their panic, every bullet missed.

Thomas Brooks, the porter on duty at the gates of Clarendon House, testified that

the footman came and called out, and not seeing the coach, I looked out and heard a noise and ran and finding my lord, endeavoured to bring him home.

They cried: 'Kill the rogue' but I got away from them with my
lord within the gates in my arms.

He had been joined by Thomas Clarke, the comptroller of Ormond's household, who was fortuitously standing in the courtyard
in front of the mansion, and, gathering together a number of servants, they raced west down Piccadilly towards the commotion.

The duke had received a 'knock over his pole [head]', a sword cut
to the hand and multiple bruises from his fall. He lay apparently
lifeless on the ground, totally exhausted from the struggle.[31] The
attack had lasted less than ten minutes.

His rescuers could only identify the victim by feeling, with their
fingers, the starburst-shaped Order of the Garter insignia pinned
on his coat 'rather than by any sound of voice he could utter'. They
carried his supine body home and laid him on a bed 'to recover his
spirits'.[32]

Blood meanwhile had fastened a noose to the gallows and, won-
dering what was delaying his accomplices and prisoner, rode back
to rejoin his empty-handed friends at the bottom of Tyburn Lane.
Four riders were sharing two horses, having lost their mounts in
the fracas. They doubled back to the western outskirts of Westminster and crossed the Thames on the horse ferry operated by Mrs
Leventhorpe[33] (where today's Lambeth Bridge crosses the river).
Then the party rode eastwards just over a mile (1.63 km) to Southwark (opposite London Bridge), hoping to have evaded the hue and
cry in their wake.

Behind them at the scene of the crime lay Thomas Hunt's silver-
mounted screw pistol, his belt (ripped off in the struggle) and
sword.

Two loose horses, one a chestnut, distinguished by 'a white stripe
and a blaze all along its face', had also been caught by Ormond's
servants. The weapons and horses were taken back to Clarendon
House as evidence. Both the pistol (later revealed to have been previously owned by Lieutenant Colonel Moore) and the sword had
the initials 'T.H.' rudely scratched upon them.

The next morning, Blood's wife, Mary, left her temporary

lodgings owned by the schoolmaster Jonathan Davies in the village of Mortlake, Surrey, and disappeared with one of her daughters.

Charles II was incandescent, both at the boldness of the outrage and the fact that it was committed disturbingly near to St James's Palace. Close watch was set on England's sea ports to ensure the fugitives could not flee the country.

London in the late seventeenth century had no recognisable police force. The forces of law and order consisted of the local watch, elected by parishes, and constables working under the direction of magistrates. There were others, more bounty-hunters than constabulary, who worked as thief-takers, receiving success fees from those who had property stolen from them. The first organised police in the capital were the Bow Street Runners, founded by the author Henry Fielding in the mid-eighteenth century; the professional Metropolitan Police were established in 1829 by the Home Secretary Sir Robert Peel. A long time to wait for a detective.

Arlington wisely took personal charge of the investigation and, utilising the resources of his secret service, demonstrated that he was no laggard in pursuing the perpetrators of the outrage against Ormond. Through shrewd and diligent sleuthing, he quickly identified the crime's main protagonists.

Arlington believed the motive behind the attack on Ormond was 'not to rob or kill [him] but to carry him to some obscure place and oblige him to ransom himself at ten or twenty thousand pounds'.[34] More ludicrously, popular report exaggerated the idea of kidnapping the duke, turning it into a cunning plan to sell him to spend the remainder of his life in slavery with the moors in North Africa.[35] Rumour naturally abounded: one maintained that only two men attacked the duke, 'carrying him some distance behind one of them',[36] while Girolamo Alberti, the Venetian ambassador to London, said that twelve men were involved, 'one of whom carried [Ormond] on his crupper,[37] vowing that he meant something more than robbery'.[38]

On 7 December, Charles II signed a proclamation at Whitehall offering the huge reward of £1,000 (or £142,000 at today's prices) 'to any who shall discover any of the six persons who ... forced the Duke of Ormond out of his coach . . . set him behind one of them on horseback with intent to have carried him to some obscure place out of town, where they might with more privacy have executed their villainous and bloody conspiracy'. The Duke, 'in his endeavour to rescue himself, [was] so wounded . . . that he now lies languishing under his wounds at his lodgings at Clarendon House'. A royal pardon, as well as this eye-watering financial incentive, was offered to any of the conspirators who broke ranks and 'declared his whole knowledge' of this 'barbarous and inhumane' plot.[39] An additional reward of £100 was available to 'any who could but tell who owned a horse and pistol which they left behind them'.

The next day's edition of the *London Gazette* named four of the attackers and described their escape across the River Thames soon after the botched kidnap. The first suspect identified was Richard Halliwell, 'a tobacco-cutter, lately dwelling in Frying Pan Alley[40] off Petticoat Lane, without Bishopsgate', in the City of London. He was said to be a 'middle-sized man, plump faced, with [smallpox] pock holes, of a demure countenance, having a short brown periwig and sad coloured clothes, about forty years of age'.

The second (whom we now know was Blood), was named as 'Thomas Allen, alias Alloyt, alias Ayliff, who pretended himself a surgeon or doctor of physic, sometimes living at Romford in Essex, but lately lodging at or near Aldgate', then a Jewish quarter near the eastern gate of the City of London. He was

a man of down look, lean-faced and full of pock holes, with a stuff coat,[41] usually wearing a worsted camlet cloak and a brown short periwig, inclining to red, about thirty-six years of age.

This description was generous, if not kind, to Blood's advancing years. In fact, he was aged fifty-two. His son, 'Thomas Hunt', was next described:

A tall and well-proportioned man, of a ruddy complexion, about thirty-three or thirty-four years of age, wearing a flaxen periwig of a large curl . . . but sometimes of late a black one. His clothes black and sometimes wearing a black worsted camlet coat, long, and has one leg a little crooked or bowed.

The last suspect was a man named only as 'Hurst' (but later established to be 'John Hurst') who was said to be 'of middle size, good complexion, with a dark coloured periwig and commonly wears a black coat'.

Arlington must have employed many of his informers in the capital's seamy underworld to come up with so much information about the miscreants so quickly. The *London Gazette* then related how Ormond's would-be attackers escaped. 'Upon inquiry, it is found that the said persons, after the . . . assassination attempt . . . made their way towards Knightsbridge and they [crossed] the Thames near to the Neat Houses[42] by Tothill Fields [Westminster].'[43] Afterwards, on the south bank, 'they made their way through Lambeth into Southwark, four of them mounted upon two horses and another singly mounted on a black mare with one white foot, about sixteen hands high, which was formerly seized at Lambeth as belonging to Thomas Hunt, who was then apprehended for attempting a robbery at Smitham Bottom[44] in Surrey.[45]

A subsequent issue of the *London Gazette* elaborated on Hunt's description 'for his better discovery'. This reduced his age by a decade to twenty-three years, and mentioned a 'mark or scar near his right eye about the bigness of a penny', probably a souvenir of his time as a highwayman.[46]

Two days after the attack, Hunt's lodgings at the apothecary John Anderson's house near the Plough tavern in Bedlam, off Bishopsgate Street, were searched by Sir Robert Viner, who enjoyed particular favour at court.[47] 'Thomas Hunt's' neighbours said that he had lived for some years in Ireland but had not been born there. One described him as a 'young, tall ruddy man' and another as 'a lusty, proper young man, full-faced, about twenty-one years of age'. They knew nothing of his father, other than that he was believed to be a 'desperate man' who was still living in London.[48]

The lord mayor, Sir Richard Ford, and Viner then raided Halliwell's house in Frying Pan Alley at two o'clock in the morning of the next day, Friday, 10 December. Halliwell escaped their clutches by swiftly dressing and clambering out through a garret window. He scrambled across the nearby roofs and down to street level as the constables searched the ground floor of his tenement.

His twelve-year-old niece, Margaret Boulter, who had lived with his family for two years, was questioned in the small hours. She told the lord mayor that Halliwell had been at home since eight or nine o'clock the previous evening and moments before his hasty exit through the attic window had begged his wife Katherine to tell the unwelcome visitors that he was not to be found in London. The child, manifestly brought up to tell the truth and shame the devil, said she had often seen 'Thomas Hunt' at the house and three men had been there at about six o'clock. One of them was the mysterious Hurst, 'a man of middle stature and no employment'.[49] A wet cloak was discovered in the house and 'treasonable material' seized, including a letter from Halliwell to his Fifth Monarchist brethren and two to Halliwell from Thomas Allen, alias Blood, found in the pocket of a coat. His wife Katherine and their young child were taken into custody.

The evidence was passed on to Arlington. Halliwell's letter rebuked his fellow 'fanatics' for their coldness and for obeying the 'filthy proclamation forbidding the churches to meet together'. It was a long, rambling and angry diatribe, which culminated in Halliwell's threat to quit the ranks of the Fifth Monarchists altogether until they fully 'repent of their sins'.[50] The two undated letters from Blood – signed 'T.A.' for Thomas Allen – appeared arcane. The first complained about not hearing anything about an unspecified coat and hose and expressed the desire to arrange a meeting. The second sought the loan of a coat, pistols and a sword. It concluded with the writer's fond hope that Halliwell 'may see a happy return' of them.[51]

While safely in hiding, Halliwell rather cheekily wrote to one of the constables who had searched his house during that early morning raid. He was a friend and near neighbour called Howell, a weaver who lived in Half Moon Alley, on the other side of Bishopsgate Street. Only too well aware that Williamson's Post Office might intercept it and read the contents, Halliwell entrusted the letter to be delivered by hand by William Mosely and his daughter Honour, of Blue Anchor Alley, off Bunhill Row.[52] He enclosed a letter which he begged Howell to deliver to Sir Richard Ford, the lord mayor. There was nothing 'unbecoming' in its contents, he assured the constable, and its purpose was only to vindicate his character.[53]

This letter was a strange compound of abject pleading and righteous indignation. Halliwell wanted to 'undeceive' Ford about him being 'an actor in the prodigious attempt against . . . Ormond'. His only involvement with Thomas Hunt was related to their business interests and the letter about a case of pistols found in his coat pocket was very old – he had not worn the garment since the previous spring. Furthermore, these weapons were required 'for an adventure at sea'. The wet cloak belonged to a young boy and been left accidentally at Halliwell's home. Several witnesses could provide him with a cast-iron alibi for the time of the attack – as he was innocently at home all that day. He then complained about the imprisonment of his wife and child 'without legal process and [who were] terrified with hard usage and want of food'. He added:

> It was to avoid such severity that I absented myself, being under prejudice in respect of my religious principles and of my formerly being in arms, notwithstanding the Act of Indemnity.[54]
> I will readily surrender if I am granted a trial but not otherwise.
> I beseech your lordship to prevent my inevitable ruin.[55]

Mrs Halliwell was to be held by the lord mayor for six weeks and was regularly questioned about 'the horrid attempt [on Ormond] whereof I praise God I am altogether innocent and hope that my husband is also, though he absents himself, for what reason I am utterly ignorant'. Then she was released into the custody of a king's messenger. Her protestations began to appear less than ingenuous when the authorities discovered she had sent a cloak to Halliwell, by a Mrs Perryn, whose address she refused to divulge.[56]

Warrants were issued on 11 December for the arrests of a Dr Ayliff, his son 'Thomas Hunt' and Richard Halliwell.

The first breakthrough in the investigation proved something of a mirage. The fourth man named as wanted in connection with the attack on Ormond was 'John Hurst', who had been seen at Halliwell's home on 9 December. Arlington was soon hard on his tracks.

His inquiries threw up one man called Hurst, the son of a Cambridge parson who had served Sir Francis Leake in Nottinghamshire for six or seven years. This Hurst had stayed at William Done's tavern, the [Golden] Fleece, in Tothill Street, Westminster, for two nights, 19 and 20 December, and had also been lodging at John Jones's White Swan in Queen Street, off Drury Lane.[57] Jones had seen Hurst on horseback at his door the previous October when he said he was a brother of a servant of Lord Howard at Arundel House named Owen,[58] 'a desperate fellow and of ill life', whom he had visited the day after the assault. Hurst had also been seen drinking at the St John's Head (or 'Heaven') tavern in the precincts of the Palace of Westminster[59] on 20 and 21 December and had sold his brother's horse to Done, saying that he was soon to depart to Jamaica with a commission to receive slaves. He was later imprisoned in the Marshalsea for a paltry debt and was brought from there to be identified by witnesses. Arlington discovered to his chagrin that this was the wrong Hurst.[60]

On 12 December Arlington interviewed several witnesses about another Hurst, a Yorkshire lawyer who had gone to Ireland in September 1669, leaving his wife Elizabeth behind in London. He had gone on to Scotland but had lately returned and was going to (?bigamously) marry a widow at Deptford, a shipyard area on the south bank of the Thames. This Hurst was described as aged about forty, 'pretty tall' with yellow hair and, according to Thomas Trishaire, was a 'great cheat'. No surprise, then, that he had had one ear cut off, or 'cropped', and had stood in the pillory – the normal punishment for writing seditious texts. Superficially, this Hurst's antecedents seemed very suspicious, fitting the profile of someone quite likely to be one of Blood's desperadoes. Indeed, a man called Taylor claimed to have seen him in company with Halliwell at the Royal Exchange more than a week after the attack.[61]

However, no evidence could be uncovered to justify linking him with the Ormond conspiracy.

The investigation turned up a third man called John Hurst, a sailor born in Sussex who had returned four months before from the island of Nevis in the West Indies where he had been based for eight years. He was interrogated on 17 December but was able to prove that he was at 'Capt. Lawrence's' house on the night of the assault. Moreover, Hurst could offer up 'Lady Lawrence of Chelsea' and other witnesses who would vouch for his unimpeachable respectability.[62]

Despite all this effort, it looked likely that the line of inquiry about Hurst was an annoying dead end. Quietly, his name was eliminated from the investigation.

This was not the only red herring. On Christmas Day, a letter arrived on Arlington's desk that seemed to clear Blood of any involvement in the outrage. Sadly, all that is left us is the postscript – the remainder of the letter is torn away.

> I am told that Allen or Ayliff mentioned in the [London] *Gazette* as one of the persons suspected in the attempt on the duke of Ormond was at sea in the *Portland* frigate[63] and that Jennings or Jennins, who was formerly surgeon to that ship is a great crony of his and a likely man to give an account of him.
>
> Jennings lives over against the Coach and Horses in St Martin's Lane and his wife works at the [Royal] Exchange. It will not be amiss to call upon him when you go that way.[64]

The note is endorsed: 'John Rogers received this letter from William Rogers of Lincoln's Inn on 24 December and that John Rogers believed it came out of Worcestershire. He does not know from whom, but will write about it to William Rogers who has gone to Gloucestershire.' 'Rogers' was an alias used by Captain John Lockyer, one of Blood's accomplices in the rescue of John Mason and his companion in his European mission to lure Edmund Ludlow to Paris. It is unlikely that this helpful correspondent was Lockyer, but it is by no means implausible that this was a clever attempt to create a false alibi for Blood and divert Arlington's questing blood-hounds from his trail. The surgeon Jennings may well have been lined up to receive a visit from Arlington or his agents and to tell of Blood's convenient adventures at sea. If he did, his account was not believed.

Meanwhile, Samuel Holmes, the apothecary who had tried un-successfully to train Blood junior in the mysteries of pharmacy, was arrested on suspicion of involvement in the attack on Ormond. On 9 December he was questioned by the lord mayor and Mr Justice Hooker and by Arlington three days later. He acknowledged that Thomas Hunt had been apprenticed to him and that he knew 'Dr Aylett' or 'Elyot', but he had not seen either man for six months. Both, he thought, were Presbyterians. He knew nothing of Hunt's father and had never heard of Thomas Blood.[65] He was remanded to the Gatehouse[66] as a close prisoner on suspicion of being 'an ac-cessory to the late attempt on the Duke of Ormond'.[67]

John Buxton, a tailor of Bell Alley, off Coleman Street, told the secretary of state that he suspected Holmes was 'in the business', as he corresponded with the three suspects and was 'a surgeon in the [parliamentary] army'. These three men, he said, 'were Fifth Monarchists and desperate'. Holmes's sister, Mrs Elizabeth Price, who had lived with Buxton, had dined with Thomas Hunt four or five months before.[68] As he seemed to know them so well, Arlington handed Buxton a warrant empowering him to apprehend all three men on sight.[69] However, after Holmes testified against Hunt, Ar-lington discharged him from prison on 23 January 1671 when he came up with cash as a security to appear when required.[70]

A week before Christmas, Arlington questioned Francis Johnson, a one-time fellow of All Souls Oxford, 'a pretended [Congregation-alist] minister' and a former chaplain to Oliver Cromwell, who lived in Gray's Inn Lane. His lodger for three years had been Lieutenant Colonel Moore, who had remained out throughout the night of 7 December. The notes of the interrogation have the endorsement that 'Moore had once the pistol' used by Hunt and left behind at the crime scene.[71]

Despite all this sound and fury, Arlington was getting nowhere.

Every strand of the tangled investigation ended in a blind alley. Three merchants on their way to France, two butchers from Gloucestershire, an Irish counterfeiter turned burglar[72] and a London cook were all detained and intensively questioned. Even one of Catherine of Braganza's royal guards was suspected of involvement.[73] All proved wholly innocent of any connection with the attempted kidnap.[74] Sir William Morton, a judge of the King's Bench, told Ormond on 31 December that he was still searching actively for Blood and Lieutenant Colonel Moore as he had heard 'they are in or about London'.[75]

On 14 January, sixty-nine temporal and spiritual members of the House of Lords[76] were appointed as a committee to 'examine the matter of fact committed in the late barbarous assaulting, wounding and robbing the person of the lord steward of his majesty's household and to make a report thereof to this House'. Their lordships, or any five of them, were to meet that afternoon in the prince's lodgings and have power to adjourn from time to time and 'to send for such persons as they shall think fit'.[77]

The Lords investigation turned up little new, aside from the distraction of a handful of reprobates who were unwise enough to utter unflattering opinions in public about the Duke of Ormond.

Thomas Woodhouse, a king's messenger, was instructed to detain Thomas Sunderland for having 'in some discourse justified the attempt to assassinate ... Ormond, or at least declared that the persons that encouraged the assassins were as good men as the duke' himself. Sunderland happily only spent two days in custody before he was freed.[78]

The charmingly named John Washwhite, a former parliamentary soldier turned cook, who had lived at Lazy Hill, near Dublin, for seventeen years had been thrown into the Gatehouse for having spoken against Ormond. He appeared before their lordships on 23 January and denied the charge levelled against him of using threatening language against the duke and openly wishing that 'he had lost his leg as well as his boot' at the Battle of Rathmines, outside Dublin, on 2 August 1649. More threateningly, he had predicted that Ormond 'would not die in his bed'. Washwhite denied all this and claimed his accusers were friends of someone he had caused to appear before Judge Morton and were trying to keep him imprisoned 'to hinder his serving' the king. The Lords believed him and his chains were ordered to be removed.[79]

Thomas Dixey, a butcher from the seedy area of Bankside in Southwark, was also accused of using abusive language about Ormond. When he was brought up in front of Judge Morton on 3 February he was accused of involvement in the assault. Defiantly, he replied: 'What's that to you?' Morton, not a man for levity, commented: 'I do suspect this fellow the more because he is a bold impudent fellow . . . and lives in Southwark whither those who did assault the duke did retire.'

The butcher was hauled up before the Lords committee on 8 and 10 February, when the constable who arrested him swore that he had said: 'All they can say is that I said the Duke of Ormond is a knave and I will justify it. I think I shall be hanged but I care not.' He confidently expected to be rescued by his brother John, known as 'Cherrybounce',[80] and Captain Careless – a mischievous reference to William Careless, Charles II's companion when he hid in an oak tree in the woods of Boscobel after his defeat at the Battle of Worcester on 3 September 1651.

Dixey was dispatched to the Gatehouse from where he wrote to Arlington, in a rather more moderate tone, sorrowfully seeking a release on bail, as 'his goods are seized and his wife and children are turned out of doors'.[81] Probably suspecting that the butcher's bark was worse than his bite, the Lords released Dixey on his providing a financial surety for his future good behaviour.[82]

The clinching evidence against the two Bloods was that silver-mounted pistol, sword and belt left behind in the mud of Piccadilly, which became the all-important link that connected 'Thomas Hunt' and, inevitably, his father with the outrage.

The link was supplied by the petition of Henry Draper, a constable, and Henry Partridge of Lambeth, who claimed the government's £100 reward because they knew the pistol belonged to the younger Blood,[83] as they had taken it from him in the hue and cry following his assault and robbery of John Constable the previous May. Moreover, they had returned all the weapons to him in October when sureties were provided after his release from the Marshalsea prison. The receipt for the equipment, signed by Hunt, was produced as additional proof.[84] Finally, the authorities knew that one of the horses used in the ambush – the 'black mare with one white foot, about sixteen hands high' – had also been seized at Lambeth and belonged to Thomas Hunt.

In late February Arlington reported to the committee that, of the men suspected, 'Jones, Blood (called Allen), young Blood his son (called Hunt under which name he was indicted last year), Halliwell, Moore and Simons, were desperate characters sheltering under the name of Fifth Monarchy men'. Always cautious, the secretary of state urged their lordships not to publish the suspects' real names: 'Would not exposing of their names by act of Parliament make them hide themselves in the country, whereas the nonconformists with whom they met and abhorred their crime, would otherwise be glad to bring them to justice?' he suggested.[85]

Apparently not. After examining a number of witnesses and reading reports of Arlington's interrogations, on 9 March 1671 the Lords finally produced their report, finding a true bill against Blood, his son and William Halliwell for the crime against Ormond – although the bill used only their pseudonyms. They were given 'a short day' to submit themselves to justice or 'upon failure of coming in, to stand convicted of the said assault'.[86]

Of course, they failed to appear. The matter was referred to the lord chief baron of the Exchequer, Sir Matthew Hale. Nothing further was accomplished.

Despite Arlington's view that the proceeds from ransoming Ormond were the prime motivation behind the attack, there seems every reason to believe that Blood intended to kill his old enemy. There are strong indications that he was going to hang the old soldier, like a criminal, from the Tyburn Tree, adding his humiliation and degradation to the heady cocktail of murder. The drama of Ormond's end would have enhanced the notoriety of the crime. Blood was looking for a place in history.

But revenge was not the only spur for the ambush. Money was

probably involved – with the cash almost certainly supplied by one of the highest in the land.

Circumstantial evidence suggests that this mystery figure who wanted Ormond dead and cold in his grave was George Villiers, Second Duke of Buckingham.

It is known that Buckingham 'hated the duke of Ormond mortally',[87] possibly because of his continuing grudge over the breakdown of a proposed marriage alliance between the two families of six years before.[88] Furthermore, Buckingham was generally believed to have set in train Ormond's recall as lord lieutenant of Ireland in February 1669.[89] He was always ruthlessly ambitious and regularly feuded with his rivals at court, particularly Arlington, and had even quarrelled with the king's brother, the Duke of York.[90] Buckingham was 'considered the most profligate person of the age and capable of any iniquity, however mean or enormous'.[91] The other person who hated Ormond at court was Barbara Palmer, First Duchess of Cleveland and Countess of Castlemaine, one of Charles II's many mistresses and one who had a penchant for meddling in politics.[92] In this, perhaps she was Buckingham's compliant ally.

Indeed, the general opinion at court was that Blood had been hired to assassinate Ormond by both Buckingham and the Duchess of Cleveland. After taking a leading role in the viceroy's removal from office, Buckingham still believed Ormond's influence with the king 'might be able to defeat the measures which he and his cabal had formed for subverting the constitution of the kingdom'. Shortly before Blood's attack, Buckingham and his cronies had spread rumours that Clarendon and Ormond's eldest son, Thomas Butler, Earl of Ossory, had employed two men to murder Villiers. Significantly perhaps, the would-be assassins had been poisoned, but before their death had confessed to the plot.[93]

Buckingham possessed numerous contacts in the political underground of dissidents, particularly in London. His 'intelligencers' moved easily in this grubby, subversive world of hidden motives, whispered confidences and madcap schemes to overthrow the government. It would not be difficult for them to find him someone both desperate enough to undertake this mission and possessing the intelligence and resolve to plan the crime and see it through. Ideally, it should be a man who harboured a burning grudge against Ormond, to conveniently muddy the waters of motivation and keep the murder at arm's length from its secret central character. Thomas Blood fitted the bill very nicely. Indeed, there was no one else in the whole of London more qualified, or probably more willing.

Circumstantial evidence of this link between Blood and Buckingham comes in a letter, turned up by Arlington's investigations, dated 17 November 1670, from Thomas Allen to Mrs Mary Hunt and addressed to 'Mr Davies' house at Mortlake'. We know Thomas Allen was Blood's alias and, furthermore, it is written in his distinctive handwriting. It reads simply:

I would have Thomas to come unto me to my lodging on Friday morning.

Let him bring his cloak with him.

We think about the beginning of the week if God gives an opportunity to sign the agreement, which is all at present.

Your friend 'T.A.'

The note is endorsed in another hand: 'John Anderson, apothecary. Near the Plough in Bishop[sgate] Street. T.H. lodges there.'[94] Who was Thomas Blood about to sign an agreement with? Whilst this can only be conjecture or speculation, was this agreement with Buckingham to implement a plan for the murder of Ormond?[95]

The most compelling evidence, albeit hearsay, comes from a rather one-sided conversation that occurred at court between Ossory and Buckingham shortly after the events in St James's Street. Ossory, seeing Buckingham standing by the king, became red-faced with anger, and told him:

My Lord, I know well that you are at the bottom of this late attempt of Blood's upon my father. Therefore I give you fair warning [that] if my father comes to a violent end by sword or pistol; if he dies by the hand of a ruffian, or by the more secret way of poison, I shall not be at a loss to know the first author of it . . .

I shall consider you the assassin.

I shall treat you as such and wherever I meet you, I shall pistol you, though you stand behind the king's chair.

I tell it [to] you in his majesty's presence that you may be sure I shall keep my word.[96]

His eloquent, heartfelt threats were recorded by Francis Turner, the king's chaplain-in-waiting, who was in the same room. Unfortunately, the reaction of Charles II – or more pertinently, Buckingham – was not recorded, but it is telling that the duke, never slow to take umbrage or seek satisfaction in a duel, on this occasion apparently failed to challenge Ossory.

Certainly, as we shall see in the next chapter, the episode created some powerful friends for Blood inside the royal household.

It was the height of irony that Blood's attack on Ormond was closely followed by another on 21 December on Sir John Coventry, elected MP for Weymouth and Melcombe Regis, Dorset in January 1667. He was assaulted in Suffolk Street at 2 a.m. while on his way home after a long night 'supping' at a Westminster tavern.

The previous day in the Commons, Coventry had proposed that a tax should be imposed on the theatres and playhouses and in his speech had made an unwise jibe about Charles II's affair with the actress Nell Gwynn.

James Scott, First Duke of Monmouth, born in 1649 as the king's first illegitimate son by his mistress Lucy Walter, felt this joke too near the knuckle and took great exception to the MP's impertinence. He commissioned Thomas Sandys, one of the officers in his troop of cavalry, to ambush Coventry and punish him for his impudence by a sound beating, if not worse. Some said afterwards that Monmouth's plan had the approval of the king himself.

After keeping the MP under surveillance for two or three hours (the tavern supper was clearly absorbing), Sandys and up to twenty accomplices, probably troopers, waylaid him, 'some of them wrapping him up in his cloak, holding him fast and others cutting and mangling his face in a barbarous manner'.[97]

In fact, they slit Coventry's nose to the bone – once a punishment

for common criminals guilty of theft or non-payment of debt and
the origin of the phrase 'paying through the nose'. The assailants
also stole the MP's periwig and the sword and belt of his servant.[98]
Aggrieved at this attack on one of their number and the grievous
affront to parliamentary privilege, the Commons passed an Act to
prevent malicious maiming and wounding.[99]

In the Ormond affair, the final question to be resolved is why
the forces of law and order could not run the suspects to ground
and arrest them. The answer was simply one of priorities and the
limited resources available with which to fulfil them. Within three
weeks of the attack on Ormond, the government learned of a conspiracy to attack Whitehall and kill the king, led by our old friend
Captain John Mason, operating under the unlikely alias of a Catholic priest, 'Father Thomas'.

Richard Wilkinson, a former Cromwellian soldier and now a
sergeant in an infantry company stationed on the Isle of Wight, exposed the plot, which clearly predated the Ormond outrage. Fifty
men had been enlisted by Mason to attack the sentries at the gates
of the Palace of Whitehall, wearing makeshift protective coats
'lined with quires of paper which would [block] carbine bullets'.
The timing of this ungainly assault (with all that protective pad-
ding) would coincide with one of the glittering entertainments at
court, such as 'masking and other jovial sports'.[100]

Prince Rupert was sent a copy of Wilkinson's letter on 23 December and told that he knew where Mason was 'and the name he
goes by'. The informant had seen one of the conspirators' declarations, which had been printed six months before.

If the matter is kept private and Wilkinson is assured of his liberty,
he undertakes to make out this and much more in a very short time
or submit to be hanged.[101]

Arlington interrogated Wilkinson in late December, when he
promised to obtain a copy of this manifesto. He had been promised
'a sight of Mason, but for want of money and the uncertainty of his
own condition, has been unwilling to seek his company'. Wilkinson

did not know whether any of the plotters had a hand in the Ormond ambush.[102]

Other spies had information suggesting that Blood, Captain John Lockyer and Timothy Butler were involved in planning this latest attack on the king. Butler was certainly in London that December and at Gravesend in Kent the following month.[103] Given Blood's friendship with Mason and his role, and that of Lockyer and Butler, in rescuing him in July 1667, it would be surprising if he had not been caught up in the conspiracy.

But for the time being he was preoccupied, planning the greatest and most daring exploit of his entire madcap career.

# 6

## *The Most Audacious Crime*

*These two being brought down to Whitehall by his majesty's command, one of them proves to be Blood, that notorious traitor and incendiary.*

London Gazette, 8–11 May 1671[1]

Always anxious to find money, Parliament in 1642 cast covetous and avaricious eyes on the Crown Jewels, or St Edward's regalia, traditionally in the custody of the dean and chapter of Westminster Abbey and held in the Pyx Chapel within its precincts. The MPs regarded them only as the disgraceful baubles of monarchy and espied an opportunity to convert these centuries-old objects into much-needed cash, despite the vociferous objections of the Abbey authorities. In a show of commendable defiance to the legislators' might and their ephemeral whim, the church dignitaries refused to part with the regalia and placed them under lock and key. By just one vote, a parliamentary resolution to search the Abbey and force the relevant lock was defeated, but a subsequent motion established a commission to create an inventory of these items of coronation ritual.[2]

Parliament's view that the Crown Jewels had become wholly redundant naturally hardened after the execution of Charles I in Whitehall in January 1649. England would become a republic and therefore no fit place for such regal paraphernalia. On 9 August that year, the House of Commons ordered that

those Gentlemen who were appointed by this House, to have the custody of the regalia, do deliver them over unto the trustees for [the] sale of the goods of the late king, queen, and prince, who are to cause the same to be totally broken.

And that they melt down the gold and silver of them; and to sell the jewels for the best advantage of the Commonwealth; and to take the like care of those that are in the Tower.[3]

All proceeds from the sale were to go towards funding new warship construction and to contribute to the burgeoning operational costs of the Commonwealth navy.

Chief among this regalia was the crown of St Edward the Confessor, king and saint, who occupied the throne of England in 1042–66. At the Reformation in the sixteenth century, its name became politically inexpedient, so it was artfully changed to 'Alfred the Great's crown', with not even a nod towards historical veracity. The collection also included an Anglo-Saxon comb and the eleventh-century crown of Queen Edith, the wife of St Edward, both probably recovered down the centuries from royal graves inside the Abbey. Precious metal from the crowns were sent to the once Royal Mint inside the walls of the Tower to be melted down and turned into coinage. Other items were sold to the highest bidder.

As far as Parliament was concerned, the most valuable item was the Tudor state crown made for Henry VII's coronation in 1485, which was decorated with twenty-eight diamonds, nineteen sapphires, thirty-seven rubies and 168 pearls. Its disposal raised the sum of £1,100 – or £128,000 at today's prices.

The only pieces that escaped this sale of the seventeenth century were a gold ampulla which contained the holy oil used to anoint the sovereign during the coronation service (first used when Henry IV was crowned in 1399) and a thirteenth-century silver gilt spoon, traditionally used in the same religious ceremony.[4]

After the demise of the Commonwealth and the reinstitution of the monarchy, new regalia was required for the coronation of Charles II on 23 April 1661. In June the following year, the Treasury (always tardy payers) paid Sir Robert Viner (whom we last met pursuing the assailants of the Duke of Ormond) for a new set of Crown Jewels and other regal accoutrements to the tune of £31,978, 9s 11d, of which just over £12,000 was for the coronation regalia.[5] These included two 'Imperial Crowns' set with precious stones, one again called St Edward's Crown 'wherewith the king was to be crowned and the other to be [worn] after his coronation before his majesty's return to Westminster Hall', according to a description drawn up by Sir Edward Walker, Garter Principal King at Arms.[6] This second 'Imperial State Crown' was adorned by the so-called 'Black Prince's Ruby', a bead-shaped spinel weighing 170 carats (34g) – or about the size of a chicken egg.[7] Among other new items were a gold orb, topped by a cross and set with precious stones, three sceptres, a ruby ring and a pair of golden spurs.[8]

After all this expenditure, arrangements had to be made for the proper safekeeping of the Crown Jewels. As we saw earlier, in previous reigns, the coronation regalia had been kept at Westminster Abbey, but the state regalia and other jewels were stored in the Tower. In 1508, Henry VII created a safe repository attached to the south side of the central White Tower and this facility was rebuilt by his son Henry VIII in 1535 with stout iron bars fitted to its windows for additional security. In 1668, the buildings attached to the White Tower began to be demolished as the smoke and sparks from their chimneys were thought to endanger the huge quantities of gunpowder stored in the massive keep or citadel.[9]

But now the security of the Crown Jewels had been dramatically reduced, perhaps in the fallacious belief that no patriotic Briton could ever dare touch the sacred crown of the newly restored sovereign, but more likely because of Charles II's perennial impecuniosity.

Meanwhile, Sir Gilbert Talbot – the same loyal Royalist who later unsuccessfully sought Thomas Blood's attainted estates following the attempt on Dublin Castle – had returned to England from exile impoverished and landless. Like so many others faithful to the Stuart crown, not unreasonably he cherished high expectations of receiving 'fortune and favour' from the new king after his lean years of steadfast but unpaid service as a gentleman usher of the privy chamber at the exiled royal court established in France and the Netherlands. With Ormond's assistance, he sought a sine-cure appointment from Charles II and was delighted to be made master and treasurer of the Jewel House soon after the Restoration.

From 1669, the Crown Jewels were kept in the three-storey Irish Tower (now called the Martin Tower), built in 1238–72 on the north-east corner of the Tower of London's inner curtain wall and topped by its own ramparts and the leads of the roof. In the past it had been used as a prison, housing one poor insomniac in Elizabeth's reign who slept 'but ten hours in seven weeks' and an unfortunate inmate called Heywood, who 'strained himself so much with immoderate laughing that he bled thirty ounces of blood'.[10] One wonders what he found so amusing.

Another prisoner was Henry Percy, Ninth Earl of Northumberland, popularly nicknamed the 'wizard earl' because of his outlandish scientific experiments and bizarre interests in alchemy. He spent seventeen years in the Martin Tower because of suspicions of his involvement in the Catholic Gunpowder Plot of 1605, but his incarceration was enlivened by an active social life within the precincts of the fortress. He even had a wooden indoor bowling alley built alongside the semicircular tower to help idle away a few of the tedious hours of his imprisonment.[11]

Talbot's official lodgings there unfortunately fell far short of his expectations or the trappings he perceived to be associated with his new status at the royal court. The master's rooms in the Martin Tower were 'two ill chambers above stairs and the passage to them [was] dark at noon day', and Talbot scornfully described the dining room below as a 'kind of wild barn without any covering except rafters'. He decided to appoint Talbot Edwards, a seventy-seven-year-old former retainer of his father's, as an assistant keeper to live there in his place, and he gratefully decamped to more salubrious accommodation in the rambling Palace of Whitehall. Apart from his advanced years, the trustworthy old soldier's credentials were impeccable for the awesome responsibility of the post.

Edwards, his wife and daughter Elizabeth thus became happy residents of the still uncomfortable and inconvenient Martin Tower. His son Wythe had been serving overseas for some years as a soldier under Sir John Talbot in Flanders and his wife had moved in with the family.[12] A plan drawn in 1702 by military engineers shows the tower's layout as it was in Edwards' time there in 1668. The dining room was on the first floor, with a closet and a cupboard provided within the massive curved stone walls and with narrow stairs climbing up from the ground floor. Off this room was the 'Little Parlour' and a very awkwardly shaped kitchen with a cooking range. Across the landing was a one-seat lavatory. Outside was a two-storey wooden shed with a flight of stairs leading up to a gallery, probably the rotting remains of Northumberland's old bowling alley.[13]

The royal regalia were stored in a recess constructed in the thickness of the wall of a room on the basement floor. Only two hinged and cross-wired doors, opening outwards, provided any modicum of security. For the last ten years, when displaying the regalia to visitors, Talbot Edwards was in the habit of standing behind these doors to prevent anyone touching the crowns.[14] There was just one door into the Crown Jewels chamber from the Tower's inner ward – and no sentry was ever stationed there to guard the entrance.

Although the assistant keeper's position was salaried, Edwards failed for years to persuade the penurious Exchequer to allow him to draw one penny of it, the officials claiming that the appointment was purely a private one and nothing to do with government.[15] Furthermore, Sir Gilbert found that as some of the recognised perquisites of the job were no longer available, he was 'not able to allow him a competent wage'.[16] As some small measure of recompense, Charles II munificently allowed Edwards to exhibit the Crown Jewels to curious tourists, 'charging such fees as each visitor might be inclined to pay'. As far as Charles was concerned, there was nothing wrong with private enterprise; it cost the king nothing and encouraged tourists to visit. Charging such 'admission fees' turned out to be a lucrative business: Sir Gilbert was offered 'five hundred old broad pieces of gold' for the position of assistant keeper when Edwards eventually died.[17]

Visiting the Tower to see the Crown Jewels was not a new practice. The state regalia had been occasionally exhibited to the tax-paying public from the Middle Ages and such events were re-corded in the early seventeenth century. It was only after the regalia were moved to the Martin Tower in 1669 that this was made a reg-ular attraction, available to casual visitors.[18]

Thus, all the elements of a potential crime of huge magnitude had fallen neatly into place like the tumblers of a lock securing a safe.

Only an old man was responsible for the safeguarding of the na-tion's Crown Jewels. There was little or no security within their repository. The Tower was an established tourist venue – drawing visitors to the Royal Menagerie within its walls[19] as well as to see the Crown Jewels. Therefore, the regalia were subject to regular access by strangers seeking to examine and perhaps even handle them after an appropriate tip was proffered. The Tower itself had an unenviable reputation during this period for the apparent ease with which prisoners could escape. Its permanent residents included many civilians, male and female, who passed through its gates with little hindrance, as did their friends. Anyone could walk in and out practically unchallenged by the sentries, who were drawn from the battalion of the King's Guards permanently based in the fortress.

For someone who craved public notoriety, the Crown Jewels seemed an irresistible temptation. That man, inevitably, was Col-onel Thomas Blood.

His contemporary biographer wrote soon after his death that, faced with his continued financial problems, 'one project yet re-mained which he was certain would either make or mar him':

> If he escaped, he thought himself made. If he failed in the attempt,
> he knew that the enterprise would make such a noise in the world
> that he was sure to be another Herostratus[20] and to live in story
> for the strangeness, if not the success of his attempts and to make
> himself whole by the spoils of the English crown.[21]

Despite its many shortcomings in security, the reputation of the Tower of London as a royal citadel would daunt any common burglar contemplating committing a felony within the twelve acres (4.86 hectares) encompassed by its substantial high walls. One would believe that the audacity and sheer effrontery of such a crime as stealing the Crown Jewels would deter even the most ambitious of thieves. But for a daredevil adventurer like Blood, ever the bold and resourceful soldier of fortune, ready to exploit any opportunity and brave in its execution, here was a golden chance to make money and to cock an impudent snook at government and the establishment. The colonel believed he would succeed where others must inevitably fail – a case perhaps of 'who dares, wins'. In any case, 'impossible' was a word he failed to countenance in any of his exploits. Others, less charitably, might see his inherent reckless daring as just insane egotism.

Blood gathered together a small team of trusted individuals for the enterprise, most of them wanted men, still on the run from the Ormond attack of the previous December. His highwayman son, of course, was included, as was Richard Halliwell, and possibly Lieutenant Colonel William Moore, although the precise role of the latter is far from clear. A newcomer to Blood's escapades was the Fifth Monarchist preacher Captain Robert Perrot, a one-time parliamentary lieutenant in Major General Thomas Harrison's regiment[22] and now a silk-dyer of Thames Street, immediately west of the Tower of London. Blood had known him earlier when he played a role in several of the apparently interminable nonconformist conspiracies against the crown in London. William Smith, another Fifth Monarchist, was recruited to act as horse-minder or 'scout' for the group's escape.[23] A further accomplice was later named as Ralph Alexander, a brewer who was implicated in the notorious Rathbone plot against the king in April 1666, but there seems no evidence to support these suspicions.[24]

In mid-April 1671, Blood arrived at the Tower ostensibly to view the Crown Jewels like any other innocent tourist up from the country, curious to see the fabulous sights of London. He was disguised as a parson, wearing 'a long cloak, cassock and canonical girdle' and employing the familiar alias of 'Dr Ayliff'.[25] His biographer provides more information about this disguise as a doctor of divinity: 'a little band [at the throat] a long false beard, a cap with ears . . . and a cloak'.[26] Accompanying him was his respectable-looking 'wife', equally excited to have sight of the famous regalia. In reality, she was an imposter in more ways than one: his wife Mary was lying ill at her old family home in Lancashire[27] and so Blood had hired a young Irish actress called Jenny Blaine to take her place.[28]

His true purpose, of course, was to reconnoitre the layout of the Martin Tower, discover any flaws or weaknesses in the security protecting the regalia and to spy out the best escape route from the fortress, across its moat, and into the anonymous safety of the surrounding teeming streets of East London. Unlike any other tourist, the colonel also needed a feasible excuse to return to the Jewel Tower on further occasions in order to hone his plans.

The historian and clergyman John Strype was later given an account of Blood's feat by the hapless custodian Talbot Edwards, which is the closest we can get to an eyewitness account of Blood's attempt to steal the Crown Jewels. The Pepys papers in the Bodleian Library in Oxford also contain a near-contemporary account of the crime.[29]

Blood's strategy was remarkably simple, if not ingenious. It was based on the sound psychological principle of winning a victim's trust in order to gain access to the desired objective.

It began with his 'wife', having admired the Crown Jewels, suddenly becoming ill and feeling faint with a distressing stomach 'qualm' or convulsion. A worried and concerned Blood then

> desired Mr Edwards to send for some spirits, who immediately caused his wife to fetch some whereof when she had drank, she courteously invited her upstairs to repose herself upon a bed.
>
> Which invitation she accepted and soon recovered.
>
> At their departure, they seemed very thankful for the civility.[30]

If ever there was a convenient illness, this was one. Three or four days later Blood was back, bearing six pairs of fine white gloves,[31] as a generous gift to Mrs Edwards as a token of his wife's great appreciation for her kindness.

Having thus begun the acquaintance, they made frequent visits to improve it, [Mrs Blood] professing that she [could] never sufficiently acknowledge the kindness [shown to her].[32]

Having made some small respite of his compliments, he returned again and said to Mrs Edwards that his wife could discourse of nothing but the kindness of those good people in the Tower . . .

She had long studied and at length bethought herself of a handsome way of requital.

The honeyed trap was about to be sprung. The colonel's tactic was no longer the expression of gratitude and the giving of gifts, but the temptation posed by a very powerful bait indeed. This was the fulfilment of every mother's secret dream: the prospect of her daughter's socially advantageous marriage to a well-off young suitor.

Blood told a delighted Mrs Edwards that her daughter Elizabeth was a 'pretty gentlewoman' and suddenly added: 'I have a young nephew who has £200 or £300 a year [income] in land [which] is at my disposal [to assign]. If your daughter be free and you approve of it, I will bring him hither to see her and we will endeavour to make it a match.'[33]

The steel jaws of Blood's trap had snapped shut.

One can imagine the happiness his surprising words sparked in the hearts of Mr and Mrs Edwards. An unexpected wedding beckoned for their daughter! Overwhelmed, the keeper 'easily assented' to Blood's gallant proposal and asked the 'parson' to dine with him that day in celebration. Naturally his invitation was accepted and, falling into his pretended role, Blood could not resist saying grace before they all sat down to dinner, performing it with

great devotion and, casting up his eyes, concluded his long-winded grace with a hearty prayer for the king, queen and royal family.

Afterwards, he was given a tour of their quarters in the Martin Tower and 'seeing a handsome case of pistols there' Blood 'expressed a great desire to buy them to present [to] a young lord who was his neighbour'. His real motive, of course, was to ensure there were no weapons available to Edwards when he next came calling.

When he departed, Blood piously blessed the Edwards family 'with a canonical benediction' and agreed the happy day and hour when he would bring his nephew to introduce him to his intended bride.[34]

This was Tuesday, 9 May 1671.

Curiously, his arrival at the Martin Tower was set at seven o'clock in the morning, an unusually early time for wooing, however ardent the bridegroom. Patently Blood wanted as few people about as possible for his exploit and old Edwards, doubtless cock-a-hoop at the forthcoming marriage and still naïvely harbouring no suspicions whatsoever, meekly agreed to the arrangement.

At the appointed hour, his daughter was up betimes to put on her best dress to impress and charm her intending husband-to-be. While her *toilette* was nearing completion, her father was surprised to see the parson arrive with three men. In fact there were four, and unknown to Edwards all were heavily armed with swordsticks (with rapier blades hidden inside the canes), daggers and a pair of pocket flintlock pistols apiece. As well as Blood, there was his son and Messrs Perrot and Halliwell, the last-named soon to unwittingly play the part of the blushing groom.[35] The fifth accomplice, William Smith, remained outside the Tower walls guarding the group's horses, ready for the escape.

The 'parson', Thomas Blood junior and Perrot entered the Jewel House tower, leaving Halliwell outside to maintain a lookout. Edwards' daughter considered it would be very immodest for her to come down to greet the party before she was summoned, so Elizabeth sent her maid 'to take a view of the company and to bring her a description of her gallant'. The servant believed that Halliwell, loitering outside and trying not to look suspicious, was the man in question 'because he was the youngest . . . and she returned to her young mistress with the character she had formed of his person'.[36] Elizabeth was apparently suitably impressed. Recalling the *London Gazette* description of him as a wanted man the year before as 'a middle-sized man, plump faced, with [smallpox] pock holes, of a demure countenance . . . about forty years of age', one must question the maid's judgement, eyesight or reaction to what she saw. Certainly, here was no 'young nephew'.

Blood meanwhile told Edwards that he and his friends would not go upstairs until his wife arrived and apologised for her lateness. To pass the time while they were awaiting her, perhaps he would be kind enough to show the Imperial Crown to them? The keeper happily agreed, possibly considering his pocketing of more fees. Another version of events repeats Blood's explanation that these men were his friends, due to leave London the next morning, 'to whom he had promised a sight of the regalia' and could Mr Edwards 'have the kindness to gratify their curiosity, though perhaps the time might not be so seasonable, as being a little too early'.[37]

In any event, within seconds the custodian had become the victim of a cruel and brutal assault.

As soon as the party gathered in the room housing the Crown Jewels, the door was slammed shut behind them and a cloak was thrown over Edwards' head as he bent to unlock the wire door protecting the regalia. As the shocked old soldier struggled, they 'clapped a gag into his mouth which was a great plug of wood with a small hole in the middle [for him] to take breath [through] . . .'. He was speedily tied by 'waxed leathers . . . around his neck and they fastened an iron hook to his nose [so] that no sound might pass from him that way neither'.

Blood helpfully informed Edwards, his eyes bulging and now painfully gasping for air, that they intended to steal the Imperial State Crown, the globe and sceptre. The choice of crown was apparently decided by its lightness and bulk, compared with the St Edward's Crown.

He was told that if 'he would quietly submit . . . they would spare his life'. Otherwise, added Blood pointedly, 'he could expect no mercy'.

Undaunted, the keeper 'forced himself to make all the noise that he possibly could' in the hope that his family upstairs would hear and raise the alarm.[38]

He was knocked to the floor by blows – 'several unkind knocks' to the head – from a wooden mallet called a 'beetle'[39] which they had brought with them 'to beat together and flatten the crown to make it more easily portable'.[40]

Blood repeated his grim warning: if Edwards 'would lie quietly they would spare his life – but if not, upon the next attempt to discover them, they would kill him'. To emphasise their murderous intent, the three men drew and pointed their stiletto daggers close to the keeper's throat and chest.

Edwards may have been elderly and possibly infirm, but he was no coward. After making 'greater noise' he was again thwacked by the robbers 'nine or ten' times on the head ('for so many bruises were found upon his skull') and finally he was stabbed in the stomach with a dagger, causing a deep puncture wound that began to bleed copiously. He was also cut ten or eleven times on the head.[41]

After his barbarous treatment he lay prone on the stone slabs of the floor, wisely pretending to be unconscious or dead. One of the party argued that Edwards should be killed immediately, but Blood 'would not permit so great a piece of barbarism, as [wearing] a disguise that would have rendered the fact doubly heinous had he added murder to robbery under the notion [appearance] of an ecclesiastical person'.[42] His accomplices may not have appreciated the intellectual niceties of his argument at such a tense moment. One knelt down by the custodian to see if he was still breathing. He commented: 'He is dead, I'll warrant him.'

Concerns for Edwards' health and welfare instantly forgotten, they got to work on the task they had come to perform. Blood took the Imperial State Crown out of the recess and passed the gold orb to Perrot, who put it into his loose-fitting breeches. His son began to file one of the sceptres in two as it was too long to fit in the small sack they had brought to conceal it and Blood used the beetle to crush flat the raised bows of the crown so it could fit into the bag he was to carry under his cloak.

Providence then took an extraordinary turn.

Edwards' son Wythe unexpectedly arrived home on leave after his ten years' soldiering overseas.

Halliwell, still on watch outside the Martin Tower, was shocked to see this stranger boldly walk up to its doorway. He inquired civilly

'With whom he would speak?' but the younger Edwards brushed him aside and went upstairs, where he was joyously welcomed by his mother, wife and sister after they recovered from their surprise at his entrance.

The gang's lookout rushed into the Crown Jewels chamber and warned Blood of the son's arrival. The last thing they wanted was to contend with a fit, able-bodied soldier who knew how to handle himself in a fight. Blood was on the floor, trying to pick up the gemstones dislodged by his beating of the crown. They ran out, carrying the stolen regalia – but leaving behind the sceptre which Blood junior had failed to file in two. Thinking Edwards was dead, they had not bothered to tie his hands. After their departure he struggled up to his feet, clutching his stomach wound and removed the wooden gag. Painfully he cried out, his voice rising in desperate urgency: 'Treason! Murder!'

His daughter heard his cries and stumbled down the stairs to find her father bruised and collapsed on the floor in a widening pool of blood. After he stammered out what had happened, Elizabeth, with a commendable sense of duty, dashed outside and shouted repeatedly: 'Treason! The Crown is stolen!'

Blood and his accomplices had meanwhile hurried, 'with more than ordinary haste', south-eastwards across an area of open ground in the Tower's inner ward which, over the previous five years, had been cleared of the old palace buildings. As they rounded the massive block of the eleventh-century White Tower, Blood and Perrot were seen to 'jog each other with their elbows as they went, which caused them to be suspected and pursued'.

Back in the Martin Tower, Wythe Edwards was now fortuitously joined by the Swedish-born Captain Martin Beckman, a former rather undistinguished spy who had served time in the Tower in 1664, but who was now rehabilitated and serving loyally as an engineer to the king's ordnance stored in the fortress.[43]

Both men had heard Elizabeth's anguished cries and rushed to the wounded keeper inside the Jewels chamber. As Talbot Edwards lay almost stupefied on the floor, they believed him dead and left the supposed corpse with his grieving wife and daughter to pursue

Blood and his party, black vengeance uppermost in their hearts.

By now the fugitives had skirted the building housing the main guard and were coming up to the Bloody Tower. Here they encountered the first of the Tower's sentries. Alerted by the urgent cries of the pursuers, the surprised soldier ordered them to 'Stand!', pointed his musket, but fired wildly. Pausing in his flight, Blood aimed one of his pistols at the sentry's face but this bullet also missed its target. The noise of the gunshot, or just plain, simple fear, panicked the sentinel and he threw himself down and lay flat on the cobbles, guessing sensibly that the danger would soon pass.[44]

Ahead of them lay the Water Gate, providing access to the wide Tower wharf alongside the River Thames. The sentry there was a former parliamentary soldier called Sill, who, believing his fellow soldier had been shot and possibly killed, failed to put up any resistance to the robbers rushing past him and through the gate. The gang then

> made all possible haste [along the wharf] towards the horses which attended St Catherine's Gate, called the Irongate [at the east end of the Tower], crying themselves, as they ran, 'Stop the Rogues!'
>
> And they were thought by all innocent, [Blood] being in the canonical habit.

Beckman, who must have been a fleet, sure-footed runner, caught up with them here and Blood paused, turned and fired his second pistol at his head. Beckman ducked and the shot passed harmlessly over him. He grabbed Blood, who still had the crown tucked up beneath his cloak, and there followed an unseemly and slightly ridiculous tug-of-war, as Beckman wrestled to snatch it from Blood's grasp.

It finally was taken from him and Blood, now held prisoner, told Beckman breathlessly: 'It was a gallant attempt, however unsuccessful . . . [but] it was for a crown.'[45]

This was now badly bent and buckled and had lost some of its precious stones that had been loosened in Blood's attempt to flatten it. A large pearl, a diamond and some of the smaller stones were later picked up by Katherine Maddox, a poor but honest cinder-sweeping woman, who returned them to Sir Gilbert Talbot and was rewarded for her pains. A barber's apprentice also handed in a diamond, and other gemstones were found in Blood's pocket.[46]

Perrot had been captured by a servant of Captain Sherborne before Blood was overpowered and the orb was recovered from his baggy breeches, as was 'a fair ballas [ruby]' from his pocket.

As with the rescue of Mason, the dénouement of Blood's attempt on the Crown Jewels began to take on almost comical aspects as, in the confused fighting, friend and foe were difficult to distinguish on the riverside strand beneath the Tower walls. Young Edwards overtook a man who was covered with blood and began grappling with him. Believing he was one who had murdered his father, he was about to run him through with his sword, when Beckman yelled out a warning: 'Hold! He is none of them!'

Beckman himself then became endangered. He had sprinted ahead of the rest of the pursuers to grab Blood and the guards, following up rather more slowly, were going to shoot him when one, who knew Beckman, shouted: 'Forbear! He is a friend!'

Thomas Blood junior escaped all this turmoil and jumped into the saddle of one of the horses still patiently held by William Smith further along the Tower wharf at the Irongate. He, with Halliwell and Smith, succeeded in clearing the precincts of the fortress. Edwards urged a Lieutenant Rainsford to mount some of his troops on those of Blood's horses that were left behind, but the subaltern refused, as he considered the mounts now forfeited to him as his property. They were led back into the fortress.[47]

The harum-scarum of the escape continued. Within two hours of leaving the Tower, Blood junior had not got far in the congested London streets when he collided with an empty cart slowly turning around in Gravel Lane, in the north-east corner of St Botolph's parish.[48] He was hit on the head by a round pole lying across the cart and knocked off his mount. There's no honour among thieves and Halliwell spurred on his horse in his haste to escape, as did Smith.

Recovering quickly, Blood placed one foot in his stirrups just as a cobbler ran up and exclaimed: 'This is Tom Hunt who was in the bloody attempt upon the person of the Duke of Ormond. Let us secure him.' Quite a mouthful for an excited man in a moment of crisis, but he probably sensed a handsome reward coming his way, as well as securing his own place in history.

A passing constable seized the younger Blood and dragged him before a local magistrate called Smith, who listened to 'confident denials' that he was not Tom Hunt, highwayman and would-be kidnapper, and was minded to release him. Then they heard the hue and cry rushing up the street outside, shouting that 'the crown is taken out of the Tower'. Wisely, the magistrate had Blood committed into custody.[49]

The two Bloods were returned to the Tower of London as prisoners of its lieutenant, Sir John Robinson.[50]

Among the evidence recovered were two thin-bladed stilettos, known as 'ballock' or 'dudgeon daggers', with their sheaths. Both are dated 1620 and appear to have been made in Scotland as they bear the marks of the Edinburgh cutlers Alexander Bruce (known to be active after 1593) and Alexander Thomson (who operated from 1588). Both are traditionally associated with Colonel Blood, who may have acquired them second-hand during his reported time in Scotland during the Pentland rebellion in 1666. The larger knife has a blade 11.4 inches (29 cm) long and the smaller weapon's blade is 9.2 inches (28.7 cm) in length. The latter is linked specifically with Robert Perrot. Both retain needle points. They are fearsome weapons, designed to be tucked into the top of a boot or in a belt and drawn quickly for lethal use. No wonder Talbot Edwards was terrified.[51]

That night the Bloods, father and son, found themselves in the unaccustomed squalor of cells in his majesty's Tower, with stinking straw for their beds.

Across London, in Whitehall, Williamson and Arlington, the guardians of the king's safety and security, were jubilant that at long last they had extracted two very painful thorns from their sides.

Williamson wrote to a friend, a Mr Braithwaite: 'The attempt of this morning to steal the crown is one of the strangest any story can tell. But considering God is pleased to make us masters of Blood, it is of ten times the value to his majesty, even of the crown itself, so desperate . . . a traitor that fellow is. God's goodness be praised for it!'[52]

But given Blood's record for escaping the rigours of justice, could everyone be entirely sure that he would meet his Maker on the executioner's scaffold on Tower Hill?

# 7

## *A Royal Pardon*

*Blood, the same villain, attempted to steal the crown and was taken
with it, yet he was pardoned . . . and a pension given him which is a
mystery that few can decipher.*

Sir Robert Southwell (1635–1702)
Privy Council clerk[1]

Robert Leigh in Dublin wrote to his master Williamson in Whitehall on 16 May 1671, scarcely believing the glad tidings that
Blood was at last safely locked up in the Tower of London. The
arrest of this 'notorious villain' after his extraordinary attempt to
steal the Crown Jewels 'makes all honest men rejoice that he is
at last taken', he declared jubilantly. There was also much opti-
mism abroad that the secretary of state and his secret service
could exploit this unique opportunity to round up more of Blood's
fellow traitors 'and those who attempted to murder the duke of
Ormond'. Leigh passionately hoped that the old renegade would
now 'receive the reward of his many wicked attempts both here and
in England'.[2]

If Thomas Blood had set out to 'make such a noise in the world',
he had clearly succeeded far more than he could ever have dreamt
of – even given his own inflated ego and the fact that he had care-
lessly gambled his life and that of his son to win universal public
attention.

News about his attempted theft of the royal regalia circulated in a
report published in the *London Gazette* and numerous private hand-
written newsletters dispatched to the provinces from individuals

living in London. A remarkably comprehensive account of the botched robbery was sent to a Mr Kirke in Cambridge[3] and another to the nonconformist lawyer Robert Aldworth, the town clerk of Bristol.[4] Both referred to the outlaw as 'Old Blood' and connected him and his son to the earlier assault on Ormond. The account sent to Bristol included a catalogue of his past exploits, beginning with the abortive rebellion in Ireland; his alleged involvement in the northern uprising, through to his rescue of Mason on the road to York. But it emphasised a belief that this latest escapade had nothing to do with politics or religious dissent. 'Their design' in attempting the theft was 'by their own confession . . . only to make their own advantage by the jewels'.

Of course, conspiracy theories about the crime abounded in countless excited conversations in the capital's coffee houses and taverns. One newsletter confirmed that the would-be robbers were English, although the Venetian ambassador Girolamo Alberti reported in a dispatch to the Doge and Senate of the *Serenissima Republica* that many Londoners had immediately 'accused the French of this treacherous act and even baser suspicions circulated . . .'. He added a trifle smugly: 'I congratulate myself on not having forwarded the various rumours on the subject which was said to be replete with important consequences, since it now seems that the sole object was to obtain a considerable sum of money.' In the end, 'I need only to say that among the gang they discovered one of the arch-rebels of Ireland who was concerned with the attack on the Duke of Ormond, mentioned by me on 19 December last.'[5]

Andrew Marvell, the Presbyterian metaphysical poet who frequently wrote satires attacking Catholics and the scandalous excesses of the royal court, penned these vituperative couplets:

> *When daring Blood his rent to have regained*
> *Upon the Royal Diadem distrained*
> *He choose the cassock, surcingle[6] and gown*
> *The fittest mask for those who rob the Crown*
> *But his lay pity[7] underneath prevailed,*
> *And while he sav'd the Keeper's life, he failed*

> *With the Priest's vestments had he but put*
> *Bishop's cruelty, the Crown was gone.*[8]

Despite its sly, scathing dig at the clergy of the Anglican Church, the poem was widely circulated and caused more than a few wry smiles.[9]

After their capture on Tower Wharf and Gravel Lane, Blood and his son were committed to the custody of Sir John Robinson, the lieutenant of the Tower of London. With a soldier's appreciation of the importance of reporting up the chain of command, Wythe Edwards immediately conveyed what had happened to his father's superior, Sir Gilbert Talbot, master of the Jewel House. A shaken and shocked Talbot 'instantly' waited on the king at Whitehall and passed on Edwards' account of the outrageous events at the Martin Tower. Charles instructed Talbot to visit the fortress that evening to question the prisoners.[10]

He found the two Bloods and Perrot in the White Tower, manacled and under armed guard. Their superficial cuts and bruises, suffered in the fighting during their attempted escape, had already been dressed by a surgeon. Colonel Blood 'lay in a corner, dogged and lowering and would not give a word of answer to any question'.[11]

The colonel had adamantly refused to be interrogated by two eager and excited local justices who had arrived to investigate his latest *cause célèbre*. With remarkable impudence (or was it discretion?) he insisted repeatedly that he should see only Charles II himself to answer the grave charges against him. Perhaps he understood too well that this very long shot was his one chance of avoiding an appointment with the public executioner.

To the amazement of all, the king readily agreed to question him – he reportedly roared with laughter when he heard of the request, so a 'Merry Monarch' after all[12] – and on 12 May, the two Bloods were escorted across London in chains to the Palace of Whitehall for the royal interrogation.[13]

Charles's motives in agreeing to see the colonel and his son remain wholly obscure. Was it just a regal whim, an irresistible curiosity to meet this 'notorious traitor and incendiary' who had attracted so much infamy in England and Ireland over the last seven years and now had the effrontery to demand to meet his sovereign?

Although the king was well known for his panache and easy accessibility, this seems improbable. His critics saw Charles II as a wily, astute and sometimes unscrupulous manipulator of public opinion and an inveterate schemer within the turbulent cockpit of domestic politics. Others, still less generous in their opinions, believed him to be a monarch whose inept handling of government business meant that he simply lurched from one crisis to another and only occasionally succeeded in his aims and objectives, more by luck than by any planning or aptitude. Certainly, the king had personally questioned rebels and informers before – and would do so again, as plot after plot against his sacred royal person was diligently uncovered by Arlington and Williamson and their agents.[14]

But there may have been other, darker forces at work behind this strange meeting between monarch and traitor, held while Charles was busy entertaining some French noblemen who were visiting the royal court.[15]

As we saw earlier, Blood's role in the Ormond episode probably obscured the malign interests of leading figures at the royal court who had set their own agenda in their relentless pursuit of power and influence.

The colonel now apparently possessed friends (or, more pertinently, employers) at court. He also knew too many embarrassing secrets that would point a damning finger of guilt at the great and gilded.

The Duke of Buckingham – perhaps in concert with his voluptuous and voracious cousin, the auburn-haired Barbara Palmer, First Duchess of Cleveland and Countess of Castlemaine – had compelling motives in supporting Blood's demands for the royal interview. Both would prefer that any shocking disclosures should be restricted to a private meeting to avoid the risk of revelations at Blood's trial that could incriminate or embarrass them. Charles would also have been both mortified and sorely damaged by public admissions that his single-minded and politically ruthless mistress – whom the diarist John Evelyn cruelly dubbed 'the curse of our nation'[16] – was intimately involved in the Ormond affair for her own tainted personal ends.[17]

Furthermore, Arlington, who probably employed Blood as a government agent in the Netherlands in 1666 and in the subsequent attempt to lure the regicide Ludlow to Paris, would also have given much to prevent details of his clandestine espionage operations being described in evidence given under oath. There may also have been a more devious motivation: Williamson had described how Blood's capture was worth 'ten times the value [of the] crown'.[18] His usefulness to the government, if not the continued safety of the realm, might be greater with him alive rather than dead, as yet another martyr in the nonconformist cause.

Therefore, those close to Charles had a range of powerful reasons, both personal and political, to argue that Blood's attempts to defend himself should be heard by a very august company behind closed doors. The king's agreement to meet him probably followed some persuasive lobbying from those around him, both courtiers and ministers.

The Duke of Ormond, an old hand (and victim) in court politics, understood full well what was going on. 'The man need not despair,' he confided to his fellow privy counsellor Sir Robert Southwell, 'for surely, no king would wish to see a malefactor but [only] with [the] intention to pardon him.'[19]

The interview, in one of the privy apartments of the palace, was also attended by James, Duke of York, Prince Rupert and a number of senior officers of the royal household, doubtless including Arlington and Williamson. The drama and surrealism of the occasion seemingly had no effect on Blood, who appeared not in the least intimidated by being in the company of the reigning House of Stuart. Because of his involvement in a long list of conspiracies to cut short the life of Charles II, he probably remained fettered, standing between several armed King's Guards.

In reply to the king's first question, Blood immediately and readily confessed that he was involved in the attack on Ormond six months before. He was then questioned about what had provoked 'so bold an assault'. Brazenly, he maintained forcibly that the duke 'had taken away his estate and executed some of his friends and that he and many others had engaged themselves by solemn oath to revenge it'.

Who were his accomplices? Blood steadfastly refused to name them, as he 'would never betray a friend's life nor deny guilt in defence of his own'.[20]

The colonel tried vainly to justify his theft of the Crown Jewels by recounting the 'wrongs, injuries and losses he had sustained ... and the disgraces and disappointments he had met with in Ireland'.[21] These he sought to remedy by robbing the king, as the representative figurehead of the state that had inflicted such injustices upon him.

The old outlaw was nonplussed to hear of the true monetary value of the coronation regalia. He had initially believed 'the crown was worth £100,000', but was horrified to learn that 'the crown, sceptre and Prince Edward's staff [had] cost the king but £6,000'. It is a mark of the scale of Blood's considerable chutzpah that when confronted by imminent public execution for treason, this was probably not the time to feel cheated about the value of your would-be ill-gotten gains. His overactive self-esteem and ego also drove him to lie about his age.

But by admitting his involvement in the Ormond assault and the attempt on the Crown Jewels, Blood recognised that he 'had sufficiently laid himself open to the law and [that] he might reasonably expect the utter rigour of it for which he was, without much concern of his own, prepared'.[22]

There were some unexpectedly generous statements made about his character. Prince Rupert testified to Blood's loyal service for the Royalist cause during the Civil War and acknowledged that 'he was a very stout, bold fellow' in his military exploits committed in defence of the king's unhappy father and his crown. Fortunately for the colonel, there was no mention of his switching sides later in the conflict.[23]

Then Blood made a dramatic statement. Looking directly at his seated sovereign, he 'voluntarily confessed' his role in another assassination attempt against him – this time by shooting the king 'with a carbine, from out of the reeds by the Thames side above Battersea where he often went to swim . . .'. He confessed

> that the cause of this resolution, in himself and others, were his majesty's severity over the consciences of the godly in suppressing the freedom of their religious assemblies.
>
> [But] when he had taken his stand in the reeds for that purpose, his heart was checked with an awe of majesty and he did not only relent but diverted the rest of his associates from the design.[24]

So the sight of Charles skinny-dipping in the river at Vauxhall caused a dramatic change of heart, as well it might.[25] Blood said he suddenly realised that the monarch's 'life was better for them than his death, lest a worst succeed him' and put down his gun.

But was this an admission of another dangerous plot against Charles's life – or just a figment of Blood's feverish imagination, timely conjured up with the gift of an Irishman's gab, to portray himself in a reformed and thus more positive light to his monarch?

If this was something more than a fantasy, the aborted attempt must have been staged either before the Ormond incident in December 1670 or just prior to mid-April 1671, when Blood made his first moves in the plot to steal the Crown Jewels – if only because the bitterly cold temperature of the Thames in winter would deter even the most hardy of kings from swimming in the river.[26]

What Blood did not bother to mention – and he later acknowledged rather lamely that he had conveniently 'forgotten' to confess to it to the king – was his entanglement in another plot to murder Charles, this time in the House of Lords during an attack on Parliament by 300 men. These, he claimed, had already been recruited and were only awaiting his call to arms. 'It never came into my mind till the k[ing]'s absence', he ingenuously admitted to Williamson later.

The following September the spymaster noted information supplied to him by Blood and other informers that Captain Roger Jones (our old friend 'Mene Tekel' who had escaped justice at York) had drawn the colonel into the conspiracy shortly 'after Lord Ormond's business'. The tobacconist John Harrison reported Ralph Alexander's claims that a 'great number of battle axes or bills with long staves' had been stored in a house in Thames Street, near the Tower, ready for the assault on the Lords. The conspirators also planned to kidnap, 'one night of a sudden', the irascible George Morley, Bishop of Winchester and Dean of the Chapel Royal, and the privy counsellor, William Craven, First Earl of Craven.[27] The motives or purpose behind these choices of target remain obscure.

The planned timing for this *coup de main* is also uncertain. Charles prorogued Parliament for a year on Saturday, 22 April 1671, and would have been present then in the Lords, 'seated on his Royal Throne, adorned with his regal crown and robes'.[28] There was no evidence whatsoever of an attack or disturbance that day and it seems very plausible that, as a major protagonist, Blood's preoccupation with the theft of the Crown Jewels forced the postponement of this assassination attempt. Alexander later disclosed that the weapons for the attack were broken and secretly thrown into the Thames after they had heard of Blood's confession.[29]

If so, this growing burden of conspiracy on Blood's time and energies makes it extremely unlikely that he tried to snipe at the king from his uncomfortable waterlogged hiding place among the Thameside reeds near Battersea. Arranging even a simple assassination attempt requires careful planning and detailed intelligence collection about the movements of the intended target. Just how many plots can one man – even the mercurial and feisty Blood – be entangled in at any one time? Yes, it seems highly likely that quick-thinking Thomas Blood made up this story on the spur of the moment to ingratiate himself with the king. Blarney is too weak a word to describe his quixotic canard.

His frank answers to the questions put to him were a curious concoction of bravado, impudence, humility and blatant threats.

Blood shamelessly cautioned the king that there were 'hundreds of his friends yet undiscovered who were all bound to each other by the indispensable oaths of conspirators to revenge the death of any of the fraternity upon those who should bring them to justice'. This inviolable blood oath, he warned bluntly, would 'expose his majesty and all his ministers to the daily fear and expectation of a massacre'.

On the other hand, 'if his majesty would spare the lives of a few, he might oblige the hearts of many who, as they have been seen to do daring mischiefs, would be as bold, if received into pardon and favour, to perform eminent services for the crown'. Blood became ever more boastful and 'pretended' to be able to wield 'such an interest and sway amongst the fanatics as though he had been the chosen general and had them all entered on his muster roll'.[30]

So there was the deal, brazenly placed on the palace table by Blood. Grant me my life, he was proposing, and I will spy for you amongst the dangerous religious dissident community. No wonder he was so keen to be questioned by the king.

Charles had shown considerable 'coolness and moderation' throughout his questioning.[31] Just to ensure everyone knew what was being offered, the king now asked: 'What if I should give you your life?' The colonel replied shortly: 'I would endeavour to deserve it.'[32]

There was no doubt that Blood's candour astonished his assembled listeners. He 'spoke so boldly that all admired him, telling the king how many of his subjects were disobliged and that he was one that took himself to be in a state of hostility and that he took not the crown as a thief but an enemy, thinking that lawful which was lawful in war'.[33]

Later, some maintained that Blood had bullied the king and 'the whole court was frighted and thought it safer to bribe him rather than to hang him'.[34] Certainly, Charles treated him 'with a leniency and moderation not to be paralleled'.[35]

The well-informed Sir Thomas Henshaw, lawyer, courtier and later diplomat, wrote to his friend Sir Robert Paston, MP and gentleman of the privy chamber, with an account of Blood's interrogation. He branded the colonel 'a gallant hardly, [but] a villain as ever herded in that sneaking sect of Anabaptists', but when he was examined by the king 'he answered so frankly and undauntedly that everyone stood amazed'. Henshaw reported that 'men guessed him to [look] about fifty years of age by the grey hairs sprinkled up and down his head and beard' but thought he was 'not above forty-five and his son twenty-one'.[36]

The interrogation in that grand palace apartment must have lasted well over an hour. At its conclusion, Blood was returned to the fetid squalor of his cell in the Tower while Charles conferred with his ministers about his next course of action to curb this doughty fighter against the forces of the crown.

Arlington and Williamson did not rely only on Blood's testimony in their attempts to fathom out the depths of the conspiracy to steal the regalia. There were several accomplices – Halliwell and Smith – still at large. The usual suspects were rounded up and interrogated.

For example, on 15 May the keeper of the Gatehouse prison in Westminster received a warrant to hold John Buxton 'for dangerous practices and combinations with Thomas Blood and his son' and was ordered to keep him a close prisoner.[37] This was the same John Buxton, of Bell Alley, Coleman Street, who had been questioned after the Ormond incident because of his friendship with the two Bloods and Halliwell and his involvement in finding a surety for 'Thomas Hunt' to buy him freedom from the Marshalsea prison.[38] Once again, no telling evidence could be found against him, and Buxton walked free from the Gatehouse within twenty-four hours.[39]

Amid all the comings and goings to Whitehall in the aftermath of the attempt on the Crown Jewels, there is one mystery document surviving in the State Papers held in the National Archives at Kew. It purports to be a letter from Blood, written from the Tower, to Charles II, dated 19 May 1671, which implicates some of the great and good in the Jewel House robbery:

May it please your majesty: this may tell and inform you that it was Sir Thomas Osborne and Sir Thomas Lyttleton, both your treasurers of your Navy, that set me to steal your crown, but he that feeds me with money was James Lyttleton esquire. 'Tis he that pays under the treasurers at your pay office.

He is a very bold villainous fellow, a very rogue, for I and my companions have had many a £100 of your majesty's money to encourage us upon this attempt.

I pray no words of this confession [be disclosed] but know your friends.

Not else but I am your majesty's prisoner and if [my] life [is] spared your dutiful subject whose name is Blood which I hope is not that your majesty seeks after.[40]

This apparent account of a wider conspiracy operating at the very heart of government was a blatant forgery, even though the last line contains a mischievous pun worthy of Colonel Blood's tortured humour. The handwriting bears no resemblance whatsoever to his familiar sloped straggly scrawl and it is no surprise that Williamson dismissed it immediately with the contemptuous endorsement: 'A foolish letter.'

This attempt to incriminate Osborne and Lyttleton must be another squalid episode in the political intrigue and constant jockeying for position that constantly pervaded the royal court. Both men were friends of Buckingham – Osborne was one of the duke's staunchest allies at this time, but later was to fall out with him. Lyttleton (1647–1709) later became speaker of the House of Commons, but the aspiring Osborne (1632–1712) was probably the main target of this forgery.

He was a combative partisan on behalf of the established Church of England who firmly opposed any kind of official toleration of either Catholics or dissenters. In 1676 Osborne tried to suppress the London coffee houses because of the 'defamation of his majesty's government' that was frequently uttered over the beverage cups. He was a man who made enemies easily. Indeed, after being created First Earl of Danby and serving as chief minister in 1673–9, Gilbert Burnet, later Bishop of Salisbury, believed him to be 'the most hated minister that had ever been about the king'.

Unknown man, formerly known as Thomas Blood, attributed to Gilbert Soest and painted in the 1670s.

Thomas Blood by George White.

James Butler, First Duke of Ormond, lord lieutenant of Ireland during the attempted seizure of Dublin Castle in 1663, and victim of Blood's attempted kidnap and murder.

Sir Joseph Williamson, secretary of state and operational head of the Stuart secret service.

Henry Bennet, First Earl of Arlington, secretary of state and pursuer of the would-be assassins of the Duke of Ormond.

Charles II, the 'Merry Monarch', who had a less than happy
time with the constant threat of rebellion or assassination posed
by radical religious dissenters or veteran republicans.

George Villiers, Second Duke of Buckingham. An ambitious arch-conspirator who probably employed Blood for unpleasant tasks but then turned against him.

Barbara Palmer, *née* Villiers, Duchess of Cleveland. The ruthless mistress of Charles II who played dangerous political games at court.

Charles II wearing the new Imperial State Crown and carrying the orb and sceptre made for his coronation – the targets of Colonel Blood and his accomplices.

The Martin Tower in the north-east corner of the Tower of London, where Charles II's new crown jewels were stored. For a small payment, anyone could see them.

Blood and his accomplices stealing the regalia from the Tower.

Colonel Blood's daggers.

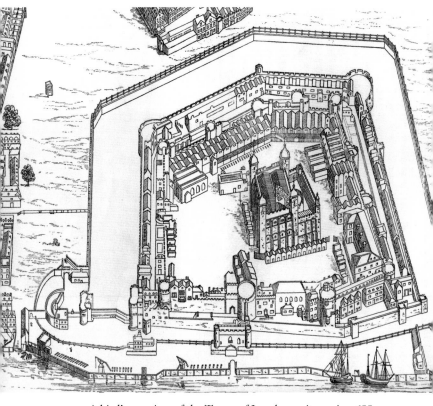

A bird's eye view of the Tower of London as it was in 1688.

The merchant James Lyttleton was a brother of Sir Thomas and cashier to the navy treasurers in 1668–71. Two years later he was employed in the unedifying task of pressing unwilling recruits into service as sailors on board Royal Navy warships.

No one accepted this forged confession as a true bill and Osborne and both the Lyttletons were not even questioned.

The key to Blood's fate must lie in the factors that drove him to try to steal the Crown Jewels. He was never a career criminal – indeed, he detested his son's felonious activities as a highwayman – and his previous adventures all had well defined political or religious objectives. His rationale in trying to steal the Crown Jewels puzzled his contemporaries and many of his friends and associates in the radical religious and republican underground. For example, Edmund Ludlow, exiled in faraway Switzerland, could not, for the life of him, perceive 'what advantage there would have been to the public cause, should they have succeeded in their enterprise'.[41]

While Blood always insisted that he was driven by purely financial gain, the difficulties of breaking up and converting such high-profile swag into ready money would have worked against his expectations of a healthy profit from the theft. The gold could have been easily melted down but too many people would have expected a generous payment for their risk in handling such recognisable gemstones. Anyway, did he have the necessary contacts within the London underworld to enable him to sell on all those diamonds, sapphires and rubies prised off the crown's gold mounting? As this was his first taste of the world of base criminality, probably not.

Then there is the purely symbolic motive aimed at damaging the monarchy: stealing the crown might allegorically remove some of the visible power from the king. This may well have appealed to a former parliamentary officer and a consort of the Fifth Monarchists who, after all, saw Charles II as an agent of Satan, but it seems too abstruse for a man of action such as Blood.

Was he trying to redeem himself with his radical Presbyterian community? There were indications that the Ormond episode had badly injured his reputation among his fellow conspirators in

London. One informer reported gleefully that 'those congregations of nonconformists which [Blood and his accomplices] . . . have formerly frequented, abhor [the attack on the duke] and would be glad to bring them to punishment if it were in their power'.[42] If that adverse reaction had troubled Blood, the Crown Jewels escapade failed to restore his good name as a fervent radical. The postponed attack on the House of Lords, caused by the jewel robbery, would not have endeared him to them either. William Dale, one of Williamson's informers, reported in early August that a 'dangerous and disaffected person and a man of great design' called William Thompson, an alias of the former Parliamentarian Captain Povey, had journeyed from London to Loughton in Essex 'muffled up and [said] that Blood should be stabbed and the rest – for they were false'.[43]

Was Blood paid to undertake the robbery? Was the theft of the regalia part of one of Buckingham's strange machinations? A precursor perhaps to the assassination of Charles II and the proclamation of a usurper whose standing would have been enhanced by his possession of the royal regalia? This particular conspiracy theory was reinforced at the time by the news of a burglary in Great Ormond Street, London, the Tuesday after the attempted robbery of the Jewel House. This was the home of the lord high chancellor, Sir Orlando Bridgeman. All his valuables were ignored by the thieves and only the Great Seal of England was stolen. Its loss was highly significant: an impression of it was routinely affixed to important state documents and its disappearance meant that much of the machinery of government would cease to function. A new one had to be made hastily.[44]

For centuries, there has been persistent speculation that Charles II himself was complicit in the crime.[45] Some believed that Blood's paymaster was the king – hence the colonel's unusual, princely treatment. One version was that Charles, perennially short of money, conceived a desperate plan to steal his own Crown Jewels and to sell them overseas to raise the required hard cash. He cast around for a suitable criminal to perform the commission and Blood's derring-do credentials fitted the royal requirements precisely.

Buckingham, with his track record of employing Blood, was asked to secretly arrange the crime.

Buckingham probably did undertake disreputable missions at Charles's behest, providing a valuable cut-out to avoid direct connection with the throne in case anything went disastrously wrong. However, there is no direct evidence to support this notion, attractive as it may appear to those romanticists amongst us, and it sadly must stay firmly in the realm of conjecture.

Another, still less plausible, theory had the king swearing, having partaken too freely at the banqueting table, that after all his painful years of exile in Europe, no one would now deprive him of the crown of England. In a moment of boisterous madness, he unwisely backed this pledge with a recklessly generous wager that none could ever make away with it. Blood heard of this bet and took the king literally at his word – intending to eventually return the regalia and claim his royal winnings with true *brio*. As conspiracy theories go, this fits the bill precisely: ingenuity coupled with just a smidgeon of lunacy.

On 6 June Sir John Robinson reported an unexpected visit to the Tower by Sir William Morton, a judge of the King's Bench, who was not only renowned for his loyalty to the monarchy but who revelled in a fearsome and well-deserved reputation for exacting harsh, exemplary justice on any wrongdoers who came up before him in court. (It was Morton who condemned to death the daredevil French 'gallant highwayman', Claude Duval, in the teeth of popular protest in January 1670.) After having played a prominent and dogged role in investigating the attack on Ormond the previous year, he was now, terrier-like, demanding to interrogate Blood.

On this occasion, Morton was thwarted again. One can imagine his frustration at being turned away by what he saw as sheer bureaucracy. Robinson told Williamson that, not having received an order allowing the judge's visit, he had to deny him permission to see his notorious prisoner. The lieutenant added, with just a hint of understatement: 'Blood, seeing him out of the window, was startled a bit.'[46]

There was great excitement over what would be made public during the trial of the colonel, his former highwayman son and Perrot. On 12 June, the Venetian ambassador wondered what revelations the colonel had produced in the course of his interrogation: 'The secrets revealed by Blood, the robber of the Crown Jewels, are hidden among the acts of his examination.' Here was a 'faithful and good servant of the late king [Charles I]' who had become a 'professed rebel ... Universal curiosity is excited by his [forthcoming] trial'.[47]

At the end of the month, Blood and his son submitted humble petitions to Arlington to allow their wife and mother to visit them – the men complaining that 'close confinement' in the Tower was impairing their health. Ever loyal, Mary Blood, apparently recovered from her illness and returned from Lancashire, concurrently sought permission to see her husband and son 'who have been now near eight weeks so closely imprisoned ... that I can neither hear of their health nor receive any directions from them'.[48]

Behind the scenes, Arlington was working assiduously to win a free pardon for Blood. This was an ancient and merciful prerogative inherent in the English monarchy. A pardon presupposes guilt or the conviction of a miscreant for a crime committed and discharges the recipient from all penalties. The process is said to make him a *novus homo* or 'new man' in the eyes of society and the law.[49] Arlington's objective was, to use the modern espionage jargon, to 'turn' Blood; to employ him as a government double agent and a major player in his campaign to defeat the ever-present menace posed by Presbyterian and other nonconformist dissidents. After the conversation with Charles II, the minister knew he was pushing at an open door as far as the outlaw was concerned.

With a third Anglo-Dutch war looming on the horizon, Arlington had to swiftly neutralise any domestic threats to the stability of the realm. The last thing he wanted was an informal alliance between the religious dissenters at home and the enemy in the Netherlands. A Dutch attack, synchronised with an insurrection by republican nonconformists, was an alarming prospect that would stretch government resources and divert attention away from a successful prosecution of the war at sea and abroad. Arlington must have already been working on drafts of a regulatory measure to provide greater religious liberty to nonconformists and Catholics as a timely sop to dissident opinion.[50]

Meanwhile, he required reliable intelligence on the intentions, plans and movements of the major players in the dangerous sectarian groups. Blood, characterised by Ludlow as 'having been acquainted with most of the secret passages [activities] that have of late been transacted in order to [revive] the Lords' witnesses',[51] was the ideal informer within this shadowy world, having worked for the secret service before on an ad hoc basis.[52]

Arlington's plan for Blood's employment was endorsed by his fellow secretary of state Joseph Williamson, who had rated his value as a spy to be 'ten times the value [of the] crown'. Although the colonel was never to win the complete trust of the two spymasters, Williamson patently believed that he and Arlington, as Blood's new masters, now possessed an agent of extraordinary power and ability.

Not content with his life being spared, the colonel tried to haggle over the terms and conditions of his pardon. Denzil Holles, First Baron Holles – that 'stiff and sullen man', according to the king – and Anthony Cooper, Lord Ashley, a supporter of official moderation towards Protestant dissenters, negotiated with the renegade immediately after his release about the agreement to spy for the government. At one point Blood apparently sought an appointment as governor of one of the North American colonies in exchange for his services, but these aspirations went unrequited. Instead, Williamson noted simply that the king 'would provide for him'.[53]

Charles placed one inviolable condition on his agreeing to Blood's pardon. The colonel must apologise humbly to the Duke of Ormond for his attack.

Apologies cost nothing and Blood happily wrote the required letter to Ormond in apparent abject atonement for his assault. The lyrical terms he employed may indicate that he included some suggested phrases – possibly offered by Arlington or Williamson – although its contents, a rambling single sentence covering sixteen lines with almost no punctuation, required some skilful editing (if not careful reading).

His one-page note says:

> The greatness of my crimes so far exceeds expression that were not my burdened soul encouraged by finding vent to its grief, though by such an acknowledgement as bears little proportion to my guilt, I had forborn this further trouble to Your Grace, but overcharged with increasing sorrow by the consideration of your renowned excellency which, I unworthy monster was so regardless of, has produced this eruption of the humble acknowledgement of my most heinous crime the which as I have a deep impression of heart compunction, so should I count it my happiness to have an opportunity in the most demonstrative way to manifest it Your Grace, who am unworthy to be accounted, though, in reality, I am
>
> Your Grace's most humble Servant
>
> Thomas Blood[54]

Arlington went to visit the duke on behalf of Charles II and asked him to forgive Blood, probably bringing this letter with him. He told Ormond that the king 'was willing to save [Blood] from execution for certain reasons which he was commanded to give him'.[55] As befits a faithful old courtier, Ormond was magnanimous in his response. The duke replied that if 'the king could forgive an attempt on his crown, I myself may easily forgive an attempt on my life and since it is his majesty's pleasure, that is reason sufficient for me and your lordship may well spare the rest of the explanations'.[56]

The condition thus fulfilled, Arlington dined with Sir John Robinson at the Tower of London on 14 July. In his pocket was a signed warrant for the release of Blood and Perrot. Thomas Blood junior was to remain a prisoner in the Tower for a little while longer, probably as a hostage to guarantee his father's immediate good behaviour and to test his commitment to his new career as a government spy.[57] The warrant for his release was finally signed on 30 August, and his free pardon, with that of Perrot, the following day.[58]

Blood was free.

On 1 August 1671, Blood was graciously granted his pardon. The six-line record in Arlington's papers read: 'Pardon to Thomas Blood the father of all treasons, misprisons[59] of treason, murders, homicides, felonies, assaults, batteries[60] and other offences whatsoever at any time since 25 May 1660,[61] committed by himself alone or together with any other person or persons . . .'.[62]

Crime sometimes does pay.

Furthermore, Blood was granted a pension of £500 a year from lands in Straffan, Co. Kildare[63] and the return of his Irish and English properties from attainder in return for his informing the government of dissident conspiracies; improving relations between the crown and nonconformists and endeavouring to 'reduce or disperse' the 'absconded persons' within that community.[64]

Blood emerged joyfully from out of the shadows. Shortly after his release from the Tower, Thomas Henshaw saw him walking in the courtyard of Whitehall Palace resplendent 'in a new suit and periwig . . . exceedingly pleasant and jocose. He has been at liberty this fortnight. He is nothing like the idea I had made to myself of him for he is a tall, rough-boned man, with small legs, a pock-freckled face[65] with little hollow blue eyes.'[66]

The diarist John Evelyn was horrified to find the colonel attending a dinner at the home of Sir Thomas Clifford, the comptroller of the royal household,[67] with 'several French noblemen'. As far as Evelyn was concerned, here was the fellow dinner guest from hell. He was mortified to see him free and so blatantly enjoying the delights of polite London society. Afterwards, he wrote:

Blood, that impudent bold fellow who not long before attempted to steal the imperial crown itself out of the Tower, pretending only curiosity of seeing the regalia there, when stabbing the keeper, though not mortally, he boldly went away with it through all the guards, taken only by the accident of his horse falling down.

How he came to be pardoned, and even received into favour, not only after this, but several other exploits almost as daring both in Ireland and here, I could never come to understand.

Some believed he became a spy of several parties, being well with the sectaries and enthusiasts, and did His Majesty services that way, which none alive could do as well as he; but it was certainly the boldest attempt, so the only treason of this sort that was ever pardoned.

This man had not only a daring but villainous unmerciful look, a false countenance, but very well spoken and dangerously insinuating.[68]

Worse yet, Blood had adopted the habit of 'perpetually' attending the court and was frequently seen happily promenading in the royal apartments of the Palace of Whitehall. With his usual arrogance and audacity, he 'affected particularly to be in the same room where the duke of Ormond was, to the indignation of all others, though neglected and overlooked by his grace'.[69] Such snubs had no effect on a man of such ego and self-confidence.

There is little doubt that Blood's release – and reward – astonished many. In Paris, William Perwich, secretary of the British embassy there, wrote to Williamson on 5 September, reporting that there were two major topics of conversation in diplomatic circles there. The first was the sorry saga of Captain Thomas Crowe, commander of the eight-gun yacht *Merlin*, who failed in his duty in not firing upon a Dutch man-of-war which discourteously 'refused to strike to the king's flag'. This had 'made a great noise here – but nothing so much as talk [about] Blood being forgiven'.[70]

In London, Sir Roger Burgoyne, up from his Bedfordshire estates and staying with his friend Sir Nathaniel Hobart in Chancery Lane, could not believe that Blood had received a pardon after 'all his villainy' and warned darkly that 'some designs, more than ordinary are on foot'.[71]

That *enfant terrible* among courtiers, the often drunken satirist poet John Wilmot, Second Earl of Rochester, may have been the author of twenty-eight stanzas attacking Charles II over a broad spectrum of complaint about his policies and personal behaviour, later described by Arlington as 'this seditious and traitorous libel'.[72] It included this acerbic passage:

Blood that wears treason in his face
Villain complete in parson's gown
How much he is at court in grace
For stealing Ormond and the crown!
Since loyalty does no man good,
Let's steal the king and outdo Blood!

There was little hope that Blood's reincarnation as a government spy could be kept secret; indeed, his showy behaviour after his release stripped away his greatest protection as an agent – anonymity and the ability to merge into his surroundings.

But this was intentional. His public rehabilitation was a conscious decision by Arlington to demonstrate the power of royal mercy to Blood's friends still on the run and to indicate that, if only they dropped their opposition to the crown, they too could expect lenient treatment and the enjoyment of normal life in open society.

That normality meant the acquisition of a home for Blood's reunited family. Now restored to funds, he acquired a house on the corner of Great Peter Street and Tufton Street in Westminster, overlooking Bowling Alley, and moved there soon after his release from the Tower.[73] This was a prosperous area of new development and the colonel enjoyed the pleasure of having a number of high-status personages from Parliament and the court as his near neighbours. He may also have bought a property in the country: an unsubstantiated tradition suggests that he lived in the manor house at Minley, a hamlet in the parish of Yateley in Hampshire.[74]

On 26 September 1671, warrants were made out for payments of royal bounty to those who had saved the Crown Jewels. After all his tribulations, the handsome sum of £200 was awarded to the faithful Talbot Edwards and further sums of £100 were each paid to Captain Martin Beckman and Wythe Edwards 'for resisting the late villainous attempt made to steal the crown'.[75]

Inevitably, with the parlous state of Charles's Exchequer, Talbot Edwards did not receive a penny. He was forced to sell on the warrants for ridiculously small amounts of cash to pay his medical expenses in treating the injuries he had sustained at the hands of Blood and his accomplices.

On 30 September 1674 he died, probably from the effects of his wounds.

# 8

## Coming in from the Cold

*Blood sees privately and cunningly [James] Innes and his friends but of that not a word, not to the king*

Notes made by Sir Joseph Williamson, 9 November 1671[1]

Thomas Blood's first task in his new guise on the government pay-roll was to operate as a spy or intermediary to support his masters' attempts to weaken the radical nonconformist underground and neutralise their threat to the Stuart crown. Arlington outlined part of his mission in evidence to the Committee of Foreign Affairs on 22 October 1671 by relating that 'upon the pardoning of Blood he went away among his brethren to bring in some of his friends on assurance of pardon'.[2]

With the prospect of war with the Dutch looming ever nearer on the horizon, accompanied by the unacceptable risk of concurrent sedition and insurrection being fomented amongst religious dissi-dents, it was imperative not only to deactivate the known renegades but also to quieten nonconformist resentment and anger at the congregations' treatment at the hand of government. Here Blood could make his mark by spying on his former friends and also by facilitating behind-the-scenes dialogue between government and dissenters.

While he still met Sir Joseph Williamson, Blood's main contact with his new paymasters, initially at least, was his old jailer, Sir John Robinson at the Tower of London. At the end of December, Sir John, profitably engaged in catching Quakers – those 'besot-ted people, fools and knaves' – reported that 'Mr Blood sometimes visits me and tells me he has been faithful in keeping his promises'.[3]

During the mid-1660s there was growing popular opposition to nonconformists being hauled up before the courts for flaunting the Act of Uniformity's insistence that none other than Church of England rites should be employed in worship. At Hereford, a grand jury presented only 150 of these 'Neros kneaded up of blood and dirt' who refused to conform[4] and similar refusals to indict continued throughout England, as at Norwich, Newcastle and Yarmouth. This general unwillingness to prosecute mirrored the king's own unease over the prosecutions: Sir Thomas Bridges of Bristol was summoned to appear before the Privy Council and told plainly that rigorous proceedings against nonconformists were not agreeable to his majesty.[5]

In the face of the continual threats posed by conspiracies and egged on by senior Anglican clergy, Charles II's government had been forced to take a firmer grip on illegal nonconformist activity. The Act to Prevent and Suppress Seditious Conventicles (or assemblies) of 1670[6] imposed stiff fines on those who attended religious services other than those of the Church of England. A fine of five shillings (25 pence) was imposed on a first offender and ten shillings (50 pence) for a subsequent breach of the law. In addition, a preacher or any other person who allowed his premises to be used for such illegal purposes risked a fine of twenty shillings (£1), or £140 in today's purchasing power, which doubled up for a second offence.

Other punishments were harsher. Two Norfolk men were arrested at an illegal conventicle at Beeston for the third time and sentenced to be transported for ten years' hard labour on one of the Caribbean islands. They were sent to the Dorset port of Lyme Regis but, no ship being available to take them overseas, they were thrown into prison and had remained there ever since. Jonathan Jennings of London also had been incarcerated for three years but eventually offered hard cash as a surety to guarantee his future behaviour as a loyal subject. An endorsement to the record of these men's miseries reads: 'Three conventiclers to be discharged; Mr Blood' – so the old reprobate, in his new role, was trying to right some natural injustices.[7]

By this intervention, Blood may have been trying to redeem his standing in the nonconformist community which, after the attack on Ormond, the attempted theft of the Crown Jewels, and his very public rehabilitation with Charles II, remained at a low ebb. The Presbyterian Arthur Annesley, First Earl of Anglesey, was still going around London 'blasting' Blood amongst the nonconformists.[8] The colonel was also unsettled by an unexpected visit to his home by a sinister stranger whom he suspected was sent 'by some ill-wisher to ensnare him'. He desired to know how the king wanted him to handle 'such cases'.[9]

Blood's activities on behalf of the government can sometimes be discerned through a series of frustratingly cryptic notes written in barely decipherable handwriting by the always frantically busy Williamson, as a kind of journal and aide-memoire for the everyday proceedings of his department. Early on, Blood was busy promoting the government's policy in the City of London 'in relation to our affairs [with] Holland and France' but was also asked to examine letters from exiled radicals in the Low Countries as 'Blood knows the key [cipher] and the [handwriting]'.[10]

He soon fell in with an Anglican clergyman named Dr Nicholas Butler, who at the time was commonly despised for his 'place-seeking and hanging [about] in the [royal] court through Prince Rupert and others'.[11] His other main associate was a Mr Church, the clerk at the Fleet prison, off what is now Farringdon Road, on the eastern bank of the River Fleet,[12] who was keen for his assistance in obtaining intelligence from Irish sources.

The colonel also began meeting James Innes, a Scottish non-conformist and former rector of the parish of St Breock, near Wadebridge in Cornwall, who was seeking to negotiate with the king to allow his brothers and sisters in the church greater religious freedom. The nonconformists had been divided in their response to the Conventicles Act. Many of their elders believed they had no choice but to obey this draconian law, as their pockets were not deep enough to defy it on a regular basis. This group of clergy, who elected to avoid holding illegal assemblies, became known in popular parlance as 'Dons'. Other brethren, often younger and more militant, chose to continue with their religious conventicles, literally at all costs. These were nicknamed, rather bizarrely, 'the Ducklings', and Innes became their main spokesman.

In early November 1671, he pleaded with Blood to humbly request the king to allow greater religious liberty. Blood refused. Innes then met Charles and begged him to permit the larger groups to openly hold their services in their meeting houses. While the king expressed sympathy with Innes' cause and showed 'all tenderness', he could not promise anything to help or comfort them in the short term. But he told him 'that they must order their meetings discreetly, that you may strengthen my hands and not weaken them'.[13] If the royal eye did not see, plainly the sheriff's officers would not be calling. But this was not enough. Basic religious freedom still went unacknowledged or, more importantly, enshrined in law.

Williamson was made aware of Blood's frequent covert meetings with Innes through the Post Office's interception of the letters between them. His notes of 9 November confirm this: 'They may not smell out we have correspondence with Innes by Blood.' He was shocked by his agent's duplicity: '*Nota bene* [mark well]. Blood sees privately and cunningly Innes and his friends but of that not a word, not to the king.'[14]

By 11 November, the secretary of state was worried by the growing prospect of a widespread uprising by the nonconformists. His jotted notes mused that the real key to suppressing the crisis was the role of the gentry: 'Gratify the gentry, for no great disturbance can be, unless they be [at the head]. The people stir not without the gentry. They are dissatisfied (1) as mostly all men are, not to be as high as others at court and (2) especially for being unrewarded for their sufferings.' After these sociological ramblings, he turned his attention to the increasingly problematical Blood, who 'disgusts his two friends [Butler and Church] by disappointing them. They think him too high and [he] values himself too much'.[15]

Then sometime between 16 November and 4 December, Blood suddenly switched his allegiance from Arlington and Williamson to the unscrupulous and licentious secretary of state for Scotland, John Maitland, Second Earl of Lauderdale. It was a strange decision to desert his paymasters, but was probably caused by Blood's realisation of the strength of Lauderdale's influence with Charles, as he was said to be 'never far from the king's ear or council' despite his responsibilities for the northern kingdom. It was also symptomatic of Blood's increasing tendency to meddle in the perilous world of court politics.

Williamson recognised the shift in his agent's loyalties very quickly. Blood, he noted, 'is going in to Lord Lauderdale, cries him up everywhere'. Faced with continuing evidence of Blood's scheming, the spymaster's patience was beginning to run very thin. His scribbled memorandum noted that the colonel 'has left himself notably to fantasies'. It was known that he had received money from secret service funds to pay off his debts, 'but [he] pays none but [only] huffs to them', the secretary of state added acidly. Blood was boasting that

> I dine once or twice a week with the archbishop of Canterbury and he did not know what should be done.

He also believed it was easy to go over Williamson's head and deal direct with Arlington. Contemptuously, the spymaster added: 'His head is turned with wine and treats and the fanatics that keep company with him take advantage of him.'[16] So much for Blood shunning strong drink and 'recreations, or pomps . . . quibbling or joking' and the other joys of good company.[17]

Williamson now harboured grave doubts about Blood's effectiveness and his value as an informer or intermediary with the dissident underground. He noted: 'Any that are known to join with him are lost to the fanatics.' He pondered whether it would be wise to end all dealings with the former outlaw: 'To break with Blood – for if he be thus mutable [fickle] as to Lord Arlington, then whether he be lost with the fanatics or no, it is not safe. To what purpose . . . to meet longer with him?' Then he added the damning four words: 'Not to be trusted.' Williamson concluded: 'That we may break off meeting with Blood for they [the nonconformists] will not absolutely trust him any longer.'[18]

This memorandum seemed to have an awful note of finality.

Three days later, Williamson recorded in his notes a meeting between Blood, Butler and Church at the clergyman's lodgings. Blood had 'magnified Lauderdale, saying that they understood one another and he was the great man ... He clapped his hand on his heart and said "[He] had not only the king but Lord Lauderdale here!"' Williamson noted: 'By all means break off with Blood. He leaps over all heads and his company may ruin them [Butler and Church] to the fanatics.'[19]

Two Scots informers then came forward to offer information about the nonconformist threat in Scotland to the privy counsellor Sir Robert Moray, a one-time spy for Cardinal Richelieu in France, a prominent Freemason and one of the founders of the Royal Society. His vocal calls for moderacy towards dissenters explains their otherwise strange choice for a point of contact within the government. He passed them on to Sir John Baber, a physician in ordinary to the king, a man well known for his absolute discretion, who was frequently used by Charles as a secret conduit for messages from the throne to the dissenters.[20] (Pepys believed him so cautious that he would 'not speak in company unless acquainted with every stranger present' in a room.)[21] The Scots were directed to Arlington, who passed them back to Baber for further questioning. With all these pillar-to-post meetings, the informers must, by now, have wondered whether their journey south was really necessary.

They told the physician that Lauderdale had lost the trust of the Scottish nonconformists and his only status in Scotland 'was by the king's favour' – his job title as secretary of state. He had 'disgusted all the nobility' and 'generally all the body of the people'. There was a 'great fermentation' in the kingdom which would 'if not prevented break out'.[22]

Blood became convinced that Baber was trying to discredit him with Arlington and he probably incited Lauderdale's bile against the despondent Scottish informants.[23] He still faced opprobrium among the dissenter community; one member warned, 'Have a care of Blood, he is a rogue', Williamson noted.[24]

The colonel needed to rebuild his fences with his paymasters and demonstrate his continuing usefulness. Williamson had earlier acknowledged that he 'had great converse of old officers', and Blood had enjoyed some success in convincing those former parliamentary army men who had a history of conspiracy and rebellion to come in from the cold, using his own treatment at the hands of the king as an example of the royal clemency that could be expected.

Now he wrote to Arlington, reminding him of his efforts to convince the nonconformist radicals exiled in the Netherlands to return home under promise of pardon to prevent them being utilised as fifth columnists by the Dutch in the event of war. One of them was Jonathan Jennings, who had been committed to Aylesbury prison in 1666 but had escaped overseas. Blood pointed out that Jennings 'having met with a stop at present in having his pardon perfected and proving a hearty friend to the king's service, I ask that some intimation be given to the jailer of the King's Bench that he has a warrant for his pardon and is suing it out, that he may not bear hard on him'.[25] He added: 'I had some other things to intimate by word of mouth to your lordship, but reserve them till I have an opportunity' of meeting.[26]

Blood's first triumph in this specific task was in September 1671 and involved Major John Gladman, said by Williamson to be 'hearty to Blood's way'.[27] Gladman agreed to seek a private audience with Charles to swear the oath of allegiance in return for a royal pardon. Captain John Lockyer (one of Blood's accomplices in the rescue of the 'general Baptist' Captain John Mason in 1667) also accepted a pardon through his intervention, although 'Mene Tekel', alias Captain Roger Jones, stoutly refused to wait on the king for his act of clemency.[28] In November 1672 Blood reported to Arlington on the audience of another radical, Major William Low, with the king:

> according to your direction I brought the gentleman to the king ... [who] was satisfied in him and bade me take care about his pardon in order to which I request your order for a warrant.
>
> Hardly anyone that has been pardoned will turn to a better account, for he is a man of parts and esteem in that [militant] party in Ireland and is so passionately taken with the king's condescending

grace that I am persuaded nothing shall stir there to his majesty's prejudice that he can hinder.

With an eye to the recruitment of a potential new agent in Dublin, Blood added: 'He shall wait on you, if you think it necessary.'[29]

He was less successful with Mason himself, now a keeper of a London coffee house and still an inveterate plotter, or with the Fifth Monarchist William Smith, who had guarded Blood's horses during the raid on the Crown Jewels. Both stuck to their radical guns and would have nothing to do with the government amnesty.

In April 1675, Blood petitioned Williamson on behalf of Captain Humphrey Spurway, of Tiverton, Devon, who was involved in the conspiracy led by Thomas Tonge (another parliamentary officer who, after the Restoration, was forced into the twin evils of selling tobacco and distilling spirits).

Spurway had planned to kill Charles while he was on his way to visit his mother at Greenwich and to seize the Dukes of York, Albermarle and Sir Richard Browne, now lord mayor of London. The conspiracy came to nothing and he fled out of the country. Financed by a small group of London merchants, he had travelled on to an overseas plantation. Now Blood wanted to win him a pardon. He was one of those 'absconded persons I took charge of to reduce or disperse who chose to remove to a remote plantation being persuaded that he might be incapable of endeavouring to promote sedition or disturbances to the government'.

His crimes were the same [as] the common drove of those his majesty pardoned at my coming out of the Tower and no other.

His is employed by [James] Nelthorpe[30] and other merchants in a remote plantation where he resolves to settle and never to return but become a loyal subject, if he may be delivered from his fears by a pardon.

I suppose his merchants will engage [vouch] for him, if there be any occasion.[31]

Spurway's pardon was granted two days later.[32]

With some of these dangerous radicals now neutralised, Charles II tried implementing a new, diametrically opposed, policy to quell the disquiet and dissatisfaction among the sombre godly ranks of his nonconformist subjects. Where coercion and oppression had failed, decriminalisation might work more effectively. Deploying his royal prerogative, the king signed the Declaration of Indulgence at the Palace of Whitehall on 15 March 1672, suspending the penal laws banning unlawful religious meeting:

Our care and endeavours for the preservation of the rights and interests of the [Anglican] Church have been sufficiently manifested ... by the whole course of our government since our happy restoration, and by the many and frequent ways of coercion that we have used for reducing all erring or dissenting persons ...

But it being evident by the sad experience of twelve years that there is very little fruit of all those forcible courses, we think ourself obliged to make use of that supreme power in ecclesiastical matters ...

And that there may be no pretence for any of our subjects to continue their illegal meetings and conventicles, we do declare that we shall from time to time allow a sufficient number of places, as they shall be desired, in all parts of this our kingdom, for the use of such as do not conform to the Church of England, to meet and assemble in order to their public worship and devotion, which places shall be open and free to all persons.

But to prevent such disorders and inconvenience as may happen by this our indulgence, if not duly regulated, and that they may be the better protected by the civil magistrate, our express will and pleasure is that none of our subjects do presume to meet in any place until such place be allowed, and the teacher of that congregation be approved by us.

The timing was tight: twelve days later, England, in alliance with Louis XIV of France, declared war on the Dutch United Provinces. Arlington sent a copy of the king's new religious policy to Sir Bernard Gascoign, the English ambassador in Vienna: 'I add also

a late Declaration his Majesty has made in favour of the nonconformists, that we might keep all quiet at home whilst we are busiest
abroad.'[33] Unwilling to face the likely wrath of Parliament, Charles
prorogued the session set for 1 April to October and then to February 1673.[34]

The longed-for official toleration of nonconformist worship
had at last arrived. The framework of a means to operate this new
policy seems to have originated with the assertive Dr Butler, who
forwarded a scheme to Williamson that envisaged a system of distributing government licences for private and public devotions.
Allowing their worship to emerge from the dark shadows of secrecy and illegality would make the nonconformists respond to
this 'little kindly treatment' by becoming more loyal to the Stuart
crown. 'A little love', he told the secretary of state, 'obliges more
than great severity' and by this means 'all will have a dependency
on his majesty.' Butler was fully confident that the threat of religious extremists would be neutralised: 'I think it would be beyond
the power of the devil or bad men to give [the king] any disturbance in his kingdoms.'[35]

There were three kinds of licences that congregations had to
apply for. One permitted the use of a building as a meeting house,
the second covered preachers at such assemblies and the third
those itinerant ministers who travelled from town to town devoutly
spreading the Word of God.

While some nonconformist ministers were wary about the impact
of the Declaration, most of their flocks were jubilant at their new-
found freedom to worship. One humble and loyal address to the
king declared: 'We cannot but look on your majesty as the breath of
our nostrils, as a repairer of our breaches and a restorer of paths to
dwell in.' Another professed that by this 'unparalleled act of grace,
you have made our hearts to leap and our souls to sing for joy of
heart and have laid such a sense of your royal condescension and
indulgence upon us if we cannot but now always, and in all places,
acknowledge and celebrate the most worthy deeds done to us your
poor subjects and as men raised out of the grave from every corner
of the land, stand and call your majesty blessed.'[36] One of those

soon to receive a licence to preach was Jonathan Jennings, having
returned to England under pardon.[37]

Another man to bless the name of the king was Thomas
Blood.

He had more venal reasons to praise, laud and magnify the name
of Charles *Rex*. The implementation of the Declaration of Indulgence, if properly arranged, might be a source of profit for someone
who understood and could manipulate the intricate workings of
government. With numerous contacts within the nonconformist
communities, he could represent himself as a kind of broker or
agent on behalf of individuals and congregations seeking licences
to legitimise their regular church services. If Blood had any com-
punction about taking money from those pursuing the basic right
of religious freedom, he did little to show it.

Within weeks, scores of applications for licences for worship
were received in Whitehall from across England. Many were forwarded on by Blood, such as on 18 April:

> Request by Mr Blood on behalf of the Anabaptists at Cranbrook,
> Kent, for licences for the houses of Thomas Beaty and Alexander
> Vines and for Richard Gun as their minister and also on behalf
> of the Anabaptist meeting in Coleman Street [London] for John
> Martin's house in White's Alley.[38]

There was another block application a few days later:

> Request by Thomas Blood for licences for Mr Kitly, Essex, person
> and house; for the house of Mr Willis in Essex, his person being
> licensed [already]; for the houses of George Locksmith and Wil-
> liam Mascall, both at Romford Essex; for Mr Gilson, Brentwood,
> Essex . . . for John Mascall's house in Monis [*sic*] Essex, for Henry
> Lever of Newcastle; for Thomas Crampton of Toxteth Park . . .
> for a meeting house at Kingsland, Middlesex; for Richard Gilpin
> and Mr Pingell of Newcastle, all Presbyterians and for Mr Durant
> of Newcastle, and for James Simonds, at a house at Lamberhurst,
> Kent, both Congregational.[39]

Blood must have become acquainted with William Mascall, a surgeon of Romford, when he briefly (and fraudulently) practised medicine there in 1667. On 14 May he wrote to Mascall, enclosing the desired licences. As barefaced as ever, the colonel told him: 'There is no charge for them, only it is agreed that five shillings for the personal licences be gotten.' The machinery of government should be well oiled to make its wheels turn faster: 'The doorkeepers and under-clerks should afterwards be remembered by a token of love', Blood insisted. Doubtless those bribes would be rendered via the old renegade himself and one must wonder whether the money ever reached the officials. Confidently, he added: 'If you need any other places to be licensed, you can have them.'[40]

Although the licences were initially free, the flood of applications severely tested the capacity of the Whitehall bureaucracy to handle the volume of paperwork. Dr Butler, who had originally insisted that the permits should be 'large and free', later changed his mind and advised Williamson that he was a fool to give himself trouble for no return.[41] Thereafter, a small fee was charged for licences for preachers, but none at all for places of worship.

After this new arrangement was imposed, Thomas Gilson of Weald, Essex, complained bitterly that Blood had only sent down 'licences for our houses which signify nothing without a parson . . . We should have taken it better if he had sent the personal licences and left it to our courtesy what we would gratify the clerks and doorkeepers with, rather than have a sum imposed contrary to the king's express command that nothing should be required.' Petulantly, Gilson added: 'Therefore, we advise him to send down presently the personal licences for us, lest we make our address some other way.'[42]

Blood showed himself to be a trifle more altruistic ten days later when he wrote to Arlington urging the release of eighteen named prisoners held for 'excommunication, nonconformity or præmunire,[43] being Presbyterians, independents or Anabaptists'. Noting that a general pardon was to be offered to Quakers who were 'imprisoned for conscience sake', Blood sought the release, by special warrant, for those 'of other persuasions [who] are like to remain in prison who are not Quakers . . . if imprisoned for no other crime'.[44]

The Declaration of Indulgence was implemented in the teeth of loud opposition from many in the Church of England. In September 1672, William Fuller, Bishop of Lincoln, complained to Williamson that 'all these licensed preachers grow insolent and increase strangely. The orthodox poor clergy are out of heart. Shall nothing be done against the Presbyterians, who grow and multiply faster than the other?'[45]

The University of Oxford was also aghast that licences were granted to Presbyterians and Anabaptists in the city. The preacher for the former was Dr Henry Langley, an erstwhile master of Pembroke College,[46] who delivered his first sermon in June and

> held forth for two hours (possibly he was to eat roast meat after and so needed not to spare his breath to cool pottage) upon the [Holy] Spirit on which subject they say he preached in the late times near two years and they say he was all the while so unintelligible that from that time to this nobody could tell whence the sound came [from] or whither [it was] going.

The University's scholars were invariably rude to these 'parlour preachers', but feelings began to run higher and its vice-chancellor, Peter Mews, had to appear in person that month to protect one preacher from the violence of the undergraduates – acknowledging that there were those 'who would have hanged him had he fallen into their hands'.[47]

Opposition and growing discontent were also endemic in Parliament, where many interpreted the suspension of penal laws covering religion as a symptom of the king's covert preferences not only for Catholicism but also for absolutist rule over his people. With an eye on the succession to the throne, many MPs were also fixated by the notion that, by slow degrees, the way was being paved for the Catholic faith to be officially approved in England. Inexorably, the delicate flower of religious tolerance withered and died in the political hothouse of Westminster. Parliament forced Charles to withdraw the Declaration in March 1673 and replaced it with the first of the so-called 'Test Acts',[48] which required anyone entering public office, civil or military, to deny the Catholic doctrine of transubstantiation,[49] take Anglican communion within three months of appointment and swear the twin oaths of Church Supremacy and Allegiance to the king. In an angry response, James, Duke of York, the king's brother and heir presumptive, openly acknowledged his Catholic faith that year and resigned all his public appointments.

At least some liberty remained for nonconformists to practise their religious beliefs. A list of conventicles in London in 1676 included details of a regular meeting of Presbyterians in the 'great almry' (the former house of the monastic almoner)[50] located behind Westminster Abbey. The congregation regularly included 'Mr Blood and his two sons', probably Charles and William.[51] Two years later they heard 'Mr Cotton' preach on a text taken from Psalms 144, verse 2: 'My goodness and my fortress, my high tower and my deliverer; my shield and He in whom I trust who subdues my people under me.' Listening in rapt attention, according to a government informer, were Sir John Hopton, 'a Scotchman and his lady . . . Lady FitzJames and [again] Mr Blood and his two sons. He was much for the defence of the Kirk [the Scottish Presbyterian church] and they sang the Scotch psalms.'[52]

Now happily rehabilitated in the eyes of his paymasters, Blood continued his spying activities, both domestic and overseas, in prosecution of the Dutch war. Some of his efforts produced valuable military intelligence, albeit time-sensitive. In March 1672, Blood was in Amsterdam and spent some time on the island of Texel, monitoring the passage of Dutch warships.[53] The following month he informed Arlington that a 'person who came through the Dutch fleet last Wednesday saw sixty-three ships, men at war and fireships together, rendezvoused at the Weling [*sic*] but could not distinguish how many there were of each. The Zeeland squadron was not come in from last Friday. I had an account also from thence with the presumption that none of their fleet would stir till after today.'[54]

Two months later the State Papers record the departure of 'Mr Newman, Blood's friend', sent to Holland 'for intelligence' on the Dover packet boat, armed with instructions and forty guineas in his purse.[55] The following February, Blood reported that seditious 'pamphlets from Holland' were expected the next week on the packet-boats. 'The bulk were to be sent to the Spanish ambassador, whose goods are to be searched by persons of the Customs house. They intend to put them in some small casks in barrels of butter . . . to the ambassador.'[56]

At home, he passed on a sealed letter in September 1672 that had come into his hands from an informant, promising that any reply could be sent via him 'if you do not have a readier way'.[57] In June 1673, Blood was back in Dublin, 'as he pretended, by my lord Arlington's leave'. Henry Ball told Williamson, now serving as a plenipotentiary at the Franco-Dutch Congress of Cologne, that Arlington was glad of Blood's absence 'because of his impertinence', but the colonel faced an uncertain welcome: 'The Presbyterian party all renounce him as one that has kept not very well his word with his majesty as to serving him.'[58]

In fact Blood had delivered a letter from Arlington to Arthur Capell, First Earl of Essex, the lord lieutenant of Ireland. The secretary of state, with his well-hidden Catholic sympathies, was worried that he had been accused of supporting the cause of Peter Talbot, the Catholic Archbishop of Dublin,[59] in his attempts to ease the grievances of the Catholic population of Ireland. Essex reassured Arlington: 'I am sure there is nothing in it but of advantage to you and your lordship may be fully satisfied that there were no questions put leading to your lordship's name.'[60]

For his espionage efforts, Blood was paid a salary of £100 a year, equivalent to £13,750 in today's purchasing power, as well as receiving his £500 a year pension from Irish lands.[61] The king also moved to restore him to his lost Irish estates, writing to Essex that Blood had not yet repossessed his property, as he required a licence for bringing a 'writ of error for reversal of his outlawry'. The viceroy was now authorised to grant that licence.[62]

In May 1673, Blood also applied to the king for a grant of £1,400 which had been paid to the former treasurer of Ireland but 'not yet disposed of by any order'.[63] Whether he eventually received this lost money is unknown.

Blood was also willing to use his position at court and at the heart of government to advance the wider interests of his family. In April 1672, he wrote to Arlington, begging his lordship to remember 'my uncle Dean [Neptune] Blood's advance in Ireland . . . He has been dean thirty years and was with the king [Charles I] at Oxford and was an active person [on his behalf].'[64] Unfortunately, in this instance, his pleas went unanswered. The following January, he suggested that his son, Thomas Blood junior, if serving alongside an 'able' lieutenant, 'could manage a company in the army' and that his third son Edmund 'was fit for an ensign or a sea officer, having been twice to the East Indies'.[65] Blood even recommended an 'able lieutenant' to act as mentor for his former highwayman son. Captain Nicholas Carter 'is very fit for a lieutenant', he observed. It is not known whether the eldest son took the king's shilling as he died around 1675, leaving a wife and an infant son, of whom his brother Holcroft became guardian. Edmund, the fourth son, was appointed purser[66] of *Jersey*, a forty-gun fourth-rate frigate of 560 tons built for the Commonwealth and launched at Maldon in Essex in 1654. Blood's second son William was a steward on the same ship. Both are known to have been serving in the Royal Navy in 1677.[67]

He also sought to advance his third son Holcroft's career in the army. In March 1678, Blood wrote to Williamson, having heard about a 'vacancy of an ensign's place in Captain Rook's company in Sir Lionel Walden's regiment. The captain accepted my son but the colonel preferred another, since he was accepted. Wherefore, I would request that he may not be put by.'[68]

There was, however, a more pressing issue preoccupying Blood's time and attention. He petitioned the king about his father-in-law's estates, still the subject of a wearying, tedious (and expensive) legal dispute. The property, he claimed, was now legally his in right of his wife, as the old parliamentary colonel's last male heir, Charles, had died in December 1672.[69] Blood had instituted his own legal proceedings against some of the Holcrofts to claim the estate, but matters had now got to the stage where violence and even two murders had been committed in attempts to finally decide the matter.

His petition pointed out that the Holcrofts 'had laboured . . . to

defraud [him] of his just right and finding their own title to be weak
have combined with Richard Calveley to promote an old title to
his part of the said estate which title for these forty years has been
overthrown at law'.

> Yet . . . the said Calveley [has] been so vexatious that when his title
> at law was rejected, they laboured by violence to get [a] footing in
> the estate . . .
>
> About six years ago, they hired several obscure persons out of
> Wales that went to the house of a gentlemen, one Hamlet Hol-
> croft . . . and with a pistol killed him dead for not giving them
> possession when they had no legal process nor officer to demand
> it by . . .
>
> Some weeks since, Richard Calveley, being attached[70] by some
> of the sheriff's bailiffs according to law concerning the prem-
> ises claimed by your petitioner, after they had him in custody . . .
> Calveley caught up a rapier and killed one of the bailiffs dead on
> the place.

Blood therefore begged Charles II

> out of your princely grace and for the better enabling your peti-
> tioner to serve your majesty . . . to confer . . . what estate Richard
> Calveley lays claim to or lately seized of the estate of John Hol-
> croft and his heirs (and consequently your petitioner's) if, upon
> Calveley's trial and conviction it shall become forfeited to your
> majesty.[71]

The outcome of Blood's appeal is not known, although it seems
likely to have failed, as the disputed estate passed to another relative and Calveley escaped justice. He is recorded as evicting a man
and his mother eight years later in a case heard during the Epiph-
any term at Lancaster Quarter Sessions.[72]

There were other means of income for the old adventurer. Blood
transformed himself into a freelance agent and 'fixer', not only involved in court rivalries and politics, but receiving fees for easing

the path of those wishing to do business with the royal household. He had been 'admitted into all the privacy and intimacy of the court'. If anyone was suffering delays in decision-making or any other hindrance to their business, 'he made his application to Blood as the most industrious and successful solicitor and many gentlemen courted his acquaintance, as the Indians pray to the Devil – that he may not hurt them'.[73]

It was a hazardous career to pursue and one that earned him powerful enemies as well as friends. His overblown confidence and arrogance remained breathtakingly obvious. If he had aggrieved one powerful figure in government, there were many others who would seek his assistance in providing information or gossip to fulfil their ambitions. He had become indispensable and boasted:

> 'It's no matter. If one lets me fall, another takes me up. I'm the best tool they have.'[74]

Every day, he attended White's coffee house near the Royal Exchange in the City of London, waiting for consultations with eager, well-heeled clients,[75] who may have included such illustrious personages as James, Duke of York and Thomas Osborne, First Earl of Danby.[76]

His greed and self-importance were to cause his eventual downfall.

There was one already suffering because of his involvement with Blood. Richard Wilkinson, another of Williamson's spies, claimed to have uncovered a conspiracy involving Blood 'against his majesty's person, crown and dignity'. (This presumably was Captain Roger Jones's plot to assassinate Charles in the House of Lords.) In February 1673, he wrote from prison at Appleby, Westmorland, complaining about his unkind treatment.

When Wilkinson revealed the plot he was 'promised not only my pardon, but a gratuity', but he was betrayed and instead of being pardoned ended up in a horrible cell.

> Since 23 September last I have been chained of my bed which is a

dark stinking hole sixteen or seventeen hours out of every twenty-four, with such a weight, namely nearly four stone[77] of iron on my legs.

If it were to save my life I cannot stir a yard from my bed.

Until recently he had neither fire nor candle, but now had one taper to light in the mornings to read by. Despite enduring these privations, he was still a faithful subject and felt obliged to warn of a planned rebellion, having been told that 'in a very short time the prison doors would be set open for me and others if I would but fight, for there were many men in most counties in great readiness who wait but for a fit opportunity'.

His friends in London had promised him a pardon but he knew he was still living under a cloud of official disapproval: 'I am very sorry that Lord Arlington is offended at me and that I am blamed because I did not manage the business better concerning Blood.'[78]

Thomas Blood still had powerful friends.

# 9

## The Ways of the Lord

*Some men are so crafty ... they dare not preach against the sin of man-catching, or trepanning men by sham evidence, false witness, sham plots ... setting snares to catch men, body and goods, life and estate ...*

The Horrid Sin of Man-Catching, July 1681[1]

London in the late 1670s and early into the next decade was a hotbed of intrigue and conspiracy, involving not only the old discontented republicans but also suspected plots by Catholics wishing to restore England to her old pre-Reformation faith. Part of this subversion and sedition was entirely fabricated – merely a trick – designed as a weapon of terror with which to seize some ephemeral personal advantage in the fevered political posturing within the royal court and Parliament.

Some died pitifully on the scaffold or were ruined as a result of the communal hysteria triggered by at least one of these fictitious conspiracies. Sensational revelations piled up, one on top of another, to unsettle or disrupt both the corporate body politic and public confidence, particularly among the population of London. No sooner was 'one sham discovered, but a new one [was] contrived to sham that', one polemicist declared artlessly.[2] Those who revealed these so-called plots were the lowest dregs of society – informers who were prepared 'to swallow oaths with as nimble convenience as Hocus[3] does ... and ready to spew them up again to murder the innocent'.[4] Their motivation or objectives were sometimes difficult to discern accurately, 'for here you have him and there you will have him ... [but] you [only] hug a cloud and embrace a shadow'.[5]

Much of this turmoil was fomented in the new political clubs that were the harbingers of today's political party system in Britain. These met noisily in hostelries, coffee houses or private homes throughout London; one of the earliest (whose eighty members nurtured resilient republican beliefs) was founded by Major John Wildman and met at his Nonsuch House tavern in Bow Street, off Covent Garden, after 1658.[6] The mercurial and devious Buckingham was a patron of Wildman, who hailed him as 'the wisest statesman in England'.[7] Catholics met at the White House nearby in the Strand or at the Pheasant in Fuller's Rents, north of King's Bench Walk in the precincts of the Inner Temple. The latter institution became notorious for some of its members' alleged proclivity for sodomy. Buckingham's supporters had their own club whose headquarters were at the Nag's Head in Cheapside in the City of London, often frequented by visiting Baptist dissenters from the west of England and Scottish Presbyterians.

Although he despised him greatly, Thomas Blood patronised the political club run by Sir William Waller,[8] that 'midnight magistrate' wickedly satirised by John Dryden in 1682[9] who was a passionate pursuer of fugitive Catholic seminary priests and whose greatest delight came from his pastime of publicly burning confiscated Catholic books and vestments. His club met regularly at the newly built St James's marketplace, between Haymarket and Piccadilly, possibly in the tavern called the Old Man's Head, located underneath the market house.[10]

One of the most powerful cliques was the radical Green Ribbon Club, chaired by the opposition MP Sir Robert Peyton, another of Buckingham's republican associates, who had been removed as a magistrate from the Middlesex Bench in 1676 for distributing seditious literature. In October the following year, Blood exposed a plot by 'Peyton and his gang' who had allied themselves with the Fifth Monarchists and the atheists in an attempt to overthrow the government and seize power. They planned that, initially at least, Richard Cromwell (third son of the Lord Protector, who succeeded him in that title for just nine months) would be appointed nominal ruler of the three kingdoms in the event of their coup succeeding.[11] The king and the Duke of York were to be murdered at Newmarket or in London by Peyton and eleven accomplices while others simultaneously captured the Tower of London. According to Williamson's notes of the information received from Blood, the group were strong opponents of the Anglo-French alliance and were aggrieved at the continuing diminution of English liberty. They also sought to impose even more punitive measures against Catholics. The spymaster believed the conspirators were

> near something, not sure how soon.
>
> Talk of the Tower, therefore look secretly to it . . . The guards to be well looked to.
>
> Have sent into Buckinghamshire, Berkshire and Bedfordshire to get their friends to a head.[12]

The MP was twice interrogated but eventually dismissed without charge. However, his colleagues in the Green Ribbon Club thought him far too dangerous a figure to continue as a member, so he was promptly dismissed as chairman and his membership terminated.[13]

Blood's investigations of this conspiracy must have continued, for in early January 1678 Williamson wrote to Archbishop Michael Boyle, lord chancellor of Ireland, about a Dublin legal case concerning Blood's interests on which he was about to adjudicate. The king had commanded that the colonel should be detained in England 'on his particular service and by his command' and Williamson earnestly requested that his enforced absence from Ireland should not prejudice his case.[14]

One of those implicated in the Peyton plot was Blood's old comrade William Smith, whom he now interrogated. He told the Duke of York:

> He has been concerned in most conspiracies that have been these fourteen years. He was with me in the business of Ormond and the business miscarried because he . . . did not follow him . . .

Then, though he was not one of the fighting party at the taking of the crown, he was employed by me as a scout and has often boasted of it.

He was not one of those that went with me to the rescue of Mason but, I suppose, was one that drudged about getting our horses and tack ready . . . and that he also boasted of.

When all my party accepted the king's pardon, he did not, being a Fifth Monarchy person but a wet one.

Smith had been involved in new plots 'contriving to assassinate persons and to surprise others' and had been sent to Westminster to spy for ten days. Blood promised to make him 'acknowledge' his role and help 'unravel the whole game . . . which, by reason of the preservation of my spies, we cannot go in a direct line to, but [should] sail with a side wind'.¹⁵ Smith was discharged from prison on 5 August.

More than a year earlier, one of Buckingham's creatures, the spy Henry North, had revealed another conspiracy against Charles II, this time involving 'diverse eminent persons'. Following the pattern of other informers, government or private, who had fallen on hard times, North had taken to the road to eke out a precarious living from preying on unwary travellers. After his arrest, he had been condemned to be hanged for highway robbery near Sleaford in Lincolnshire. Now he had decided to make a clean breast of what he knew, as 'a sincere and candid demonstration of a Christian who shall write nothing in this dying hour but what he knows to be truth'.

North was a very frightened man, terrified, not only by the prospect of dying on the scaffold, but by his rashness in making disclosures involving personages of great power and influence. In a rambling and sometimes incomprehensible two-page letter, he admitted to the king that he had been employed by Buckingham 'in a troublesome concern which I would cheerfully have performed to the utmost of my power. I sometimes spoke in his presence and understood some of his discontents.' Then his words grew yet more opaque:

I am able to demonstrate to the Duke of Buckingham, who, I persuade myself, will now believe me, of the fallacy and fraud of such as were instrumental to abuse his heroic soul with notions discrepant to his own judgment and interest, which with great zeal, I have heard him express in reference to your majesty and all your well-wishers.

Frustratingly, he skirted around the great truth he wished to impart, dropping several obscure hints about what must have been Buckingham's continuing treachery. North had long desired to tell Charles 'a secret' and had 'applied to Mr Blood about it but was advised not to trust any person'.

He added, in a bizarre emblematic reference to the depth and complexity of the conspiracy: 'The head of [the river] Nile with all his rivulets is not easily discovered.' Then there was this final cryptic statement, tinted with just a touch of anguish: 'I might have understood much more than I do and I wish had never understood anything thereof.'

Unfortunately he was executed before Williamson could discover anything more of his revelations. His letter had been delayed in the post.[16]

These two conspiracies may have constituted clear and present dangers to Charles and his government, but disclosure of a new plot in 1678 had a much greater political impact, even though it proved utterly bogus.

One of the magistrate William Waller's cronies was Titus Oates, a former naval padre in the forty-gun fourth-rate frigate *Adventure* who had been dismissed from the service with ignominy in 1677 for homosexuality. Shunning Anglicanism, he was received into the Catholic Church later that year and managed to enrol at the English Jesuit College at Valladolid in Spain, despite his ignorance of Latin. As a noviciate priest, Oates proved less than suitable, or indeed successful; he was branded 'a curse' by the college authorities and finally expelled. Undeterred by this rebuff, and still pursuing his own idea of a sacred vocation, he talked his way into a Catholic school at St Omer in the

Pas-de-Calais region of northern France, only to be thrown out again.

Rejection can metamorphose all too easily into an intense hatred. Oates was ugly, with sunken eyes and a harsh and loud voice, but was blessed with a photographic memory. He lived almost wholly in a frenzied world of rampant paranoia and fantasy, but his illusory claims and constant lies were camouflaged by an eminently believable manner. Scarred by his experiences in Spain and France, he harboured a fiery, fanatical loathing for the Catholic Church and became determined to wreak revenge on the papists who had so harshly turned him away.

In London he found a trusty ally in the shape of the half-crazed Israel Tonge, the former rector of the medieval parish church of St Mary's Staining in Oat Lane, north-east of St Paul's Cathedral, which was completely destroyed in the Great Fire of London in 1666.[17] After claiming Thomas Blood was involved in starting the conflagration,[18] Tonge had now convinced himself that responsibility for the destruction of the capital in the catastrophic inferno lay solely at the door of the Jesuit priests.

Oates and Tonge worked diligently to compile a manuscript or dossier implicating the Catholic Church in a Jesuit plot to assassinate the king. It contained the names of almost one hundred Catholics allegedly involved in the conspiracy. Upon completion, the document was bizarrely hidden behind the wainscot wall panels in the Barbican, London, home of the physician Sir Richard Barker,[19] where Tonge was staying.[20]

*Mirabile dictu*, the manuscript was 'discovered' by Tonge the next morning and shown to Barker's friend Christopher Kirby, with no explanation as to why this incendiary document had been secreted in the home of such a rabid anti-Catholic. As a chemist who had sometimes assisted Charles II with his scientific experiments, Kirby was a carefully chosen messenger to make the government aware of Oates and Tonge's sensational accusations. The loyal apothecary breathlessly told the king about the plot as he took his morning royal constitutional in the verdant splendour of St James's Park on 13 August 1678. Charles was highly sceptical about the claims, even though Kirby emphasised that those who intended to shoot him dead could be easily identified. Furthermore, he claimed that in the event of this attempt failing, Sir George Wakeman, the queen's own chief physician, would use a terrible poison to kill the king.

The lord high treasurer, Thomas Osborne, First Earl of Danby, a man renowned for his detestation of Catholics and opposition to any kind of religious toleration, did not share his monarch's incredulity. Danby urged a full investigation of the allegations, despite the robust opposition of Williamson, who was only too well aware of Tonge's bouts of insanity.

Oates duly appeared before Sir Edmund Berry Godfrey, a Westminster magistrate of some repute, to swear his deposition, preparatory to a full audience with the king and Privy Council. He recalled attending a Jesuit meeting at the White Horse in the Strand on 24 April, where the efficacy of various methods to murder Charles was eagerly debated, including shooting, stabbing by itinerant Irish louts or poisoning by Wakeman.[21]

Then, on 12 October, the magistrate suspiciously disappeared without trace.

Five days later, his body was found face down in a muddy ditch at Primrose Hill, three miles (4.82 km) north of London. He had been strangled, his neck broken and, for good measure, his body had been impaled with his own sword – but this wound was inflicted some time after death, as there was no sign of bleeding. His money and rings had not been stolen, so there was little chance of robbery being the motive. His murder was immediately blamed on the Catholics and was used as proof of the truth of Oates's wild claims.[22]

The fantasist's associate, the convicted confidence trickster Captain William Bedloe, claimed the reward for tracking down Godfrey's killer or killers by denouncing Miles Prance, a Catholic servant-in-ordinary to Queen Catherine of Braganza. Under the agony of torture, he named three labourers called Henry Berry, Robert Green and Lawrence Hill as the culprits, all in the pay of three Catholic priests.[23] Although entirely innocent, they were found guilty and executed in February 1679 at the scene of the crime.[24]

It has also been suggested that Sir Robert Peyton may have been involved in Godfrey's death. The justice of the peace was a member of the MP's republican 'gang' and he may have been murdered because he had betrayed his fellow members, or, more opportunistically, merely to stir up hatred of Catholics.

The magistrate's death certainly had that effect. Something approaching hysteria gripped the streets of London. Effigies of the pope were burnt by the angry mob. With revived memories of the Catholic Gunpowder Plot of 1605, Parliament ordered fruitless searches for non-existent explosives cunningly hidden in barrels within its cellars. Near panic ensued when it was discovered that a French physician called Choqueux was storing large quantities of black powder in a house near the Houses of Parliament. There were a few red faces when it transpired that he was no assassin but merely the king's firework-maker.

More seriously, the House of Lords demanded that, for the sake of public safety and maintaining Londoners' morale, all Catholics should be banished from an area within a radius of ten miles (16 km) around the capital and this proscription was imposed by the government on 30 October.

Thomas Blood had some dealings with Oates and Bedloe, but as he was always careful to cover his tracks, the evidence of his involvement is unclear. There is one contemporary report that he planned to destroy Oates's credibility by planting treasonous letters amongst his personal papers to demonstrate that the fanatic had been recruited by the nonconformists to damage Catholic interests. But the incriminating documents were discovered and shown to Williamson, who passed them on to the Privy Council.[25]

Blood was also on the fringes of a Catholic 'sham plot' to discredit Bedloe as a witness and to point the finger at Buckingham and Anthony Ashley-Cooper (created First Earl of Shaftesbury in 1672), as the covert instigators of Oates's 'Popish Plot'.[26] An Irish Catholic called James Netterville, formerly a clerk in Dublin's Court of Claims and latterly one of Danby's informers, had been imprisoned for seditious words he unwisely uttered in St James's Park. After appearing before the Privy Council at the Palace of Whitehall, he did not improve his chances of winning liberty by brawling in the corridor outside the chamber. After a spell in Newgate jail, he ended up as a debtor in the Marshalsea prison in Southwark.

There, he met the Dubliner Captain John Bury in January 1679 and dropped heavy hints to him about the conspiracy to undermine the veracity of Bedloe's testimony. If the good captain would help, he could expect a generous payment of up to £500 to make his efforts all the more worthwhile.[27] Bury, who was a close friend of Blood's, immediately passed on this information to the colonel, who told him to play along with Netterville and endeavour to discover where this substantial sum of money was emanating from. The liberal donor turned out to be one Russell, a servant to the French ambassador Paul Barillon, and Blood imparted this intelligence to Williamson.

Another version of events came in a ten-page letter in Latin, purportedly written by the Spanish priest James Salgado of Vine Street, near Hatton Garden, to his own father confessor. This described Netterville's confession to Salgado in which he admitted being instructed to find someone who would swear that the Popish Plot was entirely the devious brainchild of Buckingham and Shaftesbury. Netterville 'therefore bribed the man who stole the king's crown to swear to this effect for £500 and the man revealed the whole matter to the king's secretary'. The priest added: 'I do not think [Netterville] is altogether innocent, but I leave him to God.'[28]

Getting wind of this scheming, Oates, Bedloe and Waller visited Netterville in the Marshalsea and browbeat him into revealing all he knew. This latest sham plot was thus neutralised. The prisoner was singularly unimpressed by Oates, who was 'a villain', and recalled bitingly that 'he was always wanting money from the superior when he was a Jesuit [in Spain] . . .'.[29]

Eventually, Charles personally interrogated Oates. Such is the sagaciousness of monarchs, he triumphantly detected a litany of inaccuracies and lies in his testimony, and ordered his arrest. However, only days later, Parliament forced Oates's release, and rewarded his patriotism by the provision of an apartment in the Palace of Whitehall and payment of a handsome annual pension of £1,200.

After nearly three years of public unrest and phobia about treasonous Catholics permeating all sections of society, at least fifteen innocent men had been executed. Oliver Plunkett, archbishop of Armagh and primate of all Ireland, became the last to be entrapped by Oates's mesh of lies. He was accused in June 1681 of 'promoting the Roman faith' and after only fifteen minutes of deliberation, the jury brought in a guilty verdict. Plunkett was hung, drawn and quartered at Tyburn on 11 July, the last Catholic martyr to die in England.[30]

Oates at last received his richly deserved come-uppance. On 31 August, he was ordered to leave his grace-and-favour Whitehall apartment. Undeterred, he denounced the king and the Duke of York and was arrested, fined the huge sum of £100,000 and thrown into prison.[31]

Blood meanwhile was receiving some extraordinary signs of royal favour. In March 1679, he was sent for 'early' by Robert Spencer, Second Earl of Sunderland, who had replaced Williamson as secretary of state the previous month. The minister had been instructed to tell the spy 'that the king looked upon him as his friend and therefore sent for him to come to him [and] to communicate it to all his friends that his majesty would cast himself upon his Parliament'.[32]

It seemed that his reputation had reached a new pinnacle in the highest office in the land; but, unknown to him, Blood was now rapidly approaching his nemesis.

In January 1680, Jane Bradley, the barmaid of the St John's Head or 'Heaven' tavern in Old Palace Yard, Westminster, asked him to call on her, as she believed there was a major conspiracy afoot against the government. She told him that 'two shabby fellows' had told her that 'they had something of great consequence, in reference to the public welfare, to reveal but that they wanted a discreet person to manage it'. Blood told her that he would meet them and that she should pass on to them that 'if there was anything fit to take notice of, he would bring them to those that had sufficient authority to take notice of it'.

The more suspicious among us might well believe this was some form of trap, or in modern parlance a 'sting'. Blood probably shared this disquiet but treated it as an occupational hazard for a spy and informer.[33]

A meeting was arranged, but the two men, later identified as Samuel Ryther and Philemon Coddan, both Irish, fled when they saw Blood, 'averring they would have nothing to do with him for that he was the Duke of Buckingham's friend'. Jane Bradley went to Blood's house in Westminster and told him the men were 'rogues and trepans[34] and advised him to seize them and carry them before a magistrate'.

The colonel had them up before a Middlesex justice called Dr Chamberlain, who was well known to Blood. Both claimed Buckingham owed them money and one said he was willing to swear that the duke was guilty of sodomy. The justice did not believe them and the matter was apparently forgotten.[35]

What Blood was stumbling into was a conspiracy to bring down Buckingham initiated by his enemies, notably Thomas Osborne, Earl of Danby. He had been languishing in the Tower since April 1679 after being impeached for corruption and embezzlement from the Treasury, exceeding his powers 'in matters of peace and war' and 'traitorously concealing' the Oates plot. That gossipy envoy Barillon believed that Buckingham had deliberately absented himself from Danby's impeachment proceedings in the Lords because the earl had 'threatened him with prosecution for sodomy'.[36] So clearly the plot against him had been under way for some time; indeed, the previous February, Ossory – Ormond's eldest son and no friend to Buckingham – had confided to Danby that he still cherished hopes 'of procuring something very material' against the proud and arrogant courtier.[37]

The chief protagonist in the plan was probably Edward Christian, Buckingham's one-time chamberlain, who had been fired for stealing large sums of money from his master in 1673.[38] He had worked for Danby for three years as his steward and was the ideal man to organise an assault on the duke's reputation and to banish him from court. Blood had reviled Christian, from his time as Buckingham's agent, to the stage of coldly refusing him 'the civility of either drinking publicly or privately with him'.[39] The feeling was mutual.

The heart and substance of the conspiracy was the accusation that Buckingham had sodomised a London gentlewoman called Sarah Harwood and had packed her off to France to preserve her silence and to prevent the scandal becoming public.

Buckingham's reputation for violence was well known. He acknowledged that some had talked of his 'cruel, insolent, injurious carriage to my inferiors'. There was the case of the 'poor old fellow' angrily beaten by the duke after the farmer had complained that he had trampled through his cornfield while hunting. 'I protest that the story itself is wholly mistaken as some honest men, my servants that were present, are ready to witness . . . If breaking a hedge be so great a crime, I wonder what huntsmen can ever be innocent?' he asked disingenuously. Buckingham also denied categorically that he was a poisoner, even though some who had crossed him – like the informer William Leving – had died by this silent means. The attempted sodomy charge was equally serious as it had remained, since Thomas Cromwell's Buggery Act of 1533, a capital crime. Buckingham blithely, if not eloquently, denied the allegation: 'There was mention made of my attempting a crime of so horrid a nature that it ought not to be named amongst Christians.

> But for my innocency in this I can only call God to witness and rely upon the charity of all men . . . God knows I have much to answer for in the plain way but I never was so great a virtuoso in my lusts.[40]

Christian now had witnesses lined up, ready to testify that this was a wicked lie.

Philip Le Mar and his mother Frances Loveland were the first two. Le Mar was to claim that six years before Buckingham had committed buggery with him, although it was suggested that the

Countess of Danby had offered him £300 to make the allegation.[41] Coddan and Ryther were the others. All were unlikely to appear credible figures in the witness box.

Coddan and a fellow Irishman called Maurice Hickey, alias Higgins, had settled in Long Acre, near Covent Garden, where their heavy drinking and energetic arguments in Gaelic had aroused suspicions.[42] The plan was for them to convince Ryther that, in return for a large bribe, he would swear that Buckingham had sodomised the woman. If this means of persuasion failed, he would sign a confession while drugged by some narcotic. Coddan was to become the second witness who would support Ryther's allegations in court. Unfortunately, the star witness tended towards the mercurial: he agreed to testify one minute and refused the next. Another voice was necessary to steady Ryther on the difficult road to plausibility in court.

That man was Thomas Curtis, a cloth worker from Lancashire, who had earlier been briefly jailed because of his embroilment in another sham conspiracy, the so-called Meal-tub plot, named after the fact that incriminating documents had been hidden in the bottom of such a receptacle. He enjoyed an unenviable reputation for heavy drinking and, as most of his efforts to coerce the unwilling Ryther into giving evidence took place at the Crown in Ram Alley, south of Fleet Street,[43] or the Bear tavern on the Southwark shore of the Thames near London Bridge,[44] he must have relished his work.

Blood appeared at one of these meetings and pressed Coddan and Ryther about their testimony. He became persuaded that both could certainly have their day in court and would produce the required evidence.

However, both potential witnesses then suffered an attack of cold feet. Coddan promised Ryther that 'we will do this rogue Blood's business for him and get enough to swear against him by the time Sir William Waller comes to town'.[45] The next meeting was at a tavern in Bloomsbury and Hickey was given a paper for both men to sign. He was instructed to offer them £300 in gold coins but to threaten to murder them if they did not make their marks on the document as signatures. Arriving first, Ryther heard the alternatives on offer, snatched up the paper and fled out into the darkness.

He and Coddan visited Buckingham's lawyer, a Mr Whitaker, and told him what had transpired. Danby's cat was unfortunately dragged out of the bag.

On 20 January 1680, Blood was summoned by Waller to a meeting at the Buffalo Head tavern in Westminster, near the Gatehouse prison, and confronted by Coddan and Ryther's sordid tale of subornation. He was startled to see his would-be witnesses now smartly dressed 'in a genteel equipage and à la mode accoutrements'. Also present at this meeting were Whitaker, Buckingham's attorney, and the linen draper Francis Jenks, another of Buckingham's radical activists. Blood tried to bluff his way out, but Whitaker urged him to be honest, just and confess. The colonel replied: 'You have been these last two years employed to asperse me. Could you find no better invention than this?' They pressed Waller for justice and the magistrate 'very civilly' asked the colonel to find bail.[46]

Blood resisted detention until 22 January when he met a constable at the upper end of King Street, Westminster, who told him he had a warrant for his arrest. Remarkably, they both went to the Dog tavern, alongside the Gatehouse, and over the next few hours had several drinks together. Waller meanwhile discovered the officer was armed only with a *mittimus*[47] and hurriedly sent over a warrant as the constable was worried that it was in the power of Mr Blood 'to bring me under great trouble for my inadvertency in the thing'[48] by bringing action for false imprisonment. Addressed to 'all constables', the warrant read:

Whereas oath has been made by two witnesses that Colonel Thomas Blood has been a confederate in a late conspiracy of falsely accusing and charging his grace the Duke of Buckingham of sodomy and has refused to give bail for his appearance at the next general sessions to be held for the city and liberty of Westminster.

These are therefore to will and require that you seize and apprehend the said Colonel Thomas Blood and if he shall refuse to give in bail, to carry him and deliver him into the hand of Mr Church, keeper of the Gatehouse in Westminster, according to the tenor of the *mittimus* in your hands.[49]

Blood, in default of bail, was taken to prison.

The colonel, Christian, Curtis and Hickey were tried for blasphemy, confederacy and subornation in King's Bench court and found guilty. They were fined and imprisoned. Later in May 1680, Le Mar and his mother were convicted of being suborned to swear sodomy against Buckingham.[50] Le Mar had been made drunk and given drugs during the conspiracy and he was later to die from the effects of these narcotics in the Marshalsea prison.[51] His mother was put into the pillory on 19 June, 'where she was severely dealt with by the people throwing dirt and rotten eggs at her'.[52] The attorney general, Sir Creswell Levinz, investigated the Le Mar case and the examining magistrate, called Barnsley, was removed from the commission of the peace for his 'undue practices'.[53]

Sir William Waller was also sacked as a magistrate for similar irregularities and misdemeanours and he later fled to Holland.

Buckingham meanwhile was intent on vengeance against his erstwhile employee Blood. He brought an action for defamation – a civil suit for *scandalum magnatum* – against the colonel, Christian and Curtis claiming £10,000 damages.[54] The jury found for Buckingham.

Blood was growing desperate. Whenever a situation becomes especially fraught, one calls in favours from every quarter, so on 14 July he sent his son Charles to see James, Duke of York, to seek his royal intercession on his behalf. The next day, Blood wrote to the duke politely thanking him for 'the great favour' in granting the audience and asking if his brother the king would order the Treasury to pay his salary, which 'Lord Sunderland has often done without effect'. The hard-pressed colonel could not possibly find the wherewithal for a bail payment and he wondered if the king 'would encourage some to [stand] bail for me'.

He was becoming ever more frustrated by Whitehall's bureaucratic ineptitude. 'You ordered my son to go to Sir Leoline Jenkins

[appointed secretary of state in April 1680] to understand what instructions he had from the king concerning me – and he said he
knew not a word of it.

> I therefore humbly beg that I may not be left in this cause to fall,
> which is because I keep the Commonwealth party in awe and
> broke the neck of Sir William Waller.
>
> I intend to have a *habeas corpus* today and to put in bail before
> Judge Dolben.[55]
>
> If you can favour me with any interest in him, it will be my great
> advantage.[56]

The ever-dilatory Treasury still failed to come up with his salary
and three days later Blood, frustrated and fuming, wrote to Jenkins
with a frantic plea for his immediate assistance.

> I have been left destitute of the usual supply of money from the
> court and tantalised from day to day and week to week … [The]
> lords of the Treasury have promised me from three days to three
> days the payment of that £600[57] which the king allowed me for
> my salary to enable me to do his business. [This has] all ended in
> words, [so] they may be effectively spoken to.
>
> Next I desire an immediate supply of thirty or forty guineas to
> bear the charges of my disentanglement for I am quite destitute,
> having pawned my [silver] plate. I would also entreat you to en-
> courage some persons to be bail for me.

Blood was writing from within the walls of the Gatehouse prison
in Westminster. The sheriff's officers would not acknowledge or
accept 'his privilege' and dragged him off into the prison, leading to
a complaint about his treatment being made to the king. Blood angrily maintained that Buckingham and the Commonwealth party
had spent £10,000 'to get me out of their way, knowing I have been
a check on their disloyal actions these nine years and remain so
still'. Having got the 'better of them as to the criminal part of the
cause, in spite and envy, they arrest me in an action for £10,000,

supposing that sum was so great that it would fright any tradesman from bailing me'.[58]

He received his writ of *habeas corpus* on 21 July and removed himself to the King's Bench prison for debtors in Southwark.[59] Happily he was bailed the following morning. Some well-disposed individual put up a surety for his release (did the money come from secret service funds?) and he was freed, amid voluble protests that he had been illegally proceeded against.[60]

When Blood was incarcerated in the Tower, following his abortive attempt to steal the Crown Jewels, a small book of his was confiscated by his jailers. The original is now lost but a copy is preserved in the Pepys papers in the Bodleian Library at Oxford.[61] It seems to have been compiled during Blood's more ruminative moments while still in captivity or just after being released in 1671 – there is one line on the first page that mentions 'my son who is wont [to be known] by the name of Thomas Hunt, now a prisoner in the Tower'.[62]

Under the heading 'Deliverances since I was for the Lord's cause', his seventy escapes from arrest or danger are listed for the period 1663–71, annoyingly with a frustrating lack of detail. These include his adventures in Dublin after the coup attempt ('I escaped when most were taken'), boarding a ship 'when none knew me' and arriving at a port where he was well known; eluding capture when visiting his mother-in-law in Lancashire and again during his wanderings around Manchester and being pursued by a pack of dogs.

His exploits also included being 'a prisoner [in] Zeeland' and escaping arrest in Bishopsgate Street during the Great Fire of London. There are other escapades, the circumstances of which we can sadly only guess at: 'my swimming'; 'the guard at the bridge' the 'Life Guard man'; 'from friends at Ipswich' and being 'taken by a constable at Essex'. His rescue of Captain Mason is probably covered by the entries: 'from the trepan beyond Newark'; 'from them in the little hours'; 'in the battle'; 'Leving confession' and being 'healed of my wounds'. Even after going into semi-retirement as a quack apothecary, he faced 'discovery at Romford'; 'a design by some to cast me off' and from 'discontented friends'.

There was also another deliverance at the 'Bull in the Strand'.[63]

Interleaved in these notes are two entries referring to his son's decision to take to a life of crime, clearly a source of great disappointment to his father: 'my son's wickedness – this was Hunt's robbing on ye highway' and 'My son's being stopped and coming before [Justice] Keeling'. Were these deliverances or trials?[64]

All these feats created the absolute certainty in Blood's mind that he should never 'forsake the cause of God for any difficulties'. His notes also contain twenty-two one-line moral and religious tenets for life that he plainly tried to adhere to and which also indicate Blood's belief in the existence and power of Providence (which had served him so badly at the Martin Tower). These included: 'To [spend] each day in serious consideration of my interest in Christ and what he has done'; 'To avoid disputing or crossing in discourse or undervaluing of persons in religious or civic things' and 'To labour to be content with my condition, considering nothing comes by chance'. These precepts also urged his avoidance of strong wine and drink and any 'recreations or pomps or excess in apparel . . . quibbling or joking . . . all obscene and scurrilous talk'. There were also three rules, very pertinent to the uncertain life of a spy: 'To be faithful in trust remitted and wary to whom I commit it'; 'Not to reveal secrets' and 'Not to break engagements'. Blood was clearly a deeply religious man, inclined to searing self-analysis and the need to discover some pattern in his life and personal objectives, laid down by God Himself.[65]

The colonel needed that religious belief and fortitude now, as never before. He returned to his home on the corner of Great Peter and Tufton streets in Westminster and here 'reflected upon his condition, both as to his personal reputation and the interests of his family'.

His faithful wife Mary was already dead, as was his eldest son, Thomas. His two daughters were prosperously married and his other sons were gainfully engaged in careers in the service of the king. But Blood's standing in society had been 'extremely blasted' by the 'malice of enemies' and was ruined by the failure of his debtors to reimburse him – a particular blow when he was faced with having to pay a gigantic bill for damages to Buckingham.

Blood could not now see any means of 'getting out of the mire by his former methods of contriving and daring'. In the past, he had 'trusted to his hands' and his sagacity to rescue him in any emergency but now he realised he was completely 'manacled'.

These 'dismal thoughts' degenerated into 'a pensive melancholy' and this, combined with the hot weather of the season, caused a 'fatal, though not violent distemper' – a disturbed condition of the mind.

His sickness lasted fourteen days and throughout this period Blood was visited by his loyal friends and a Presbyterian minister who found him in a 'sedate temper as to the concerns of his soul' and not 'startled by the apprehension of approaching death'. Blood told him he had set his thoughts in order and 'was ready and willing to obey, when it pleased God to give him the last call'. These were the only words he uttered, as he seemed unwilling to talk to his other visitors, and the only noises he made were 'involuntary sighs' between increasingly frequent spells of sleep. On the Monday before his death, he was struck speechless and barely able to move, presumably having suffered a stroke, and his breathing grew ever more laboured.

On Monday, 22 August he dictated his last will and testament, 'being at the time sensible of the frailty and mortality of man' and afflicted by 'a weariness of body'. Blood therefore bequeathed his soul 'into the hands of almighty God . . . in full assurance of that blessed resurrection held forth in the Holy Scriptures' and his body 'to the earth from whence it came'.

As a debtor, the terms of his will were necessarily curtailed. Long gone were the halcyon days of riches and affluence, with Blood strutting arrogantly around town dressed in the latest fashions and wearing the finest periwig. His 'small temporal estate' now consisted only of the simple goods and chattels that he still possessed. Everything else of value had been pawned or disposed of. Those items 'capable of being sold' were to be turned into cash immediately and the proceeds were to be divided equally into three parts. His daughters Mary and Elizabeth were to receive one part each and the third was to be shared by his three surviving sons Holcroft, William and Charles and his daughter-in-law, the widow of Thomas Blood junior. The only bequest outside the family was the twenty shillings (£1) to be paid 'to my old friend John Fisher'. His executors were named as 'my faithful and loving friends' Robert Blakeys, of London, clerk, and Thomas Lisle of Westminster, 'not doubting their old friendship and kindness in undertaking' these duties. The will was witnessed by Sarah [?Frend] and John Ward, Blood's servant.[66]

An inventory of his remaining goods and chattels in May the following year lists the items left in each room of his house: 'the dining room'; 'the little parlour and entry'; 'the little chamber backward' and the like. There was precious little remaining: a few chairs, a leather jack (a jug for beer), some hangings, a chopping knife and some brass candlesticks in the kitchen, a bedstead, blankets and some rugs. All in all, they were valued at £300 14s 2d, which was probably more than Blood realised.[67]

At three o'clock on the afternoon of Wednesday, 24 August, Colonel Thomas Blood died. He was aged sixty-two.

After a life of striving to 'make a noise in the world' by assiduously courting popular notoriety and infamy, his passing was marked more by a pathetic whimper than the anticipated bang.

Or was it? One last event that caught the public's imagination marked his demise.

The old colonel would have been gratified that lurid rumours about his death swept London. Some gossips maintained that he had used a 'narcotic and stupefying' drug to hasten his end, but his contemporary biographer believed this was a harsh judgement on a man 'who had the courage not to despair in the worst circumstances of life and far less should be thought to do it on a deathbed of no painful sickness'. Others claimed he died a devout Catholic after a last-gasp conversion. This again was untrue: 'It would be needless to produce the testimonies of persons beyond exception who were constantly with him in his sickness to refute this . . . calumny raised by those enemies of his'.[68] At least Blood did not die alone and friendless.

Two days later Blood was 'decently interred' a few hundred yards away from his home in the chapel in Tothill Fields[69] near the grave of his wife.

If he had pious hopes of a joyful resurrection awaiting him, these were realised sooner than he could have wished.

As we saw at the beginning, there was much talk that his final illness, death and burial were nothing more than another trick to throw off his enemies and avoid paying Buckingham his punitive damages. Some people testified that they had seen him alive and well in his familiar haunts in Westminster and the Palace of Whitehall. Was his apparent death nothing but a devious 'farce and piece of pageantry to carry on some design' planned by Blood? Such was the pitch of excitement in London that the authorities decided the only way to scotch such uncontrolled speculation was to exhume Blood's body, to prove, once and for all, that he was truly dead.

Accordingly, the grave was reopened on the following Thursday. A coroner and jury from Westminster – made up of twenty-three honest citizens who knew him in life – were convened in an inquest to view the disinterred and odorous body.

Such civic duties can never be pleasant and this was particularly gruesome. After six days below ground in that warm season, the jurymen were horrified to find his 'face so altered and swollen' and so 'few lineaments and features of their old acquaintance' remaining that they were unable to recognise the corpse formally, or even informally. An army captain was called in who maintained, under oath, that the thumb of the cadaver's left hand demonstrated conclusively that this was Blood's body. All who knew him had 'taken notice' of this distinguishing feature which had grown 'to a prodigious bigness' after an old injury. However, this was not enough to convince the sceptical jury and no verdict was returned.[70]

The body was decently returned to its grave, although some reports long afterwards suggested that the colonel was reburied not in Tothill Fields, but in the graveyard of St Andrew's parish church in Hornchurch, Essex. Alongside the church on the High Street side is an anonymous grave marked only by a weather-beaten and effaced slab bearing a skull and crossbones which is pointed out as that of Blood. Despite Hornchurch's proximity to his old stomping ground in Romford, this seems highly unlikely.

A number of satirical broadsheets marking his death were quickly published by those wanting to capitalise on the end of someone quite so infamous. The seventy-six lines of doggerel verses *An Elegy on Colonel Blood, Notorious for Stealing the Crown*, rushed out by J. Shorter only six days after Blood's death, began with the damning:

> *Thanks, ye kind fates for your last favour shown*
> *Of stealing BLOOD who lately stole the Crown*
> *We'll not exclaim so much against you since*
> *As well as BEDLOE you have fetched him hence,*
> *He who has been a plague to all mankind*
> *And never was to anyone a friend . . .*

and ended with the suggestion that this should be his epitaph:

> *Here lies the man who boldly has run through*
> *More villainies than ever England knew*
> *And nere to any friend he had was true*
> *Here let him then by all unpitied lie*
> *And let's rejoice his time was come to die.*[71]

Unkind words indeed.

Perhaps a more appropriate epitaph would be the summary of his life written by Richard Halliwell, his contemporary biographer, who generously declared that Blood never pursued

mean . . . and sneaking actions that leave an indelible character of ignominy upon those who would be thought gentlemen when they tread in the steps of villains.

He was indeed for forbidden game, but never on the king's highway, always in royal parks and forests. Crowns, sceptres and government were his booty and the surprising of castles and viceroys his recreation.

His exploits, he wrote, were 'to live in story for [their] strangeness, if not by the success of his attempts'.[72]

They do indeed. His arrogance and daring were spellbinding, particularly so as, despite the plaudits of his former accomplice, he rarely enjoyed any real success in his adventures. Some might see the colonel as a psychologically flawed attention-seeker, perhaps wholly narcissistic, as the symptoms of this personality disorder apparently include an exaggerated sense of one's own abilities and achievements, a constant need for affirmation and a sense of entitlement and expectation of special treatment. When examining his exploits, these may sound uncannily familiar.

But aside from the complexities of his psychology, a strong case can also be made that his primary motivation was a volatile mix of religious fervour, a sense of injustice and the burning need for vengeance – like so many others in seventeenth-century Britain. However, the colonel stands out as a different kind of desperado to those grim-faced fanatics that populated his twilight world of espionage and treachery in Dublin and London.

Unlike them, Blood was an eccentric gambler who was never daunted by the odds that fate threw up against him and who took a rash delight in staging an outrage purely for its own sake. In his turbulent career, Blood tried to assassinate viceroys, rescue friends and stole the unthinkable (or unattainable) just because the challenges were perceived as too great by other mere mortals. What drove him on was the same irrepressible motivation that later forced people to climb mountains purely because they were there.

Fame was his spur.

He ranks high in the pantheon of true adventurers, with his escapades frequently the excited talk of three kingdoms. His colourful, madcap exploits enliven and enrich the pages of seventeenth-century British history. We remain amazed by his daredevil audacity, his astonishing effrontery and smile at his harum-scarum escapes from the hand of destiny.

Although the governments of Ireland and England of the time would disagree, thank God he was there.

# Epilogue

*Most dangerous conspiracies are still carrying on against your person and interest, [made] far more general and dangerous ... by the incredible numbers of the commonalty and gentry of both city and country.*

Charles Blood to James, Duke of York, 1681[1]

George Villiers, Second Duke of Buckingham, was finally restored to Charles II's favour in 1684 but his enjoyment of this royal approval was short-lived as the king died on 6 February the following year, a few days after suffering an apoplectic fit. After the accession of the Duke of York as James II of England and James VII of Scotland, the old schemer returned briefly to public life, diligently attending routine parliamentary business and writing *A Short Discourse on the Reasonableness of Man's having a Religion* in 1685, a pamphlet that advocated greater religious freedom for both Catholics and Protestants.

Because of ill-health and his omnipresent financial troubles, Buckingham retired to the relatively cloistered world of his small estate at Helmsley, Yorkshire and lived there quietly for eighteen months. He died on 16 April 1687, supposedly from a chill caught while out hunting,[2] at the home of one of his tenants in Kirkbymoorside, believing himself 'despised by my country and, I fear, forsaken by my God'. Buckingham was aged fifty-nine. His was a life of wanton dissipation, coupled disastrously with serial embezzlement by those he imprudently trusted. By 1671, all his properties had been mortgaged, sometimes three or four times over, and that year a trust was established to administer what remained, yielding him an annual income of only £5,000. Buckingham died intestate, his once grand estates dispersed and his fortune long gone. Without a legitimate male heir, his title became extinct. He was buried in Westminster Abbey.

That indomitable old republican Edmund Ludlow felt that with William III's accession to the throne in 1688, it might be safe to quit the protective haven of Switzerland and return to London. Accordingly on 25 July 1689 he formally bade farewell to the obliging magistrates of Vevey, declaring that God had called him home 'to strengthen the hand of the English Gideon'. No doubt the city fathers nodded approvingly at this righteous motive.

He arrived safely without let or hindrance and his London home inevitably attracted visits by the last survivors of the old republican party. It was just as predictable that his presence in the capital would cause scandal and unrest in political circles. On 6 November, Sir Joseph Tredenham, MP for St Mawes in Cornwall, stood up in the Commons and drew its attention to Ludlow's unashamed residence so close to Westminster and the seat of government. The MPs needed little debate on the issue and almost immediately resolved

> that a humble address be presented to his majesty that he will be pleased to issue out a proclamation for the apprehending of Colonel Ludlow who stands attainted of high treason by Act of Parliament for the murder of King Charles I.
>
> And that he will be pleased to propose an award to such as apprehend him.

The Commons ordered that a loyal address should be presented to the king by Tredenham's brother-in-law, Sir Edward Seymour, MP for Exeter and a former speaker of the house.[3]

William III thought the Commons had an entirely reasonable and just point of view and therefore published their sought-for proclamation, offering £200 for Ludlow's arrest. The fugitive fled England for the second and final time, again finding refuge in the

Netherlands before returning to Switzerland. He died at Vevey on 26 November 1692, aged seventy-three. His life in lonely exile far from home was filled with pathos after his heady days in the godly Commonwealth and this is reflected in the inscription he hung up over the door of his home at 49 Rue du Lac. It read: '*Omne solum forti quia patris*' which Ludlow had adapted from a line by the Roman poet Ovid: 'To the brave man, every land is a fatherland because God his Father made it.'[4]

Ludlow, like his fellow regicide John Phelps, was buried in the Swiss Reformed church of St Martin in Vevey, where his widow erected a monument to his memory in 1693.

Ormond was restored to the viceroyalty of Ireland in 1667 but his caution and conservatism hindered progress towards the long-overdue reform of the standing army and English administration in Dublin. One contemporary told the Anglo-Irish diplomat Sir Robert Southwell that the 'diverse reforms to be made in Ireland . . . his majesty thinks will be too hard a thing to put on my lord of Ormond'.[5] He clung grimly on to office until the death of Charles II automatically terminated his commission.

On 9 November 1682 he had been created an English duke and this rarefied status impelled him to buy the grandest mansion in St James's Square, London, at the cost of £9,000. He retired to Cornbury in Oxfordshire and died on 21 July 1688 at Kingston Lacey, Dorset, aged seventy-seven. Ormond had survived a tumultuous career with his honour firmly intact. He always had an eye for the judgement of history and wrote: 'However ill I may stand at court, I am resolved to lie well in the chronicle.' Leaving debts estimated at between £100,000 and £150,000, he too was buried in Westminster Abbey.

As we saw earlier, Arlington resigned as secretary of state on 11 September 1674 after a 'burdensome employment . . . [of] almost twelve years, with more labour and envy than I would willingly undergo, or indeed can support in my declining age'. He was appointed lord chamberlain of the royal household and five years later a commissioner of the Treasury. His five-year-old daughter was betrothed on 1 August 1672 to nine-year-old Henry Fitzroy (later created Duke of Grafton),[6] the second illegitimate son of Charles II and Barbara Villiers, Duchess of Cleveland. They married in November 1679. Arlington died on 28 July 1685, aged sixty-seven, finally acknowledging his adherence to Catholicism. He was buried at Euston, Suffolk where he had a large estate.[7] His London residence was Arlington House in St James's, which burned down in 1674 and was on the site of the south wing of today's royal residence, Buckingham Palace.

Williamson was dismissed as secretary of state in 1679 when, for the first time, he dramatically (and fatally) overreached himself. During the furore over the Popish Plot, he had ordered a search of Catherine of Braganza's official residence at Somerset House in the Strand, without obtaining permission from the king.[8] Williamson was an MP in both the English and Irish Houses of Commons and died at Cobham, Kent, on 3 October 1701, aged sixty-eight. He left £6,000 and his library to his old *alma mater*, Queen's College, Oxford, and £5,000 to found Sir Joseph Williamson's Mathematical School at Rochester, Kent.[9]

The plots against the government by Blood's old associates continued unabated after his death. In 1683, James Harris of Paved Alley in St James's warned Secretary Jenkins of a conspiracy involving, amongst others, Ralph Alexander, Robert Perrot, John Mason (now a brewer in Wapping) and Richard Halliwell (who had moved to Spitalfields). Under the pretence of being Catholics, they planned to rouse the population on the symbolic date of Sunday, 5 November (in memory of the Gunpowder Plot of 1605) and seize the king, the Duke of York, the Dukes of Ormond and Albermarle and members of the government and Privy Council. Most of the miscreants had previously been pardoned, but, as Harris pointed out, 'Any spark of loyalty may see that his majesty's pardons have made no impression of honesty or gratitude upon them.'

However, Halliwell objected vociferously to the coup being mounted on a Sabbath day for religious reasons: 'We cannot fall on the fifth, according to our covenant', he told his fellow plotters. 'But we steadfastly resolve to secure as many as we can of the court party on the seventeenth (being Bess' Day)[10] and we will deal with them and Ormond as we formerly intended against him.' Grudges clearly ran very deep.

Sir Robert Viner, whom we last met hunting down Ormond's assailants and recreating the Crown Jewels, had a trusted informer familiar with the 'fanatics' and details of their conspiracy. This spy, a tobacconist called John Harrison, nursed his own grudge: he had revealed plans for an attempt 'some years ago' on the lives of Charles and the Duke of York when they were travelling by boat up the Thames. He had supplied this information to Blood, 'who had a reward and, he heard, was commanded to reward him, but he never had anything'. The sum involved was £100, half of which was to come to Harrison, 'but Blood was in trouble and died not long afterwards, but [he] never had a penny for the service'.[11]

One of the conspirators, William Hone, who lived near Redcross Street,[12] Southwark, was questioned by the king and Privy Council on 30 June and talked about another plot 'within these last seven years' to kill Charles by firing a crossbow bolt at him from the tower of Bow church (St Mary-le-bow in Cheapside) as the procession of the annual lord mayor's show passed by. Hone denied any involvement in this: 'A fellow talked something of it that was a butcher once and belonged [was in the pay] of Blood.'

Another more active plan envisaged kidnapping the king and Duke of York at Newmarket 'three weeks or a month ago', according to Hone, who acknowledged he was on the fringes of the conspiracy. For security reasons, the royal victims were code-named 'Blackbird' and 'Bullfinch' by the conspirators.[13] This was the so-called 'Rye House' plot, named after the moated house near Hoddesdon, Hertfordshire, where the attack was to be staged.

There was no royal abduction planned here. The plotters intended to murder Charles and his heir presumptive. Assassins were to be hidden in the Rye House grounds to ambush the royal party with muskets or carbines as they returned to London by coach from the horse races at Newmarket, now in Suffolk, on 1 April 1683. However, there was a major fire in the town on 22 March, which destroyed the north side of its High Street. As a result of this disaster, the races were cancelled so Charles and the Duke of

York returned a week early and the planned attack never took place. Eleven were executed as conspirators, including two MPs, and the same number imprisoned. Arthur Capell, First Earl of Essex, the former lord lieutenant of Ireland, was caught up in the hunt for plotters and committed suicide horribly by cutting his throat in the Tower of London on 13 July 1683.

Most of Blood's old comrades seemed to escape scot-free. Robert Perrot, however, ended up on the gallows. When the Duke of Monmouth staged his insurrection against the Catholic James II, Perrot joined his army as a major in the rebels' Yellow Regiment, commanded by the former Guards officer Colonel Edward Matthews, who was something of a hard-drinking tearaway. Perrot's luck finally ran out when he fought on the losing side at the Battle of Sedgemoor, at Westonzoyland, near Bridgwater, Somerset, on 6 July 1685 and was wounded. He was captured while hiding in the Brendon Hills some weeks later and executed with 144 of his comrades at Taunton, Somerset.[14] Monmouth himself was beheaded on Tower Hill on 15 July by the notoriously cack-handed public executioner Jack Ketch, who reportedly took five blows to complete the messy decapitation.

One really cannot like the government spy Philip Alden, and not just because he was an opportunistic shady lawyer. This reprehensible creature had lived in London and spied on religious radicals after his adventures in Ireland. Afterwards he smugly boasted of his successes in 1665–6, 'being so skilful and serviceable . . . [and] having a constant correspondence from Ludlow and others out of Switzerland and having mixed again with that villain Blood and his partners and more considerable rebels, so that most of their designs . . . were discovered [by Alden] to his majesty or ministers'.[15]

However, in 1666 his loyalties came under increasing suspicion by those he regularly informed upon and he felt himself coming under threat of exposure and terrible retribution. What finally sealed his fate was when an officer attached to the staff of General George Monck, Duke of Albermarle, found a trunk of Alden's in a house near Moor Park, Hertfordshire, while he was searching for the disaffected. Inside were letters from Colonel Ned Vernon and the Irish Secretary Sir George Lane to the spy, making his undercover activities painfully apparent. Unfortunately, the officer made the contents public before he showed them to Albermarle. Alden's cover was finally and irrevocably blown. For 'his safety [he] was taken off that employ' and he was forced to return to Ireland. A grateful government granted him a pension of £100 a year, which predictably was paid only erratically by the Treasury. He experienced great difficulty in claiming back his sizeable arrears in payment.[16] Perhaps there is some justice in this world after all.

The former spy Martin Beckman, the fast-running military engineer who apprehended Blood in his attempt to steal the coronation regalia, married Talbot Edwards' daughter Elizabeth. They had several children, of whom none sadly lived to adulthood, and she died in 1677. He later remarried. That year Beckman was appointed 'chief engineer of all of his majesty's castles, forts, blockhouses and other fortifications in England, Wales and Berwick',[17] coupling his military work with organising impressive firework displays. He died at the Tower on 24 June 1702.[18]

If Blood's old accomplices could not shake off their proclivity for traitorous plots, one of his family continued the established family business of spying. His fifth son Charles was an informer for the Duke of York after his father's death, and sent at least two reports, probably in 1681–3, warning him of current plots against his life and potential insurrections when he succeeded his brother on the throne.

His first warning was of

> most dangerous conspiracies ... still carrying on against your person and interest, far more general and dangerous than the late association [plot], not only by the members of the same but by incredible numbers of the commonalty and gentry of both city and country. If you be pleased that I shall communicate their wicked intentions to you, I am fully assured that I can have information, though not without difficulty, of every circumstantial part of their proceedings.[19]

Like father, like son. Charles understood full well how to sell his value as a spy, and to hint that the collection of intelligence was an expensive activity, worthy of generous remuneration.

Charles Blood's second surviving report warned that Protestants were determined to oppose James's accession, 'to the hazard of their lives and fortunes'. Buckingham and his associate Francis Jenks were among those who had 'formed an association' and had recruited 'great numbers' who were 'qualified to provide arms as [well as] bear them'. These weapons, which had been given free to those who could not buy them, included one resembling a halberd[20] 'but far more dangerous'. Blood claimed 'vast quantities' had been manufactured to be given to those who did not know how to use a musket. The revolutionaries had purchased horses and firearms, including blunderbusses, and were protected by a kind of silk armour 'that would resist a carbine bullet'.[21]

Therein lies a clue. Captain Ralph Alexander was famous for inventing 'silk armour', presumably metal plates covered by the material, 'which he has made many suits for the richer sort . . . as well as some for the court'.[22] His armour and the manufacturer of halberds featured in the reports of the 1683 conspiracy by the gang of Blood's old associates and his son's intelligence must relate to the same plot.

Charles later became a barrister in London.

Of Blood's two sons serving in the navy,[23] William died in 1688 in *Mary*,[24] at sea off the coast of the present-day Republic of Guinea in West Africa.[25] An inventory of his goods and chattels, taken later that year and approved by his younger sister Elizabeth Everard, valued them at only £15.[26] Edmund had died in 1679 in London, leaving half his estate to William and the other to Thomas Chamberlain, son of Matthew Chamberlain, silk thrower of London.[27]

Holcroft, the third son, enlisted in the Royal Navy without his father's knowledge or permission in 1672 and served at sea during the Third Anglo-Dutch War. He later joined Louis XIV's French Guards as a cadet, using the *nom de guerre* of 'Leture', and studied engineering in the French military academy. His father obtained him the post of clerk of the peace in Co. Clare in April 1676.[28] Two years later, Charles II granted him a licence of absence as he had been 'absent by the king's command and has remained in England on the king's service'.[29]

In 1686, he married Elizabeth Fowler, widowed daughter of the barrister Richard King, at St Pancras church, London, and in October 1688 was appointed captain of pioneers in James II's artillery train. After the Glorious Revolution and the accession of William of Orange and his wife Mary, Holcroft was promoted second engineer in the artillery and sent to Ireland. Holcroft fought in the major sieges and battles against James II's Jacobite forces in Ireland and was wounded at the capture of Carrickfergus in Co. Antrim in August 1689, at Cashel, in Co. Tipperary the following February and at the decisive Battle of the Boyne on 1 July 1690.[30] In February 1696 he was unexpectedly promoted second engineer of England at a salary of £250 a year[31] and that May was rewarded with a payment of £180 for his role in arresting the chief protagonists in a conspiracy to assassinate William.

Under the Duke of Marlborough, he fought as colonel of the train of artillery in the war against France. At the siege of Venloo in south-east Holland in September 1702, Lord Cutts successfully stormed the town's outwork defences, reporting that engineers and pioneers

> under Col. Blood, who acted as first engineer . . . was to have made the lodgment [captured position] continuous. When he saw that I had quitted that design, he showed the part of a brave officer, charging with the men, sword in hand, and killing an officer of grenadiers who made a vigorous opposition with his party.[32]

After successfully commanding the allied artillery at the victory of Blenheim on 2 August 1704, Blood was promoted brigadier general.

Holcroft had enjoyed a lengthy affair with a Mrs Mary Andrews and his wife had quit the marital home in London in disgust at his infidelity. In October that year, he attempted a reconciliation that ended fruitlessly and embarrassingly in a public brawl between husband and wife. She tried to take out warrants for his arrest for assault but her attempts were thwarted by his barrister brother Charles. She then sued for separation for his adultery and cruelty in the London consistory court, but after Holcroft proved her own unfaithfulness, her suit was dismissed.[33]

Blood returned to military service in Flanders and died in Brussels on 19 August 1707, aged fifty. His will left £200 a year for ninety-nine years to his natural son Holcroft[34] of St Anne's Soho, Westminster, and an annuity of £100 to his mother, 'my dear and entirely beloved friend Mrs Dorothy Cook of the city of Dort in the province of Holland'. She also received 'all money, plate, jewels, watches, household goods and camp furniture'.

His wife Elizabeth was left forty shillings (£2).[35]

Nothing further is known of the lives of Blood's two daughters, Mary and Elizabeth, except that they were still alive in 1707, as they received bequests of £50 each in Holcroft's will.

Holcroft had taken Edmund, the eldest of his deceased brother Thomas's two offspring, into his protection when the child was only three or four months old.[36] The child's mother died in Dublin while he was staying with his uncle in Holland. Edmund later served with the British army in Albany, the capital of New York state, and told a relative, a Mrs Mary Blood of Meath Street, Dublin in July 1734 that since he was aged eight, 'I have been abroad in the service of the crown.'

The subject of his letter was the sad story of a long-lost inheritance: the Blood lands in Counties Meath and Wicklow granted by Charles I. After Colonel Blood's attainder, the property was granted to Captain Toby Barnes in April 1666[37] for thirty-one years. After Blood's royal pardon, Charles II directed the lord lieutenant and justices of Ireland to allow him to bring an action for a writ of error to reverse the attainder for treason against him. Unfortunately, that reversal was either not provided or had been lost in the government archives in Dublin Castle.

Barnes died in 1688, with his heirs living in England. The tenants of the properties were 'papists ... and the [lands] became waste'. Adam Loftus, First Viscount Lisburne,[38] master of the Court of

Requests, granted their title to a Mary Sloane, who afterwards made them over to a Joseph Henry who left them, presumably, to his son Hugh. By November 1734, they were worth £500 a year.[39]

Edmund Blood sought their return, as direct descendant, through his highwayman father, of his grandfather Colonel Blood. He told Mary Blood that Hugh Henry's title to the estates should be investigated and 'if he is unwilling to show his title himself he must be compelled to discover the same by a short bill of equity'. Edmund's son-in-law [Richard] Williams 'is lately come from Dublin ... and together with your kind assistance may make the best inquiries and do whatever is requisite in the affair'.

> I beg you ... let me hear from you and know what is doing therein. Whatever expenses you are at in the affair be pleased to let me know and I shall make punctual remittances either to London or Dublin as conveniency offers.

He asked that her reply should be directed to 'Capt. Edmund Blood at Mr Henry Holland, merchant, in Albany, North America, to be forwarded by Mr Joseph Nico, merchant in London'.[40]

Despite their best efforts, the Bloods apparently never recovered their lost lands in Ireland.

After the colonel's attempted theft of the Crown Jewels in 1671, new security arrangements were immediately put in place. In 1710, Zacharias von Uffenbach, a foreign tourist visiting the Tower, described entering a 'gloomy and cramped den' that housed the regalia. After visitors had entered, the strong outer door was both bolted from inside and locked by sentries outside. He and his fellow tourists sat on wooden benches and viewed the jewels through 'a trellis of strong iron'. More than seventy years later, William Hutton was taken to a 'door in an obscure corner' of the Tower that led to a 'dismal hole resembling the cell of the condemned'.

In the nineteenth century, visitors were confronted by a rather pompous lady custodian, carrying a candle, described somewhat unkindly by an American visitor as 'an old hag' who 'presided like a high priestess over the glories' of the Crown Jewels. These security measures continued until 1840 when a new Gothic Revival Jewel House was built by the Royal Engineers, funded by visitors' admission fees to the fortress. Unfortunately the new building proved to be damp and not fireproof and it was demolished in 1870. Work on converting the Wakefield Tower to house the regalia began in 1867. Thereafter they were displayed behind a 'great cage', together with railings and barriers.[41] In 1910–11 the ironwork was replaced by a reinforced glass case. However, by the 1960s the volume of visitors had increased enormously and a new purpose-built area was opened beneath the Waterloo Barracks in 1967 and this was succeeded by the Tower's current facility in 1994.[42]

One of the few casualties of Blood's exploits was Talbot Edwards, the aged custodian of the Crown Jewels. As we have seen, he died in 1674, probably as a result of his injuries at the hands of Blood and his accomplices, and was buried in the Chapel Royal of St Peter ad Vincula,[43] the parish church of the Tower of London, situated in the inner ward.[44] The slab placed over his grave read:

Here lieth y[e] body of Talbot Edwards gent[n] late keeper of his Mat[s] Regalia who dyed y[e] 30 of September 1674 aged 80 yeares and 9 moneths

If nothing in life is uncertain, neither is anything after death.

Edwards' tombstone was ripped from his grave by the Home Secretary Sir James Graham 'with others from the Tower' in 1842 to be used to repair the latrines in the Queen's Bench prison, Southwark, after the closure of the Fleet prison. The historic inscription was recognised during this recycling work and the resultant row caused it to be returned to the Tower.[45]

Unfortunately, it was not replaced in the Chapel Royal but instead was used as a paving stone in one of the houses in front of the Beauchamp Tower. There it was found in 1852 by General William FitzGerald-de-Ros, deputy lieutenant of the Tower, who caused it to be replaced in St Peter's, mounted on its south wall.[46]

# Chronology

**1595:** Edmund Blood, founder of the Irish branch of the family, sails to Ireland as a cavalry captain in Elizabeth I's army to fight against an Irish rebellion. He resigns his commission, acquires property in Co. Clare and is elected in **1613** as one of two members of the Irish Parliament for the borough of Ennis.

**Early 1618:** Thomas Blood born at Sarney, Co. Meath, son of Thomas Blood, third son of Edmund.

**1640:** Thomas Blood junior is appointed a justice of the peace in Co. Meath.

**1641: October** Rebellion of Catholics in Ulster; the Irish Confederation becomes the *de facto* government of Ireland.

**1642: 19 March** 'Adventurers' Act' (16 Caro I, *cap.* 34–5) passed at Westminster authorising money to be raised to suppress the Irish rebellion; anyone subscribing £200 would receive 1,000 acres (404.7 hectares) of land confiscated from rebels.

**1642: 22 August** Charles I raises royal standard at Nottingham; beginning of Civil War against Parliament in England. Blood probably serves on Royalist side as a captain from **May 1643** and probably fought at the siege of Sherborne Castle in Dorset in **August 1645**.

**1648: 28 October** Blood probably a member of besieged garrison of Pontefract Castle, Yorkshire and may have been involved in the Royalists' botched attempted kidnap and death of the parliamentary commander Colonel Thomas Rainborowe at his billet in Doncaster.

**1649: 30 January** Execution of Charles I outside the Banqueting House, Whitehall.

**1649: 15 August** Cromwell lands at Dublin with 12,000 men of the New Model Army together with an extensive siege artillery train to put down the Irish Confederation rebellion.

**1649: 11 September** Drogheda captured after eight-day siege; most of the 3,000-strong garrison are slaughtered, together with a number of Catholic priests and civilians.

**1649: 11 October** Wexford captured after a nine-day siege; 2,000 defenders and around fifteen hundred civilians massacred.

**1650:** Blood switches sides in the Civil War, serving initially as a cavalry cornet and then is promoted lieutenant in the parliamentary army, probably serving briefly with Cromwell in Ireland before going to Lancashire.

**1650: 21 June** Blood marries seventeen-year-old Mary Holcroft, elder daughter of parliamentary MP and hero Lieutenant Colonel John Holcroft and his wife Margaret at Newchurch, Lancashire.

**1651: 30 March** Baptism of the Bloods' first child, Thomas, at Newchurch, Lancashire.

**1652: 12 August** Act of Settlement for Ireland passed at Westminster.

**1653: April** Last Irish Confederation troops surrender to parliamentary forces in Co. Cavan.

**1653: July** Order for the transplantation of Irish landowners to Connacht and other areas west of the River Shannon.

**1655–8:** The 'Down Survey' of Ireland ensures the most efficient redistribution of sequestered Irish lands.

**1656: 22 April** Blood's father-in-law, Lieutenant Colonel John Holcroft, is buried at Newchurch, Lancashire, leaving a flurry of legal actions over his estates.

**1658: 3 September** Death of Oliver Cromwell at Whitehall, aged fifty-nine.

**1660: 8 May** Restoration of the monarchy: Charles II enters London (on his birthday) and is crowned at Westminster Abbey on **23 April 1661**. New regalia is made for his coronation to replace that earlier sold or destroyed by the Commonwealth.

**1662: 19 May** Act of Uniformity, reinforcing Anglican rites, passed at Westminster.

**1662: 27 September** Act of Settlement passed by Irish Parliament in Dublin. Blood loses most of his property.

**1662: September** Blood conceives plan to seize control of Ireland.

**1663: 9/10 March** Original date of first attempt on Dublin Castle and coup d'état, but news of the conspiracy leaks out and the attack is postponed.

**1663: March** Formation of London council of nonconformist extremists. Plot to kill the king, the Dukes of York and Albemarle and the lord chancellor, Edward Hyde, Earl of Clarendon.

**1663: mid-April** James Butler, First Duke of Ormond, lord lieutenant of Ireland, hears of revived plan to seize Dublin Castle and take him hostage.

**1663: 21 May** Conspirators plan to seize Dublin Castle but the attack is delayed until the following week to allow further rebel troops to arrive in the city.

Troops arrest twenty-four plotters in early-morning raids in Dublin, including the government undercover informer, Philip Alden. Blood and the remainder of the conspirators flee, some to Scotland. Further arrests are made during the last week of May.

Ormond prorogues Irish Parliament until 21 July.

**1663: 23 May** Proclamation is published offering a reward of £100 for the apprehension of nine named fugitive former officers, including 'Lieutenant Thomas Blood', and two Presbyterian ministers concerned in the conspiracy.

**1663: 30 May** Ormond signs a warrant for the 'removal of certain inhabitants of Dublin for the better security of the city'.

**1663: 14 June** Seventy plotters under arrest. Blood, who has recklessly returned to Dublin to see his wife, again flees from the city and dons a variety of disguises – including that of a Catholic priest. He eludes arrest on a number of occasions while hiding in the hills and mountains of Ulster and Wicklow.

**1663:** before **18 June** Government informer Philip Alden breaks through a barred window and escapes from 'the highest turret' in Dublin Castle.

**1663: 25 June** Trial begins of Edward Warren, Richard Thompson and Alexander Jephson, MP for Trim, for high treason at the King's Bench court in Dublin. A fourth defendant, the Presbyterian minister William Leckie (Blood's Scottish brother-in-law) is also arraigned but appears insane (subsequently found to be feigned).

**1663: 1 July** Leckie convicted of high treason but proceedings halted because of his insanity.

**1663: 8 July** Warren, Thompson and Jephson convicted and sentenced to be hung, drawn and quartered.

**1663: 15 July** Thompson, Warren and Jephson are executed at Gallows Green (now Lower Baggot Street, Dublin, near the present-day bridge over the Grand Canal). After Jephson is hanged there is a 'hot alarm' – possibly a rescue attempt – and the crowd scatters in panic. Thompson blames Blood for 'drawing' him into the conspiracy.

**1663: 12 October** Planned date of uprising in north of England. The insurrection, largely organised by former parliamentary officers, is averted by pre-emptive arrests of many of the ringleaders.

**1663: 14 November** Leckie escapes from Dublin's Newgate prison disguised in his wife's clothes but is recaptured shortly afterwards and is executed on **12 December**.

**1664:** Blood flees to the Netherlands and meets the Dutch naval hero Michiel de Rutyer, returning to London in March to associate with Fifth Monarchists.

**1664: September** Blood involved in an abortive London plot to attack Charles II at the Palace of Whitehall and to seize the Tower of London.

**1664: December** Blood reported in Ireland.

**1665: May** Outbreak of bubonic plague in the capital. The Great Plague of London, which finally died away in **February 1666**, kills around 120,000 citizens, or about 15 per cent of the city's population.

**1665: October** Presbyterian factions hold a secret meeting in Liverpool to plan strategy. The Irish contingent is led by Blood and his fellow Dublin Castle plotter, Lieutenant Colonel William Moore.

**1666: February** Blood in Ireland and with Colonel 'Gibby' Carr (another former accomplice) plots to seize the city of Limerick.

Blood and his friend John Lockyer travel to the Dutch United Provinces and are arrested as spies. After his release, Blood visits the republican regicide Edmund Ludlow in Switzerland in an unsuccessful attempt to persuade him to return from exile and join a conspiracy to overthrow the government of Charles II.

He may have been a double agent, working for Sir Joseph Williamson, operational head of Charles II's secret service.

**1666: April** Charles II grants Blood's remaining property in Ireland to Captain Toby Barnes.

**1666: August** Blood involved in new Irish conspiracy.

**1666: 2–5 September** Blood in London and again escapes arrest.

Great Fire of London breaks out after a tinder-dry summer and a drought lasting from November 1665. It destroys more than 13,000 houses in the largely medieval city, together with eighty-seven parish churches and Old St Paul's Cathedral. Subsequently, Blood is (wrongly) accused of starting the fire which, after investigation, is said to have been accidental.

**1666: 28 November** Blood probably involved in the failed Pentland uprising in Scotland which is suppressed by the rout at the Battle of Rullion Green in Lothian. He escapes unharmed and crosses the border to England, living in the Warrington and Manchester areas of Lancashire.

**1667:** Blood returns to London with his family and practices as a quack doctor and apothecary under the alias 'Dr Ayliff' in Romford, Essex. His wife lives in an apothecary's shop in Shoreditch, Middlesex.

**1667: 25 July** Rescue of fellow conspirator Captain John Mason at Darrington, near Doncaster, Yorkshire, from a military escort taking him to trial at York. Blood badly wounded.

**1670:** Blood's eldest son Thomas abandons his apprenticeship as an apothecary and after fitful, unsuccessful attempts to earn a living as a grocer and mercer becomes a highwayman in Surrey. He is caught and convicted on **4 July** at Surrey assizes and is briefly incarcerated in the Marshalsea prison, Southwark.

**1670: 6 December** Attempted kidnap or murder of James Butler, First Duke of Ormond, in St James's, London as he returns from a state banquet entertaining the Prince of Orange at the Guildhall.

Blood may be acting as hired assassin of George Villiers, Second Duke of Buckingham.

**1671: 9 May** Attempted theft of the Crown Jewels from the Tower of London.

**1671: 1 August** Blood receives a full pardon for all his crimes and the grant of lands in Ireland yielding £500 a year.

He becomes a government spy in England and Holland and a private agent for those at court who need information to fulfil their ambitions.

*c.***1675:** Blood's eldest son Thomas dies in unknown circumstances, leaving a widow and an infant son who is brought up by his brother Holcroft.

**1679:** Blood may have provided bribes to suborn witnesses against George Villiers, Second Duke of Buckingham, who is accused of sodomy. Tried on charges of blasphemy, confederacy and subornation and fined and imprisoned.

Buckingham brings an action for defamation against Blood and his accomplices, claiming £10,000 in damages.

Blood contracts a fever in prison and is freed in **July 1680**.

**1680: 24 August** Blood dies at his home overlooking Bowling Alley, Westminster, aged sixty-two after an illness lasting fourteen days. He may have suffered a stroke.

**1680: 1 September** Inquest in Westminster to determine whether the body exhumed from Blood's grave is really that of Colonel Thomas Blood. The corpse is so swollen and disfigured that the twenty-three-man jury – made up of those who knew Blood – cannot reach a verdict, even though an army captain swears that the cadaver's thumb is enlarged which, he claims, was a distinguishing mark identifying Blood.

# *Dramatis Personæ*

## THOMAS BLOOD AND HIS FAMILY

**Blood, Charles.** Fifth son of *Thomas Blood* and *Mary* his wife. Around 1681, supplied intelligence to *James, Duke of York* warning him of 'most dangerous conspiracies against him' and about a conspiracy to launch an insurrection on the death of *Charles II*. Later became a barrister, defending his brother *Holcroft Blood* against accusations of assault by his estranged wife Elizabeth in October 1700.

**Blood, Edmund.** (? – *c*.1645), of Makeney, Derbyshire. Sailed to Ireland in 1595 as a cavalry captain in Elizabeth I's army fighting Irish rebels led by Hugh O'Neill. Resigned commission and acquired land in Co Clare and elected one of the two MPs for the borough of Ennis in the Irish House of Commons in April 1613. He had three sons by his first wife Margaret: *Neptune* (born 1595); *Edmund* (died 1615) and *Thomas Blood senior*. After his wife's death, he married Mary Holdcroft or Holcroft of Lancashire and by her had a fourth son, William, born in 1600. He may have married a third time.

**Blood, Edmund.** Fourth son of *Thomas Blood* and *Mary* his wife. As a witness, signed the receipt for the recovery of his eldest brother's sword, belt and pistols, dated 17 October 1670 at Lambeth. Had journeyed to the East Indies twice – possibly in the service of the East India Company. Purser on board the frigate *Jersey*. Died in London in 1679.

**Blood, Elizabeth**. Younger daughter of *Thomas Blood* and *Mary* his wife. Married Edward Everard. Signed inventory of her brother William's goods in 1688. Recipient of £50 bequest in her brother *Holcroft*'s will in 1707. No further details known.

**Blood, Holcroft.** (*c*.1657–1707) Third son of *Thomas Blood* and *Mary* his wife. Enlisted in Royal Navy in 1672 without his father's permission and served during the Third Anglo-Dutch War. Later enlisted as a cadet officer in the French Guards under the alias of 'Leture' and studied military engineering. Guardian of Edmund, the young son of his elder brother *Thomas* after the latter's death around 1675. Appointed clerk of the peace and JP in Co. Clare, April 1676. Married Elizabeth Fowler, widowed daughter of the barrister Richard King in 1686. Three years later promoted second engineer to the artillery train in the Irish wars and was wounded at the capture of Carrickfergus in Co. Antrim in August 1689; at Cashel, Co. Tipperary the following February and at the Battle of the Boyne in July 1690. Appointed second engineer of England in February 1696 and commander of artillery in the Duke of Marlborough's campaigns, including fighting at the Battle of Blenheim on 2 August 1704. Promoted brigadier general. Because of his infidelity he became estranged from his wife, who sought his prosecution for an assault on her, which was successfully defended by his barrister brother *Charles* in 1700. Died in Brussels, 19 August 1707, leaving an illegitimate son, Holcroft, of St Anne's Soho, London (died 1724) by his mistress Dorothy Cook of Dort, Holland.

**Blood, Mary** *née* Holcroft (1633–*c*.1672). Elder daughter of *Lieutenant Colonel John Holcroft* and his wife Margaret. Married *Thomas Blood* at Newchurch, Lancashire, 21 June 1650 and the couple had seven children. In 1667, lived with her eldest son *Thomas Blood* in an apothecary's shop at Shoreditch, north of London, under the alias of Weston. In 1670, stayed at the home of schoolteacher Jonathan Davies in Mortlake, Surrey, with one of her daughters but prudently disappeared the day after the assault on *Ormond*. In 1671, said to be ill in Lancashire.

**Blood, Mary**. Eldest daughter of *Thomas Blood* and *Mary* his wife. Married —Corbett. Received a £50 bequest in her brother Holcroft's will in 1707. No further details known.

**Blood, Neptune** (1595–1692). Eldest son of *Edmund Blood* and his first wife Margaret. Born during passage across St George's Channel to Ireland. Ordained minister in March 1623 and appointed dean of Kilfenora in 1663. Served with Charles I at Oxford during the first Civil War. Uncle of *Thomas Blood junior*. Married three times and was succeeded as dean by another Neptune Blood, his fourth son by his third wife.

**Blood**, **Thomas senior** (1598–1645). Third son of *Edmund Blood* (died *c*.1645) of Makeney, Derbyshire and Kilnaboy, Co. Clare, Ireland and his first wife Margaret. Born in Kilnaboy, and became an ironmaster in Sarney, Dunboyne, Co. Meath. Details of wife unknown. Two sons and at least one daughter. Died at Sarney, 1645.

**Blood**, **Colonel Thomas junior** (1618–80), aliases include Allen, Ayliff and Morton. Born at Sarney, Dunboyne, Co. Meath, probably elder son of *Thomas Blood senior*. Appointed JP in 1640 and fought against the rebels in the Irish Confederation insurrection after 1642. Fought for the Royalist side in the Civil War, probably at the sieges of Sherborne Castle, Dorset in 1645 and Pontefract Castle, Yorkshire three years later. By 1650, had changed sides, fighting for parliamentary forces in Ireland. Married *Mary Holcroft*, eldest daughter of Lieutenant Colonel John Holcroft of Lancashire, 21 June 1650, and had five sons – *Thomas*, *William*, *Holcroft*, *Edmund* and *Charles* – and two daughters, *Mary* and *Elizabeth*. Lost possession or share in 1,426 acres granted in Ireland under the 1652 Act of Settlement and, thus embittered, embarked on a long career of rebellion and violent intrigue against the government in Ireland, Scotland and England to further the Presbyterian cause. After attempting to assassinate the *Duke of Ormond* in December 1670 and to steal the Crown Jewels from the Tower of London the following year, he was pardoned and granted a pension from Irish lands. He became a government spy in England and Holland (1672) and was employed privately by some in the royal court to further their ambitions. Caught up in various popish plots after 1679 and may have provided bribes to suborn witnesses against *George Villiers, Second Duke of Buckingham*, who sued him and his accomplices for defamation, claiming £10,000 in damages. Tried on charges of blasphemy, confederacy and suborn-ation; fined and imprisoned. Caught a fever and was freed in July 1680. He died at his home overlooking Bowling Alley, Westminster, but as some thought reports of his death were just another of Blood's tricks, his body was exhumed and identified by the inordinate size of one of his thumbs.

**Blood**, **Thomas III** alias '**Thomas Hunt**' (1651–*c*.1675). Eldest son of *Thomas Blood junior* and *Mary* his wife. Born in Newchurch, Lancashire. In 1667, lived with his mother in an apothecary's shop in Shoreditch under the name 'Weston' and later that year was apprenticed to a Scots apothecary, Samuel Holmes, a former parliamentary army surgeon, in Southwark. He quit after six months' training and joined his father in Romford, Essex, assisting him in his charlatan medical practice before striking out alone, firstly as a grocer and latterly as a mercer. Heavily in debt, he became a highwayman in Surrey, under the alias 'Thomas Hunt'. Fined £67 and jailed in the Marshalsea prison, Southwark on 4 July 1670 at Surrey assizes, Guilford, for assaulting, with intent to rob, John Constable the previous May. Freed after his father found two sureties. Took part in the assault on the *Duke of Ormond* and the attempt to steal the Crown Jewels; subsequently pardoned. Married a Miss Delafaye or Delahaye and possibly had two children, of whom the eldest, *Edmund*, was brought up by his mother and uncle, *Holcroft Blood*, and later was living in Albany, capital of New York State, in 1734 as a captain in the British army.

**Blood, William**. Second son of *Thomas Blood* and *Mary* his wife. Steward on board the frigate *Jersey*. Died in the frigate *Mary* in 1688, off the coast of today's Republic of Guinea in West Africa. Left goods and chattels worth only £15.

**Holcroft, Lieutenant Colonel John** (died 1656). Member of a knightly family in Lancashire who profited from the spoils of the Reformation. MP for Liverpool, 1640; mayor of the city 1644 and MP for Wigan 1646. Excluded from Parliament in Pride's Purge in December 1648. Involved in one of the first skirmishes of the Civil War in Manchester in July 1642 and defended Lancaster for Parliament in March 1643. Married Margaret, daughter and co-heiress of John Hunt of Manchester. By her he had two sons and three daughters, one of whom died an infant. The eldest daughter *Mary* married *Thomas Blood junior*. After his death, there were a number of expensive legal actions over the ownership of properties he had acquired and the settlement of his estate.

## BLOOD'S FELLOW CONSPIRATORS

**Atkinson, John**. Former parliamentary army officer. After the restoration of the monarchy in 1660, became a stocking-weaver or 'stockinger'. Following the collapse of the 1663 northern rebellion, he fled to

Durham dressed as a labourer. In 1664, he went to London under the alias 'Dr Peter Johnson' and lived at Worcester Court on Garlick Hill in the east of the city. Described by the government spy *William Leving* as a 'little man [with] sad brown hair ... thin ... about forty years old'. He was arrested in London in September 1664 but released. He planned to escape to the Low Countries in early 1665 but was arrested and sent for trial at York assizes. His fate is unknown, but presumably he was convicted and paid the penalty for treason.

**Butler**, **Timothy**. One of the conspirators in the numerous plots against the government in London in the 1660s, acting as quartermaster and 'entrusted in the buying of arms'. One of Blood's accomplices in the release of Captain John Mason on 25 July 1667.

**Carr**, **Colonel Gilbert 'Gibby'**. Involved in a conspiracy to rescue Archibald Campbell, First Marquis of Argyll from the Tower of London. Leading plotter in the botched attempt to capture Dublin Castle in 1663 and possibly fled to Scotland after its discovery. Produced an alibi that he was in Rotterdam, in the Dutch United Provinces, at the time of the conspiracy. Involved again with Blood in plans to seize the city of Limerick in February 1666.

**Chambers**, **Robert**. Presbyterian minister who had published a treasonous pamphlet in 1660. Conspirator in the Dublin Castle plot, but evaded arrest and remained in hiding in Ireland until 1669 when his wife secured a pardon on his promise of future good behaviour, backed by a financial security.

**Charnock**, **Stephen** (1628–80). Born in parish of St Katherine Cree, London. Studied at Emmanuel College, Cambridge and fellow at New College Oxford. Minister of St Werburgh's church, Dublin 1656–60 and former chaplain to Henry Cromwell, parliamentary lord deputy in Ireland. Involved in Dublin Castle plot of 1663 and fled to London afterwards, via Chester, hiding at the home of the stationer Robert Littlebury, at the sign of the Unicorn in Little Britain. Lost his library in Great Fire of London, September 1666. Charnock began a Presbyterian co-pastorship at Crosby Hall in Bishopsgate, London in 1675; this was his last ministry before his death in 1680. He was buried in St Michael Cornhill, London.

**Halliwell**, **Captain Richard**. Fifth Monarchist tobacco-cutter of Frying

Pan Alley, Bishopsgate, London. Former parliamentary officer who served in Flanders and Virginia. Involved in the attack on *Ormond* – when he was described as a 'middle-sized man, plump faced, with [smallpox] pock holes, of a demure countenance, having a short brown periwig and sad coloured clothes, about forty years of age' – as well as the botched robbery of the Crown Jewels, when he acted as lookout. Escaped arrest. Probably the compiler 'R.H.' who wrote the contemporary biography of Thomas Blood, 'Remarks on the Life and Death of the Fam'd Mr Blood', published in London in 1680. Later took part in other conspiracies against the government of *Charles II*.

**Leckie** or **Lackey**, **William**. Fellow of Trinity College, Dublin, Presbyterian minister in Co. Meath and schoolmaster, Blood's Scottish brother-in-law and one of the main conspirators in the Dublin Castle plot. Feigned madness at his trial, escaped from the city's Newgate prison on 14 November 1663, wearing his wife's clothes, but swiftly recaptured and executed in Dublin on 12 December.

**Lee**, **Major**. One-handed former parliamentary officer who was a member of the rebel council in London that fomented a number of conspiracies against the government in the 1660s.

**Lockyer**, **John** alias **Rogers**. Fifth Monarchist. Member of London council of religious extremists formed in March 1663 by *John Atkinson*. Accompanied Blood in visit to Edmund Ludlow in Lausanne, Switzerland in March 1666. One of Blood's accomplices in the rescue of *Captain John Mason* at Darrington, Yorkshire on 25 July 1667. Later pardoned.

**Jephson**, **Colonel Alexander**. MP for Trim, Co. Meath, in Irish House of Commons. One of the conspirators in the Dublin Castle plot of 1663. Executed for treason in Dublin, 15 July 1663.

**Jones**, **Roger**. Parliamentary army captain, alias Mene Tekel from his authorship of the radical underground pamphlet *Mene Tekel, or the Downfall of Tyranny*, printed in 1663. One of the conspirators in the abortive northern rising of that year, also led the uprising in Co. Durham. After a lengthy period on the run, captured and sent for trial at York assizes, but escaped justice and later took part in other conspiracies against the government, such as the plot to assassinate Charles II at the House of Lords in 1671. Fate unknown.

**Mason, John**. Captain in parliamentary army. 'General Baptist'. One of the plotters for the Northern rising in 1663. Arrested in Newark upon Trent, Nottinghamshire on 15 November 1663. Escaped from Clifford's Tower, York in early July 1664 with fellow conspirators Robert Davies and Colonel Thomas Wogan, but recaptured in 1667. Freed on 5 July 1667 at Darrington, near Doncaster when his military escort, taking him to trial and probable execution at York assizes, was ambushed by Blood and his accomplices. Later became a coffee house owner and tavern-keeper, still involved in anti-government conspiracies, including a plot to attack the Palace of Whitehall in 1670. Refused a pardon in the government amnesty of the early 1670s.

**McCormack, Andrew**. Scots Presbyterian minister and a leading figure in the Dublin Castle plot. Fled to Scotland and fought in the Pentlands uprising of 1666, being among the fifty killed in the rout after the Battle of Rullion Green in Lothian on 28 November 1666.

**Moore, Colonel William**. Apparently the son of Sir William Moore of Scotland. In 1648, his regiment of infantry, which had been serving in Ulster for two years, joined Michael Jones's parliamentary forces to fight the Irish Confederates. Six years later Moore was involved in the transportation of the Irish to the West Indies. When his regiment was based in the Caribbean in 1657, only the threat of a court martial kept him from deserting. Left army after being garrisoned at Galway and Athlone. Involved in the Dublin Castle plot and sent to Ireland by the nonconformist council meeting secretly in London in 1665. In 1668 lived in Gray's Inn Lane, London, and may have been involved in both the assault on *Ormond* and the attempt on the Crown Jewels.

**Perrot, Robert**. Fifth Monarchist. Lieutenant in Harrison's regiment of horse in the New Model Army. Silk-dyer of Thames Street, London. Took part in the attempted theft of the Crown Jewels and regalia from the Tower of London on 9 May 1671. Sailed with Duke of Monmouth and fought as a major in the rebels' Yellow Regiment (commanded by former Guards officer Colonel Edward Matthews) at the Battle of Sedgemoor. He was wounded, captured a few weeks later hiding in the Brendon Hills in Somerset and executed at Taunton.

**Smith, William**. Fifth Monarchist. May have assisted in arranging rescue of *Captain John Mason* in July 1667 and been accomplice in attack on *Ormond* in 1670. Guardian of getaway horses in attempt to steal Crown Jewels and escaped. Refused an offer of pardon. Interrogated by *Blood* after his arrest in 1678.

**Staples**, **Major Alexander**. Born Londonderry, MP for Strabane. Although involved, said to have warned of the plot to seize Dublin Castle and was eventually pardoned, despite *Charles II*'s misgivings about granting him mercy.

**Tanner**, **James**. Born Dublin, formerly a clerk to the secretary of Henry Cromwell, Parliament's lord deputy of Ireland. Involved in Dublin Castle plot of May 1663 but turned king's evidence.

**Thompson**, **Lieutenant Richard**. Deputy provost-marshal for Leinster. Involved in Dublin Castle plot. Confessed and sentence commuted to simple hanging, rather than hanging drawing and quartering. Executed Dublin 15 July 1663, blaming *Blood* for drawing him into the plot.

**Warren**, **Colonel Edward**. Former parliamentary army officer, involved in Dublin Castle plot of May 1663. Executed Dublin, 15 July 1663.

## GOVERNMENT SPIES AND INFORMERS

**Alden**, **Philip**. Shady lawyer, dealer in forfeited Irish estates and agent of former parliamentary general Edmund Ludlow. Became government agent under the control of Colonel Edward Vernon. Exposed the Dublin plot of 1663; arrested with the conspirators to preserve his cover but escaped from the prison inside the castle. Moved to England where he spied on the radicals before they began to suspect his allegiance in 1666. Retired to Ireland, granted a pardon and a £100 a year pension, only fitfully paid by the Treasury.

**Betson**, **John**. Associate of *William Leving* who complained about the levels of his remuneration while on the trail of *Captain John Mason*.

**Freer** or **Fryer**, **William**. Associate of *William Leving* and accompanied him to Ireland in 1666. To earn money, resorted to highway robbery in Leicestershire and Yorkshire.

**Grice**, **Captain John**. Spied for Sir Arthur Heselrige, parliamentary governor of Newcastle during Civil War when serving as a cavalry cornet. Then spied for Williamson in England and Ireland amongst the radical

Presbyterian and Fifth Monarchist communities. Died, in mysterious circumstances, in 1667.

**Harrison, John**. Tobacconist. Provided information about a conspiracy to assassinate Charles II and the Duke of York 'as they go abroad by water' (?on the Thames). *Blood* passed on the intelligence and promised him £50 reward but he was left empty-handed.

**Leving, William** alias **Leonard Williams**. Born in Durham. Junior officer in Sir Arthur Heselrige's cavalry regiment during the Civil War but dismissed for his support for Colonel John Lambert's attempts to resist parliamentary control of the army. Leving was imprisoned in York Castle after taking part in the abortive Durham rebellion of 1663 and became a government spy in England and for a short period in Ireland. Involved in investigation into *Buckingham*'s alleged treasonable activities in 1667. Resorted to highway robbery in Leicestershire and Yorkshire in May 1665 and early 1667. Lost most of his family in London in the Great Plague of 1665–6. Found dead in York Castle in early August 1667, having been poisoned, possibly by agents of *Buckingham*. Buried in York.

**North, Henry**. Spy for *Duke of Buckingham* and associate of *William Leving* with *William Freer*. Informed against *Leving* to Blood's gang in London. Arrested during investigation into *Buckingham*'s alleged treasonable activities in 1667. Executed in 1677 for highway robbery near Sleaford, Lincolnshire. Tried to expose a conspiracy probably concerning his old master *Buckingham* but was executed before he was able to disclose the full details.

**Wilkinson, Richard**. Revealed plot to assassinate *Charles II* in House of Lords in 1670. Instead of his expected pardon and reward, he was thrown into prison at Appleby, Westmorland. His brother was involved in the 1663 northern uprising in England.

## FREELANCE SPIES

**Beckman** or **Börkman, Captain Martin**. Swedish military engineer and hydrographer employed by the English crown in the Civil War from 1645. He was injured in an explosion while preparing fireworks to mark *Charles II*'s coronation in April 1661, receiving £100 compensation. In

June 1661, Beckman accompanied the Earl of Sandwich's expedition to Tangier on the north African coast and became chief military engineer to the English garrison. In October 1663 he offered to spy for Philip IV of Spain and then tried to pass on intelligence about Spanish plans to the English consul in Cadiz. Imprisoned in the Tower of London for six months from late 1663. On release, he joined the Swedish army but returned to England in 1667 and was appointed engineer to the ordnance on 19 October 1670. Beckman lived in the Tower and joined in the hue and cry after Blood ran off with the royal regalia in May 1671, receiving a £100 reward 'for resisting that late villainous attempt made to steal the crown'. He married Elizabeth, daughter of Talbot Edwards, the deputy keeper of regalia, and in 1677 was appointed chief engineer of 'all his Majesty's castles, forts, blockhouses and other fortifications', the year Elizabeth died. Knighted 20 March 1686 and naturalised 7 November 1691. Beckman married a widow, Ruth Mudd, of Stepney, Middlesex, on 31 August 1693 and died 24 June 1702 at the Tower of London.

## ROYALTY

**Charles II** (1630–85). King of England, Scotland and Ireland. Eldest son of Charles I, deposed by Parliament and executed outside his Banqueting House in Whitehall on 30 January 1649. Left England in 1646 for exile in France and The Hague in the Netherlands. After the death of Cromwell, the monarchy was restored and he was crowned Charles II on 23 April 1661 in Westminster Abbey. Married the Portuguese princess Catherine of Braganza on 21 May 1662 in two ceremonies in Portsmouth. As she was a Catholic, the first was according to Roman rites and held in secret, but the second was a public Anglican service. She was unable to provide an heir and had to suffer a licentious husband who fathered an acknowledged fourteen illegitimate children, some by the queen's lady of the bedchamber, *Barbara Palmer, Duchess of Cleveland*. Charles suffered an apoplectic fit and died four days later, probably from uraemia, at the Palace of Whitehall, having been received into the Catholic Church the previous evening.

**James II of England and VII of Scotland** (1633–1701). Second surviving son of Charles I. Created Duke of York January 1644. After the

Restoration, placed in charge of fire-fighting operations during the Great Fire of London in September 1666. Converted to Catholicism in 1668/9 although he still attended Anglican services until 1676. On death of his elder brother *Charles II*, he was crowned king on 23 April 1685. Faced a number of rebellions but in June 1688 the Protestant William, Prince of Orange, was invited to invade England. He landed on 5 November and on 11 December James fled, reputedly throwing the Great Seal of England into the River Thames. He landed in Ireland in 1689 with a small army, assisted by French troops, but was defeated by William III at the Battle of the Boyne on 1 July 1690. He died of a haemorrhage at the Château de Saint-German-en-laye in the Île de France, now in the western suburbs of Paris, on 16 September 1701.

**James Scott, First Duke of Monmouth and First Duke of Buccleuch** (1649–85). Illegitimate son of *Charles II* and his mistress Lucy Walter. Fought in Second and Third Dutch wars. Exiled after claims that he was implicated in the Rye House plots. In 1685 led a rebellion to depose his Catholic uncle *James II* but was defeated at the Battle of Sedgemoor, in Somerset, on 6 July 1685 – the last pitched battle to be fought on English soil. Beheaded for treason by five blows of the headsman's axe on Tower Hill on 15 July 1688.

## THE ROYAL COURT

**Palmer, Barbara, First Duchess of Cleveland** (1640–1709). Married Roger Palmer, First Earl of Castlemaine but separated in 1662 after the birth of their first son. From 1660, mistress of *Charles II* who acknowledged his responsibility for five children by her, some born while she was lady of the bedchamber to the queen, Catherine of Braganza, after 1662. Converted to Catholicism in 1663. Ambitious, ruthless intriguer at court who was far from averse to meddling in politics. Cousin of *George Villiers, Second Duke of Buckingham*. As a result of the 1673 Test Act, which effectively banned Catholics from public office, she lost her position as lady of the bedchamber and Charles dropped her as his favourite mistress, taking Louise de Kéroualle as her successor. In 1705 her husband died and she married Major General Robert Fielding, whom she later prosecuted for bigamy.

**Villiers, George, Second Duke of Buckingham** (1628–87). Son of First
Duke of Buckingham, favourite of James I and Charles I, who was assassinated by stabbing in a Portsmouth tavern in August 1628 when
his son was just seven months old. After Restoration, Buckingham was
effectively debarred from reaching high office by the lord chancellor
and chief minister, *Edward Hyde, First Earl of Clarendon,* who despised
him as a schemer and conspirator. Always with ties to the radical nonconformist movement and associating with known rebels, the duke was
accused of treasonable intrigues in 1667 and of casting the king's horo-
scope – predicting the monarch's death had been treason since Tudor
times. His arrest was ordered on 26 February, but he evaded capture
until surrendering on 27 June and was sent to the Tower. Buckingham
was free by 19 July and restored to favour. However, his affair with
the Countess of Shrewsbury led to a duel with her husband in January
1668 in which the Earl of Shrewsbury was fatally wounded. The comfortable installation of the widow in his own house caused great public
offence. In January 1674 Buckingham was attacked in Parliament. The
Lords complained that Buckingham continued his affair with the countess and that their son had been buried in Westminster Abbey under
the title of Earl of Coventry. The duke and his mistress were forced to
apologise and offer sureties totalling £10,000 not to continue to co-
habit. In the Commons, he came under fire as the promoter both of a
French alliance and of popery in England and the House petitioned the
king to remove Buckingham not only from his presence but from royal
employment for ever. Charles promptly agreed. After the accession of
*James II,* the old intriguer returned briefly to public life, but because
of ill-health and his financial troubles, retired to his small estate at
Helmsley, Yorkshire. He lived there quietly for eighteen months and
died on 16 April 1687, supposedly from a chill caught while out hunting, at the home of one of his tenants in Kirkbymoorside.

## CHARLES II'S GOVERNMENT

**Bennet, Henry, First Earl of Arlington** (1618–85). Second son of Sir
John Bennet, of Harlington, Middlesex. Fought in Civil War as a Royalist volunteer in a skirmish at Andover, Hampshire in 1644. In exile,

appointed secretary to James, Duke of York, and later served in a diplomatic post in Madrid. Returned to London in April 1661 and appointed keeper of the king's privy purse. Replaced Sir Edward Nicholas as secretary of state in October 1662 and was appointed postmaster general, 1666–77. Created First Earl of Arlington, 14 March 1665. Rival to *George Villiers, Second Duke of Buckingham*. Sold his secretaryship to Sir Joseph Williamson for £6,000 in September 1674 and became lord chamberlain of the royal household. He hid his Catholic beliefs during his lifetime, only calling for a priest on his deathbed while stipulating that his conversion should be kept secret until after his death.

**Hyde, Edward, First Earl of Clarendon** (1608–74). Appointed chancellor of the Exchequer by Charles I in 1645 and guardian to the Prince of Wales (later *Charles II*), accompanying him when he fled to the Channel Island of Jersey in 1646. While in exile, appointed lord chancellor in 1658 and negotiated with Presbyterians in England who supported the return of Charles as king. Hyde played a major role in the creation in the 'Declaration of Breda' in 1660 – the manifesto for the restoration of the monarchy. On the restoration, appointed first lord of the Treasury and continued as lord chancellor, in practice, the chief minister of Charles II's government. His daughter Anne married *James, Duke of York*. Created First Earl of Clarendon, 1661. In late 1660s, fell out of royal favour after the disasters of the Second Anglo-Dutch War of 1665–7. Due to the enmity and machinations of *Buckingham* and Charles's mistress, *Barbara, Duchess of Cleveland*, dismissed from office in 1667 and fled to France. Died, Rouen in Upper Normandy, 9 December 1674. His body was later taken to England and buried in a private ceremony in Westminster Abbey.

**Osborne, Thomas, First Earl of Danby** (1631–1712). Ally of *Buckingham* in his attacks on *Clarendon* in 1667. Joint treasurer of the navy with Sir Thomas Lyttleton in 1668 and later sole treasurer. Appointed lord treasurer of England in June 1673 and created First Earl of Danby in 1674. Notorious for his detestation of all things Catholic and his opposition to any kind of religious toleration. His political enemy, Anthony Ashley-Cooper, First Earl of Shaftesbury, did not mince his words in his verdict on Danby, calling him an 'inveterate liar, proud, ambitious, revengeful, false, prodigal and covetous to the highest degree'.

Impeached by Parliament for his corruption and embezzlement in the Treasury, assuming royal powers in matters of peace and war and concealing Titus Oates's 'Popish Plot' and spent nearly five years in the Tower of London. While there, probably instigated the plot to cause the downfall of his political rival *Buckingham*. In June 1688 one of the Protestant lords who signed the invitation to the Protestant William of Orange to invade England and claim the crown. Created Marquis of Carmarthen, April 1689. Impeached unsuccessfully in 1695 for accepting a bribe of more than £5,000 to procure a new charter for the East India Company. Died at Easton Neston, Northamptonshire on 26 July 1712.

**Williamson, Sir Joseph** (1633–1701). Son of an impoverished Anglican clergyman, the vicar of Bridekirk, near Cockermouth, Cumberland. In December 1661 appointed keeper of the king's library at the Palace of Whitehall and the State Paper Office and became secretary of state, together with *Bennet* in 1662. His responsibilities included leading the intelligence-gathering activity of *Charles II*'s government, together with interception of the mail at the General Post Office. Appointed clerk to the Privy Council in January 1672 and knighted. Dismissed as secretary of state in 1679 after ordering a search of Catherine of Braganza's official residence at Somerset House in the Strand, London, without the king's permission. Died at Cobham, Kent on 3 October 1701, aged sixty-eight.

## THE GOVERNMENT AND JUDICIARY OF IRELAND

**Aungier, Francis,** later **First Earl of Longford** (*c.*1632–1700). Grandson of a Master of the Rolls in Ireland. Governor of West Meath and Longford, 1661 and Carrickfergus, 1678–84. Vice-treasurer of Ireland, 1670–78. Master of Ordnance 1679–84. Irish Privy Council 1660–87. MP for Surrey, 1660 and for Arundel, Sussex, 1661. Created viscount 1675 and Earl of Longford 1677.

**Barry, Sir James, First Baron Santry** (1603–73). Lord chief justice of the court of King's Bench. Eldest of three sons of Alderman Richard Barry, mayor of Dublin and later MP three times for the city. Appointed recorder of Dublin, sergeant-at-law, second baron of the Exchequer and in November 1660, lord chief justice. Knighted 1634 and created Baron Santry on 18 February 1661.

**Boyle, Sir Roger, First Earl of Orrery** (1621–79). President of the province of Munster from 1660 until the post was abolished in 1672. Governor of Co. Clare, 1661–72. Knighted 1 April 1628. Created Baron Broghill in February 1628 and Earl of Orrery, September 1660. MP for Arundel, Sussex, 1660 and 1661. *Arlington* thought him 'a deceitful and vain man who loved to appear in business [but] dealt so much underhand that he had not much credit with any side'. *Ormond* found his 'vanity, ostentation and itch to popularity' very irksome, together with his 'peevish, malicious jealousy'.

Orrery was manifestly a dangerous opponent and, in alliance with *Buckingham*, he secured *Ormond*'s dismissal as lord lieutenant of Ireland in 1669. He died of gout in October 1679 and was buried at Youghal, Co. Cork.

**Butler, James, First Duke of Ormond** (1610–88). Eldest son of Thomas Butler, Viscount Thurles, a member of the major Anglo-Norman settler families in Ireland. Fought the Irish Confederation rebels and negotiated a ceasefire in September 1643. Lord lieutenant of Ireland 1644–49; routed by parliamentary forces at Battle of Rathmines, near Dublin, 2 August 1649. Exiled in Europe from 1650 but after the Restoration reappointed lord lieutenant of Ireland in February 1662–9 and again 1677–85. Died at Kingston Lacey, Dorset, aged seventy-seven, leaving debts estimated at between £100,000 and £150,000.

**Clarges, Sir Thomas** (?1618–95). Member of Irish Privy Council from 1663 but predominantly an English parliamentarian. Son of John Clarges, a farrier of Drury Lane, Westminster. Apprenticed to an Oxford apothecary and served in that capacity with the Royalist army during the Civil Wars. MP for Westminster (1660), Southwark (by-election 1666), Christchurch (1679) and University of Oxford (1689). Knighted: 8 May 1660.

Gilbert Burnet, later Bishop of Salisbury, said Clarges was 'an honest but haughty man who valued himself on his frugality in managing the public money ... After he was become very rich, he seemed to take care that nobody else should grow as rich as he was.' Clarges died of apoplexy on 4 October 1695, leaving property in four counties and in

St James's and Westminster: Clarges Street in Mayfair is named after him.

**Domville, Sir William** (1609–89). Of Leighlinstown, Co. Dublin. Knighted and appointed attorney general for Ireland at the Restoration of the monarchy in 1660, a post held until 1686. MP for Dublin City in the Irish House of Commons.

**Lane, Sir George** (*c.*1620–1683). Secretary of state for Ireland 1665–78. MP for Roscommon in the Irish House of Commons 1662–6; sworn a member of the Irish Privy Council November 1664. Created Viscount Lanesborough in the Irish peerage 31 July 1676.

**Temple, Sir John** (1632–1705). Solicitor general for Ireland from 10 July 1660. Second son of Sir John Temple, Master of the Rolls in Ireland. MP for Carlow in the Irish House of Commons in 1661. Knighted 15 August 1663. Appointed attorney general for Ireland, 1690.

# *Notes*

## PROLOGUE

1    Vol. 2, p.818. This was the first 'who was who' of major figures in British history, published by Andrew Kippis in six volumes between 1747 and 1766. As an indication of Blood's enduring notoriety, his biography takes up nine pages, sandwiched between those of Admiral Robert Blake, the Cromwellian founder of British naval supremacy, and 'the very ancient, once noble and still truly honourable' family of Blount.

2    TNA, SP 44/34/110, f.111.

3    Blood was thus described in the *London Gazette*, issue no. 572, 8–11 May 1671, p.2, col.2.

4    'Adam the Leper' was the leader of a gang of robbers in the 1330s–40s who specialised in stealing the property of members of the royal court and their retainers, mainly in towns in south-east England. Adam and his gang besieged the London home of a merchant who was safeguarding the queen's jewels. When he refused to hand them over, the house was set ablaze and the jewels were seized. See: William Donaldson, *Rogues, Villains and Eccentrics* (London, 2005), pp.6–7 and Luke Owen Price, *A History of Crime in England, illustrating the Changes in Laws in the Progress of Civilisation* (2 vols., London, 1873–6), vol. 1, p.245. Adam died in the 1360s.

5    Edward I was away fighting the Scots when the burglary occurred. See: Dean Stanley's *Historical Memorials of Westminster Abbey*, 3rd ed. (London, 1869), pp.428–30. English monarchs had stored their treasure in the Chapel of the Pyx from a few years after the Norman Conquest in 1066. The name 'Pyx' comes from the wooden chests stored there, which held randomly chosen samples of the coinage of

the realm. These are still tested for metal content (and thus value) annually in a ceremony presided over by an official with the impressive title of 'Queen's Remembrancer of the Royal Courts of Justice'. This was undertaken in the Palace of Westminster, but in 1870 the ceremony was transferred to the Goldsmiths' Hall in the City of London and continues there today.

6    Richard of Pudlicott or 'Dick Pudlicote' was a wool merchant who, having fallen on hard times, decided to undertake a little grand larceny to better his lifestyle. His haul from Edward's wardrobe treasury was valued at £100,000 or £73,350,000 in today's monetary values. He was executed in 1305. See: Paul Doherty, *The Great Crown Jewel Robbery of 1303: The Extraordinary Story of the First Big Bank Raid in History* (London, 2005) and T. F. Tout, *A Medieval Burglary* (Manchester, 1916), pp.13–5. Sadly for the more bloodthirsty amongst us, expert analysis in 2005 found the skin on the wooden door to be cow hide. The door is probably the oldest surviving one in Britain – dating from the 1050s.

7    Bod. Lib. Rawlinson MS A. 185, ff.473*v*–474*r*.

8    Montgomery-Massingberd (ed.), *Burke's Irish Family Records*, p.142. Duffield is five miles (8 km) from Derby. England's first smelt mill to extract lead from its galena ore was established at Makeney in 1554 by the German mining engineer Burchard Kranich and in 1581 Sir John Zouch, of nearby Codnor Castle, built a wire-drawing works there. Perhaps Edmund Blood decided to escape the noise and smells of early industrialisation and seek pastures new? See: Brian Cooper, *Transformation of a Valley: The Derbyshire Derwent* (London, 1983).

9    More than 18,000 English troops fought against the Irish rebels – the largest military operation on land conducted during Elizabeth's reign. (The English expeditionary force assisting the Dutch rebels against Spain in the Low Countries under the Treaty of Nonsuch of August 1585 was never more than 12,000-strong.) Like other Irish rebellions, this one failed to oust the English from Ireland.

10    The confusingly named Murrough McMurrough O'Brien (1562–97), fourth baron Inchiquin, was a member of one of the oldest families in the Irish peerage. In 1597, during a skirmish, he was shot

under the arm while fording the River Erne near Sligo. He fell off his horse and, encumbered by his armour, drowned. Inchiquin was buried in Donegal Abbey. His two-year-old son Dermot succeeded to the title.

11 Kilnaboy Castle was destroyed in 1641 by Cromwellian forces. The site is off the R476 Kilfenora–Ballyvaughan road, north of Inchiquin Lough.

12 Burke, *Genealogical and Heraldic History of the Landed Gentry of Ireland*, p.56.

13 NAI, MS 12,816, f.29. Catholic resentment at this gerrymandering spilled over when the new Parliament first met on 18 May 1613, resulting in an unseemly brawl in the Commons chamber in Dublin Castle. As a result of these protests, some constituencies were scrapped, leaving a Protestant majority of only six seats.

14 The arms of Blood are: *Or, 3 bucks couchant vulned with arrows proper*, with the crest *A buck's head erased with an arrow in its mouth*.

15 NAI, MS 12,816, f.32 includes a family tree, dated 1879, that adds a fourth brother, Robert, with the comment: 'supposed to have settled at Tamworth [Staffordshire]. Buried there 16 September 1646. The Bloods of Birmingham claimed descent from this Robert Blood.' However, there is no other mention of Robert Blood in this MS but he appears in another family tree in NAI, MS 451, f.11.

16 NAI MS 451, f.11; MS 12,816 f.18. Mary Holcroft was supposedly related to the Hyde family of Norbury, Cheshire, from whom descended Sir Edward Hyde, First Earl of Clarendon, lord chancellor to Charles II. Her relationship to the Holcroft family into which Thomas Blood married is uncertain.

17 NAI, MS 12,816, f.7.

18 *CSP Domestic 1671–2*, pp.372–3.

19 Hanrahan, *Colonel Blood . . .*, p.2.

20 The chalice at Kilfenora has this inscription engraved upon it: '*Calix Ecclesia Cathedralis Fineboensis empt[or] expensa diocensis valet £4 15s 3d Neptuna Blood decano Anno Domini 1665*' – 'This chalice from St Fin Barr's Cathedral was purchased for £4 15s 3d by Neptune Blood, dean, 1665'. See: NAI MS 12,816, f.30. Neptune married three times and died in 1692, three years short of his 100th birthday. He

was succeeded as dean of Kilfenora by his fourth son by his third wife, another Neptune. His brothers and sisters, with ages ranging from five to sixteen, are commemorated by a large tablet with a long Latin inscription on the north wall of the cathedral. See: *Jnl of the Royal Society of Antiquaries of Ireland*, vol. 30 (1900), p.396.

21   NAI, MS 12,816, f.35.

22   Marshall, 'Colonel Thomas Blood' in *ODNB*, vol. 6, p.270. Other authorities suggest Blood was born ten years later, e.g. Montgomery-Massingberd (ed.), *Burke's Irish Family Records*, p.142, but this seems unlikely.

23   'Remarks . . .', p.219.

24   NAI, MS 12,816, f.21. A survey in 1654–6 indicated that Thomas Blood, 'Protestant', had held 220 acres (89 hectares) of land in Sarney since at least 1640. Robert Simington (ed.), *Civil Survey 1654–6; County of Meath*, vol. 5, p.126.

25   *Civil Survey 1654–6; County of Meath*, vol. 5, p.129; NAI, MS 12,816, f.35.

26   *CSP Ireland* 1666–9, p.88. NAI, MS 12,816, f.20 in an account dated 1791 also records 120 acres (48.5 hectares) in 'Seatown and Bea-town' and 103 acres (41.3 hectares) in Westfieldstown, East Fingal. Glenmalure is a remote wooded valley in the Wicklow Mountains, with the River Avonbeg running through. It was the site of a battle on 25 August 1580 when an English force under Arthur Grey, Fourteenth Baron Grey of Wilton, was routed as they advanced to capture Balinacor, the stronghold of the rebel chieftain Fiach McHugh O'Byrne. See: Richard Brooks, *Cassell's Battlefield of Britain and Ireland* (London, 2005), p.331–2.

27   NAI, MS 12,816, f.35.

28   The Irish Confederation rebellion is also known as the 'Eleven Years War'.

29   Frost, *History and Topography of the County of Clare*, pp.369–70.

30   Tibbutt (ed.), *Life and Letters of Sir Lewis Dyve 1599–1669*, p.148. A Captain Blood was reported as serving in 'the old King's army under Sir Lewis Dyves' in 1671 (BL Add. MS. 36,916 f.233) and a 'Capt Bludd' was noted as quartermaster in his regiment in the indigent officers' list of 1663 (Anon., *A List of Officers Claiming to the Sixty*

*Thousand Pounds Granted by his Sacred Majesty . . .*, p.39). However, Blood is absent in the published regimental lists of both the Royalist and parliamentary armies in 1642, so he must have rallied to the king's colours after this date. See: Peacock (ed.), *The Army Lists of the Roundheads and Cavaliers*.

31 Blood's name does not appear in the brief account of the Sherborne siege by a parliamentary author. John Rylands Library, Manchester, Tatton Park MS 68.20, f.210.

32 'Remarks . . .', p.220.

33 Also spelt 'Rainsborough'.

34 Paulden and Col. Morrison, wearing disguises, had gained entry to the fortress by fooling the parliamentary sentries and snatched control of Pontefract Castle on 3 June 1648.

35 Bod. Lib. Clarendon MS 34, f.27*v*. 'R.H.' in his account of Blood's life, maintained that Rainborowe had been 'pistolled [shot] in his chamber'. See 'Remarks . . .', p.220. Rainborowe's fellows in the Leveller faction (which advocated religious tolerance, extended suffrage and equality under the law) claimed that he had been assassinated on Cromwell's orders. A subsequent investigation produced no evidence to support this allegation. Three thousand people took part in his funeral procession through the streets of the City of London before Rainborowe was buried at Wapping. Subsequent street pamphlets, such as *Colonell Rainborowe's Ghost*, vociferously demanded revenge to be inflicted upon the royalists.

36 The defeat at the Battle of Preston quashed any lingering hopes of a Royalist victory. Pontefract, the last cavalier stronghold, hung on grimly. After Charles I was executed, his son was proclaimed king within the besieged castle. This is the origin of Pontefract's motto, *Post mortem patris pro filio* – 'After the death of the father, support the son'. The 100 survivors of the garrison finally surrendered on 25 March 1649 and the castle was slighted.

37 'Remarks . . .', p.220. Blood's entry in Andrew Kippis' *Biographia Britannica* (vol. 2, p.817), written seven decades after his death, implies his involvement in the Rainborowe attempted kidnapping by pointing out that 'he was in England' in 1648 when the colonel 'was surprised and killed at Pontefract' [*sic*].

38  Sergeant, _Rogues and Scoundrels_, p.111.

39  _CSP Domestic 1671–2_, p.373; RCHM _Sixth Report_, p.370.

40  John Rylands Library, Manchester, Tatton Park MS 68.20, f.210.

41  Kippis, _Biographia Britannia_, vol. 2, p.817. For more information on those who switched allegiance, see Andrew Hopper's _Turncoats and Renegadoes: Changing Sides during the English Civil War_ (Oxford, 2012). A cornet is the most junior commissioned rank in a cavalry regiment.

42  Cromwell remains a figure of intense odium in Ireland because of the sheer brutality of this campaign. Irish Catholic Confederate battlefield casualties probably totalled almost 20,000. After the fall of Drogheda, Cromwell commented: 'I am persuaded that this is a righteous judgment of God upon these barbarous wretches, who have imbrued their hands in so much innocent blood and that it will tend to prevent the effusion of blood for the future, which are satisfactory grounds for such actions, which otherwise cannot but work remorse and regret.' In total, around 200,000 civilians died in the famine and in a bubonic plague pandemic that followed the fighting – although some authorities estimate that Ireland's then population of 1.6 million was reduced by as much as half a million. In addition, 50,000 Irish were forcibly deported to the West Indies as indentured labourers. See: Sean O'Callaghan: _To Hell or Barbados: The Ethnic Cleansing of Ireland_ (Dingle, Co. Kerry, 2000), p.85. The last Irish and Royalist troops surrendered in Co. Cavan in 1653.

43  W. Johnson-Kaye & E. W. Wittenburg-Kaye (eds.), _Register of Newchurch in the Parish of Culcheth: Christenings, Weddings and Burials_, p.217.

44  Off Holcroft Lane, Culcheth, Warrington, Lancashire. National Grid Reference: SJ 67979 95162. Postcode: WA3 4ND. Holcroft's wife was the daughter of John Hunt of Lymehurst and his wife Margaret: BL Harley MS 2,161, f.158.

45  Hanrahan, _Colonel Blood_ . . ., p.14.

46  An action for recovery of £200 debt was brought in 1367 in the Chancery Court against Thomas, son of John de Holcroft of Lancashire, by his creditor, Henry de Tildeslegh of Ditton [Widnes]. See: TNA, C/241/147/39; 17 February 1367.

47  *VCH Lancs*, vol. 4, fn. p.161.

48  Manchester Archives MS L89/1/23/1.

49  Douglas Brunton and D. H. Pennington, *Members of the Long Parliament* (London, 1954), p.234, and Browne Willis, *Notitia Parliamentaria: Part II – A Series of Lists of the Representatives in the Several Parliaments held from the Reformation 1541 to the Restoration 1660*, pp.229–39. Dissident troops under the command of Colonel Thomas Pride had forcibly removed opponents to their political aims. Some forty-five were imprisoned for a time, initially in a nearby tavern called 'Hell'. It is difficult to determine how many MPs were prevented from sitting: there were 471 active members before the events of 6 December and 200 afterwards. Some eighty-six had absented themselves voluntarily and a further eighty-three were allowed back. The way had been cleared for Parliament to establish a Republic and to try the king for treason. Holcroft's name does not appear on the list of those excluded but neither does it appear in the HoC *Jnl* reports of the proceedings of the Rump Parliament.

50  *Lancashire Civil War Tracts*, pp.32–3; Lancashire Record Office MS DDX 2670/1.

51  *Lancashire Civil War Tracts*, p.85.

52  W. Johnson-Kaye & E. W. Wittenburg-Kaye (eds.), *Register of Newchurch in the Parish of Culcheth: Christenings, Weddings and Burials*, p.15.

53  Montgomery-Massingberd, *Irish Family Records*, p.142.

54  Kippis, *Biographia Britannia*, p.817.

55  'Remarks . . .', pp.219–20.

56  Sergeant, *Rogues and Scoundrels*, p.112.

## CHAPTER I: CAPTURE THE CASTLE

1  TNA, SP 63/313/168, f.346.

2  The Commonwealth Parliament was perennially short of money to pay its troops. In 1646, it resolved to sell the gilded bronze effigy of Henry VIII that lay on top of the black marble sarcophagus marking his grave in St George's Chapel, Windsor. Around £600 for the statue was paid to 'Colonel [Christopher] Whichcot, governor of

Windsor Castle, to be by him employed for the pay of that garrison'. (In one of those delicious ironies of history, Henry had filched the sarcophagus from the unfinished tomb of Cardinal Thomas Wolsey after his downfall in 1529 and the tomb-chest was recycled in 1808 for the huge monument to Nelson in St Paul's Cathedral, where it remains today.) See Robert Hutchinson, *Last Days of Henry VIII* (London, 2005), pp.268–70.

3 See C. H. Firth and R. S. Rait, *Acts and Ordinances of the Interregnum 1642–60*, vol. 2, pp.598–603 (3 vols. London, 1911), for more information on this draconian legislation and pp.722–53 for the subsequent Act of Satisfaction. Under the so-called Adventurers' Act, passed 19 March 1642, funds for the suppression of the Irish rebellion could be solicited from speculators. Anyone who invested £200 would receive 1,000 acres (404.7 hectares) of property confiscated from rebel landowners – or four shillings (twenty pence in modern English money), an acre. Cromwell subscribed £600.

4 John Scott, an English traveller in the West Indies during the Commonwealth period, saw Irish labourers working in gangs in the fields, alongside black slaves 'without stockings under the scorching sun'. He reported that the Irish were derided by 'the negroes and branded with the epithet "white slaves"' (TNA, CO 1/21, 1667, no.170). See: Hilary Beckles, 'A "riotous and unruly lot": Irish indentured servants and Freemen in the English West Indies, 1644–1713', *William and Mary Quarterly*, vol. 47 (1990) pp.503–22. Irish traditions and heritage survive in the Caribbean – St Patrick's Day is still celebrated as a national holiday in Montserrat, the only nation to do so outside Ireland.

5 A star fort known as 'Cromwell's Barracks', dating from this period, defends the harbour of Inishbofin.

6 Sir William Petty (1623–87), who had leave of absence from his position as professor of anatomy at Brasenose College, Oxford, was paid £18,532 for his pains, but had to accept 30,000 acres near Kenmare, Co. Kerry, in lieu of the last £3,181 of his fee as, inevitably, Parliament's treasury was bare.

7 For full details of Blood's holdings after the Down Survey and

previous landowners, see the Trinity College, Dublin, website: http://downsurvey.tcd.ie/landowners.

8   Irish House of Commons 14 & 15 Car 2 *cap.*2.

9   See: Wilson, 'Ireland under Charles II', p.79.

10  The commissioners appointed were: Sir Richard Rainsford, Sir Thomas Beverley, Sir Edward Dering, Sir Edward Smith, Sir Allan Broderick, Winston Churchill and Colonel Edward Cooke, 'all men of good parts, learned in the law and clear in their reputation for virtue and integrity', Carte, *Life of . . . Ormond*, vol. 4, book 6, p.123.

11  Sergeant, *Rogues and Scoundrels*, p.114 and Greaves, *God's Other Children*, p.21. Leckie is described in a number of sources as Blood's 'brother-in-law', but we have no firm record of Blood having had a sister.

12  Abbott, *Colonel Thomas Blood . . .*, p.42.

13  Lancashire Record Office MS, DDX 2670/1.

14  TNA, E 134/1652/Mich2. Pursfurlong had been purchased by Sir John Holcroft in 1549 and it was sold in 1605 to Ralph Calveley but later reverted to the Holcrofts. See: *VCH Lancs.*, vol. 4, pp.159–60.

15  Lancashire Record Office DP 397/25/4, f.4.

16  Lancashire Record Office QSP/147/3.

17  TNA, E 134/12Chas2/Mich6.

18  TNA, E 134/13Chas2/East21 and E 134/13/Chas2/Trin6.

19  13 & 14 Car 2 *cap.* 4.

20  TNA, SP 63/313/230, f.465; 13 June 1663.

21  Greaves, *Deliver Us from Evil*, p.159.

22  *CSP Ireland 1663–65*, pp. 22–7.

23  Carte, *Life of . . . Ormond*, vol. 4, book 6, p.129.

24  *CSP Ireland 1663–65*, p.31. The king to the commissioners, Whitehall, 28 February 1663.

25  *CSP Ireland 1663–5*, p.31. Ormond to the king, Dublin Castle, 7 February 1663.

26  Bod. Lib. Carte MS 44, ff.708–9, with a fuller version in Carte MS 64, ff.392v–339v.

27  Greaves, *Deliver Us from Evil*, pp.140–41. Ludlow had been appointed lieutenant general of horse during Parliament's war against the Irish Confederation. After Henry Ireton died in November 1651,

he became commander in chief. During the bitter counter-insurgency campaign of 1651–2, Ludlow complained of his operations in the ninety-seven square miles (250 sq. km) of the Burren, Co. Clare, that it was 'a country where there is not enough water to drown a man, wood enough to hang him, nor earth enough to bury him'. A small portion of the area is now an Irish national park. Ludlow later became one of the four commissioners imposing the land seizures under the Act of Settlement of Ireland 1652. In September 1660 a proclamation ordered the apprehension of 'Edmund Ludlow esquire, commonly called Col. Ludlow'; SAL Proclamations, vol. 13, 1660–06, f.27.

28    Bod. Lib. Carte MS 214, f.448. Vernon was told of the conspiracy by an unidentified correspondent, a member of the Pigott family (?Thomas Pigott, an Irish MP) in a letter of 11 March: 'I suppose you will hear from others of the late design of surprising the castle here by some fanatic. The design was desperate and would have been bloody in its execution for most as yet observed to be engaged in it were formerly officers and since discontented tradesmen. Every day makes new discoveries so that many know not and most fear where it will end.' Addressed to Colonel Edward Vernon 'at Mr Henry Nutings, his house in Plow Yard, in Fetter Lane, London'. *CSP Ireland 1663–5*, p.37.

29    Bod. Lib. Carte MS 214, f.446; in cipher with decoded text interleaved. Minute in the hand of Sir George Lane, Irish Secretary. Dublin Castle, 4 March 1663.

30    HMC 'Ormond', vol. 2, p.251.

31    Abbott, 'English Conspiracy and Dissent 1660–74', p. 519.

32    Carte, *Life of Ormond*, vol. 4, book 6, pp.124–5.

33    Bod. Lib. Carte MS 143, ff.96–7; Dublin Castle, 7 March 1663.

34    On 30 January 1649 Hewlett was the officer in charge of the troops providing security at the execution of Charles I. After the restoration of the monarchy, he was convicted for his part in the king's beheading but was not executed with the two other officers who were found guilty at the same time – Daniel Axtell and Francis Hacker. Another prisoner in Dublin Castle was Henry Porter, who had been locked up for two years, charged with being one of the

two disguised and masked executioners of Charles I in Whitehall in 1649. On 29 April, Ormond and his Irish Council wrote to Secretary Bennet pointing out that if he was on the scaffold, 'he should be tried in England and he is clamouring for a *habeas corpus*' – a court appearance to free him without charge. They added: 'We are anxious for his majesty's direction in the matter' (TNA, 63/313/120, f.243). The issue was apparently ignored in Whitehall. The public executioner at the time of Charles's death was Richard Brandon (son of Gregory Brandon, the common hangman), who had beheaded Thomas Wentworth, First Earl of Strafford in 1641 and Archbishop Laud in 1645. Initially, he reportedly refused to behead the king, but was persuaded otherwise and was paid £30, all in half-crowns, within an hour of the execution – and was given a handkerchief taken from the king's pocket and an orange, which he sold for £10 at his home in Rosemary Lane, Whitechapel. Brandon died on 20 June 1649 and was buried at Whitechapel. See: H.V. Morton, *In Search of London* (London, 1951) pp.198–9. In 1813, the vault in St George's Chapel, Windsor containing the body of Charles I was opened and it was confirmed that the king had been decapitated with one clean strike – surely the work of an experienced executioner.

35   *CSP Ireland 1663–5*, p.34.

36   *CSP Ireland 1663–5*, p.37.

37   Bod. Lib. Carte MS 214, f.442; Dublin Castle, 18 March 1663.

38   'Pepys Diary', vol. 3, p.67; 20 March 1663. A token from a coffee house at the west end of St Paul's is described in Boyne's *Trade Tokens issued in Seventeenth-century London*, ed. G.C. Williamson (2 vols., London, 1889) vol. 1, p.736.

39   *CSP Ireland 1663–5*, p.51.

40   *CSP Ireland 1663–5*, p.51. Ormond to the king, 28 March 1663. Later, he told Charles that he had found out no more about the earlier plot. 'There certainly was one and if I decided to let it come to a head, as one of my spies [?Alden] suggested, I might have made great discoveries. But Parliament was sitting at the time in very ill humour and there were many dangerous people in Dublin and I did not care to let the game go so long'; *CSP Ireland 1663–5*, p.83. Ormond to the king, 8 May 1663.

41    The mythical circular island of Brasil or Hy-Brasil, rumoured to be located in the Atlantic Ocean, west of Ireland, was said to be cloaked in magical mists which cleared for only one day in seven years, the only time it could be seen by sailors. In 1674 Captain John Nisbet claimed to have seen it, finding it inhabited only by giant black rabbits and a solitary sorcerer who lived alone in a stone castle. Porcupine Bank, a rocky shoal in the Atlantic about 120 miles (200 km) west of Ireland, which was charted in 1862, has been suggested as the site of Hy-Brasil.

42    *CSP Ireland 1663–5*, p.47. In fact, the ship had Colonel Henry Pretty, former parliamentary governor of Carlow, on board, who was also under suspicion of involvement in the conspiracy. The ship escaped from Limerick but was captured in mid-May while hiding among the Aran Islands off Ireland's west coast. Ludlow was not on the ship. See: Greaves, *Deliver Us from Evil*, p.141.

43    Bod. Lib. Carte MS 34, f. 674*r* – 'Advice of Incidents in Ireland'. The information was sent anonymously to Ormond.

44    Bod. Lib. Carte MS 143, f.128–31. Ormond to the king, 8 May 1663.

45    Bod. Lib. Carte MS 46, ff.51–2. Bennet to Ormond, Whitehall, 15 May 1663.

46    Marshall, *Intelligence and Espionage . . .*, p.188.

47    *CSP Ireland 1663–5*, p.111.

48    HMC 'Ormond', vol. 2, p.252.

49    'Veitch & Brysson Memoirs', appendix 9, pp.508–9.

50    *CSP Ireland 1663–5*, p.115.

51    *CSP Ireland 1663–5*, p.79. Vernon to Bennet, Dublin, 6 May 1663.

52    Bod. Lib. Carte MS 32, ff.384–5 and 388.

53    *CSP Ireland 1663–5*, p.92. Ormond to the king, Dublin Castle, 18 May 1663.

54    Bod. Lib. Carte MS 68, f.580; Dublin Castle, 19 May 1663.

55    The commander of an army's reconnaissance troops.

56    Donagh MacCarthy, First Earl of Clancarty, Second Viscount Muskerry (died 1665), was among the last Irish commanders to surrender to the English after Cromwell's invasion. He was defeated by Roger Boyle, later Earl of Orrery, at the Battle of Knocknaclashy in 1651 and retreated into the Kerry Mountains. He surrendered the

following June, his 5,000-man army disbanded, and he fled Ireland. Charles II granted MacCarthy the title of Earl of Clancarty and his estates were restored under the Act of Settlement 1662. He died in London.

57 RCHM *Eighth Report, Appendix*, pt. 1, pp.263–4; Bod. Lib. Carte MS 118, f.63.

58 HMC 'Ormond', vol. 2, p.253.

59 Greaves, *Deliver Us from Evil*, p.144.

60 *CSP Ireland 1663–5*, p.112.

61 *CSP Ireland 1663–5*, pp.97; TNA, SP 63/313/170, f.351 and Bod. Lib. Carte MS 68, f.564.

62 TNA, SP 63/313/164, f.335.

## CHAPTER 2: ESCAPE AND EVASION

1 TNA, SP 63/313/221 f.451.

2 Following damage caused by a munitions explosion in the castle armoury in 1764, the Bermingham Tower was demolished down to its first-floor level and rebuilt in 1777.

3 Greaves, *Deliver Us from Evil*, p.145.

4 Blood was exaggerating for effect. Sir William Petty estimated the Protestant death toll in the Irish Confederation rebellion to be 37,000 (Sir Richard Musgrave, *Memoirs of the different Rebellions in Ireland* [London, 1801] p.30).

5 This is a reference to the 1643 agreement between the English and Scottish Parliaments to preserve the Presbyterian religion in Scotland and its adoption in England. After the restoration of the monarchy, the Sedition Act of 1661 (13 Caro II St.1 *cap.* 1) declared the agreement unlawful and it was burnt publicly in London by the common hangman.

6 'Veitch & Brysson Memoirs', pp.508–9.

7 'Veitch & Brysson Memoirs', p.509. A letter to Ormond of 11 June 1663 with information on the conspirators refers to him as 'Cornet Blood' – the lowest officer rank in the cavalry. See: Bod. Lib. Carte MS 32, f.553. The rebels' declaration was later burnt in Dublin by the public executioner.

8    TNA, SP 63/313/170, f.351 and Bod. Lib. Carte MS 68, f.564.

9    TNA, SP 63/313/225, f.458.

10   TNA, SP 63/313/173, f.355; Ormond to [Secretary Bennet], Dublin
     Castle, 23 May 1663; SP 63/313/174, f.357; Ormond to Bennet,
     Dublin Castle, 24 May 1663.

11   TNA, SP 63/313165 f.340.

12   Bod. Lib. Carte MS 32, f.446. Sir Arthur Forbes to Ormond, 22 May
     1663.

13   Aungier was created Viscount Longford in the Irish peerage in 1675
     and Earl of Longford two years later.

14   TNA, SP 63/313/172, f.354.

15   Churchill, one-time MP for Weymouth and Melcombe Regis, was
     knighted in 1664. He was the father of John Churchill, First Duke of
     Marlborough, and ancestor of his namesake, the twentieth-century
     statesman and prime minister.

16   CSP Ireland 1663–5, pp. 104.

17   TNA, SP 63/312/174, f.357. Ormond to Bennet, Dublin Castle, 24
     May 1663.

18   TNA, SP 63/313/221, f.451. Talbot to Williamson, 13 June 1663.

19   CSP Ireland 1663–5, pp.97–8; Dublin Castle, 21 May 1663.

20   TNA, SP 63/313/164, f.335.

21   SAL Proclamations, Ireland 1572–1670, vol. 17, f.75. Another copy is
     in Bod. Lib. Carte MS 54, f.537.

22   TNA, SP 63/313/169, f.349. Vernon to Secretary Bennet, Dublin,
     23 May 1663.

23   An adherent of the religious group founded in Germany and Swit-
     zerland in the sixteenth century which only recognised the baptism
     of adult believers and rejected Anglican doctrines.

24   TNA, SP 63/313/168, f. 346.

25   SAL Proclamations Ireland 1572–1670, vol. 17, f.75 and Bod. Lib.
     Carte MS 71, ff.388–9; 'Proclamation upon the occasion of the late
     conspiracy by the lord lieutenant and council of Ireland'.

26   Bod. Lib. Carte MS 49, f.193.

27   Morrice, Collection State Letters of Roger Boyle . . ., pp.69–70.

28   The suspects 'ride always by night and on Sunday mornings, but
     never by the highways. Sometimes there are six or seven in a

company'. Bod. Lib. Carte MS 32, f.460, Dublin, 25 May 1663.

29   Bod. Lib. Carte MS 32, f.608, Loughbrickland, 29 June 1663.

30   Bod. Lib. Carte MS 214, f.438, Dublin, 22 May 1633.

31   Bod. Lib. Carte MS 165, f.111. Warrant to evict Dublin citizens from accommodation overlooking the city's quays and replacing them with soldiers; Dublin Castle, 30 May 1663.

32   TNA, SP 63/313/180 f.366; Bod. Lib, Carte MS 143, f.133*v*.

33   Bod. Lib. Carte MS 143, f.133*r*.

34   TNA, SP 63/313/186, f.376. Vernon to [Secretary Bennet] Dublin, 30 May 1663.

35   TNA, SP 63/313/187, f.378. Deposition of James Tanner; Dublin, 31 May 1663.

36   *CSP Ireland 1663–5*, p.116; Ormond to Bennet, Dublin Castle, 3 June 1663.

37   TNA, SP 63/313/193, f.395; Sir Nicholas Armorer to Joseph Williamson, Dublin, 3 June 1663. Armourer was a Royalist spymaster during the English Civil Wars and after the Restoration was appointed a captain in the Irish Guards and governor of Duncannon fort, a star-shaped fortification built to protect Waterford harbour at New Ross in Co. Wexford.

38   *CSP Ireland 1663–5*, p. 117; Sir Thomas Clarges to Secretary Bennet, 3 June 1663.

39   TNA, SP 63/313/198, f.430. Vernon to Joseph Williamson, 5 June 1663.

40   Bod. Lib. Carte MS 221, ff.52–3. Bennet to Ormond, Whitehall, 6 June 1663; Carte MS 46, f.55; 1 June 1663.

41   TNA, SP 63/313/207, f.419. Ormond to Bennet, Dublin Castle, 10 June 1663. Ormond, worried about successfully prosecuting the conspirators, had toyed with the idea of trying them under martial law unconstrained by normal legal requirements. But he concluded that 'in time and place of war it was, and could be again, practised without scruple but in time of peace, a court martial will hardly be found that will sentence a soldier to death . . .' Bod. Lib. Carte MS 143, ff.142*r* and *v*. Ormond to Bennet, 13 June 1663.

42   Little Britain connects St Martin's Le Grand in the east with West Smithfield in the northern part of the City of London.

43   TNA, SP 63/313/209, f.422. Dublin Castle, 10 June 1663.

44   TNA, SP 63/313/209, f.425.

45   Bod. Lib. Carte MS 114, f.505. Edward Tanner to Lieutenant Colonel Staples, 15 June 1663.

46   Proudfoot's Castle was formerly known as Fyan's Castle, from its previous owners: Thomas Fyan was sheriff of Dublin in 1640. Later in the seventeenth century, the tower was acquired by the merchant George Proudfoot, cousin to the chief justice, Sir James Barry, First Baron Santry (Gilbert, *History of the City of Dublin*, vol. 1, p.375). Proudfoot apparently rented the structure to Francis Sleigh, a Dublin tanner, who agreed, in turn, to lease it to Philip Carpenter, the sergeant-at-arms, at £30 a year and on payment of £70 'for keeping therein such prisoners as shall be committed to Carpenter's charge' (*CSP Ireland 1663–5*, p.138).

47   Darcy (1598–1668) was a Catholic lawyer who was admitted as a student at London's Middle Temple in July 1617 before practising on the Connacht circuit from *c*.1627. He was instrumental in drawing up the constitution of the Irish Catholic Confederation in 1642 and, after Cromwell's invasion, was imprisoned in the Marshalsea jail, Dublin. He was buried in Kilconnell Abbey, Co. Galway, with this epitaph inscribed upon his tomb: *Hic misera patria sola columna jacet* – 'Here, wretched country, lies your sole support'.

48   Bod. Lib. Carte MS 32, ff. 666, 668 and 669.

49   Santry (1603–72) was the eldest of three sons of Alderman Richard Barry of Dublin. He was recorder of the City of Dublin, sergeant-at-law, second baron of the Irish Exchequer, before being appointed chief justice of the court of King's Bench in November 1660 as a reward for his 'many good services to Charles I and his eminent loyalty to Charles II'. He was created First Baron Santry of Santry, Co. Dublin, in February 1661. See: E. Barry, *Records of the Barrys of Co. Cork*, p.135 and Ball, 'Notes on the Irish Judiciary in the Reign of Charles II', p.90.

50   *CSP Ireland 1663–5*, p.131. Ormond to Secretary Bennet, Dublin, 13 June 1663.

51   TNA, SP 63/33/245, f.495. Ormond to Secretary Bennet, Dublin Castle, 25 June 1663.

52  The Irish Parliament, sitting at Drogheda, passed two laws in 1495 relating to treason. The first (10 Henry VII, *cap.* 25) made it treason to 'stir the Irishry to war' and the second (10 Henry VII, *cap.* 37) decreed that murder 'of malice pretensed' was also treason. It seems likely that the former legislation was used against the conspirators. See David B. Quinn, 'Bills and Statutes of Irish Parliament of Henry VII and Henry VIII' in *Analecta Hibernica*, no. 10 (July 1944), pp.71–169.

53  *CSP Ireland 1663–5*, p. 138. Vernon to Williamson, 17 June 1663.

54  HMC 'Ormond', vol. 3, pp.57–8. Eleven ministers were arrested in Carrickfergus, Co. Antrim, and sent to Carlingford, but nine could not be found, including two – 'Henry Hunter and Mr Bruces' – who had escaped to Scotland. The troops also failed to find one of the named plotters, the 'pretended minister' Andrew McCormack (Bod. Lib. Carte MS 32, f.655).

55  Bod. Lib. Carte MS 59, f.86 and TNA 63/313/226, f.460.

56  Bod. Lib. Carte MS 43, f.192. King to Ormond, [10] June 1663.

57  Ormond was probably not a party to Vernon's plans to free Alden. On 20 June, the lord lieutenant reported the informer's escape; 'owing to the negligence of the constable of the castle I believe he is gone into England but hope to have news of him through one of my spies'. *CSP Ireland 1663–5*, p.142.

58  *CSP Ireland 1663–5*, p.139; 19 June 1663. The previous day Ormond signed a warrant for the recapture of Alden 'late a prisoner in Dublin Castle, under charge of high treason'; Bod. Lib. Carte MS 165, f.116*v*.

59  Bod. Lib. Carte MS 68, f.562. It was housed in the Four Courts building, so called because cases in the Chancery, King's Bench, Exchequer and Common Pleas courts were heard there. The present building was constructed in 1786–96.

60  TNA, SP 63/313/243, f.491. Sir George Lane to [Secretary Bennet], Dublin Castle, 25 June 1663.

61  *CSP Ireland 1663–5*, p.121. Vernon to [Joseph Williamson], 6 June 1663.

62  Bod. Lib. Carte MS 32, f.602, Dublin, 22 June 1663.

63  Ponsonby (*c.*1609–78), from Haile in Cheshire, came with Cromwell

to Ireland in 1649 as a colonel of horse and received substantial lands around Bessborough in Co. Kilkenny as a reward for his military service. He was also MP for the county in the Dublin Parliament and was active in seeking to maintain Protestant domination of Ireland.

64   Bod. Lib. Carte MS 32, f.604r. The letter is marked: 'For your grace only'.

65   The ancient law of the Hebrews, attributed to Moses and contained in the Pentateuch or Torah, the first five books of the Hebrew Bible.

66   TNA, SP 63/314/2, f.3. Vernon to Joseph Williamson, 1 July 1663.

67   Bod. Lib. Carte MS 32, f.673; Dublin, 3 July 1663.

68   Bod. Lib. Carte MS 32, ff.691–4. Lord Santry's speech in passing judgment upon Jephson and others; Court of King's Bench, Dublin, 7 July 1663.

69   *CSP Ireland 1663–5*, p.169. Robert Leigh to Joseph Williamson, 8 July 1663.

70   TNA, SP 63/314/11, f.32. Sir George Lane to Secretary Bennet, Dublin Castle, 11 July 1663.

71   *CSP Ireland 1663–5*, p.167. Robert Leigh to Williamson, Dublin, 11 July 1663.

72   Thompson is also referred to as a 'major' or a 'captain' in contemporary documents.

73   Campbell (c.1607–61) was accused of treason for collaborating with the Commonwealth during the interregnum and his role in the suppression of the Royalist uprising in Scotland in 1653–4, led by William Cunningham, Eighth Earl of Glencairn. Campbell was beheaded in Edinburgh on 27 May 1661 by 'the Scottish Maiden', an early form of guillotine which was used to execute more than 150 persons in the city between 1564 and 1710. One is preserved today in the Museum of Scotland, Edinburgh.

74   Bod. Lib. Carte MS 32, f.688; Dublin Castle, 5 July 1663.

75   Greaves, *Deliver Us from Evil*, p.149. Early the following November, a widow called Mary Roberts petitioned Ormond for payment of a debt owed her by Thompson, out of his estate that had become forfeit to the crown. Bod. Lib. Carte MS 144, f.123v.

76   Bod. Lib. Carte MS 32, ff.589–90. Certificate by the borough

masters of Rotterdam about the residence in that city of Colonel Gibby Carr; Rotterdam, 10–20 June 1663.

77    *CSP Ireland 1663–5*, p.166. Ormond to Bennet, Whitehall, 10 July 1663.

78    Bod. Lib. Carte MS 46, ff.61–4. Bennet to Ormond, Whitehall, 27 June 1663.

79    Bod. Lib. Carte MS 32, f.202. Examination of James Milligan of Antrim by the Earl of Mount Alexander and William Leslie esq., in relation to the concealment of Thomas Blood; Antrim, 24 August 1663.

80    Bod. Lib. Carte MS 32, f.202*r*. Interrogation of James Milligan.

81    Bod. Lib. Carte MS 214, f.534. Earl of Mount Alexander to Ormond, Newtown, 25 August 1663. In early August, a former soldier E[dward] Bagot, wrote to Ormond from Blithfield in Staffordshire to warn the lord lieutenant that former parliamentary troops in Ireland were plotting to kill him. 'Some of these men have told my intelligencer [spy] that, when their blow shall be struck in Ireland, there [is] a party in England ready to second them.' Bod. Lib. Carte MS 33, f.18.

82    Bod. Lib. Rawlinson MS A.185, f.374*r*.

83    Bod. Lib. Carte MS 32, f.210. Blood to John Chamberlin. ?August 1663.

84    Bod. Lib. Carte MS 32, f.211. Undated, but endorsed: 'Copied, 14 August 1663 at Wicklow'.

85    Bod. Lib. Rawlinson MS A.185, f.473.

86    TNA, SP 63/314/16, f.42. Ormond to the king, 14 July 1663.

87    Bod. Lib. Carte MS 49, f.216.

88    *CSP Ireland 1663–5*, p.181.

89    Bod. Lib. Carte MS 68, f.574. Alexander Jephson's last speech on the scaffold.

90    Bod. Lib. Carte MS 68, ff.576–8.

91    *CSP Ireland 1663–5*, pp.176–7.

92    Bod. Lib. Carte MS 159, f.66.

93    TNA, SP, 63/315/25, f.49. Sir George Lane to Bennet, Dublin Castle, 18 November 1663.

94    'Remarks . . .', pp.220–21.

95    Morres, *History of the Principal Transactions of the Irish Parliament 1634–66*, (2 vols., London, 1742), vol. 2, p.136.

96    *CSP Ireland 1663–5*, p.308. His mother, Charity, wrote to Ormond in August 1663, prostrate at his feet and 'knowing scarcely how to articulate her anguish', that her son 'should have had his hand in treason' and blaming his 'tenderness of years and to the frailty of a nature beguiled by the subtlety of some grand imposter'. Bod. Lib. Carte MS 33, f.90.

#### CHAPTER 3: A TASTE FOR CONSPIRACY

1    *CSP Ireland 1663–5*, p.662.

2    For information about the Elizabethan intelligence organisation, see my *Elizabeth's Spymaster* (London, 2006).

3    Both Houses of Parliament decided on 19 December 1644 to impose the observance of Christmas Day as a fast day, banning such fripperies as mince pies. They decreed that 'this day in particular is to be kept with more solemn humiliation because it may call to remembrance our sins and the sins of our forefathers who turned this feast, pretending the memory of Christ into extreme forgetfulness of him, by giving liberty to carnal and sensual delights' ('Lords *Jnls*', vol. 7, p.106). The Royalist satirist and poet John Taylor (1580–1653) wrote a book ridiculing this ordinance, having Father Christmas visit the 'schismatic and rebellious' cities and towns of London, Yarmouth, Newbury and Gloucester and finding 'All the liberty and harmless sports, with the merry gambols, dances and friscals [capers] [by] which the toiling plough-swain and labourer were wont to be recreated and their spirits and hopes revived for a whole twelve month are now extinct and put out of use in such a fashion as if they never had been. Thus are the merry lords of misrule suppressed by the mad lords of bad rule at Westminster.' (*Complaint of Christmas*, Oxford, 1646). The performance of plays had been banned in 1642. Maypole and Morris dancing accompanied Charles II's triumphal entry into London in May 1660.

4    Later King James II.

5    J. R. Magrath (ed.), *The Flemings in Oxford, being the Documents selected*

*from the Rydal Papers in illustration of the Lives and Ways of Oxford*
*Men 1650–7* (3 vols., Oxford Historical Society, 1904–24), vol. 1,
p.160.

6    *An Act for Erecting and Establishing a Post Office*, 12 Car II, *cap*. 35.
     Postal charges were levied at the rate of two, four and six old pence
     for a single-sheet, folded letter carried up to 80, 140 or more miles
     to the addressee.

7    His father was in charge of the post after 1635 when the service was
     created by Charles I. Witherings the elder wrote to the Mayor of
     Hull announcing the posts which would be carried along the five
     principal roads in the kingdom: to Dover, Edinburgh, Holyhead,
     Plymouth and Bristol (TNA, POST 23/1; 28 January 1636). For
     further information see: Turner, 'The Secrecy of the Post', *EHR*, vol.
     33, pp.320–27.

8    TNA, SP 29/168/151, f.158. ?24 August 1666.

9    Wallis (1616–1703) was the third Savilian professor of geometry at
     the University of Oxford. He had worked as a cryptographer for
     Cromwell's spymaster John Thurloe during the republic in 1659–60
     and then for Williamson after the Restoration, being described as a
     'jewel for a Prince's use and service' in code-breaking. Later he was
     accused of deciphering the correspondence of Charles I, captured by
     parliamentary forces after the Royalist defeat at the Battle of Naseby
     on 14 June 1645 – charges which he vehemently denied in a letter
     to his friend, John Fell, Bishop of Oxford in a letter dated 8 April
     1685 (BL Add. MS. 32,499, f.377). For details of Wallis' life, see an
     eighteenth-century account in Bod. Lib. Rawlinson MS C. 978.

10   Marshall, *Intelligence and Espionage* ..., pp.79–80. Oldenburg
     (*c.*1619–77) was secretary of the Royal Society, founded on 28 Nov-
     ember 1660, and founding editor of its peer-reviewed *Philosophical
     Transactions*, the world's oldest scientific journal, which is still going
     strong today. Oldenburg, who was harshly critical of the govern-
     ment's handling of the Second Dutch War in 1665–7, fell foul of the
     government because of his views, expressed in intercepted corre-
     spondence with his Royal Society contacts. It was a case of the biter
     bit, as he spent two months imprisoned in the Tower of London in
     1667 as a salutary lesson.

11  Morland's *Brief discourse containing the nature and reason of intelligence*, Egmont Papers vol. 214, BL Add MSS 47,133, ff.8–13.

12  A seventeenth-century description of Morland's 'speaking trumpet' was sold at Sotheby's in London on 4 November 1969, lot. 260.

13  See: Susan E. Whyman, *Postal Censorship in England*; HMC 'Finch', vol. 2, p.265; HMC 'Downshire', vol. 1, pt. 2, pp.594–5.

14  A customs officer who boarded and inspected ships on arrival and collected the dues on their cargoes.

15  BL Egerton MSS 2,539, f.101.

16  There was a private entrance to Bennet's and Williamson's offices from the privy garden of the palace. Otherwise, a visitor would have to enter from the Stone Gallery through an outer door into a porch, guarded by a door-keeper. See: Marshall, 'Sir Joseph Williamson and the Conduct of Administration in Restoration England', *HR*, vol. 69, pp.21–2.

17  Was one safe house the home of the astronomer Sir Paul Neale (1613–86)? He received £38 from secret funds for his 'lodging in Whitehall' from 23 November 1678 to 31 July 1679. Neale had become MP for Newark in 1673 but because the election was contested, he was not allowed to take his seat in the Commons and the vote was declared void in 1677. See Akerman (ed.), *Moneys received and paid for Secret Services of Charles II and James II from 30 March 1679 to 25 December 1688*, p.5. Williamson had his own house in Scotland Yard, off Parliament Street.

18  Marshall, *Intelligence and Espionage . . .*, p.160.

19  Expenditure on Britain's three intelligence agencies – the Secret Intelligence Service (MI6) the Security Service (MI5) and the Government Communications Headquarters (GCHQ, the equivalent of the USA's National Security Agency) – is contained in the 'Single Intelligence Account' which totalled £1·9 billion in 2014–15, plus a further £123 million for cyber-security funding. For security reasons, the individual budgets of the agencies are not published.

20  BL Add. MS. 28,077, f.139. The hearth tax was imposed in 1662–89 and involved a householder paying one shilling (5 pence) for every hearth or stove twice a year, at Michaelmas (25 September) and on Lady Day (25 March). In 1674, John Cecil, Fifth Earl of Exeter,

had to pay for seventy hearths in Burghley House, at Stamford, Lincolnshire.

21  Akerman (ed.), *Moneys received and paid for Secret Services of Charles II and James II from 30 March 1679 to 25 December 1688*, pp. x and 7.

22  RCHM *Fifteenth Report*, appendix, pt. 7, p.170.

23  Book of Daniel, chapter 2, verse 44.

24  Book of Revelations, chapter 13, verses 17–18.

25  At least they were consistent in the vilification of their rulers: Cromwell, they declared, had been a Babylonian tyrant.

26  Samuel Pepys records in his Diary for 9 January 1661: 'Waked in the morning about six o'clock by people running up and down . . . talking that the fanatics were up in arms in the City. So I rose and went forth, where in the street I found everybody in arms at the doors. So I returned (though with no good courage . . .) and got my sword and pistol, [for] which I had no powder to charge . . .'. The next day, he was horrified to hear that the 'fanatics . . . have routed all the Trained Bands [London militia] that they met with, put the king's life guards to the run, killed about twenty men . . . and all this in the daytime when all the City was in arms'. 'Pepys Diary', vol. 1, pp.298–9.

27  Capp, '*A Door of Hope* Re-opened: the Fifth Monarchy, King Charles and King Jesus', *Jnl of Religious History*, vol. 32, pp.16–30. For more information on the Fifth Monarchists, see Capp's *The Fifth Monarchy Men: A Study in Seventeenth century English Millenarianism* (London, 1977) and Champlin Burrage, 'The Fifth Monarchy Insurrections', *EHR*, vol. 25, pp.741–3.

28  The first issue of the newspaper, on 7 November 1665, was published under the title *Oxford Gazette*, as the court had fled to that city because of the epidemic of bubonic plague raging in London. It reported that the 'bill of mortality' (or death toll) in London that week was 1,359, of which 1,050 were from plague – a decrease of 428. It became the *London Gazette* on 5 February 1666.

29  'Magalotti, *Relazione*', pp.44–5.

30  'Pepys Diary', vol. 3, pp.30–31. 6 February 1663.

31  'Pepys Diary', vol. 5, p.223. 1 March 1666.

32  'Evelyn Diary', vol. 2, p.300.

33  'Magalotti, *Relazione*', p.44, although the Italian's estimate was

probably exaggerated. See also Marshall, *Intelligence and Espionage* . . ., p.36 and, by the same author, 'Sir Joseph Williamson', *ODNB*, vol. 59, pp.352–6 and 'Sir Joseph Williamson and the Conduct of Administration in Restoration England', *HR*, vol. 69, pp.18–41.

34   B. L. Egerton MS 2,539, ff.142–3. For details of the pay of the secretaries of state, see F. M. Greir Evans, 'Emoluments of the Principal Secretaries of State in the seventeenth century', *EHR*, vol. 35, pp.513–28.

35   Marshall, 'Henry Bennet, first earl of Arlington, *ODNB*, vol. 5, p.102.

36   Greaves, *Deliver Us from Evil*, p.174.

37   Greaves, *Deliver Us from Evil*, pp.178–9.

38   For more information on the northern rebellion, see Gee, 'A Durham and Newcastle plot in 1663', *Archaeologia Aeolian*, third s., vol. 14 (1917), pp.145–56 and Walker, 'The Yorkshire Plot, 1663', *Yorkshire Archaeological Jnl*, vol. 31 (1932–4), pp.348–59, who notes that the fears of Whitehall officials seemed to have 'caused something in the nature of a panic which were not justified' (pp.358–9). For the grisly fate of some of those caught up in the northern rebellion, see Raine, J. (ed.), *Depositions from the Castle of York relating to Offences Committed in the Northern Counties* . . ., Surtees Society, vol. 40.

39   *CSP Domestic 1663–4*, p.652.

40   Marshall, 'William Leving', *ODNB*, vol. 33, p.345. Jones was the author of the radical underground pamphlet verbosely titled 'Mene Tekel or the Downfall of Tyranny wherein liberty and equity are vindicated, and tyranny condemned by the law of God and right reason, and the people's power and duty to execute justice without and upon wicked governors, asserted by Laophilus Misotyrannus'. This angry, seditious document, published earlier in 1663, argued that kings were the servants of the people, were set up by the people and therefore could be removed by the people. With memories of the bloody fate of Charles I still fresh, it was inevitable that its publication touched a raw nerve in the Restoration government.

41   Lambert (1619–84) was accused of high treason at the Restoration and spent the last twenty-four years of his life a prisoner, firstly in the Channel Island of Guernsey and latterly on Drake's Island in Plymouth Sound where he died in March 1674.

42   Marshall, *Intelligence and Espionage . . .*, p.156.

43   TNA, SP 29/97/41, f.54; Sir Roger Langley to Bennet, 3 April 1664. SP 29/97/201, f.32; Sir Roger Langley to Secretary Bennet, York, 23 April 1664.

44   TNA, SP 29/97/75, f.130. One of the earliest documented examples of a career as an informer in England was George Whelplay, a London haberdasher, who conceived the idea after being sent to Southampton to investigate the customs service in the port, by Henry VIII's enforcer, Thomas Cromwell. See G.R. Elton, 'Informing for Profit: A Sidelight on Tudor Methods of Law Enforcement', *Cambridge HJ*, vol. 11 (1954), pp.149–67. Elton points out that Whelplay received 'precious little out of bustling activity which, despite its essentially sordid air, had not a little of the pathetic about it'.

45   *CSP Domestic 1663–4*, p.629.

46   'Remarks . . .', p.221. If this story is true, Blood must have met de Rutyer before his departure in early May on a naval expedition to the coast of West Africa where he recaptured some of the Dutch slave stations briefly held by the English. He then crossed the Atlantic to raid English colonies in North America. In April 1665, de Rutyer was in Barbados.

47   'Remarks . . .', p.222.

48   TNA, SP 29/102/48, f.57.

49   TNA, SP 29/102/49, f.59. Order by the commissioners for the repair of the Tower of London; 12 September 1664.

50   *CSP Ireland 1663–5*, p.459. Major Rawdon to Viscount Conway, Lisburn, 20 December 1664.

51   TNA, SP 29/121/131, f.175. List of thirty-one disaffected persons in London.

52   *CSP Domestic 1664–5*, p.259. Williams to Secretary Bennet, ?18 March 1665.

53   *CSP Domestic 1664–5*, p.259. Williams to Secretary Bennet, 18 March, 1665.

54   The alias of the Fifth Monarchist Captain Edward Carey, who escaped from a messenger (an arresting officer) in 1664.

55   *CSP Domestic 1664–5*, p.259. Williams and John Betson to Sir Roger Langley, London, 18 March 1665.

56    Marshall, *Intelligence and Espionage* . . ., p.158. Petty France was so
      called because of the number of French merchants who lived there.
      The street was later renamed York Street.

57    This was probably the chamber mentioned during the interroga-
      tion of William Ashenhurst, a prisoner in the White Lion prison
      in Southwark. He said the conspirators 'sometimes stayed there
      all night and some bring arms [and] looking through the keyhole,
      he heard them in earnest discourse [about] something to be done'
      the following April (TNA, SP 29/115/44, f.124). The White Lion
      was one of four prisons located between Newcomen Street and St
      George's church on the east side of Borough High Street, South-
      wark, the others being the King's Bench and Marshalsea (both dating
      back to the fourteenth century) and the House of Correction.

58    Blood's notebook suggests that the court martial was held there
      (Bod Lib. Rawlinson MS A.185, ff.473–5). Coleman Street runs
      from Gresham Street to London Wall and a congregation of Ana-
      baptists was active there during this period. Swan Lane was also a
      known haunt of Fifth Monarchists. (See: Champlin Burrage, 'The
      Fifth Monarchy Insurrections', *EHR*, vol. 25, pp.724–5.

59    'Remarks . . .', pp.222–3; Burghclere, *Life of Ormond*, vol. 2, p.183.

60    The winter of 1664/5 was particularly cold, with the ground frozen
      from December to March and the River Thames twice blocked to
      river traffic by thick ice.

61    Marshall, *Intelligence and Espionage* . . ., pp.161–2; *CSP Domestic
      1664–5*, p.271.

62    TNA, SP 29/103/21, f.13.

63    Marshall, 'William Leving', *ODNB*, vol. 33, p.545. The earliest cases
      occurred in the spring of 1665 in a parish outside the city walls
      called St Giles-in-the-Fields. The death rate began to rise during
      the summer months and peaked in September when 7,165 London-
      ers died in one week.

64    Bod. Lib. Rawlinson MS A. 185, f.474.

65    *CSP Ireland 1663–5*, p.101. Browne was involved in the Dublin
      Castle plot, liaising between 'the fanatics of England and Ireland'.

66    The French periwig or 'peruke' became fashionable for men of high
      social standing after Charles II was restored to the throne in 1660.

Wearing the wig, which had shoulder-length or longer human hair, had its own problems. Pepys, in his Diary for 18 July 1664, noted: 'Thence to Westminster to my barber's [Mr Jervas] to have my periwig [that] he lately made me cleansed of its nits which vexed me cruelly that he should put such a thing into my hands.' (vol. 4, p.178).

67  *CSP Ireland 1663–5*, p.662. Orrery to Secretary Arlington, Dublin, 8 November 1665.

68  The naval war against the United Provinces of the Netherlands was fought between 4 March 1665 and 31 July 1667. The Royal Navy won an initial victory at the Battle of Lowestoft on 13 June 1665 and although both sides claimed victory in the so-called 'Four Days Battle' of 1–4 June 1666, the English ships suffered considerable damage. After the Dutch had blockaded the Thames estuary, the St James's Day Battle (25 July 1666) off Kent's North Foreland was another victory for the English fleet. When fighting resumed in the spring of 1667 the Dutch sailed into the Thames and destroyed warships in the River Medway in one of the most humiliating defeats suffered by the Royal Navy.

69  TNA, SP 29/147/115, f.147.

70  This area, once in the suburbs of Dublin, surrounds a small valley with a tributary of the River Poddle, otherwise known as the Coombe Stream. In the late seventeenth century it was the centre of the local weaving or clothing industry.

71  TNA, SP 63/320/45, f.1. Earl of Orrery to Ormond, Charleville, Co. Cork, 12 February 1666. Charleville was founded by Orrery in 1661 and named after Charles II.

72  TNA, SP 63/320/45, f.2. ?Dame Dorcas Lane to her husband, Sir George Lane, 8 February 1666.

73  Was this Blood's little joke? Morton was the name of an assiduous London magistrate.

74  In April 1662, the canton of Berne granted Ludlow protection for him to live in the area.

75  Blood's notebook records him being 'a prisoner in Zeeland'. Bod. Lib. Rawlinson MS A.185 f.473*v*. entry no. 39.

76  Phelps (*c.*1619–after 1666) was clerk of the high court trying Charles

I for his life. At the Restoration, he escaped prosecution. He lived in exile in Lausanne and Vevey, Switzerland. A black marble monument to his memory was erected in the Swiss Reformed church of St Martin, Vevey, in 1882 by William Phelps of New Jersey, American ambassador to Prague, Czechoslovakia, and Dr Charles A. Phelps of Massachusetts, 'descendants from across the seas'.

77 TNA, SP 9/32/313. Williamson's address book.

78 Marshall, *Intelligence and Espionage . . .*, pp.201–2 and, by the same author, 'Colonel Thomas Blood and the Restoration Political Scene', *HJ*, vol. 32, pp.576–8.

79 *CSP Ireland 1666–9*, p.80. Ormond to Arlington, Dublin Castle, 2 April 1666. The matter had taken some time to reach this stage: Captain Barnes had petitioned Ormond to become custodian of Blood's lands in February 1664 (Bod. Lib. Carte MS 159, ff.175 and 175*v*).

80 Bod. Lib. Carte MS 43, f.505. The king to Ormond, Whitehall, 11 April 1666. TNA, SP 63/320/129, f.2.

81 Marshall, 'Colonel Thomas Blood and the Restoration Political Scene', *HJ*, vol. 32, p.576; TNA, 84/180/62, intercepted letter from Ludlow.

82 All three were executed in London on 19 April 1662. At the Restoration, Downing had been rewarded for his loyalty by the grant of land adjoining St James's Park which became Downing Street.

83 Blood's opinion of Ludlow appears in *A Modest Vindication*, p.2.

84 Bod. Lib. Carte MS 46, ff.357. Arlington to Ormond, Whitehall, 26 August 1666.

85 TNA, SP 29/168/148, f.148. Grice to [Williamson], 24 August 1666. Grice clearly had been involved on the periphery of the Dublin Castle plot, as he named seven of its conspirators (including Lieutenant Colonel Jones, late governor of the castle) on condition the promise to him that he would not be called as a witness was kept. Grice, a former parliamentary cavalry cornet, had spied for Sir Arthur Heselrige, governor of Newcastle, during the Civil War. See: TNA, SP 46/95/72 and 46/95/78.

86 *CSP Domestic 1666–7*, p.64. Grice had his enemies. The marshal, Gilbert Thomas, told Arlington the following October that Grice

'is too large in his discourses' and was a 'babbling fellow'. *Ibid.*, p.178.

87  A note from Gilbert Thomas, marshal of the Gatehouse prison in Westminster, to Arlington, dated 2 May 1666 reports where 'Allen, if he be Blood, doth lodge or lye'. TNA, SP 29/155/17, f.24.

88  TNA, SP 63/321/164, f.55. Orrery to Arlington, Charleville, 22 September 1666.

89  Bod. Lib. Carte MS 35, f.52r. Notes on persons suspected of complicity in seditious plots in Ireland.

90  It destroyed 13,200 homes, eighty-seven parish churches and St Paul's Cathedral, as well as a number of official buildings such as the Royal Exchange.

91  *London Gazette*, no. 85, Monday, 10 September 1666, p.1, col.1. Some of the French and Dutch had 'little hand-grenades about the size of a ball which they carried in their pockets' (HMC, 'le Fleming', p.41). Patrick Hubert, a French-born watchmaker, claimed to have started the fire as an agent of Pope Alexander VII. Despite doubts about his mental state and fitness to plead, he was hanged on 28 September.

92  HMC 'Ormond', vol. 4, p.462. Sir Robert Southwell to Ormond, 22 October 1678.

93  TBA, SP 29/173/132, f.206. Arlington also told Ormond on 7 September that 'we are reasonably secure the quiet of the kingdom will not be discomposed [by the fire] not being able, by any of the circumstances, to trace out or suspect that it was either contrived or fomented by any of the discontented party' (Bod. Lib. Carte MS 46, ff.363–4). A correspondent of Lord Conway also assured him 'there was nothing of a plot in this, though the people would think otherwise and lay it on the French or Dutch or on the fanatics breaking out so near 3 September their celebrated day of triumph. Others lay it on the papists because some of them are said to be now in arms but it is merely as militia men. The stories of making and casting of fireballs, when traced, are found to be fictitious.' TNA, SP 29/450/712, f.46.

94  Bod. Lib. Carte MS 35, f.54v. Arlington to Sir George Lane. Blood had been in Lancashire and had come close to arrest after the Great Fire of London. Whitehall, 6 September 1666.

95    Bod. Lib. Carte MS 46, f.383. Arlington to Ormond, Whitehall, 12 October 1666.

96    Bod. Lib. Carte MS 35, f.128.

97    *CSP Domestic 1666–7*, p.349. Leving to Arlington, 15 December 1666.

98    *London Gazette*, issue 106, 19–22 November 1666, p.2 col.2; HMC 'le Fleming, p.43.

99    B.L. Add. MS 23,125, f.198r. Declaration by the Pentland rebels.

100   B.L. Add. MS 23,125, f.149r. Sir Peter Wedderburn, clerk to the Privy Council, to the Duke of Lauderdale.

101   *London Gazette*, issue 110, 3–6 December 1666, p.2, cols. 1 and 2.

102   Sergeant, *Rogues and Scoundrels*, p.125.

103   Greaves, *Enemies Under His Feet*, p.75.

104   TNA, SP 29/196/6, f.6. Sir P. M[usgrave] to Williamson, 1 April 1667. Lady Burghclere, in her biography of Ormond, maintains that Blood 'was present at the Battle of Pentland Hills on 26 November 1666 and when the insurgents were routed, he contrived, after his usual fashion to make good his escape' (*Life of Ormond*, vol. 2, p.184).

105   Bod. Lib. Carte MS 35, f.146r. List of persons declared rebels [in Scotland] by proclamation.

106   *CSP Domestic 1666–7*, p.545.

107   *CSP Domestic 1666–7*, p.463.

108   'Remarks . . .', p.223.

CHAPTER 4: A FRIEND IN NEED

1     'Remarks . . .', p.225.

2     *CSP Domestic 1666–7*, p.537: 'All proclaimed persons [were] to be brought before Lord Arlington, should [they] be found in London and Westminster. It should also warrant a search for arms in the houses where they are taken'. The warrant was granted on 2 March.

3     Leving claimed to be paid £20 a year as a spy – equivalent in modern purchasing power to just over £2,500 per annum.

4     Thomas Gardiner, controller of the Post Office in London, had reports of 'several robberies about Leeds lately. Leving, one of the thieves is taken; Freer, another, has gone to London and has been

several times with Lord Arlington.' *CSP Domestic 1667*, p.114. A warrant for Freer's arrest 'for dangerous and seditious practices' had been issued earlier that month; *ibid.*, p.114

5   *CSP Domestic 1667*, p. 114. A reward of £10 was offered for Freer's arrest. A warrant for his detention was issued 'at court at White-hall' in May, for his 'dangerous and seditious practices'. TNA, SP 29/201/93, f.108.

6   TNA, SP 29/201/39, f.46. John Mascall to Williamson, York, 18 May 1667.

7   TNA, SP 29/209/44, f.54. W. L[eving] to Lord Arlington, Newgate, 11 July 1667.

8   *CSP Domestic 1667*, p.310. Mason had been held in the Tower since 15 June. Two weeks later, his married sister Joan Prestwood received permission to visit him. *CSP Domestic 1667*, pp.193 and 245.

9   Now the Life Guards, the senior regiment of the British Army, which, with the Blues and Royals, forms the sovereign's Household Cavalry. The regiment was formed in 1658 and its third troop, made up of exiled Royalists, became the Duke of York's troop. It was originally recruited from gentlemen and its corporals were commissioned, and had a rank equivalent to lieutenants in the remainder of the army.

10  Darrington is split in two by the London–Scotland A1 trunk road (or the old Great North Road), with the M62 motorway junction nearby.

11  HMC 'le Fleming', p.52.

12  TNA, SP 29/211/60, f.61.

13  It has been claimed, without evidence, that Lockyer was married to one of Blood's sisters (Sergeant, *Rogues and Scoundrels*, fn. p.236).

14  Possibly the present-day Spread Eagle, or the demolished Crown Inn, once located on the crossroads in Darrington.

15  Burghclere, *Life of Ormond*, vol. 2, p.184.

16  From the now illegal sport of cock-fighting (popular in the seventeenth century in England), meaning to fight pluckily.

17  'Remarks . . .', pp. 223–5.

18  Under the Statute of Winchester of 1285 (13 Edward 1, *caps*. 1 & 4) the 'Hue and Cry', under common law, required every able-bodied citizen to assist in the arrest of someone witnessed in committing

a crime. This pursuit could run from town to town and county to county until the felon was detained and handed over to a sheriff. In Mason's case, the crime would be escaping from custody.

19    TNA, SP 29/210/151, f.173. William Leving to Arlington, 25 July 1667.

20    TNA, SP 29/211/17, f.18. Mascall to Williamson, York, 27 July 1667.

21    Wheeler was also an MP, having defeated Sir Christopher Wren by a narrow majority in a by-election for the Cambridge University seat on 8 March that year.

22    TNA, SP 29/211/60, ff.61–2. Darcy to Sir Charles Wheeler, York, 29 July 1667. Some of the troopers reportedly died later from their wounds (Abbott, *Colonel Thomas Blood . . .*, p.60).

23    Andrew Browning (ed.), *Memoirs of Sir John Reresby* (Glasgow, 1936) pp.69–70.

24    Bod. Lib. English History MS C.487, Ludlow, *Voyce from the Watch Tower*, f.1265

25    'Remarks . . .', pp.225–6.

26    Bod. Lib. Rawlinson MS A.185, f.473v, entries 47–53.

27    *CSP Domestic 1667*, p.285.

28    TNA, SP 29/212/6, f.6. Betson to Arlington, 1 August 1667.

29    TNA, SP 45/12/246 (damaged); SAL Proclamations, Charles II, vol. 14 (1667–84), f15. Whitehall, 8 August 1667.

30    *CSP Domestic 1667*, p.345.

31    TNA, SP 2/212/70, f.74. Leving to Robert Benson, York Castle, 5 August 1667.

32    Bod. Lib. Rawlinson MS A.185, f.473v, entry 51.

33    Marshall, *Intelligence and Espionage . . .*, pp.167–8.

34    Buckingham had been accused of 'holding secret correspondence about the raising of mutinies' within the army and 'seditions among the people, he having resisted the messenger sent to apprehend him and withdrawn to some obscure place' according to the proclamation seeking his arrest. *CSP Domestic, 1666–7*, p.553.

35    A Pritchard, 'A Defence of His Private Life by the Second Duke of Buckingham', *HLQ*, vol. 44, pp.157–77 and Marshall, *Intelligence and Espionage . . .*, p.168.

36  *CSP Domestic 1667*, p.427. Freer to Williamson, Bradford, 31 August 1667.

37  TNA, SP 29/218/18, f.27. Freer to Arlington, York Castle, 28 September 1667.

38  *CSP Domestic 1667*, p.465.

39  *CSP Domestic 1667*, p.465.

40  Abbott, *Colonel Thomas Blood . . .*, p.63.

41  'Remarks . . .', p.226.

42  HoL Record Office HL/PO/JO/10/1/344/352(e6). Testimony of Samuel Holmes.

43  *Ibid.*, (e7). Testimony of Holmes's servant.

44  *Ibid.*, (e9). Testimony of Samuel Weyer.

45  Bod. Lib. Rawlinson MS A.85, f.474.

46  HoL Record Office HL/PO/JO/10/1/344/352(e5). Testimony of Mrs Elizabeth Price.

47  TNA, ASSI 35/111/5, f.4 and HoL Record Office HL/PO/JO/10/1/344/352(g3).

48  HoL Record Office HL/PO/JO/10/1/344/352(e13). Testimony of Barnaby Bloxton, tailor.

49  *Ibid.*, (e10) and (e11). Testimonies of William Gant and William Mumford.

50  *Ibid.*, (g4). Receipt of Thomas Hunt for sword, belt and pistol.

51  Its first appearance in literature seems to have been in Eugene Sue's novel *Memoirs of Matilda*, published in 1846, although it was being used in common parlance much earlier.

CHAPTER 5: AN INCIDENT IN ST JAMES'S

1   TNA, SP 29/281/75 f.101. Benson to Williamson, Wrenthorpe, near Wakefield, West Yorkshire, 24 December 1670.

2   The curious name of 'Piccadilly' is traditionally believed to be a reference to the ruff collars called 'pickadels' made in the area in the seventeenth century. An alternative explanation refers to its location on the outskirts of built-up London, from the old Dutch *pickedillekens*, meaning the extremity or utmost part of anything. Dasent, *Piccadilly in Three Centuries*, pp. 8–9. The first reference to it

as a street name is about 1673, although there is a reference in the rate-book of St Martin-in-the-Fields in 1627 to 'Picadilly'. Part of it was officially known as Portugal Street, named in honour of Charles II's Portuguese-born queen Catherine of Braganza, although this name was not used by the general populace.

3   Tyburn Lane is today's Park Lane. Executions were staged here from the twelfth century. In 1571, the 'Tyburn Tree' was erected on the execution site. This consisted of a horizontal wooden triangle supported by three tall uprights which allowed three felons to be hanged simultaneously. In January 1661, the disinterred corpses of Oliver Cromwell, John Bradshaw (who presided over the trial of Charles I) and the parliamentary general Henry Ireton, who died of a fever at Limerick in November 1651, were hanged from this triple gibbet in a macabre act of royal revenge. The name of Tyburn originated in the stream that rises in South Hampstead, flows south through Regent's Park and empties in St James's Park. Today its course runs through underground conduits.

4   In today's purchasing power, the cost would be between £5,240,000 and £6,550,000. Clarendon had bought stone originally purchased to repair the medieval St Paul's Cathedral, destroyed in the Great Fire of London in 1666. Doubtless the price for this building material was cheap. Sir Roger Pratt, the architect, employed more than 300 masons, bricklayers and labourers.

5   Clarendon House was demolished in 1683 and speculative builders constructed Bond, Dover and Albermarle Streets on its site.

6   Ormond was removed as lord lieutenant in March 1669, largely through the intrigues of his political enemies, Buckingham and the Earl of Orrery. See: Barnard, 'James Butler, first duke of Ormond', *ODNB*, vol. 9, 153–63; Beckett, 'The Irish Viceroyalty in the Restoration Period', *TRHS*, vol. 20, pp.53–72 and McGuire, 'Why was Ormond Dismissed in 1669?' *Irish Historical Studies*, vol. 18, pp.295–312. In the early 1660s, Ormond purchased Moor Park in Hertfordshire and sold it at a profit in 1670, briefly renting Clarendon House as his London base.

7   Dasent, *Piccadilly in Three Centuries*, pp.38–9.

8   The hospital was dedicated to St James the Less, hence the name both of the palace and this area of London.

9   Ben Weinreb & Christopher Hibbert (eds.), *London Encyclopædia*, p.721; Norman Brett-James, *Growth of Stuart London*, p.369. In 1670 an Act was passed for the repair of London's highways 'now generally soiled by the extraordinary and unreasonable loading of waggons and other carriages and the neglect of repairing and preserving the same' (London Streets, Paving, Cleansing Act, 22 Caro. II, *cap.* 17).

10  The treaty formally recognised English claims to the Dutch colony of New Netherlands on the eastern seaboard of North America. New Amsterdam, at the mouth of the Manhattan River, was captured by a small English naval force in 1664 and was renamed New York, after James, Duke of York. It was retaken by Dutch forces in August 1673 during the Third Anglo-Dutch War, but returned to England by the Treaty of Westminster in February 1674.

11  Charles II eventually had fourteen illegitimate children by seven mistresses.

12  They married in 1677 and the Dutch prince became William III of England and Orange in 1689. See: Trost, *William III the Stadtholder King: A Political Biography*, pp.62–4.

13  HMC 'le Fleming', p.73.

14  Burghclere, *Life of Ormond*, vol. 2, p186; Chancellor, *Memorials of St James's Street*, p.188.

15  *CSP Venice 1669–70*, p.305.

16  The forerunner of the Covent Garden fruit, vegetable and flower market was located at the southern end of this piazza from 1657.

17  Livesey was rumoured to have been murdered by Royalists in the Netherlands in 1660 but he was reported alive and well in Hanau in Hesse, Germany, soon after and later in Rotterdam in 1665, where he probably died in the same year.

18  'Lords *Jnls*', vol. 12, 1666–75, p.448. 9 March 1671.

19  Sometimes called the 'Buffalo Head' tavern.

20  The Bull Head tavern, which occupied the eastern portion of the tenement at 57 Charing Cross, had been a public house since at least 1636. See: G. H. Gater and E. P. Wheeler (eds.), *Survey of London*,

vol. 16, 'St Martin-in-the-Fields. 1 – Charing Cross' (London, 1935), p.122. The diarist Samuel Pepys was an occasional imbiber within its portals. He recorded on 1 September 1660 that he dined at the Bull Head with friends 'upon the best venison pasty that ever I eat of in my life and with one dish more, it was the best dinner I ever was at' ('Pepys Diary', vol. 1, p.216). The pasty was so good, he returned three days later to finish it off.

21   Canary wine, or 'sack' was a fortified white wine with a yellowish tint, imported from the Canary Islands off the north-western coast of Africa. It must have resembled present-day malmsey. Shakespeare refers to canary wine in *Twelfth Night* (Act 1, scene 3, line 74) and *The Merry Wives of Windsor* (Act 3, scene 2, line 83).

22   A person who grazes or feeds cattle up for market.

23   HoL Record Office MS HL/PO/JO/10/1/344/352(b). The affidavit was signed by William Pretty, but William Wilson, who plainly could not write, could only scrawl an 'X' as his mark. It was witnessed by Robert Joyner, landlord of the Bull Head tavern, and his wife Margery.

24   HoL Record Office MS HL/PO/JO/10/1/344/352(o): Information 'given to Arlington concerning the persons who assaulted the duke of Ormond'. The persons named were 'all ... desperate men, who shelter themselves under the notion of Fifth Monarchy men'.

25   RCHM, *Eighth Report*, pt. 1, appendix, p.155.

26   Ormond's account of the attack unfortunately does not survive.

27   Knight, *Encyclopaedia of London*, pp.230–2 and Caulfield, *Portraits, Memoirs and Characters . . .*, vol. 2, pp.177–81.

28   Greaves, *Enemies Under His Feet*, p.206.

29   'Remarks . . .', p.226.

30   Berkeley House was constructed in 1665 for Lord Berkeley of Stratton, a Royalist army officer in the Civil Wars whose name appears in Berkeley Square, Berkeley and Stratton Streets in the vicinity. In 1733, Berkeley House was gutted by a fire started when a workman's pot of glue boiled over. The shell was pulled down and Devonshire House erected on the site in 1734–7 for William Cavendish, Third Duke of Devonshire, as his London residence. It was sold by the Ninth Duke in 1918 and was demolished in 1924, with a new block,

also called Devonshire House, built on frontage overlooking Piccadilly, opposite the Ritz Hotel.

31 Carte, *Life of Ormond*, vol. 2, pp.188–9; Chancellor, *Memorials of St
James's Street*, p.189.

32 Carte, *Life of Ormond*, vol. 2, p.443.

33 The horse ferry, originally owned by the Archbishop of Canterbury,
was leased to Mrs Leventhorpe in 1664 and operated by her family
for many years. Lambeth Bridge was first built in 1862. The nearby
Horseferry Road takes its name from the ferry.

34 RCHM, *Eighth Report*, pt. 1, appendix, p.155.

35 Carte, *Life of Ormond*, vol. 2, p.189.

36 *CSP Domestic 1670*, p.571.

37 An old term for the hindquarters of a horse.

38 *CSP Venice*, p.36.

39 *CSP Domestic 1670*, p.567.

40 Frying Pan Alley, between Bell Lane and Sandy's Row, remains
today, a narrow thoroughfare overshadowed on its eastern end by
the thirty-three floors of the modern Nido Tower. It got its name
because it was originally occupied by numerous ironmongers and
braziers who hung frying pans outside their shops as a symbol of
their trade.

41 'Stuff' is a coarse, thickly woven cloth formerly manufactured in
Kidderminster, Worcestershire. Originally it was probably made entirely of wool, but later with a warp of linen, yarn and a worsted web.
Lawyers' gowns in England are still made of 'stuff' while those worn
by queen's counsels are of silk – hence the distinguishing nickname
for QCs of 'silks'.

42 This refers to a row of red-brick houses erected by the Earl of
Craven in 1665 to receive victims of the Great Plague of London
on the site of a defensive battery and breastwork erected in 1642 by
order of Parliament to protect the western outskirts of London. The
pest houses were also known more prosaically as 'Five Houses' or
'Seven Chimneys'.

43 Tothill Fields occupied a roughly diamond-shaped area, south of St
James's Park, which today would be bounded by Vauxhall Bridge
Road, Francis and Regency Streets. Vincent Square occupies the

central portion. The name 'Tothill' is probably derived from a 'toot', or beacon mound, and the name was most likely given to this district from a beacon being placed here on the highest spot in the flat lands of Westminster. See: Walter Thornbury and Edward Walford, *Old and New London*, vol. 4, pp. 14–26.

44 Smitham Bottom, which today is part of Coulsdon and has the A23 Brighton Road running through it, is located at the junction of three dry valleys which flooded in the seventeenth century. It expanded greatly in the nineteenth century because of the construction of the London–Brighton railway.

45 *London Gazette*, issue 529, 8–12 December 1670, p.2, col. 2.

46 *London Gazette*, issue 531, 15 December–19 December 1670, p.2, col. 2.

47 Viner lent large sums of money to pay for the extravagances at court. He showed Pepys over his fine mansion at Swakeleys at Ickenham in Middlesex, including 'a black boy that he had [as a servant] that died of a consumption. He caused him to be dried in an oven and lies there entire in a box.' 'Pepys Diary', vol. 5, p.64; 7 September 1665.

48 RCHM, *Eighth Report*, pt. 1, appendix, p.155.

49 HoL Record Office MS HL/PO/JO/10/1/344/352(e3). Deposition of Margaret Boulter, 10 December 1670.

50 HoL Record Office MS HL/PO/JO/10/1/344/352 (h4). Halliwell's letter, endorsed: 'Fifth Monarchy', seized by Sir Robert Viner at Halliwell's home in Frying Pan Alley.

51 HoL Record Office MS HL/PO/JO/10/1/344/352(h1) and (h2).

52 HoL Record Office MS HL/PO/JO/10/1/344/352(h8).

53 HoL Record Office MS HL/PO/JO/10/1/344/352(h6). Halliwell's letter to Howell, a constable.

54 The Act of Free and General Pardon, Indemnity and Oblivion (12 Caro. II, *cap*.11) became law on 29 August 1660 and pardoned all those fighting for Parliament during the Civil War, save those with a direct hand in the execution of Charles I.

55 HoL Record Office MS HL/PO/JO/10/1/344/352(h7) – Halliwell's letter to Sir Richard Ford, lord mayor. Halliwell was a cavalry cornet in the parliamentary army. The 'Act of Free and General Pardon' forgave treasons and other offences committed since 1 January 1637.

56 HoL Record Office MS HL/PO/JO/10/1/344/352 (e12 and h9). Statement by Katherine Halliwell before Arlington, 10 December 1670, and petition of Katherine Halliwell, 26 January 1671.

57 HoL Record Office MS HL/PO/JO/10/1/344/352(c1). Information of William Done and (c2) information of John Jones, victualler of the White Swan.

58 Arundel House, demolished in the late 1670s, was located between the Strand and the River Thames, near the church of St Clement Danes.

59 The 'Heaven' tavern adjoined Westminster Hall. There were two other alehouses nearby, called 'Hell' and 'Purgatory', that dated from the Tudor period.

60 RCHM, *Eighth Report*, pt. 1, appendix, pp.155–6.

61 HoL Record Office MS HL/PO/JO/10/1/344/352(c4). Information of Thomas Trishaire and W. Taylor.

62 HoL Record Office MS HL/PO/JO/10/1/344/352(d1). Examination of John Hurst, taken before Arlington on 17 December.

63 HMS *Portland* was a fifty-gun fourth-rate frigate launched at Wapping in 1653 and burnt to avoid capture in 1692. The eighth Royal Navy ship to bear this name, a 'Duke' class Type 23 frigate, was launched in 1999 and commissioned in May 2004.

64 TNA, SP 29/281/77 f.103.

65 HoL Record Office MS HL/PO/JO/10/1/344/352(e6). Evidence of Samuel Holmes.

66 The Gatehouse prison was built in 1370 as the gatehouse of Westminster Abbey and first used as a prison by the abbot. It was used to detain those awaiting trial for felonies and petty offences as well as state prisoners. It was demolished in 1776 and its site is now marked by the column of Westminster School's Crimean War and Indian Mutiny memorial, erected in 1861 in Broad Sanctuary.

67 *CSP Domestic 1670*, p.573.

68 HoL Record Office MS HL/PO/JO/10/1/344/352(e2 and e4). Evidence of John Buxton.

69 *CSP Domestic 1670*, p.573.

70 RCHM, *Eighth Report*, part 1, appendix, p.156.

71 HoL Record Office MS HL/PO/JO/10/1/344/352(l). Examination of Francis Johnson by Arlington, 19 December 1660.

72 This was Sebastian Jones, who had been condemned in Ireland for producing counterfeit coins and was afterwards convicted, with eight others, of stealing £1,500 of silver plate from the Earl of Meath and from Alderman Pennington's home in Dublin. The others were executed, but Jones was due to be transported to the West Indies. He was pardoned, bailed and fled to England. He had offered a man called Sharpe, living in Soho, £50 to go to Ireland and retrieve the stolen plate 'which was hidden underground'. Judge Morton employed Jones to find Blood and Moore in London 'since he knew them in Ireland . . . and knew some acquaintances of theirs here'. *CSP Domestic 1671*, p.37.

73 Henry Davis, 'one of the guards in the Queen's troop', had a sword which Thomas Peachy, one of Williamson's informers, believed 'to be the same as was taken from the attempted assassin of the Duke of Ormond and is deposited at Clarendon House' (TNA, SP 29/281/24, f.28). Later, he retracted his suspicions of Davis's involvement 'in the horrid business connected with the Duke of Ormond' and begged Williamson: 'Do not inform Davis that I gave information against him.' (TNA, SP 29/281/99, f.132.)

74 Greaves, *Enemies Under His Feet*, p. 208.

75 HoL Record Office MS HL/PO/JO/10/1/344/352(g1). Judge Morton to Ormond.

76 The committee was nominally led by the lord chamberlain of the royal household, the sixty-eight-year-old Edward Montague, Second Earl of Manchester. It consisted of two marquises, twenty-three earls, two viscounts, twenty-seven dukes, the archbishops of Canterbury and York and ten Anglican bishops. Not all would have attended the committee hearings.

77 'Lords *Jnls*', vol. 12, 1666–75, p.404.

78 *CSP Domestic 1670*, pp.576 and 582.

79 RCHM, *Eighth Report*, pt. 1, appendix, pp.156 and 158.

80 An alcoholic drink made by infusing cherries and sugar in brandy. Perhaps Dixey's brother was an imbiber?

81 *CSP Domestic 1670*, pp.615–16.

82  RCHM, *Eighth Report*, part 1, appendix, p.156.

83  TNA, SP 29/289/283 f.284. Petition of Thomas Drayton, constable, and Henry Partridge of Lambeth for £100 reward. ?April 1671.

84  HoL Record Office MS HL/PO/JO/10/1/344/352(g4). Receipt of Thomas Hunt, dated 17 October 1670, for sword, belt and pistol, from the custody of Thomas Drayton, constable of Lambeth.

85  Abbott, *Colonel Thomas Blood*, p.19

86  'Lords *Jnls*', vol. 12, 1666–75, pp.447–8.

87  Carte, *Life of Ormond*, vol. 2, p.424.

88  Haley, *The First Earl of Shaftsbury*, p.188.

89  In November 1668, Sir Ellis Leighton, Buckingham's secretary, told the French ambassador that Ormond was about to be removed and that this demonstrated the extent of Buckingham's power and influence. (McGuire, 'Why was Ormond Dismissed in 1669?' *Irish Historical Studies*, vol. 18, p.299.)

90  Marshall, 'Colonel Thomas Blood and the Restoration Political Scene', *HJ*, vol. 32, p.565.

91  Carte, *Life of Ormond*, vol. 4, p.448.

92  Carte, *Life of Ormond*, vol. 4, p.424.

93  Carte, *Life of Ormond*, vol. 4, pp.447–8.

94  HoL Record Office MS HL/PO/JO/10/1/344/352(g6). Thomas Allen to Mrs Mary Hunt at Mr Davies' house at Mortlake, Surrey, 17 November 1670.

95  Marshall, 'Colonel Thomas Blood and the Restoration Political Scene', *HJ*, vol. 32, p.566.

96  Carte, *Life of Ormond*, vol. 2, p.449.

97  'HoC *Jnls*', vol. 9, 1667–87, p.188.

98  'Burnet's History', vol. 1, p.488 and Kennett, *Compleat History of England . . .*, vol. 3, p.280.

99  22 & 23 Caro. II, *cap.* 1. It was repealed in 1828.

100 Greaves, *Enemies Under His Feet*, p. 208.

101 TNA, SP 29/281/74, f.100. Robert Pitt to Prince Rupert, 23 December 1670.

102 TNA, SP 29/281/911, f.120.

103 Greaves, *Enemies Under His Feet*, p. 209.

CHAPTER 6: THE MOST AUDACIOUS CRIME

1    *London Gazette*, issue 572, 8–11 May 1671, p.2, col.2

2    Sitwell, *Crown Jewels . . .*, p.79.

3    'HoC *Jnls*', vol. 6, p.276, 9 August 1649. Other royal regalia were
     stored in the Tower Wardrobe, the department of state that held
     hangings, jewellery and other items for the royal court.

4    These were purchased by a private individual at the sale of King
     Charles's goods in 1649 and returned to his son Charles II after he
     was restored to the throne in 1660.

5    Sitwell, *Crown Jewels . . .*, p.79 and Cole, 'Particulars relative to that
     portion of the Regalia of England which was made for the Coro-
     nation of King Charles the Second', *Archaeologia*, vol. 29, p.262–5.
     Sitwell, *Crown Jewels . . .*, p.48.

6    Sitwell, *Crown Jewels . . .*, p.48 and p.44.

7    The 'Black Prince's Ruby' was worn by Henry V on his helmet at
     the Battle of Agincourt in 1415 and was incorporated in the state
     crown by James I early in the seventeenth century. After the Crown
     Jewels were broken up under the Commonwealth, the gem was
     purchased by a London jeweller and goldsmith who sold it back to
     the monarchy at the Restoration. The Imperial State Crown was
     remodelled for the coronation of George VI (the present Queen's
     father) in 1937, and incorporates more than 3,000 gemstones. See
     Treasury order for payment to Viner (BL Add. MSS 44,915, ff.1–2
     and his receipt on f.3) and the list of regalia provided for Charles II's
     coronation in Sir Gilbert Talbot's custody (*ibid.*, ff.5–12).

8    No regalia for the coronation of a queen was made as Charles II had
     not then married. When James II was crowned on 23 April 1685,
     new regalia had to be made for his queen, Mary of Modena. Lists of
     regalia for this coronation and their valuation are in BL Add. MSS
     44,915, ff.43r.

9    Impey and Parnell, *The Tower of London . . .*, p.106.

10   Strype, *A Survey of the Cities of London and Westminster . . .*, vol. 1,
     p.97.

11   Dixon, *Her Majesty's Tower*, vol. 2, pp. 244–7. Eleven German spies
     were imprisoned in the Martin Tower in 1914–16 and executed in

the Tower of London, nine of them shot in the fortress's indoor rifle firing range. Hence, the First World War saw more executions in the Tower than occurred in the reigns of the Tudors.

12    John Talbot was the nephew of Sir Gilbert Talbot. For Wythe Edwards' wife, see Strype, *A Survey of the Cities of London and Westminster . . .*, vol. 1, p.98.

13    TNA, WORK 31/22. Plans of Jewel House in Tower of London, 15 August 1702, and plan of first storey showing dining room, parlour, kitchen and staircase, dated 1668, both bearing the stamp 'I.G.F.' for Inspector General of Fortifications. A second drawing, WORK 31/68, shows a plan and section of the Jewel Tower in the early eighteenth century.

14    'Remarks . . .', p.227.

15    Charlton, *Tower of London: Its Buildings and Institutions*, p.63.

16    The king gave with one hand and took away with the other. Talbot expected annual profits of £1,200 from the post, but received only £200 a year.

17    Younghusband, *The Jewel House: an Account of the Many Romances connected with the Royal Regalia . . .*, pp.177 and 247.

18    Charlton, *Tower of London: Its Buildings and Institutions*, p.63.

19    The Tower's Royal Menagerie was founded in 1200 during the reign of King John (1199–1216) and was established for 600 years, drawing hundreds of visitors each year to see the animals there. In 1251 a 'white bear' was brought from Norway which was allowed to fish in the River Thames on the end of a stout cord. Four years later, Louis IX of France donated an African elephant. Acknowledging the menagerie's value as an attraction, James I built stone viewing platforms in 1622. Finally, in 1831–2 the animals were transferred to the Zoological Society of London's new buildings in Regent's Park and the menagerie was closed in 1835.

20    Herostratus sought notoriety by burning down the temple of Artemis at Ephesus in 356 BC, one of the seven wonders of the ancient world. He was executed and mere mention of his name thereafter was forbidden under penalty of death. 'Herostratus' therefore has become a metonym for anyone who commits a crime in order to become notorious.

21　'Remarks . . .', p.227.

22　Harrison was hung, drawn and quartered as a regicide at Charing Cross on 13 October 1660, 'he looking as cheerful as any man who could do in that condition' according to the diarist Samuel Pepys, who witnessed his execution ('Pepys Diary', vol. 1, p.241).

23　Greaves, *Enemies Under His Feet*, p.209.

24　BL Lansdowne MS 1,152, vol. 1, f.238r. A former parliamentary colonel, John Rathbone, and seven other New Model Army officers and soldiers were found guilty at the Old Bailey in April 1666 of conspiring the death of Charles II and the overthrow of his government. The plot involved capture of the Tower of London, setting fire to the City of London and the Horse Guards being surprised in the inns where they were quartered, several ostlers having been suborned for that purpose. Alexander, who escaped capture, had acted as paymaster for the conspirators. The date of 3 September was chosen for the attempt because *Lilly's Almanack* deemed this date to be especially lucky, as a ruling planet predicted the downfall of the monarchy.

25　BL Harley MS 6859, f.1. Bod. Lib. Rawlinson MS A.185, f.471r.

26　'Remarks . . .', p.227.

27　Bod. Lib. Rawlinson MS A.185, f. 471r.

28　Strype, *A Survey of the Cities of London and Westminster* . . ., vol. 1, p.97; Hanrahan, *Colonel Blood* . . ., p.110.

29　Bod. Lib. Rawlinson MS A.185, ff. 471v–472v.

30　Strype, *A Survey of the Cities of London and Westminster* . . ., vol. 1, p.97.

31　Bod. Lib. Rawlinson MS A.185, ff. 471v. Some accounts say it was four pairs of gloves.

32　Blood visited three or four more times, according to one account. (Bod. Lib. Rawlinson MS A.185, ff. 471v).

33　Strype, *A Survey of the Cities of London and Westminster* . . ., vol. 1, p.97.

34　Strype, *A Survey of the Cities of London and Westminster* . . ., vol. 1, p.97.

35　BL Harley MS 6,859, f.5.

36　Strype, *A Survey of the Cities of London and Westminster* . . ., vol. 1, p.97.

37  'Remarks . . .', p.227.

38  Strype, *A Survey of the Cities of London and Westminster* . . ., vol. 1, p.97.

39  A wooden tool with a heavy head and handle for ramming, or driving wedges.

40  *London Gazette*, 8–11 May 1671, issue 572, p.2, col. 2.

41  Bod. Lib. Rawlinson MS A.185, ff. 471*r*.

42  'Remarks . . .', p.228.

43  Throughout Beckman's life he had been fascinated by loud bangs and was injured in an accidental explosion which occurred while he was rigging up a firework display to celebrate the coronation of Charles II at Westminster on 23 April 1660. Later he turned to military engineering and mapped the defences of Tangier (the Moroccan port held by the English in 1661–84 after it had been ceded as part of the dowry of Charles II's queen, Catherine of Braganza. See BL Sloane MS 2,448, f.15 – 'Necessities for fortifying Tangier' by 'T. S. Bekman'). In October 1663, he traitorously offered to help Spain capture Tangier and accepted part-payment for his information from the Duke of Medinaceli and later supplied the duke's letters to the English consul at Cadiz. In early 1664 he returned to England, expecting a warm welcome. However, Arlington had been alerted about his dubious character, being warned by Colonel John Fitzgerald, deputy governor of Tangier, that 'Beckman the intelligencer is to be feared'. His suspicions were confirmed when, unaware of the surveillance both he and the envoy were under, he visited the Dutch ambassador in London, offering a 'free discourse of Tangier'. Charles himself ordered an investigation of Beckman's movements and loyalties to be undertaken (Bod. Lib. Rawlinson MSS D.916, f.101. Marshal, *Intelligence and Espionage* . . ., pp.180 and 184). Beckman found himself in the Tower for six months, from where he complained: 'I have been a near half year a close prisoner only from one person's [?Colonel Fitzgerald's] malicious and false tongue.' After this period in prison, Beckman was released and sent back to Tangier to draw up plans for stronger defences of the city, together with the Dutch engineer Bernard de Gomme (Jonathan Spain, 'Sir Martin Beckman', *ODNB*, vol. 6, p.741).

44 *London Gazette*, 8–11 May 1671, issue 572, p.2, col. 2; de Ros, *Memorials of the Tower of London*, p.198.

45 BL Harley MS 6,859, f.5; Strype, *A Survey of the Cities of London and Westminster . . .*, vol. 1, p.98.

46 Sergeant, *Rogues and Scoundrels*, p.142; 'Remarks . . .', p.228; Greaves, *Enemies Under His Feet*, p.210. While other gems were recovered by a yeoman warder and 'faithfully restored', some were lost for ever. (Strype, *A Survey of the Cities of London and Westminster . . .*, vol. 1, p.99). See also Bod. Lib. Rawlinson MS A.185, ff. 472*v* and Nigel Jones, 'Blood, Theft and Arrears: Stealing the Crown Jewels', *History Today*, vol. 61, pp.10–17.

47 Strype, *A Survey of the Cities of London and Westminster . . .*, vol. 1, p.98.

48 TNA, SP 29/289/187, f.366. Newsletter to Mr Kirke at Cambridge; Kennett, *A Compleat History of England . . .*, vol. 3, p.283.

49 Strype, *A Survey of the Cities of London and Westminster . . .*, vol. 1, p.98.

50 Robinson (1615–80), was lieutenant of the Tower of London in 1660–79 when he was dismissed. One of his duties was acting as jailer to political prisoners and he was accused in 1664 of taking 'excessive fees' from them. He was lord mayor of London in 1662–3 and Samuel Pepys was scornful of his talents, describing him as 'a talking bragging bufflehead [fat-headed, foolish or stupid] . . . as very a coxcomb as I would have thought had been in the City . . . nor has he brains to outwit any ordinary tradesman' ('Pepys Diary', 16 March 1663, vol. 3, p.65).

51 The larger knife remains in the Royal Armouries at Leeds, with the number X.214a. The smaller, which had the number X.214b, has been missing since 1983 and was finally deemed lost in 2002. Both daggers were deposited in the Armouries by the Royal Literary Fund in 1926, having being bequeathed to them in 1807 by Thomas Newton, a descendant of the scientist and mathematician Sir Isaac Newton. Sir Isaac may have come by them through his post as firstly warden (1696) and later master of the Royal Mint (1699) located within the Tower of London. My grateful thanks are due to my good friend Philip J. Lankester and to Robert C. Woosnam-Savage,

Curator of European Edged Weapons at the Royal Armouries, for much help and assistance with the issue of the daggers. See also: Ffoulkes, 'Daggers Attributed to Colonel Blood', *Antiquaries Jnl*, vol. 7, pp.139–40 and Caldwell and Wallace, 'Ballocks, Dudgeons and Quhingearis: Three Scottish Daggers recently acquired by the Scottish Museum', *History Scotland*, November–December 2003, pp.15–19.

52 Bod. Lib. English Letters D.37, f.84.

### CHAPTER 7: A ROYAL PARDON

1 Hervey Redmond Morres, Second Viscount Mountmorres, *History of the Principle Transactions of the Irish Parliament*, vol. 1, p. 273.

2 *CSP Domestic 1671*, p.244.

3 TNA, SP 29/289/187, f.366. Newsletter to Mr Kirke at Cambridge. London; 9 May 1671.

4 *CSP Domestic 1671*, p.247.

5 *CSP Venice 1671–2*, p.49. Alberti to the Doge and Senate of Venice. London, 22 May 1671.

6 The belt fastening clerical garb.

7 Humanity or sympathy.

8 Egmont Papers. BL Add. MS 47,128, f.13r. Poem attributed to Andrew Marvell.

9 See copies in the papers of Dr Nehemiah Grew of London (BL Sloane MS 1,941, f.18, in English and Latin) and in the papers of Dr Walter Charleton (d.1707) of Norwich (BL Sloane MS 3,413, f.29r, also in English and Latin).

10 BL Harley MSS 6,859, ff.1–17.

11 Strype, *A Survey of the Cities of London and Westminster ...*, vol. 1, p.99.

12 Younghusband, *The Jewel House ...*, p.187.

13 *London Gazette*, issue 572, 8–11 May 1671, p.2, col.2; HMC 'le Fleming', p.78. One account maintains that Perrot, not Thomas Blood junior, accompanied the colonel to the audience with Charles II.

14 Marshall, *Intelligence and Espionage ...*, p.194.

15 HMC 'le Fleming', p.78.

16   'Evelyn Diary', vol. 2, p.259, 1 March 1671.

17   See Burghclere, *Life of Ormond*, vol. 2, pp. 190–91.

18   Bod. Lib. MSS English Letters D.37, f.84.

19   Burghclere, *Life of Ormond*, vol. 2, p.190.

20   Abbott, *Colonel Thomas Blood*, p.76.

21   'Remarks . . .', pp.228–9.

22   Strype, *A Survey of the Cities of London and Westminster . . .*, vol. 1, p.99.

23   RCHM, *Sixth Report* pt. 1, appendix, p.370. MSS of Sir Henry Ingilby, Ripley Castle, Yorkshire.

24   Strype, *A Survey of the Cities of London and Westminster . . .*, vol. 1, p.99; Carte, *Life of Ormond*, vol. 4, pp.422–3; RCHM, *Fourth Report*, pt. 1, report and appendix, p.370.

25   In the seventeenth century, the waters of the River Thames were still so clean that noblemen who lived in the string of great houses along the Strand in Westminster used to bathe in it frequently. In the reign of Charles I this was the regular practice of Lord Northampton; and Sir Dudley North swam so 'constantly that he could live in the water an afternoon with as much ease as others walk upon land' (Thornbury, *Old and New London*, vol. 3, p, 309). Charles II was a keen swimmer.

26   Because the Thames was broader and shallower before it was embanked in the Victorian period, its flow was much slower and it was frequently frozen over for some days in the seventeenth centuries, as in 1663, 1666 and 1677. The mean temperatures in centigrade for November and December 1670 have been estimated at 6° and 3°, and for January, February and March 1671, 4°, 3.5° and 5° respectively (see: Gordon Manley, 'Central England Monthly Mean Temperatures 1659–1973', *Quarterly Jnl Royal Meteorological Society*, vol. 100 (1974), p.393.

27   TNA, SP 29/293/28, f.31. 'Notes by Williamson of information received by Blood and others', 21 September 1671.

28   'Lords *Jnls*', vol. 12, p.514, col. 2. 22 April 1671.

29   Greaves, *Enemies Under His Feet*, p.210.

30   Strype, *A Survey of the Cities of London and Westminster . . .*, vol. 1, p.99.

31  Kippis, *Biographia Britannia*, vol. 2, p.823.

32  'Remarks . . .', p.229.

33  Baxter, *Reliquiæ Baxterianæ*, p.89; Greaves, *Enemies Under His Feet*, pp.210–1.

34  John Oldmixon, *History of England during the reigns of the House of Stuart* (London, 1730), vol. 1, p.500.

35  'Remarks . . .', p.228.

36  RCHM *Sixth Report*, pt.1, appendix, p.370.

37  TNA, SP 44/34/86, f.87. Warrant to keeper of Gatehouse prison to receive John Buxton, 15 May 1671.

38  Greaves, *Enemies Under His Feet*, p.212.

39  *CSP Domestic 1671*, p.244.

40  TNA, SP 29/290/11, f.15. 'Colonel Blood to the King'. The Tower, 19 May 1671.

41  Marshall, *Intelligence and Espionage . . .*, p.205.

42  RCHM *Eighth Report*, pt. 1, appendix, p.159.

43  *CSP Domestic 1671*, p.413.

44  J. Hartley, *History of the Westminster Election . . .* (second edn., London, 1765), p.79.

45  For example, *N&Q*, vol. 154 (1928), p.10; Jones, 'Blood, Theft and Arrears: Stealing the Crown Jewels', *History Today*, vol. 61, pp.10–17.

46  *CSP Domestic 1671*, p.300. Ironically, Morton wanted to question Blood and Perrot about a Colonel Barrow, alias Johnson, who was suspected of sedition and conspiracy. He had called at Barrow's home but the suspect escaped. Later Morton applied to Williamson for a warrant to question Perrot, citing Barrow's involvement in the plot to capture Dublin Castle and also naming him as an associate of Blood 'in the intended rising on the plague time in London' (Sergeant, *Rogues and Scoundrels*, p.147).

47  *CSP Venice 1671–2*, p.74. Alberti to the Doge and Senate, London, 12 June 1671.

48  *CSP Domestic 1671*, p.351.

49  'R.S.P.' – 'Free pardon', *N&Q*, vol. 175 (1938), p.104.

50  This measure became the Declaration of Indulgence in March 1672, which the following year was withdrawn, following parliamentary

pressure. For further information see Bate, *The Declaration of Indulgence 1672* . . .

51	Bod. Lib. MS English history, C.487, Ludlow, *A Voyce from the Watchtower*, f.1265.

52	Marshall, *Intelligence and Espionage* . . ., pp.195–6.

53	Hanrahan, *Colonel Blood* . . ., p. 136; Abbott, *Colonel Thomas Blood* . . ., p. 88. *CSP Domestic 1671*, p.496.

54	Bod. Lib. Carte MS 69, f.164*r*. Blood's apology to Ormond.

55	Strype, *A Survey of the Cities of London and Westminster* . . ., vol. 1, p.100.

56	Carte, *Life of Ormond*, vol. 4, pp.446–7.

57	*CSP Domestic 1671*, p. 385.

58	*CSP Domestic 1671*, pp.457 and TNA, SP 44/34/115, f.116. Their lands were also restored: see Shaw (ed.), *Calendar of Treasury Books*, vol. 3 (1669–72), p.1168.

59	The crime of failing to report a treasonable offence.

60	The unlawful striking or beating of one person by another.

61	The date of Charles II's landing at Dover at the beginning of the restoration of the monarchy.

62	TNA SP 44/34/110 f.111. Pardon of Thomas Blood, 1 August 1671.

63	NAI, MS 12,816, f.27. Straffan is a village on the River Liffey, sixteen miles (25 km) north-west of Dublin.

64	Greaves, *Enemies Under His Feet*, p.214.

65	Blood had suffered from smallpox which can leave pock-marks from the scabs on the face.

66	RCHM, *Sixth Report*, pt. 1, appendix, p.370.

67	'Williamson Letters', vol. 1, p. 14 fn.

68	'Evelyn Diaries', vol. 2, pp.259–60.

69	RCHM, *Sixth Report*, pt. 1, appendix, p.370; Carte, *Life of Ormond*, vol. 4, p.447.

70	Curran, *Dispatches of William Perwich* . . ., p.165.

71	RCHM, *Seventh Report*, pt. 1, report and appendices, p.464.

72	*History of Insipids* is commonly attributed to Wilmot. For a discussion on attribution, see Vivian de S. Pinto, 'The History of Insipids: Rochester, Freke and Marvell', *Modern Language Review*, vol. 65 (1970), pp.11–5. Wilmot (1647–80) was notorious for his drunken behaviour and extravagant frolics at court. At Christmas 1673 at Whitehall Palace, he delivered a satire about Charles II, entitled *In the Isle of Britain*, in which he criticised the king's 'obsession' with sex at the expense of his kingdoms. He was exiled from court for a month. In January 1675, Wilmot, in a drunken frolic, destroyed the sundial in the middle of the Privy Gardens at Whitehall 'which was esteemed to be the rarest in Europe'.

73 This was south of College Street, where there was a bowling green. The house, distinguished by a shield and a coat of arms raised in relief in the brickwork of the front, was reported to be 'no longer standing' in 1820 (Thornbury and Walford, *Old and New London*, vol. 4, p.35). Fifty-three houses in Bowling Alley and thirty-six in Great Peter Street were recorded in this period (H.F. Westlake, *St Margaret's Westminster* [London, 1914], p.79).

74 See note by 'R.C.' in *N&Q*, second s., vol. 7, 18659, p.131. The present manor house at Minley was built in the French style in 1858–60 for Raikes Currie, a partner in Glynn Mills bank.

75 Shaw (ed.), *Calendar of Treasury Books*, vol. 3, 1669–72, p.937.

## CHAPTER 8: COMING IN FROM THE COLD

1 TNA, SP 29/294/14, f.20.

2 Marshall, *Intelligence and Espionage . . .*, p.196.

3 TNA, SP 29/294/16, f.274. Sir John Robinson to Williamson, Tower of London, 23 December 1671. He had just closed down two Quaker meeting houses 'and if any preach, I take them up and send them to Newgate [prison] for six months . . . Some are rich men and there's no further way to proceed against them but to . . . seize their estates and imprison them during the king's pleasure. If this rule was generally followed, it would break them without any noise or tumult.'

4 *CSP Domestic 1663–4*, p.295.

5 *CSP Domestic 1663–4*, p.287.

6 The so-called 'Coventicles Act'. 22 Caro. II *cap*.1.

7 TNA, SP 29/140/93 f. 136: 'Discharge of three conventiclers'. The original document is dated December ?1665, but the discharge was almost certainly granted in late 1671.

8    TNA, SP 29/293/28 f.31. Notes of Williamson about information received from Blood and others, 21 September 1671.

9    TNA, SP 29/29/12, f.15. Blood to Williamson, London, 18 September 1671.

10   TNA, SP 29/293/28, f.31.

11   Bate, *The Declaration of Indulgence*, fn, p.91.

12   The Fleet prison was burnt down on the third day of the Great Fire of London in September 1666, the prisoners escaping the flames at the last possible moment. The warden, Sir Jeremy Whichcote, purchased Caroon House in south Lambeth (once the residence of the Dutch ambassador in the reigns of Elizabeth I and James I) to house the prison's debtors while it was rebuilt on the original site at his own expense.

13   TNA, SP 29/294/15, f.21. Notes in Williamson's hand, 11 November 1671.

14   TNA, SP 29/294/14, f.20.

15   TNA SP 29/294/15 f.21. Notes in Williamson's hand, 11 November 1671.

16   TNA, SP 29/294/139, f.169. Notes in Williamson's hand, 4 December 1671.

17   Bod. Lib. Rawlinson MS A.185, f.474, entries 10, 15 and 16.

18   TNA, SP 29/294/139, f.169.

19   *CSP Domestic 1671–2*, p.14.

20   Baber (1625–1704) lived in King Street, and was a near neighbour to Dr Thomas Manton, the nonconformist rector of St Paul's church in Covent Garden. Baber's son John was not nearly so discreet; in 1683 he eloped with the daughter of Sir Thomas Draper and married her. See John Wilson, *Court Satires of the Restoration* (Columbus, Ohio, 1976), p.95.

21   Eliot, 'A new MSS of George Saville, first marquis of Halifax', *Macmillan's Magazine*, vol. 36, p.456.

22   TNA, SP 29/293/235, f.295. Notes by Williamson, 27 December 1671.

23   Greaves, *Enemies Under His Feet*, p.221.

24   TNA, SP 29/293/235, f.295.

25   'Suing it out' means the completion of a legal process, i.e., in this

case, the drawing up of a document granting a free pardon to the recipient.

26 *CSP Domestic 1671–2*, p.47. Blood to Arlington, 28 December 1671.

27 TNA, SP 29/293/28, f.31.

28 Greaves, *Enemies Under His Feet*, p. 221.

29 *CSP Domestic 1672*, p.111.

30 Nelthorpe's son Richard was a conspirator against the government in the 1680s. See: Greaves, *Enemies Under His Feet*, p. 222.

31 *CSP Domestic 11 March 1675–29 February 1676*, p. 56.

32 *CSP Domestic 11 March 1675–29 February 1676*, p.60.

33 Brown, *Miscellanea Aulica*, p.66. Arlington to Gascoign, resident at the imperial court at Vienna, Whitehall, 19 March 1672.

34 Abbott, 'English Conspiracy and Dissent', *American Historical Review*, vol. 14, p.719.

35 Bate, *The Declaration of Indulgence*, p.92.

36 *CSP Domestic 1671–2*, pp.37 and 184.

37 Marshall, *Intelligence and Espionage . . .*, p.201.

38 *CSP Domestic 1671–2*, p.343. The Coleman Street application was unsurprisingly rejected, given its reputation for sedition.

39 *CSP Domestic 1671–2*, p.434.

40 *CSP Domestic 1671–2*, p.568.

41 *CSP Domestic 1671–2*, p.366.

42 *CSP Domestic 1671–2*, p.589.

43 A writ of *præmunire* charged a sheriff to summon a person accused of asserting or maintaining papal jurisdiction in England, so denying the monarch's ecclesiastical supremacy. The statute of Richard II, on which this writ was based, was later applied to actions seen as questioning or diminishing royal jurisdiction. This probably was the case here.

44 *CSP Domestic 1672*, p.45. A total of 480 Quakers were released in May 1672.

45 *CSP Domestic 1672*, p.589.

46 Langley was appointed by Parliament in 1647 but ejected by the University visitors in 1660.

47 Bod. Lib. Western MSS 28,184, f.250.

48 'An Act for Preventing Dangers which may Happen from Papist Recusants', 25 Caro. II, *cap.* 2.

49 The doctrine of transubstantiation declares that the blessed bread and wine used in the Sacrament of the Eucharist is in reality the Body and Blood of Christ, while appearing unchanged in appearance to worshippers' sight. The oath attached to the Act read: *I,* [name] *do declare that I do believe that there is not any transubstantiation in the sacrament of the Lord's Supper, or in the elements of the bread and wine at or after the consecration thereof by any person whatsoever.*

50 The monk responsible for handing out alms to the poor before the dissolution of the monasteries in the sixteenth century. The Presbyterian congregation may have used the old disused chapel of St Ann within the almoner's house. See: H. F. Westlake, *St Margaret's Westminster* (London, 1914), p.6.

51 HMC 'Leeds', p.15.

52 *CSP Domestic 1678*, pp.226–7.

53 TNA, SP 84/188/125.

54 *CSP Domestic 1671–2*, p.372.

55 *CSP Domestic 1672*, p.683.

56 TNA, SP 29/333/181, f.245. Notes in Blood's handwriting, ?February 1673.

57 *CSP Domestic 1672*, p.601, Colonel Thomas Blood to Williamson, 12 September 1672.

58 'Williamson Letters', vol. 1, pp.14–5. Henry Ball to Williamson, Whitehall, 2 June 1673. The lord lieutenant, Arthur Capell, First Earl of Essex, told Arlington from Dublin that 'Mr Blood arrived here last Saturday but I have not yet seen him'. *CSP Domestic January 1663–August 1664*, p.335.

59 Peter Talbot (1620–80) had been appointed queen's almoner after Charles's marriage but was accused of conspiring, with four Jesuit priests, and planning to assassinate the Duke of Ormond. He resigned his office and retired to France, but was appointed archbishop of Dublin in 1669. He convened a meeting of Irish Catholic gentry which decided to make representations to the king about Catholic grievances and this so alarmed Irish Protestants that harsher

measures against the Catholic population were imposed and Talbot sought exile in Paris.

60 'Essex Papers', pp.90–1. Earl of Essex to Arlington, Dublin Castle, 17 June 1673.

61 TNA, SP 29/366/181, f.11.

62 *CSP Domestic January 1663–August 1664*, p.410.

63 *CSP Domestic January 1663–August 1664*, p.304.

64 *CSP Domestic 1671–2*, p.373. In August 1677, Neptune Blood petitioned the Duke of Ormond to grant him the two rectories of Castletown Kindalen and Churchtown, Co. Clare, formerly belonging to the Abbey of Mullingar, at an annual rent of £6 (*CSP Domestic 1677–8*, p.234).

65 *CSP Domestic January 1663–August 1664*, p.502. Were his voyages with the East India Company?

66 An officer on board ship who keeps the accounts and sometimes has charge of the provisions.

67 In March 1669, the diarist Samuel Pepys, a member of the Navy Board, was temporarily named captain of *Jersey* as a legal manoeuvre to render him eligible to become a member of a court martial over the loss of HMS *Defiance*. The appointment gave him 'much mirth'. HMS *Jersey*, the first of eight ships to bear the name in the Royal Navy, was captured by the French in the West Indies on 18 December 1691 and renamed, rather unimaginatively *Le Jersey*. She remained in French naval service until 1716. See: Brian Lavery, *The Ship of the Line*, vol. 1, *Development of the Battlefleet 1650–1850* (London, 2003), p. 160. Her name comes from one of the Channel Islands and an image of the ship appeared on a 23p Jersey stamp in 2001. See also: BL Add. MS. 10,115 (Williamson papers on projected war with France in 1677), f.73 – Blood's two sons serving in Royal Navy.

68 *CSP Domestic March–December 1678*, p.20.

69 Henry Ball told Williamson in June 1673 that Blood 'pretends to have a great estate left his wife but Dr Butler tells me this was "a flam [a deceit] and he has none at all on that side".' 'Williamson Letters', vol. 1, p.15.

70 Place or take under the control of a court.

71  Lancashire Record Office MS DDX 26/70/1. This petition is also calendared in the State Papers under the year 1665 but as Charles Holcroft died in December 1672, it must date from 1673 at the earliest.

72  Kaye, *Romance and Adventures of Colonel Blood* . . ., pp.250–3; Lancashire Record Office MS QSP/547/15.

73  'Williamson Letters' vol. 1, p.15 fn.

74  TNA, SP 29/294/235, f.295.

75  Lillywhite, *London Coffee Houses*, p.639.

76  Marshall, 'Colonel Thomas Blood and the Restoration Political Scene', *HJ*, vol. 32, p.571.

77  Fifty-six pounds or 25.4 kg.

78  TNA, SP 29/333/82, f.126. Richard Wilkinson to Colonel John Russell, Appleby, 10 February 1673.

## CHAPTER 9: THE WAYS OF THE LORD

1  Explained in a sermon, preached at Colchester [Essex] by Edmund Hickeringill, rector of All Saints, p.1.

2  'T.S.', *The Horrid Sin of Man-catching* . . ., p.1.

3  To deceive or trick.

4  'Sham Plots', p.1. Samuel Bold (1649–1737), the vicar of Shapwick in Dorset and an earnest advocate of religious toleration preached a sermon against religious persecution when a brief was read out in support of Huguenot refugees in 1682, declaring that informers were the 'brutish and degenerate part of mankind' and were men 'of desperate fortunes'. His sermon was subsequently published as *A Sermon against Persecutions, preached 26 March 1682* (London, 1682), pp.7–9. For an excellent overview, see Marshall, *Intelligence and Espionage* . . ., p.207.

5  'Sham Plots' p.1.

6  Allen, 'Political Clubs in Restoration London', *HJ*, vol. 19, pp.563 and 566.

7  *CSP Domestic 1667–8*, p.89.

8  Waller (c.1637–99) was the son of the parliamentary general of the same name who fought in the Civil War and his second wife.

9    Dryden, *Absalom and Achitophel*, pt. 2, line 53.

10   Waller's club is mentioned in the Catholic midwife Elizabeth Cel-
     lier's *Malice Defeated*. For Blood's infrequent attendances there, see
     'Counter-plots', 1679, p.6.

11   After Richard Cromwell's fall from power, he was unkindly nick-
     named 'Queen Dick' by Royalists and was now exiled in France.

12   TNA, SP 29/397/7, f.7. Williamson's notes of information received
     from Mr Blood, 2 October 1678.

13   Peyton (*c.*1633–89) fled to Holland after the succession of James II
     but a botched attempt to kidnap him and bring him back to England
     caused a diplomatic incident between the two countries. In 1688, he
     commanded a regiment in William of Orange's invasion force after
     it landed in Dorset. The following year Peyton died in London from
     a fever, reportedly two days after drinking bad claret.

14   *CSP Domestic 1677–8*, p.571. Williamson to Boyle, Whitehall, 12
     January 1678. It may have been connected with his old lands at
     Sarney. On 5 June 1679, a note was issued to the lord lieutenant of
     Ireland about 'the petition of Thomas Blood for a grant of the chief
     rent payable out of land belonging to him called Sarney, Co. Meath,
     of £6 per annum, not claimed for thirty-eight years and the arrears
     thereof'. See: *CSP Domestic January 1679–August 1680*, p.164.

15   *CSP Domestic 1678*, p.290. Blood to Duke of York, 16 July 1678.

16   *CSP Domestic 1677–8*, pp.30–1. Ralph Burnett, the postmaster at
     Lincoln, sent on North's letter to the king two days after it was
     written with a note saying the 'enclosed is upon life and death and
     on other great concerns. I therefore pray you to take special notice
     that it may be delivered very carefully so that answer may come by
     Thursday's post.'

17   The church was not rebuilt after the fire and the parish was united
     with that of St Michael, Wood Street in 1670. Since 1965, there has
     been a garden on its site.

18   HMC, 'Ormond', vol. 4, p.462.

19   Barker was fined £50 for 'illegal practice' by the College of Phys-
     icians in 1656. In December 1673 he was appointed a physician in
     ordinary to Charles II – an honorary position, apparently without
     any fees.

20   Pollock, *The Popish Plot . . .*, p.13.

21   Williams, 'The Pope-Burning Processions of 1679, 1680 and 1681', *Jnl Warburg and Courtauld Institutes*, vol. 21, p.108.

22   Kenyon, *The Popish Plot*, p.78.

23   That old gossip Aubrey believed that Hill was also a member of the queen's household (Aubrey's *Brief Lives*, vol. 1, p.320). The murder had been committed in the courtyard of Somerset House, off the Strand, and the body later dumped at Primrose Hill (Kenyon, *The Popish Plot*, p.150). Miles Prance pleaded guilty to perjury in 1686 and was fined £100 and ordered to stand in the pillory (*ibid.*, p.295).

24   Primrose Hill was popularly known afterwards for a short time as 'Greenberry Hill' after the names of the men executed there. Their corpses would have been suspended on the gallows for some time afterwards.

25   'T.S.', *The Horrid Sin of Man-catching . . .*, p.20.

26   HMC 'Fitzherbert', pp.114–5.

27   See: Bury, *A True Narrative of the Late Design of the Papists . . .*, p.8; Marshall, *Intelligence and Espionage . . .*, p.211.

28   HMC 'Fitzherbert', pp.114–5.

29   HMC 'Fitzherbert', p.115.

30   He was canonised in 1975.

31   Oates was retried for perjury in 1685 and sentenced to be whipped through London twice, imprisoned for life and pilloried every year. At the accession of William of Orange and Mary in 1689, he was pardoned and granted an annual pension of £260. Oates died on 12 or 13 July 1705.

32   Bod. Lib. Carte MS 228, f.151. Newsletter addressed to Thomas Wharton at Winchendon, Buckinghamshire, reporting Lord Sunderland's interview with Blood, 3 March 1679.

33   'Remarks . . .', p.229 and 'Narrative' p.4.

34   A 'trepan' is a seventeenth-century noun for a person who lures or tricks another into a disadvantageous or ruinous act or position.

35   Marshall, *Intelligence and Espionage . . .*, p.222.

36   Dalrymple, *Memoirs of Great Britain . . .*, vol. 2, p.231.

37   HMC 'Ormond' vol. 4, pp.328–9. Hester Chapman has claimed that

Blood was the chief protagonist of the plot against Buckingham, but this seems unlikely. See her *Great Villiers . . .*, pp.262–4.

38  Melton, 'A Rake Reformed . . .', *HLQ*, vol. 51, pp. 300–1.

39  'Narrative', p.28.

40  Pritchard, 'A Defence of His Private Life . . .', *HLQ*, vol. 44, pp.164 and 168.

41  HMC 'Ormond', vol. 5, pp.296–7.

42  'Narrative', p.18.

43  Ram Alley, later renamed Hare Place, was a place of sanctuary for debtors in the seventeenth century and a very insalubrious area.

44  More properly known as the 'Bear at Bridgefoot'.

45  'Le Mar', p.14.

46  'Remarks . . .', p.231.

47  A written precept, under a magistrate's seal, directing a constable to take a suspected felon to prison. From the Latin, meaning 'we send'.

48  'Narrative', p.10.

49  'Narrative', p.12.

50  HMC 'Ormond', vol. 5, p.324.

51  Marshall, *Intelligence and Espionage . . .*, p.222.

52  *CSP Domestic 1679–80*, p.521.

53  *London Gazette*, issue 1500, 1–5 April 1680, p.2, cols. 1 and 2.

54  *CSP Domestic 1679–80*, p.560. Newsletter to Sir Francis Radcliffe at Dilston, Northumberland, 18 July 1680.

55  Sir William Dolben (*c.*1625–94) was appointed a justice of the Court of King's Bench on 23 October 1678. He was a man of small stature with a surprisingly loud voice and was known popularly as 'an arrant old snarler'.

56  TNA, SP 29/414/23, f.40. Blood to James, Duke of York, 15 July 1680.

57  There was clearly some arrears in this payment.

58  TNA, SP 29/414/26, f.46. Blood to Secretary Jenkins, 18 July 1680.

59  The prison, situated in Angel Place, off Borough High Street, had been rebuilt in Henry VIII's reign with a high brick wall enclosing a courtyard and buildings. This was demolished in 1761 after the completion of a new prison on a four-acre (1.62 hectare) site close to St George's Fields, Southwark.

60 *CSP Domestic 1679–80*, p.568. Newsletter to Roger Garstell, Newcastle, 22 July 1680.

61 Bod. Lib. Rawlinson MSS A.185 (Pepys Papers), ff.473*r*–475 – Copy of notes from Blood's pocketbook.

62 Bod. Lib. A.185, f.474*r*.

63 Bod. Lib. A.185, ff. 473*r*–474*r*, entries 2, 5, 6, 16, 18, 21, 33, 39–43, 47–52, 54, 59, 67. The Bull's Head tavern was located between Maiden Lane and the Strand. It was pulled down in 1897 and replaced by the Nell Gwynne public house.

64 Bod Lib. A.185, f.474*r*.

65 Bod. Lib. A.185, f.473v–474*r*, entries 4–7, 10, 15–16, 21. See also Marshall, *Intelligence and Espionage . . .*, pp.198, 202, 204.

66 TNA, PROB/11/364/248. Probate was granted on 4 November 1680.

67 TNA PROB 4/5301. Inventory of Thomas Blood of the parish of St Margaret, Westminster, 7 May 1681.

68 'Remarks . . .', pp.233–4.

69 This was built in 1638–42 as a chapel of ease and burial ground for St Margaret's church, Westminster. It was demolished and replaced in the nineteenth century by a new church, Christchurch. This was destroyed by bombing in the 1941 London Blitz and the burial ground was converted into a public garden in 1950 at the junction of Broadway and Victoria Street and designated a conservation area in 1985. A monument commemorating the Suffragette Movement was erected in the gardens in 1970.

70 'Remarks . . .', p.234.

71 Chappell, *Roxburghe Ballads*, Ballad Society, vol. 6, pp.787–8.

72 'Remarks . . .', pp.235 and 227.

## EPILOGUE

1 TNA, SP 29/417/207, f.443.

2 Buckingham founded the Bilsdale Hunt in Yorkshire in 1668, reputedly the oldest hunt in England.

3 'HoC *Jnls*', vol. 10, p.280, 6 November 1678

4 Firth (rev. Blair Warden), 'Edmund Ludlow', *ODNB*, vol. 34, p.717.

5    Bod. Lib. MS English Letters C.53, f.131. P. Maddocks to Sir Robert Southwell, 14 November 1684.

6    Diana, Princess of Wales, was one of his descendants.

7    Marshall, 'Henry Bennet, first earl of Arlington', *ODNB*, vol. 5, pp.101–5.

8    Kenyon, *The Popish Plot*, p.155.

9    Marshall, 'Sir Joseph Williamson', *ODNB*, vol. 59, p.356.

10   The anniversary of the accession of Protestant Elizabeth I to the throne of England in 1558 on the death of her Catholic half-sister Mary I.

11   *CSP Domestic January–June 1683*, pp.66 and 104.

12   Now known as Red Cross Way.

13   *CSP Domestic January–June 1683*, pp.382–3.

14   See: Peter Earle, *Monmouth's Rebels* . . ., p.32; BL Lansdowne MS 1,152, vol. 1, f.238*v* – Nicholas Cooke and Henry Lavening to Sir Bourchier Wrey, MP for Devon, reporting the capture of Perrot, 30 July,1685.

15   HMC 'Ormond', vol. 2, p.253.

16   See: *CSP Domestic 1671*, p.267; *CSP Domestic 1670*, p.174 and Marshall, *Intelligence and Espionage* . . ., p.140.

17   A town on the border of England and Scotland.

18   Spain, 'Martin Beckman', *ODNB*, vol. 6, pp.740–3.

19   TNA, SP 29/417/207, f.443.

20   A pole arm, with an axe head below the spear-like point.

21   TNA, SP 29/417/207 f.445.

22   *CSP Domestic January–June 1683*, p.66.

23   They were both serving in the navy in 1677. See BL Add. MSS, 10,115, f.73.

24   The warship was launched as the fifty-gun third-rate frigate *Speaker* in the Commonwealth navy in 1650 and renamed *Mary* after the Restoration. In 1677 she was refitted as a sixty-two-gun ship and was rebuilt in 1688. *Mary* was lost on the Goodwin Sands shoals, off the coast of Kent, during the Great Storm of 1703.

25   Montgomery-Massingberd, *Burke's Irish Family Records*, p.142

26   TNA, PROB 4/54/476. Dated November 1688.

27   TNA, PROB 11/360/467, ff.304–5. Will of Edmund Blood.

28   *CSP Domestic March 1676–February 1677*, p.77.

29   *CSP Domestic 1678*, p.241.

30   Montgomery-Massingberd, *Burke's Irish Family Records*, p.143. Today, the battle is commemorated in Northern Ireland on 12 July, the day after its date under the 'New Style' Gregorian calendar, adopted in Britain in 1752.

31   *CSP Domestic William III 1696*, p.33. Warrant for Lieutenant Colonel Holcroft Blood to be second engineer in place of Captain Thomas Philips deceased. Kensington, 1 February 1696.

32   Porter, *History of the Corps of Royal Engineers*, vol. 1, p.111.

33   Spain, 'Holcroft Blood', *ODNB*, vol. 6, pp.268–70.

34   Holcroft Blood junior died in 1724.

35   TNA, PROB 11/504/89, will of Holcroft Blood.

36   Thomas Blood had two children, according to Edmund Blood's will (TNA SP PROB 11/360/467, f.304); presumably one died young.

37   NAI MS 12,816, f.20, calls him 'Tobias Baines'.

38   Lisburne (1647–91) also commanded an English regiment during the Williamite wars in Ireland and was killed outright by a cannon-ball at the siege of Limerick in September 1691.

39   NAI MS 12,816, f.21.

40   NAI MS 12,816, ff.31–2.

41   TNA, WORK 14/2/1. Paper on the adaption of the Wakefield Tower as a new jewel house and the provision of glass cases to display the regalia, 1852–69.

42   Impey and Parnell, *The Tower of London . . .*, pp.108–10.

43   Literally, 'St Peter in chains', a reference to the prisoners held in the Tower of London.

44   The burial register entry reads: '1674: Mr Edwards ye crown keeper, buryed October ye second'.

45   TNA, War Office papers WO 94/58/24, f.1. Letter from a Mr Wray Hunt, of Wargrave, Berkshire, 3 December 1936.

46   Bell, *Notices of the Historic Persons buried in . . . St Peter ad Vincula . . .*, p.37. Lord de Ros, perhaps modestly, provides a different version of the way Edwards' gravestone was rescued. It was recognised by a Colonel Wyndham 'in a heap of rubbish and by the [Tower of London] constable's order fixed against in safety against the south

wall. In one of those reckless reparations which so often were allowed in the Tower, the masons employed in repairing the chapel floor threw this tablet aside but it was luckily observed' (de Ros, *Memorials of the Tower of London*, p.202).

# *Bibliography*

## LIST OF ABBREVIATIONS

*Note: All dates employ the 'Old Style' Julian calendar, in use before the introduction of the Gregorian calendar, under the Calendar Act 1752.*

| | | | |
|---|---|---|---|
| Add. MS. | Additional Manuscript | JP | Justice of the Peace |
| bart | baronet | MP | Member of Parliament |
| BL | British Library | MS(S) | Manuscript(s) |
| Bod. Lib. | Bodleian Library | NAI | National Archives of Ireland |
| *c.* | circa | *N&Q* | *Notes & Queries* |
| Co. | County | no. | number |
| col. | column | ODNB | Oxford Dictionary of National Biography |
| CS | Camden Society | pt. | part |
| *CSP* | *Calendar of State Papers* | r | recto |
| ed. | edited | rev. | revised |
| edn. | edition | RCHM | Royal Commission on Historical Manuscripts |
| *EHR* | *English Historical Review* | s. | series |
| fn. | footnote | SAL | Society of Antiquaries of London |
| *HJ* | *Historical Journal* | TNA | The National Archives |
| *HLQ* | *Huntington Library Quarterly* | *Trans* | *Transactions* |
| HMC | Historical Manuscripts Commission | *TRHS* | *Trans. Royal Historical Society* |
| HoC | House of Commons | transl. | translated |
| HoL | House of Lords | v | verso, versus |
| *HR* | *Historical Research* | *VCH* | *Victoria County History* |
| IMC | Irish Manuscripts Commission | | |
| Jnl | Journal | | |

# *Primary sources*

## MANUSCRIPT

### Bodleian Library
### Broad Street, Oxford OX1 3BG

**Carte MSS**

**32** f.202*r* – Examination of James Milligan of Antrim by the earl of Mount-Alexander and William Leslie esq. about the concealment of Thomas Blood, alias Thomas Pilsen, in Antrim; 24 August 1663.

f. 210 – Letter from Thomas Blood to John Chamberlin, reporting that he hoped to recruit disbanded cavalry troopers but he had no confidence in the 'Scots . . . they stick so to a King's interest, though I have laboured with some of them of a small sort to come along with me, I can prevail little – yet, I doubt not to pick up some'; ?August 1663.

f.211 – Instructions for the bearer of above letter, listing persons who can give information and assistance, undated but endorsed: 'copied 14 August 1663 at Wicklow'.

ff.384–5 – Order in Council by Ormond regulating military pay; Dublin, 4 May 1663.

f.388 – Order in Council by Ormond directing the return of arms to his majesty's military stores in Dublin and various other cities; Dublin, 4 May 1663.

f.446 – Sir Arthur Forbes to Ormond, reporting evidence to expect 'some sudden design' against the State and the apprehension of the people; Newton, Co. Meath, 22 May 1663.

f.460 – Robert Green to Colonel James Walsh, reporting that 'disguised men have been passing about these parts' and the night meetings held before the discovery of the Dublin Castle plot; Dublin, 25 May 1663.

f.538*r* – Jared Hancock to Ormond, reporting the departure of a ship from Wexford, belonging to Samuel Abernattin, 'a known fanatic', with several passengers on board; Wexford, 2 June 1663.

f.550 – Ormond to Bennet; Stephen Charnock, 'a pretended minister, and chaplain to Henry Cromwell, is deeply involved in the guilt of the late conspiracies here' and was lodged in London at Robert Littlebury's house 'at the sign of the Unicorn in Little Britain'; Dublin, 10 June 1663.

f.553 – Eglinton to Ormond with information on the conspirators, Lieutenant Colonel Moore and Cornet Blood; 11 June 1663.

ff.589–90 – Certificate by the borough masters and governors concerning testimony given by Jacob 'Borstius' [Vorstius] and others about the residence in that city of Colonel Gilbert Carr; Rotterdam, 10/20 June 1663.

f.602 – Patrick Darcy, learned counsel, to Ormond, submitting lists of the members of the grand juries of the city and county of Dublin but fearing 'not many of them [are] fit for the business now to be agitated'; 22 June 1663.

f.604*r* – Patrick Darcy to Ormond, passing on information that Sir John Ponsonby 'has said openly . . . that at the trial of the prisoners [the government] would find themselves deceived'. Endorsed: 'For your grace only'; 22 June 1663.

f.605*v* – List of members of grand juries of the city of Dublin and Co. Dublin; 22 June 1663.

f.608 – J[ohn] T[homson?] to William Jackson reporting that much mischief was being done here by unruly persons 'spoiling people's houses in the night, under [the] pretence of taking prisoners for being [in] on the plot'; Loughbrickland, Co. Down, 29 June 1663.

f.645 – Petition of Major Thomas Barrington to Ormond, providing details of his service and that of Colonel Edward Warren in the uncovering of the late treasonable plot and seeking clemency in granting Warren's life and estate; [June] 1663.

f.655 – Schedule of ministers' names that are taken and sent to Carrickfergus and Carlingford relating to the late treasonous plots in Ireland; [June 1663].

f.666 – Opinion of Patrick Darcy, learned counsel, upon a point of law submitted by the Irish Government, about the penalties faced by the Dublin Castle conspirators; Dublin, 23 May 1663.

f.668 – Patrick Darcy to Ormond; Boar's Head, Dublin, 4 June 1663.

f.669 – The case against conspirators to 'surprise His Majesty's Castle of Dublin in respect of the penalties by law incurred thereby with questions thereon stated to learned counsel'; [?1 June] 1663.

f.669 – Further opinion of Patrick Darcy; 23 June 1663.

f.673 – Patrick Darcy to Ormond about the progress of the trial of the conspirators; Dublin, 3 July 1663.

f.686 – Information from Lieutenant Richard Thompson about his knowledge of the late conspiracy in which he 'was unhappily involved'; written from Dublin Castle prison, 5 July 1663.

f.688 – Lieutenant Richard Thompson to Ormond. Please 'accept these last words of a dying man . . . [I] was drawn in by Mr. Blood into the plot for which great sin I beg pardon'; Dublin Castle 5 July 1663.

ff.691–4 – Lord Santry's speech when passing judgment upon Alexander Jephson and others; Dublin, 7 July 1663.

33 f.18 – E[dward] Bagot, a former soldier, to Ormond, warning of a plot against the Lord Lieutenant's life; Blithfield, Staffordshire, 2 August 1663.

f.90 – Mrs. Charity Staples to Ormond. Prostrating herself at his feet, 'knowing scarcely how to syllable or articulate her anguish that my son [Major Alexander Staples of Londonderry] should have his hand in treason' . . . [I] beseech [Ormond] to have a regard to his tenderness of years and to the frailty of a nature beguiled by the subtlety of some grand impostor'; ?Ballysheskin, 28 August 1663.

34 f.674r – 'Advice of Incidents in Ireland' sent anonymously to Ormond and by him endorsed with the initials 'P.A.', April 1663.

35 f.52r – Notes on persons suspected of complicity in seditious plots in Ireland 'given by R.A.' apparently to Sir George Lane; 6 September 1666.

f.54r – 'Persons lately going into Ireland'.

f.54v – Arlington to Sir George Lane: Blood reported in Lancashire and came near to arrest after Fire of London; Westminster, 6 September 1666.

f.128r – William Leving, government spy, to Ormond, providing information about [Thomas] Blood and other conspirators who had fled Ireland; 15 November 1666.

f.146v – List of Persons declared rebels [in Scotland] by proclamation; 4 December 1666.

**39** f.27 – The king to Ormond; the office of clerk of the crown and peace in Co. Clare, once held by Thomas Blood and 'passed in his son Holcroft Blood's name' is now void because of Blood's absence from Ireland; Whitehall, 12 March 1679.

**43** f.192 – The king to Ormond; Colonel Shapcott, now in custody in Ireland upon charges of complicity in the late conspiracy, is to be taken to England for further interrogation; Whitehall, [day left blank] June 1663.

f.505 – The king to Ormond; Captain Toby Barnes to have the lease of towns and lands in Sarney, Beatown and Foylestown in the barony of Dunboyne and Co. Meath with certain unprofitable mountain-lands in Co. Wicklow, formerly belonging to Thomas Blood, now attainted of high treason; Whitehall, 11 April 1666.

**44** ff.708–9 – Ormond's speech to the Irish House of Commons; 9 March 1663.

**46** ff.51–2 – Bennet to Ormond; the king 'wonders if [Ormond] could get further [details about] the last plot' and discover whether it had 'any connections with England and Scotland in both which there is certainly much combustible matter, if a fire should ever break forth, from which God keep us'; Whitehall, 15 May 1663.

f.55 – Bennet to Ormond; the king 'approves in general of [Ormond's] vigour and steadiness in abiding the plot'; Whitehall, 1 June 1663.

ff.61–4 – Bennet to Ormond. Despite diligent inquiries, no trace of Charnock has been found in London. Colonel Gibby Carr's wife, also in London, has produced testimony from magistrates in Rotterdam that he had been 'constantly seen there these six months' . . . but 'perhaps 'tis a bought testimonial only'; Whitehall, 27 June 1663.

ff.357–8 – Arlington to Ormond. Reports on the arrival in Ireland of 'Blood and other notorious conspirators' who were 'hoping to work effectually their wicked ends upon the . . . militia especially'. Some of his informers had offered to go to Ireland; Whitehall, 28 August 1666.

ff.363–4 – Arlington to Ormond. The government was unable 'to trace out or suspect that [the Great Fire of London] was either contrived or fomented by any of the discontented party'; Whitehall, 7 September 1666.

f.383 – Arlington to Ormond. The bearer of this letter, is sent into Ireland, with the intention of taking Blood; Whitehall, 12 October 1666.

**49** f.193 – Ormond to Colonel Gorges, urging 'uttermost vigilance' – it was certain that the plotters had intelligence from Derry by means of one Staples, some of whose former company remain in the city's garrison; Dublin Castle, 25 May 1663.

f. 216 – Ormond to Clarendon, announcing Colonel Vernon's departure to London; Dublin Castle, 14 July 1663.

**59** f.86 – Instructions by the lord lieutenant for the seizure of firearms in Ireland; 16 June 1663.

**68** f.562 – Report of the trial of prisoners upon commission of oyer and terminer; 23 February 1664.

f.564 – Ormond and Council of Ireland to Bennet; reporting that some two months ago, intelligence had been supplied to the lord lieutenant of a conspiracy to seize Dublin Castle and his own person. Due precautions were taken and some conspirators seized; Dublin, 23 May 1663.

f.574 – Alexander Jephson's last speech on the gallows; Dublin, [July] 1663.

ff.576–8 – Edward Warren's speech at his execution; Dublin, 15 July 1663.

f.580 – Instructions by the Lord Lieutenant of Ireland to the governors of Carrickfergus, Derry and Galway to search diligently for conspirators and to secure the security of their garrisons; Dublin Castle; 19 May 1663.

**69** f.164r – Blood's apology to Ormond.

**71** ff.388–9 – Proclamation 'upon the occasion of the late conspiracy' signed by the lord lieutenant and members of the Council of Ireland.

**114** f.505 – Edward Tanner to Lieutenant Colonel Thomas Staples, recommending that Staples throws himself on Ormond's mercy and 'make an ingenuous confession of his whole knowledge of the plot. The evidence is clear and the law will condemn us all'; 15 June 1663.

**118** f.63 – Narrative of the discourse between Alexander Jephson of Trim, Co. Meath and Sir Theophilus Jones; Lucan, 19 May 1663.

**143** ff. 96–97 – Ormond to Edward Hyde, lord chancellor, on how the plot against Dublin Castle was discovered; Dublin Castle, 7 March 1633.

ff.128–31 – Ormond to the king: memorandum on the constitution of his majesty's army in Ireland and proposals to 'bring it to the condition' his majesty would have it in, with details of what had been discovered about the late plot; Dublin Castle, 8 May 1663.

f.133*v* – Ormond to the king, reporting that the conspiracy was more widespread than he first believed and warning that a coup d'état could still be mounted, with an intercepted letter about the plot; Dublin Castle, 30 May 1663.

f.133*r* – Ormond to Bennet, urging that some conspirators should be pardoned to entice them to turn king's evidence and praising Colonel Edward Vernon's role in uncovering the plot; Dublin Castle, 30 May 1663.

ff.142*r–v* – Ormond to Bennet, warning of the problems of bringing prosecutions under martial law; Dublin Castle, 13 June 1663.

**144** f.26*v* – Order signed by Ormond for the immediate return of all officers of His Majesty's Army in Ireland to their respective garrisons and quarters; Dublin Castle, May 1663.

f.123 – Petition of Mary Roberts, widow, to Ormond, praying for the satisfaction of a debt owed to her by Lieutenant Richard Thompson, executed for treason, from his estate forfeited to the crown; *c.*10 November 1663.

**159** f.66 – Elizabeth Warren, widow to Ormond: Edward Warren, her late husband, 'in time of great sickness was wrought upon by the pestilential insinuation of one Blood to join with him in his plot against the castle of Dublin for which offence he hath satisfied the sentence of the law by the loss of his life . . .'. Her marriage portion of £400 was used to purchase land in Ballybrittan, Co. Meath, which, 'with other [confiscated] lands, worth about £500, a year, were since lost to him, and restored to the proprietors, by decree of the Court of Claims . . .'. She begs that her late husband's small remaining estate, now forfeited, may be remitted to her and her seven children.

f.175 – Petition of Captain Toby Barnes to Ormond to become custodian of Blood's former lands in Counties Meath and Wicklow; [?1 February] 1664.

f.175*v* – Warrant signed by Ormond to the Barons of the Exchequer for the grant of custodian of Blood's former lands, if found to be at his majesty's disposal; 4 February 1664.

**165** f.111 – Warrant signed by Ormond for the removal of Dubliners living in rooms overlooking the city's ports and replacing them with soldiers 'for the better security of the city'; Dublin Castle, 30 May 1663.

f.116*v* – Warrant, signed by Ormond, for the recapture of Philip Alden, 'late a prisoner in Dublin Castle' under charge of high treason; Dublin Castle, 18 June 1663.

**214** f. 438 – Major Thomas Barrington to Sir George Lane, reporting rumours that his name was mentioned during the investigation of the Dublin Castle plot and that he expected every hour to be arrested 'to his disparagement'. If Sir George sent a guard, he would 'instantly wait upon him'; Dublin, 22 May 1663.

f.442 – Ormond to Philip Alden, sent via Colonel Vernon 'for security' seeking more information about the plot to help find 'the bottom of the plot . . . in some way that it may not spoil the use of future intelligence'; Dublin Castle, 18 March, 1663.

f.446 – Ormond to Philip Alden, seeking information on 'who are at the head of the design for taking the castle'; Dublin, 4 March 1663.

f.448 – Philip Alden to Ormond, disclosing details of a plot to capture Dublin Castle; 4 March 1663.

f.534 – Earl of Mount-Alexander to Ormond, announcing the capture of 'Blood's only guide and protector in the County of Antrim' and entreating Ormond always 'to have about his person a sufficient guard'; Newtown, 25 August 1663.

**221** ff.52–3 – Bennet to Ormond: the king has had Ormond's letter to him about the late conspiracy read twice to him and has agreed to extend mercy to those willing to turn king's evidence; Whitehall, 6 June 1663.

**228** f.151 – Newsletter addressed to Thomas Wharton at Winchendon, Buckinghamshire, about Lord Sunderland's interview with Thomas Blood; Whitehall, 3 March 1679.

## Clarendon MSS

**34** f.27v – Account of the attempted kidnapping of Colonel Thomas Rainborowe at Doncaster, Yorkshire; 29 October 1648.

## MSS English History

**C.487** – Edmund Ludlow, *A Voyce from the Watchtower*.

## MSS English Letters

**C.53** f.131. P. Maddocks to Sir Robert Southwell, 14 November 1684 about Ormond's reactions to reform of the standing army in Ireland and of the administration in Dublin.

**D.3** f.84 – Letter from Williamson describing Blood's attempted theft of the Crown Jewels as 'one of the strangest any story can tell' and that his capture was worth 'ten times the value [of the] Crown'.

## Rawlinson MSS

**A.185 (Pepys Papers)** f.471*r*–472*r* – Narrative describing Blood's attempt to steal the crown.

f.473*v* – Joseph Williamson's 'address-book'; correspondence with a 'Mr. T.B.' in Zeeland in the Dutch United Provinces in 1666; entries 38–44.

ff.473r-475 – Copy of notes from Blood's pocketbook, listing his 'deliverances since I was for the Lord's cause' including his wanderings in the north of England in late 1663 and his near-arrest in London around the time of the Great Fire of 1666; also his religious resolutions and duties.

**C.978** – Life of John Wallis, Savilian professor of geometry at Oxford, by Rev. John Lewis, minister at Margate, 1735. (Another copy is in BL Add. MS. 32,601.)

**D.916** f.99 – Description of Captain Martin Beckman.

f.101 – Instructions by Charles II to investigate Beckman's contacts with the Dutch ambassador in London.

## Western MSS

**28,184** f.250 – Account of the two licensed nonconformist congregations in Oxford, 1672.

## The British Library
### 96 Euston Road, London NW1 2DB

**Additional Manuscripts**

**10,115** – Williamson papers on projected war with France in 1677.

f.73 – Blood's two sons serving in Royal Navy.

**28,077** – Minute book recording business in the office of Thomas Osborne, Earl of Danby, lord high treasurer; 19 June 1673–31 March 1675.

f.139 Payment of £4,000 to secretaries of state for intelligence purposes, to be paid from funds collected by the hearth tax or 'chimney money'; October 1674.

**32,99** f.377 – Letter from Dr John Wallis, Savilian professor of geometry, to his friend, John Fell, Bishop of Oxford, denying the truth of charges made against him of deciphering letters of Charles I, captured by parliamentary forces after the Battle of Naseby; Oxford, 8 April 1685.

**36,916** – Ashton Papers. Newsletters sent to Sir Willoughby Aston by John Starkey and H. Skipwith from London; 17 October 1667–9 January 1672.

f.233 – Capture of Blood reported and his description as 'formerly a captain in the old king's army under Sir Lewis Dyve'.

**41,254** – Letter book of Thomas Belasyse, Second Viscount Fauconberg, lord lieutenant of North Yorkshire; 16 June 1665 to 18 August 1684.

f.7r – Letter to Charles II naming John Mason as being involved in the Great Fire of London.

**44,915** – Papers collected by Robert Cole on the provision of the new regalia for the coronation of Charles II.

f.1–2 – Treasury order for payment to Robert Viner (later lord mayor of London) of £21,97 9s 11d for the new regalia.

f.3 – Receipt signed by Robert Viner for £5,000 in part payment for the regalia.

ff.5–12 – Lists of the regalia provided for Charles II's coronation in the custody of Sir Gilbert Talbot, master and treasurer of the jewels and plate.

**47,128** – Egmont Papers. Miscellaneous poems copied by First Lord Egmont before 1748.

f.13*r* – Poem beginning: 'When daring Blood his Rent to have regained . . .' attributed to Andrew Marvell, 1671.

**47,133** – Egmont Papers. Morland's *Brief Discourse containing the nature and reason of intelligence*, ff.8–13.


### Egerton MSS

**2,539** – Official and private correspondence of Sir Edward Nicholas, secretary of state, and his son, Sir John, clerk to the Privy Council, 1660–1704.

f.101 – Petition of William Garret to Williamson for the position of 'tide-waiter' in reward for his past service in sending intelligence to Williamson's predecessor as secretary of state; October, 1662.

ff.142–3 – Letter from Sir John Nicholas to his father.


### Harley MSS

**2,161** f.158 – Pedigree of Richard Hunt of Limehurst, showing Margaret Hunt's marriage to John Holcroft.

**6,859** – Memoirs and narratives by Sir Gilbert Talbot.

ff.1–17 – Account of Blood's attempt to steal the Crown Jewels.


### Lansdowne MSS

**1,152, vol. 1** – Papers of William Bridgeman, later under-secretary of state to the Earl of Sunderland in the reign of James II.

f.238*v* – Nicholas Cooke and Henry Lavening to Sir Bourchier Wrey, bart., on the capture of [Captain Robert Perrot], one of the Monmouth rebels, Brendon, Somerset; 30 July 1685.

f.238*r* – Ralph Alexander named as being suspected of involvement in the attempted theft of the Crown Jewels.


### Sloane MSS

**2,448** – ff.15 –'Necessities for fortifying Tangier' noted by 'T.S. Bekman' [Captain Martin Beckman] *c*.1661.

**1,941** – Papers of Dr Nehemiah Grew of London, mainly seventeenth-century poems and songs.

f.18 – A stanza 'upon Blood's attempting to steal the crown' in Latin and English.

**3,413** – Papers of Dr Walter Charleton [d.1707] of Norwich.

- f.29r – Poem by Andrew Marvell on Blood's attempted theft of the Crown. Latin and English.

**Stowe MSS**

202 Essex Papers, May–August 1673.

f.81 – Warrant in favour of Thomas Blood senior in Ireland, 1673.

### John Rylands Library
### 150 Deansgate, Manchester M3 3EH

**Tatton Park MS 68.20** – Nehemiah Wallington, *Great Marcys Continued: or yet God is good to Israel*; f.210, an account of the siege of Sherborne Castle, Dorset, 1645.

### Lancashire Record Office
### Bow Lane, Preston PR1 2RE

**DDX 2670/1** – Notes on the Holcroft family, compiled by J. Paul Rylands, 1877.

**DP/23** – Depositions of Leonard Egerton esquire of Shawe; Holcroft Linford gentleman, of Little Walden and John Peers, yeoman, of Glasbrooke, in Egerton *v* John Holcroft esquire of Holcroft concerning money borrowed for the purchase of the manors of Holcroft and Pursfurlong; November 1666; certified by Hugh Standish and William Berrington, 6 May 1683.

**DP/397/25/4** – Notes on defendants' title in lawsuit over the manors and lands of Holcroft, Pesfurlong, Culneth and Risley, Lancashire, *c.*4 December 1657.

**QSP/147/3** – Information of Margaret, widow of Colonel John Holcroft esq., against Thomas Holcroft esq., Hamlet Holcroft the younger, gent., Joseph Key, Robert Drinkwater, husbandman and Richard Deane, miller, all of Holcroft, Culcheth; Quarter Sessions petitions, Ormskirk, Lancashire, midsummer 1657. Damaged.

**QSP/547/15** – Ejection of John Southworth of Cadeshead, Lancashire, and his mother Margaret by Richard Caveley, *c.*1681–2.

## House of Lords Record Office
## Houses of Parliament, London SW1A OPW

**HL/PO/JO/10/1/344/352** – Records of House of Lords' inquiry into the assault on the duke of Ormond; 14 January 1671.

**(b)** Attestations of Mathew Pretty and William Wilson at the Bull Head tavern, London.

**(c1)** Information of William Done.

**(c2)** Information of John Jones, victualler at the White Swan tavern in Queen's Street, London.

**(c4)** Information of Thomas Trishaire, W. Tayler and Michael Beresford.

**(d1)** Examination of John Hurst.

**(e1)** Deposition of Thomas Drayton, a constable of Lambeth, Surrey.

**(e2)** Deposition of John Buxton, of Bell Alley, Coleman Street, London.

**(e3)** Deposition of Margaret Boulter, aged twelve years, niece of Richard Halliwell.

**(e4)** Deposition of John Buxton.

**(e5)** Deposition of Elizabeth Price.

**(e6)** Deposition of Samuel Holmes.

**(e7)** Deposition of Holmes's servant.

**(e9)** Deposition of Thomas Weyer.

**(e10)** Deposition of William Gant.

**(e11)** Deposition of Mrs Price and William Mumford.

**(e12)** Deposition of Katherine Halliwell.

**(e13)** Deposition of Barnaby Bloxton, tailor.

**(g1)** Letter of Judge Morton to the Duke of Ormond.

**(g2)** Copy of JPs' warrant.

**(g3)** Record of conviction against Hunt.

**(g4)** Receipt of Thomas Hunt, dated 17 October 1670, relating to the recovery of his pistol, sword and belt, in the custody of Thomas Drayton, constable of Lambeth.

**(g6)** Letter from T[homas] A[llen] to Mrs Mary Hunt, dated 17 November 1670, and addressed to 'Mr Davyes' house at Moreclack' (Mortlake, Surrey).

**(h)** Summary of previous depositions relating to Halliwell.

**(h1)** Letter from T[homas] A[llen] to Mr Holloway [Halliwell].

**(h2)** Letter from T[homas] A[llen] to Mr Holloway [Halliwell].

**(h4)** Paper endorsed 'Fifth Monarchy'.

**(h6)** Letter from Richard Halliwell.

**(h7)** Letter from Richard Halliwell to the lord mayor.

**(h8)** Depositions of William Mosely and his daughter Honour Mosely, of Blue Anchor Alley, Bunhill, London.

**(h9)** Petition of Katherine Halliwell, wife of Richard Halliwell, tobacco-cutter.

**(l)** Examination of Francis Johnson, 'a pretended minister', living in Gray's Inn Lane, London, 19 December 1670.

**(m)** Information of John Wybourne and George Baker about John Washwhite.

**(m1)** Petition of John Washwhite.

**(m2)** Petition of John Washwhite.

**(n3)** Examination of Thomas Dixey (named in the information John Dixey).

**(n4)** Letter from Judge Morton to Mr James Clarke.

**(o)** Paper endorsed: 'An information given to the Lord Arlington concerning the persons that assaulted the Duke of Ormond'.

**(p)** Report of the House of Lords' Committee; 17 February.

**(q)** Draft order of the House of Lords; 9 March.

### Manchester Archives
### Marshall Street, Manchester M4 5FU

**L89/1/23/1** – Commission on Chantries addressed to Sir Thomas Holcroft, John Holcroft and two others relating to chantries of Stretford and Manchester; 13 February 1546.

### National Archives of Ireland
### Kildare Street, Dublin 2

**MSS**

**451** – Pedigrees and other genealogical data compiled by Alfred Molony relating to the Brereton, Blood and Blount families.

**12,816** – An account of the family of Blood, mainly of Co. Clare, descended from Edmond Blood MP, with blazons of arms.

## The National Archives
## Kew, Richmond, Surrey TW9 4DU

### America and Colonial Papers
**CO/21**, no 170. West Indies papers, 1667.

### Assize Records
**ASSI 35/111/5**, f.4 – Surrey assizes at Guildford; Indictment of Thomas Hunt, alias Thomas Blood, for highway robbery at Croydon; 4 July 1670. Damaged.

### Chancery Court Records
**C 241/147/39** – Action for recovery of a debt of £200 brought by the creditor, Henry de Tildeslegh of Ditton in [Widnes], Lancashire, against Thomas, son of John de Holcroft of Lancashire; 17 February 1367.

### Exchequer Records
**E 134/1652/Mich2** – Depositions in the dispute over the estates, debtors and last will of Edward Calveley esquire, died November 1636.

**E 134/12Chas2/Mich6** – Robert King *v* John Benbow and Mary Holcroft, relict of John Holcroft, over a conveyance made by Christopher Trentham of his estate in Cheshire to John Holcroft and others; 1660.

**E 134/13Chas2/East21** – John Calveley *v* Thomas Holcroft, Margaret Holcroft, widow, John Kerford, Charles Holcroft, Thomas Broome, John Shaw, Thomas Busworth, John Barton; manors of Holcroft, Cadawshed, Barton-upon-Irwell and Pursfurlong and lands in Culcheth, Riseley, Atherton and Wigshaw, Lancashire; 1661.

**E 134/13Chas2/Trin6** – John Calveley *v* Thomas Holcroft, Margaret Holcroft, widow, Charles Holcroft, Thomas Broome, John Shaw, Thomas Unworth, John Kerford John Barton; manors of Holcroft, Cadawshed, Barton-upon-Irwell and Pursfurlong and lands in Culcheth, Riseley, Atherton and Wigshaw, Lancashire; 1661.

## Postal archives

**POST 23/1** – Letter to mayor of Hull announcing that regular posts would be carried along five principal roads in England and Wales, viz. to Dover, Edinburgh, Holyhead, Plymouth and Bristol; London 28 January 1636.

## Privy Council Records

**PC 2/68** – Proceedings of Privy Council 21 April 1679–29 May 1680.
f.471 – Removal of Sir William Waller from the Commission of the Peace.

## State Paper series

**9/32/313** – Sir Joseph Williamson's 'address book'.

**29/97/20**, f.32 – Sir Roger Langley, high sheriff of Yorkshire, to Bennet; York, 23 April 1664.

**29/97/41**, f.54 – Sir Roger Langley, high sheriff of Yorkshire, to Bennet, suggesting the services of William Leving as a spy; 3 April 1664.

**29/97/75**, f.130 – Leving to Arlington; Tower of London, 30 April 1664.

**29/98/132**, f.244 – Sir Roger Langley, high sheriff of Yorkshire, to Bennet; May 1664.

**29/102/48**, f.57 – Names of thirteen persons in London in disguise with their aliases.

**29/102/49**, f.59 – Orders for the repair of the Tower of London; Whitehall, 12 September 1664.

**29/103/21**, f.13 – Bennet's certificate of employment for William Leving and request that he should 'not be molested or restrained'; 5 October 1664.

**29/115/44**, f.124 – Interrogation of William Ashenshaw, a prisoner in the White Lion prison.

**29/121/131**, f.175 – List of thirty-one disaffected persons in London; 22 May 1665.

**29/121/132**, f.176 – List of seventeen seditious persons suspected to be in London; 22 May 1665.

**29/140/93**, f.136 – Discharge of three conventiclers [?with assistance of Colonel Blood] – dated December 1665 in *CSP Domestic* but almost certainly after 1671.

**29/147/111**, f.147 – 'Notes from the person sent by my lord of Orrery'.

**29/155/17**, f.24 – Gilbert Thomas, marshal of the Gatehouse prison to Arlington; 2 May 1666.

**29/168/148**, f.154 – Captain John Grice to Williamson; Blood has departed for Ireland with others to 'do mischief'; 24 August 1666.

**29/168/151**, f.158 – Instructions from Williamson to intercept all letters coming from Ireland addressed to John Knipe [of] Aldersgate Street [London] or going to Ireland, addressed to Daniel Egerton, of Cock [Cook] Street, Whitehall; ?24 August 1666.

**29/168/211**, f.154 – Captain John Grice to Williamson about Blood's involvement in a new Irish conspiracy; 26 August 1666.

**29/173/131**, f.205 – Request for permit from Arlington, endorsed 'Blood's Memorial' dated August 1665 in *CSP Domestic* but after 1671.

**29/173/132**, f.206 – Memorandum [by Williamson] reporting that 'nothing [had been] found' to justify that the Great Fire of London had been caused 'other than by the Hand of God, a great wind and a dry season'; London, 1666.

**29/196/6**, f.6 – Sir Philip Musgrave to Williamson reporting that Blood 'was among the Scottish rebels' and had been in Westmoreland 'at a rigid Anabaptist's [house]'; 1 April ?1667.

**29/201/39**, f.46 – Jonathan Mascall to Williamson, reporting that William Leving was held as a prisoner; York, 18 May 1667.

**29/201/93**, f.108 – Warrant to apprehend William Freer for 'dangerous and seditious practices'; 'given at court at Whitehall'; partially undated [?May] 1667.

**29/209/44**, f.54 – William Leving to Arlington; Newgate prison, London, 11 July 1667.

**29/209/88**, f.103 – William Leving to Williamson; Newgate prison, London, 13 July 1667.

**29/210/141**, f.162 – Petition of Captain John Grice to Arlington, seeking an allowance and a pass for Ireland; 25 July 1667.

**29/210/151**, f.173 – William Leving to Arlington, providing his account of the rescue of Mason; 25 July 1667.

**29/211/17**, f.18 – Jonathan Mascall to Williamson, giving another account of Mason's rescue; York, 27 July 1667.

**29/211/60**, f.61 – Corporal William Darcy to Sir Charles Wheeler, Old Palace Yard, Westminster; York, 24 July 1667.

310

**29/212/6**, f.6 – John Betson, government spy, to Arlington; 1 August 1667.

**29/212/70**, f.74 – William Leving to Robert Benson, clerk of assizes, with note attached reporting that Leving was dead and had been poisoned; 5 August 1667.

**29/218/18**, f.27 – Freer to Williams, wrongly reporting the death of Blood; York Castle, 28 September 1667.

**29/281/74**, f.100 – Robert Pitt to Prince Rupert; 23 December 1670.

**29/281/77**, f.103 – Postscript to a torn letter to an unknown addressee reporting that 'Allen or Ayliff, mentioned in the [*London*] *Gazette* ... had been at sea in the *Portland* frigate'; 25 December 1670.

**29/281/15**, f.17 – [Henry Muddiman] to Mr. Worth, collector at Falmouth; Whitehall, 8 December, 1670.

**29/281/24**, f.28 – Thomas Peachy supplying information about Henry Davis, one of the Queen's troop of guards (in Williamson's handwriting); London, 13 December, 1670.

**29/281/75**, f.101 – Robert Benson to Williamson; Wrenthorp, near Wakefield, Yorkshire, 24 December 1670.

**29/281/99**, f.132 – Thomas Peachey to Williamson, retracting his suspicions about Henry Davis; 'The Mews' ?London, 30 December 1670.

**29/287/911**, f.120 – Examination of Richard Wilkinson before Lord Arlington; [undated] 1670.

**29/289/187**, f.366 – Account of attempted theft of Crown Jewels in a newsletter to Mr Kirke in Cambridge; London, 9 May 1671.

**29/289/283**, f.284 – Claim by Thomas Drayton and Henry Partridge of Lambeth, Surrey, for the £100 reward for information leading to the identification of the attackers of the Duke of Ormond; ?April 1671.

**29/290/11**, f. 15 – Blood to the king; Tower of London, 19 May 1671. [A forgery – not in Blood's hand.]

**29/293/12**, f.15 – Blood to Williamson, describing a visit by a stranger who may be trying to ensnare him; London, 18 September 1671.

**29/293/28**, f.31 – Notes by Williamson on information on conspiracies supplied by Blood; 21 September 1671.

**29/294/14**, f.20 – Notes in Williamson's hand on methods of defeating conspiracies; London, 9 November 1671.

**29/294/15**, f.21 – Williamson's notes on Blood's work amongst the Presbyterians; London, 11 November 1671.

**29/294/36**, f.43 – Williamson's aide-memoire on conspiracies; London, 16 November 1671.

**29/294/124**, f.152 – Richard Wilkinson, government informer, to Williamson; 1 December 1671.

**29/294/139**, f.169 – Williamson's notes claiming that Blood 'has left himself notably to fantasies', has received money to pay debts and his 'head is turned with wine and treats'; London, 4 December 1671.

**29/294/216**, f.274 – Sir John Robinson, lieutenant of the Tower of London, to Williamson, describing his meetings with Blood; Tower, 23 December 1671.

**29/294/235**, f.295 – Williamson's notes of threats to Blood; London, 27 December 1671.

**29/333/82**, f.126 – Richard Wilkinson, government informer, to Colonel John Russell about his poor treatment in prison; Appleby, 10 February 1673.

**29/333/181**, f.249 – Note in Colonel Blood's handwriting that pamphlets from Holland were due to be delivered, most going to the Spanish ambassador; [February] 1673.

**29/366/25**, f.11 – Williamson's notes: Blood's pension as a spy; 12 September 1675.

**29/397/7**, f.7 – Notes by Williamson about information supplied by Blood of a Fifth Monarchists' plot to attack the Tower of London and kill Charles II and his brother at Newmarket or London and set up Richard Cromwell as nominal ruler; London, 2 October 1677.

**29/414/23**, f.40 – Blood to James, Duke of York with a plea for his assistance in gaining freedom; 15 July 1680.

**29/414/26**, f.46 – Blood to Sir Leoline Jenkins with a request for £600 from the Lords of the Treasury in lieu of his salary and 'an immediate supply' for thirty or forty guineas 'for I am quite destitute'; London, 18 July 1680.

**29/417/207**, f.443 – Charles Blood to the Duke of York warning of 'most dangerous conspiracies' against him; undated, ?1681.

**29/417/207.1**, f.445 – Charles Blood's information about a plot to stage an insurrection against the king; undated, ?1683.

**29/450/712**, f.46 – Letter to Lord Conway assuring him that there was no plot involved in starting the Great Fire of London; [8 September] 1666.

**44/34/86**, f.87 – Warrant to the keeper of the Gatehouse prison to receive John Buxton for 'dangerous practices and combinations with Thomas Blood and his son' and to keep him a close prisoner; London, 15 May 1671.

**44/34/110**, f.111 – Pardon to Thomas Blood 'the Father of all Treasons' of 'all Treasons, misprisons of treason, murders … felonies, assaults, batteries and other offences w[ha]soever at any time since 29 day of May 1660, com[m]itted by himself alone, or together w[it]h any other p[er]sons …' recorded in Arlington papers, dated 1 August 1671.

**44/34/115**, f.116 – Grant of pardon to Thomas Blood junior in the same form as his father's pardon; London, 31 August 1671.

**45/12/246** – Proclamation offering reward for the capture of the rescuers of Captain John Mason; 8 August 1667.

**46/95/72** – Warrants from P[aul] Hobson (major in Sir Arthur Hesilrige's Regiment of Foot) to Alderman Thomas Ledgard, military treasurer to Sir Arthur Hesilrige, governor of Newcastle, for payments to Cornet John Grice for money for the soldiers to buy oats for their horses; receipted, 11 May 1649.

**46/95/78** – Warrants from Sir Arthur Hesilrige to Alderman Ledgard for payments to Cornet John Grice for intelligence; receipted, 22 June 1649.

**84/180/62** – Intercepted letter: Ludlow 'heard that several persons sent out of England to destroy friends wheresoever they may be met with'.

**84/188/125** – Blood reports on passage of Dutch warships on River Texel; March 1672.

### State Papers series, Ireland

**63/313/120**, f.243 – Ormond and Irish Council to Bennet concerning the prisoner Henry Porter, alleged executioner of Charles I; Dublin Castle, 29 April 1663.

**63/313/164**, f.335 – Colonel Edward Vernon to Bennet; 21 May 1663.

**63/313/166**, f.340 – Colonel Edward Vernon to Williamson; 21 May 1663.

**63/313/168**, f.346 – Earl of Orrery to the king; Newtown, 23 May 1663.

**63/313/169**, f.349 – Colonel Edward Vernon to Bennet; 23 May 1663.

**63/313/170**, f.351 – Ormond and Council to Bennet; Dublin Castle, 23 May 1663.

**63/313/172**, f.354 – Lord Aungier to Bennet; 23 May 1663.

**63/313/173**, f.355 – Ormond to Bennet; Dublin Castle, 23 May 1663.

**63/313/176**, f.361 – Sir George Lane to Bennet; Dublin Castle, 25 May 1663.

**63/313/174**, f.357 – Ormond to Bennet; Dublin Castle, 24 May 1663.

**63/313/180**, f.366 – Ormond to the king; Dublin, 30 May 1663.

**63/313/186**, f.376 – Colonel Edward Vernon to Bennet; Dublin, 30 May 1663.

**63/313/187**, f.378 – Deposition of James Tanner taken before the lord lieutenant; Dublin, 31 May 1663.

**63/313/193**, f.395 – Sir Nicholas Armorer to Williamson; Dublin, 3 June 1663.

**63/313/198**, f.403 – Colonel Edward Vernon to Williamson; Dublin, 5 June 1663.

**63/313201**, f.408 – Ormond to Bennet; Dublin, 6 June 1663.

**63/313/207**, f.419 – Ormond to Bennet; Dublin Castle, 10 June 1663.

**63/313/209**, f.422 – Ormond to Bennet; Dublin Castle, 10 June 1663.

**63/313/209**, f.425 – Sir George Lane to James Tanner with reply and note to Robert Littlebury in London; 6–10 June 1663.

**63/313/211**, f.430 – Sir Thomas Clarges to Bennet; Dublin, 11 June 1663.

**63/313/215**, f.435 – Sir George Lane to Bennet; Dublin Castle, 13 June 1663.

**63/313/217**, f.439 – Ormond to Bennet; Dublin Castle, 13 June, 1663.

**63/313/220**, f.449 – Thomas Bate to Robert Littlebury at the sign of the Unicorn, Little Britain, London; Dublin, 13 June 1663.

**63/313/221**, f.451 – Sir Gilbert Talbot seeks the grant of Blood's estates in Ireland from Williamson; 13 June 1663.

**63/313/224**, f.456, [–] 'from my chamber in the "Round World"' to Sir Jordan Crosland 'at his house in Holborn [London] between the Griffin and the Bowl'; 14 June 1663.

**63/313/225**, f.458 – Colonel Edward Vernon to Bennet; Dublin, 14 June 1663.

**63/313/226**, f.460 – Instructions for the search for arms in Co. Dublin, signatures torn off; Dublin, after 16 June 1663.

**63/313/230**, f.465 – Account of all His Majesty's military stores and weaponry in Ireland, as at August 1662 and July 1663; 18 June 1663.

**63/313/234**, f.474 – Robert Leigh to Williamson; Dublin, 20 June 1663.

**63/313/243**, f.491 – Sir George Lane to Bennet; Dublin Castle, 25 June 1663.

**63/313/245**, f.495 – Ormond to Bennet; Dublin, 25 June 1663.

**63/314/2**, f.3 – Colonel Edward Vernon to Williamson; 1 July 1663.

**63/314/6**, f. 42 – Draft of a letter from Ormond to the king; Dublin, 14 July 1663.

**63/314/11**, f.32 – Sir George Lane to Secretary Bennet; Dublin Castle, 11 July 1663.

**63/314/17**, f.44 – Colonel Edward Vernon to Williamson; Dublin, 14 July 1663.

**63/314/18**, f.46 – Ormond to Bennet; Council Chamber, Dublin, 15 July 1663.

**63/315/21**, f.42 – Ormond to Bennet; Dublin Castle, 16 November 1663.

**63/315/22**, f.44 – Earl of Orrery to [Bennet]; Newtown, 17 November 1663.

**63/315/25**, f.49 – Sir George Lane's account of the recapture of William Lackey on 15 November, 1663; Dublin Castle, 18 November 1663.

**63/320/34**, f. 72 – Earl of Orrery to the king; Charleville, 7 February 1666.

**63/320/45**, f.1 – Copy of a letter from Earl of Orrery to Ormond; Charleville, 12 February 1666.

f.2 Dame Dorcas Lane to her husband, Sir George Lane, 8 February 1666.

**63/321/164**, f.10 – Earl of Orrery to Arlington; Charleville, 22 September 1666.

**63/320/129**, f.2 – The king to Ormond, with instructions to grant Captain Toby Barnes a lease of the town and lands of Sarney, Braystown and Foylestown in the barony of Dunboyne, Co. Meath and 500 acres of 'unprofitable mountain' in Glenmalure, Co Wicklow, formerly belonging to Thomas Blood, lately attainted of high treason; White-hall, 11 April 1666.

**War Office Papers**

**WO 94/58/24** – Correspondence relating to the memorial to Talbot Edwards, 1936.

**Works Departments Records**

**WORK 14/2/1** – Papers on the adaptation of Wakefield Tower as a new Jewel House and provision of glass cases to display the Regalia; 1 January 1852 to 31 December 1869.

**WORK 31/22** – Plans of Jewel House in Tower of London, 15 August 1702 and plan of first storey showing dining room, parlour, kitchen and staircase, dated 1668, both bearing the stamp 'I.G.F.' for Inspector General of Fortifications.

**WORK 31/68** – Plan and section of Jewel Tower; early eighteenth century.

**Wills and Probate Records**

**PROB 11/364/248** – Will of Thomas Blood; Westminster, 22 August 1680.

**PROB 4/5301** – Engrossed inventories, exhibited from 1660, of Thomas Blood of St Margaret, Westminster; 7 May 1681.

**PROB 4/5476** – Inventory of the goods and chattels of William Blood, of *Mary*, signed by his sister Elizabeth Everard, November 1688.

**PROB 11/360/467**, f.304 – Edmund Blood, purser of *Jersey*, 3 April 1678.

**PROB 11/504/89** – Brig. Holcroft Blood, Brussels, 26 July 1708.


## PUBLISHED

Akerman, John (ed.), *Moneys received and paid for Secret Services of Charles II and James II from 30 March 1679 to 25 December 1688* (London [CS] 1851).

Anon., *A List of Officers Claiming to the Sixty Thousand Pounds Granted by his Sacred Majesty for the Relief of the Truly Loyal and Indigent Party* (London, 1663).

'Aubrey's Brief Lives' – *Brief Lives, chiefly of contemporaries set down by John Aubrey between the years 1669 and 1696*, ed. Andrew Clark (2 vols., Oxford, 1898).

Baxter, Richard, *Reliquiæ Baxterianæ: or, Mr. Richard Baxter's narrative of the most memorable passages of his life and times. Faithfully publish'd from his own original manuscript, by Matthew Sylvester* (London, 1696).

Brown, Thomas (ed.), *Miscellanea Aulica, or a collection of State Treaties, Never before published* (London, 1702).

'Burnet's History' – *Burnet's History of My Own Time*, ed. Osmund Airy (new edn., 2 vols., Oxford, 1897–1900).

Bury, John, *A True Narrative of the late Design of the Papists to charge their horrid plot upon the Protestants. by endeavouring to corrupt Captain Bury and Alderman Brooks of Dublin, and to take off the evidence of Mr. Oats and Mr. Bedlow, &c. as appears by the depositions [of Bury and Brooks]* (London, 1679).

Cellier, Elizabeth, *Malice Defeated: or a Brief relation of the accusation and deliverance of Elizabeth Cellier, wherein her proceedings . . . are particulary related, and the mystery of the meal-tub fully discovered. Together with an abstract of her arraignment and tryal, written by herself* (London, 1680).

Chappell, William (ed.), *Roxburghe Ballads*, Hertford (Ballad Society vol. 6), 1890–1.

'Counter-plots' – *A just narrative of the hellish new counter-plots of the Papists to cast the odium of their horrid treasons upon the Presbyterians and under that notion, to involve many hundreds of the most considerable Protestant nobility and gentry in a general ruin. With an account of their particular intrigues, carried on to ensnare Mr Blood and several other considerable persons with the happy discoveries thereof* (London, 1679).

*CSP* – *Calendar of State Papers Domestic in the Reign of Charles II, 1660–85*, ed. Mary Anne Everett Green, F. H. Blackburne Daniell and Francis Bickley (28 vols., including Addenda, London, 1860–1939).

*Calendar of State Papers Domestic in the Reign of William III, 1 January–31 December 1696*, ed. William Hardy (London, 1913).

*CSP Ireland* – *Calendar of State Papers relating to Ireland preserved in the Public Record Office, 1663–65, and 1666–69*, ed. Robert Pentland Mahaffy (London and Dublin, 1907 and 1908).

*CSP Venice* – *Calendar of State Papers and Manuscripts relating to English*

*Affairs existing in the Archives and Collections of Venice and in other librar-
ies of Northern Italy*, vol. 36, 1669–70 and vol. 37, 1671–2, ed. Allen B.
Hinds (London, 1937 and 1939).

Curran, Beryl (ed.), *Dispatches of William Perwich, English Agent in Paris
1669–77* (London [CS] 1908).

*Essex Papers 1672–9*, ed. Osmund Airy (London [CS] 1890).

'Evelyn Diary' – *The Diary of John Evelyn Esq.* ed. William Bray (new edn.,
4 vols., London, 1879).

Firth, C. H., *Memoirs of Edmund Ludlow . . . 1625–1672* (2 vols., Oxford
1894).

Hickeringill, Revd. Edmund, *The Horrid Sin of Man-Catching Explained
in a Sermon, upon Jeremiah 5, 25–6, preached at Colchester 10 July 1681*
(Colchester, Essex, 1681).

HMC (Historical Manuscripts Commission)

'Downshire' – *Report on the Manuscripts of the Marquis of Downshire*, vol.
1, pt. 2 (London, 1924).

'Finch' – *Report on the Manuscripts of the late Allan George Finch of
Burley-on-the-Hill, Rutland*, vol. 2 (London, 1922).

'Fitzherbert' – *Manuscripts of Sir William Fitzherbert, bart., and others*
(London, 1893).

'le Fleming' – *Manuscripts of S.H. le Fleming Esq., of Rydal Hall* (London,
1890).

'Leeds' – *Manuscripts of the Duke of Leeds, the Bridgewater Trust, Reading
Corporation, the Inner Temple* (London, 1888).

'Ormond' – *Manuscripts of the Marquis of Ormond preserved at the Castle,
Kilkenny*, vol. 2, ed. John T. Gilbert and Rosa Gilbert (London,
1899); new s., vol. 3, ed. Caesar Litton Falkiner (London, 1904);
vol. 4, ed. Caesar Litton Falkiner (London, 1906); vol. 5, ed. Caesar.
Litton Falkiner (London, 1908).

'HoC Jnls' – *House of Commons Jnls*, vol. 8, 1660–87 and vol. 9, 1667–87
(London, 1802).

'HoC Ireland Jnls' – *Jnls of the House of Commons in Ireland* (Dublin,
1796).

Johnson-Kaye, W. and Wittenburg-Kaye, F. W., *Register of Newchurch in
the Parish of Culcheth: Christenings, Weddings and Burials* (Cambridge
[Lancashire Parish Register Society], 1905).

'Lancashire Civil War Tracts' – *Tracts relating to Military Proceedings in Lancashire during the Great Civil War, commencing with the removal by Parliament of James, lord Strange, afterwards earl of Derby, from his Lieutenancy of Lancashire* . . . ed. George Ormerod, Chetham Society, old s., vol. 2 (Manchester, 1844).

'Le Mar' – *Narrative of the Design lately laid by Philip Le Mar and several others against his grace George Duke of Buckingham* (London, 1680).

*London Gazette*, published by authority:

no. 85, 3–10 September 1666.

no. 106, 19–22 November 1666.

no. 528, 5–8 December 1670.

no. 529, 8–12 December 1670.

no. 531, 15–19 December 1670.

no. 572, 8–11 May 1671.

no. 1500, 1–5 April 1680.

'Lords Jnls' – *House of Lord Jnls*, vol. 12, 1666–71 (London, 1767).

'Magalotti, *Relazione*' – *Lorenzo Magalotti at the Court of Charles II; his Relazione d'Inghilterre of 1668–9*, transl. and ed. W. E. Knowles-Middleton (Waterloo, Ontario, 1980).

Morres, Hervey, Second Viscount Mountmorres of Castle Morres, *History of the Principal Transactions of the Irish Parliament 1643–66* (2 vols., London, 1797).

Morrice, Thomas, *A Collection of the State Letters of* . . . *Roger Boyle, first earl of Orrery, Lord President of Munster in Ireland* (London and Dublin, 1743).

'Narrative' – *The Narrative of Colonel Thomas Blood concerning the design reported to be lately laid against the life and honour of George, Duke of Buckingham* . . . (London, 1680).

Peacock, Edward (ed.), *The Army Lists of the Roundheads and Cavaliers, containing the names of the officers in the Royal and Parliamentary Armies of 1642* (second edn., London, 1874).

'Pepys Diary' – *The Diary of Samuel Pepys*, ed. Henry B. Wheatley (8 vols., London, 1928).

Raine, J. (ed.), *Depositions from the Castle of York relating to Offences Committed in the Northern Counties in the Seventeenth Century*, Surtees Society, vol. 40 (London, 1861).

'Remarks . . .' – 'Remarks on the Life and Death of the Fam'd Mr. Blood' by R.H. (London, 1680) contained in *'Somers Tracts'*, vol. 3 (1748–51), 219–35.

RCHM – Royal Commission on Historical Manuscripts, *Fourth–Fifteenth Reports*, pt. 1, reports and appendices (London, 1876–96).

'SAL Proclamations'

Proclamations, Charles II, vol. 13, 1660–6, f.27: *A Proclamation for the Apprehension of Edmund Ludlow Esquire, commonly called Colonel Ludlow* (London, 1 September 1660).

Vol. 14, 1667–84, f.15 – *A Proclamation for the discovery and Apprehension of John Lockier, Timothy Butler Thomas Blood, commonly called Captain Blood, John Mason and others . . .* (Whitehall, 8 August 1667).

Ireland 1572–1670, vol. 17, f.75 – *Whereas we have, by the Blessing of God, discovered and disappointed a traitorous conspiracy for surprising and taking His Majesties castle of Dublin . . . which the said conspirators had designed to do on the 21th day of this present month of May . . .* (Dublin, 23 May 1663).

'Sham Plots' – *The Character of a Sham-Plotter or Man-Catcher* (London, 1681).

Shaw, William A. (ed.), *Calendar of Treasury Books 1660–1718*, 32 vols., vol. 3, 1669–72 (London, 1908).

Simington, Robert, *The Civil Survey AD 1654–6, County of Meath*, vol. 5, IMC (Dublin, 1940).

'Somers Tracts' – *A Collection of Scarce and Valuable Tracts on the most interesting and entertaining subjects but chiefly such as relate to the History and Constitution of these Kingdoms. Selected from an infinite number in print and manuscript, in the Royal, Cotton, Sion, and other Public, as well as private libraries; particularly that of the late Lord Som(m)ers*, second edn., vol. 8, pp.219–35, ed. Sir Walter Scott (13 vols., London, 1809–15).

Strype, John, *A Survey of the Cities of London and Westminster and Borough of Southwark . . . by John Stow, Citizen and Native of London, corrected, improved and very much enlarged in the year 1720 by John Strype* (2 vols., London, 1754).

Tibbutt, H. G. (ed.), *The Life and Letters of Sir Lewis Dyve 1559–1669*, vol. 27 (Bedfordshire Historical Record Society, Streatley, Beds., 1948).

'T.S.' – *The Horrid Sin of Man-Catching, the second part; or, further discoveries and arguments to prove, that there is no Protestant-Plot* . . . (London, 1681).

'Veitch & Brysson Memoirs' – *Memoirs of Mr William Veitch and George Brysson, written by themselves with other narratives illustrative of the history of Scotland from the Restoration to the Revolution* (Edinburgh, *c.*1825).

'Williamson Letters' – *Letters addressed from London to Sir Joseph Williamson while Plenipotentiary at the Congress of Cologne in the years 1673–4*, ed. W. D. Christie (2 vols., C. S., London, 1875).

Willis, Browne, *Notitia Parliamentaria: Part II – A Series of Lists of the Representatives in the Several Parliaments held from the Reformation 1541 to the Restoration 1660* (London, 1750).

# Secondary sources

*Present day values of seventeenth-century money have been determined using calculators available at*
*http://www.measuringworth.com/ukcompare/index.php.*

Abbott, Wilbur, 'English Conspiracy and Dissent 1660–74', *American Historical Review*, vol. 14 (1909), pp.503–28 and 696–722.
— *Colonel Thomas Blood, Crown-stealer* (Rochester, New York, 1910).

Allen, David, 'Political Clubs in Restoration London', *HJ*, vol. 19 (1976), pp. 561–80.

Ball, F. E., 'Notes on the Irish Judiciary in the Reign of Charles II, 1660–85', *Jnl Cork Historical and Archaeological Society*, 2nd s., vol. 7 (1902), p.90.

Barnard, Toby, 'James Butler, first duke of Ormond' in *ODNB*, vol. 9, pp.153–63.

Barry, E., *Barrymore: Records of the Barrys of Co. Cork* (Cork, 1902).

Bate, Frank, *The Declaration of Indulgence 1672: A Study in the Rise of Organised Dissent* (London, 1908).

Beckett, J.C., *The Making of Modern Ireland 1602–1923* (London, 1996).
— 'The Irish Viceroyalty in the Restoration Period, *TRHS*, 5th s., vol. 20 (1970), pp.53–72.

Bell, D.C., *Notices of the Historic Persons buried in the Chapel of St Peter ad Vincula in the Tower of London* (London, 1877).

Brett-James, Norman, *The Growth of Stuart London* (London, 1935).

Brunton, Douglas and Pennington, D.H., *Members of the Long Parliament* (London, 1954).

Burghclere, Lady Winifred, *George Villiers, second duke of Buckingham 1628–87: a study in the History of the Restoration* (London, 1903).

— *The Life of James, first duke of Ormond, 1610–88* (2 vols., London, 1912).

Burke, Sir Bernard – *A Genealogical and Heraldic History of Landed Gentry of Ireland*, new edn., rev. A. C. Fox-Davies (London, 1912).

Burrage, Champlin, 'The Fifth Monarchy Insurrections', *EHR*, vol. 25 (1910), pp.722–47.

Caldwell, D. H. and Wallace, J., 'Ballocks, Dudgeons and Quhingearis: Three Scottish Daggers recently acquired by the National Museum', *History Scotland*, November-December 2003, pp.15–19.

Capp, Bernard, *The Fifth Monarchy Men: A Study in Seventeenth-century English Millenarianism* (London, 1977).

—'A Door of Hope Re-opened: the Fifth Monarchy, King Charles and King Jesus', *Journal of Religious History*, vol. 32 (2008), pp.16–30.

Carte, Thomas, *The Life of James duke of Ormond, containing an account of the most remarkable affairs of his time and particularly of Ireland under his government* (new edn., 5 vols., Oxford, 1851).

Caulfield, James, *Portraits, Memoirs and Characters of Remarkable Personages from the Reign of Edward III to the Revolution* (3 vols., London, 1813).

Chancellor, E. Beresford, *Memorials of St James's Street* (London, 1922).

Chapman, Hester, *Great Villiers: A study of George Villiers, second duke of Buckingham 1627–87* (London, 1949).

Charlton, John (ed.), *The Tower of London: Its Buildings and Institutions* (London, 1978).

Cole, Robert, 'Particulars relative to that Portion of the Regalia of England which was made for the Coronation of King Charles II', *Archaeologia*, vol. 29 (1842), pp. 262–6.

Cunningham, Peter, *A Handbook to London Past and Present* (new edn., London, 1850).

Dalrymple, Sir John, *Memoirs of Great Britain and Ireland. From the Last Dissolution of the last Parliament of Charles II until the sea battle of La Hogue* (2 vols., Dublin, 1773).

Dasent, Arthur, *Piccadilly in Three Centuries* (London, 1920).

Dixon, William, *Her Majesty's Tower* (4 vols., London, 1870).

Earle, Peter, *Monmouth's Rebels: The Road to Sedgemoor 1685* (London, 1977).

Eliot, Hugh, 'A new MS of George Saville, first marquis of Halifax', *Macmillan's Magazine*, vol. 36 (1877), pp.452–63.

Elton, G., 'Informing for Profit: A Sidelight on Tudor Methods of Law Enforcement', *Cambridge HJ*, vol. 11 (1954), pp.149–67.

Evans, F. M. Greir, 'Emoluments of the Principal Secretaries of State in the Seventeenth Century', *EHR*, vol. 35 (1920), pp.513–28.

Ffoulkes, Charles, 'Daggers attributed to Colonel Blood', *Antiquaries Jnl*, vol. 7 (1927), pp.139–40.

Firth, C. F. (rev. Blair Warden), 'Edmund Ludlow' in *ODNB*, vol. 34, pp.713–18.

Fraser, Peter, *The Intelligence of the Secretaries of State and their Monopoly of Licensed News 1660–88* (Cambridge, 1956).

Frost, James, *History and Topography of the County of Clare* (Dublin, 1893).

Gee, H., 'A Durham and Newcastle plot in 1663', *Archaeologia Aeliana*, 3rd s., vol. 14 (1917), pp.145–56.

Gilbert, J. T., *History of the City of Dublin* (2 vols., Dublin, 1854).

Greaves, Richard L., *Deliver Us from Evil: The Radical Underground in Britain, 1660–63* (Oxford, 1986).

— *Enemies Under His Feet: Radicals and Nonconformists in Britain 1664–77* (Stanford, California, 1990).

— *God's Other Children: Protestant Non-conformists and the Emergence of Denominational churches in Ireland 1660–1700* (Stanford, 1997).

Haley, K. H. D., *The First Earl of Shaftesbury* (Oxford, 1968).

Hanrahan, David, *Colonel Blood, the Man who Stole the Crown Jewels* (Stroud, 2004).

Hutchinson, Robert, *Elizabeth's Spymaster* (London, 2006).

Impey, Edward and Parnell, Geoffrey, *The Tower of London: the Official Illustrated History* (London, 2000).

Jones, Nigel, 'Blood, Theft and Arrears: Stealing the Crown Jewels', *History Today*, vol. 61 (October 2011), pp.10–17.

Kaye, Eugene, *The Romance and Adventures of the Notorious Colonel Blood who attempted to Steal the Crown Jewels from the Tower of London in the Reign of Charles II* (Manchester, 1913).

Kennett, White, *A Compleat History of England with the lives of all the Kings and Queens thereof* (3 vols., London, 1706).

Kenyon, John, *The Popish Plot* (2nd edn., London, 2000).

Kippis, Andrew, *Biographia Britannica, or the Lives of the most eminent personages who flourished in Great Britain and Ireland from the earliest ages down to the present times* (6 vols., London, 1747–66).

Knight, Charles, *Encyclopedia of London* (London, 1851).

Lillywhite, Bryant, *London Coffee Houses; A Reference Book of Coffee Houses in the seventeenth, eighteenth and nineteenth centuries* (London, 1963).

Marshall, Alan, 'Colonel Thomas Blood and the Restoration Political Scene', *HJ*, vol. 32 (1989), pp.561–82.

— *Intelligence and Espionage in the Reign of Charles II, 1660–85* (Cambridge, 1994).

— 'Sir Joseph Williamson and the Conduct of Administration in Restoration England', *HR*, vol. 69 (1996), pp.18–41.

— 'Henry Bennet, first earl of Arlington' in *ODNB*, vol. 5, pp.101–5.

— 'Colonel Thomas Blood', *ibid.*, vol. 6, pp.270–75.

— 'William Leving', *ibid.*, vol. 33, pp. 545–6.

— 'Sir Joseph Williamson', *ibid.*, vol. 59, pp. 352–6.

McGuire, J. T., 'Why was Ormond Dismissed in 1669?', *Irish Historical Studies*, vol. 18 (1973), pp.295–312.

Melton, F. T., 'A Rake Reformed: The fortunes of George Villiers, second duke of Buckingham 1671–85', *HLQ*, vol. 51 (1988), pp. 297–318.

Montgomery-Massingberd, Hugh (ed.), *Burke's Irish Family Records* (London, 1976).

Moses, D. A. H., 'Colonel Blood's Theft of Crown Jewels', *N&Q*, vol. 154, (7 January 1928), p.10.

O'Brien, Richard, *Studies in Irish History 1603–49* (Dublin, 1906).

*ODNB – Oxford Dictionary of National Biography*, ed. H.G. Matthew and Brian Harrison (Oxford, 2004).

Osborough W. N., 'James Barry, first baron Santry', in *ODNB*, vol. 4, pp.132–3.

Pollock, John, *The Popish Plot: A Study in the History of the Reign of Charles II* (London, 1903).

Porter, Whitworth *et al.*, *History of the Corps of Royal Engineers* (3 vols., London, 1889).

Pritchard, A., 'A Defence of his Private Life by the second duke of Buckingham', *HLQ*, vol. 44 (1980–1), 157–71.

Rogers, P. G., *The Fifth Monarchy Men* (London, 1966).

de Ros, William, *Memorials of the Tower of London* (London, 1867).

'R.S.P' – 'Free Pardon' with comment by Wilfred H. Holden, *N&Q*, vol. 175 (6 August 1938), 104.

Sergeant, Philip W., *Rogues and Scoundrels* (London, 1924).

Sitwell, H. D. W., *The Crown Jewels and other Regalia in the Tower of London*, ed. Clarence Winchester (London, 1953).

Spain, Jonathan, 'Sir Martin Beckman' in *ODNB*, vol. 6, pp.740–3.

—'Holcroft Blood' *ibid.*, vol. 6, pp.268–70.

Thornbury, Walter and Walford, Edward, *Old and New London* (8 vols., London, 1879).

Trost, Wouter, *William III the Stadtholder King: A Political Biography*, transl. J. C. Grayson (Aldershot, 2005).

Turner, Edward, 'The Secrecy of the Post', *EHR*, vol. 33 (1918), pp.320–27.

*VCH Lancs.* – *VCH Lancashire*, vol. 4, ed. William Farrer and J. Brownbill (London, 1911).

Walker, J., 'The Yorkshire Plot, 1663', *Yorkshire Archaeological Journal*, vol. 31 (1932–4), pp. 348–59.

Weinreb, Ben and Hibbert, Christopher (eds.), *The London Encyclopædia* (London, 1983).

Wheatley, Henry B., *Round about Piccadilly and Pall Mall, or a ramble from the Haymarket to Hyde Park* . . . (London, 1870).

Whyman, Susan E., *Postal Censorship in England 1635–1844*, Princeton. edu/sites/English/csbm . . . /postal-censorship-england.doc. (accessed May 2014).

Williams, Sheila, 'The Pope-Burning Processions of 1679, 1680 and 1681', *Jnl Warburg and Courtauld Institutes*, vol. 21 (1958), pp.104–18.

Wilson, Philip, 'Ireland under Charles II, 1660–85' in O'Brien, *Studies in Irish History 1649–1775*, pp.67–124.

Younghusband, Sir George, *The Jewel House: an Account of the Many Romances connected with the Royal Regalia, together with Sir Gilbert Talbot's account of Colonel Blood's Plot here reproduced for the first time* (New York, 1920).

# Index